Legal Accounting

Legal Accounting

Principles and Applications

Douglas C. Michael
Thomas P. Lewis Professor of Law
University of Kentucky
J. David Rosenberg College of Law

Carolina Academic Press
Durham, North Carolina

Library of Congress Cataloging-in-Publication Data

Names: Michael, Douglas C., 1957- author.
Title: Legal accounting : principles and applications / by Douglas C. Michael.
Description: Durham, North Carolina : Carolina Academic Press, LLC, 2022.
Identifiers: LCCN 2021046274 (print) | LCCN 2021046275 (ebook) | ISBN 9781531006211 (paperback) | ISBN 9781531006228 (ebook)
Subjects: LCSH: Accounting--Law and legislation--United States.
Classification: LCC KF1357 .M53 2022 (print) | LCC KF1357 (ebook) | DDC 346.73/063--dc23/eng/20211220
LC record available at https://lccn.loc.gov/2021046274
LC ebook record available at https://lccn.loc.gov/2021046275

Carolina Academic Press
700 Kent Street
Durham, North Carolina 27701
(919) 489-7486
www.cap-press.com

Printed in the United States of America

Contents

Table of Cases

Principal cases in **bold**

Table of Companies Listed in Examples

Permissions

Excerpts from Edward J. Janger, *Brandeis, Business Ethics and Enron* in Nancy B. Rappaport and Bala G. Dharan (2004) pp. 63 and 65-66 reprinted with permission of West Academic Publishing.

Excerpts from THE SMARTEST GUYS IN THE ROOM: THE AMAZING RISE AND SCANDALOUS FALL OF ENRON by Bethany McLean and Peter Elkind, Copyright © 2003, 2004, by Fortune, a division of Time, Inc. Used by permission of Portfolio, an imprint of Penguin Publishing Group, a division of Penguin Random House LLC. All rights reserved.

The Financial Accounting Standards Board (FASB) material is copyrighted by the Financial Accounting Foundation (FAF), 401 Merritt 7, PO Box 5116, Norwalk, Connecticut 06856-5116, U.S.A., and is reproduced with permission. A complete copy of the *FASB Standards Codification®* is available from the FAF.

Internal Control — Integrated Framework Executive Summary © 2013 and Enterprise Risk Management — Integrating with Strategy and Performance © 2017 Committee of Sponsoring Organizations of the Treadway Commission (COSO). All rights reserved. Used with permission.

Excerpts from *Accounting Ethics and the Near Collapse of the World's Financial System* by Michael Pakaluk and Mark Cheffers, copyright © 2011 by Allen David Press. Used with permission.

Codification of Statements on Auditing Standards, AU-C section 501, *Audit Evidence — Specific Consideration for Selected Items*, Copyright © 2021, American Institute of Certified Public Accountants.

Excerpts from *Statement of Policy Regarding Lawyers' Responses to Auditors' Requests for Information*, 31 Bus. Law. 1709 (1976), ©1976 by the American Bar Association. Reprinted with permission. All rights reserved. This information or any or portion thereof may not be copied or disseminated in any form or by any means or stored in an electronic database or retrieval system without the express written consent of the American Bar Association.

Part One

The Basic Skills

This book proceeds in three parts, in order for you to become proficient in the use of accounting and financial information as it affects the practice of law. The latter two parts of the book deal with accounting issues with legal implications and, conversely, legal issues which deeply involve accounting concepts. But before we can discuss any of that, you must have a basic understanding of what financial information is, how it is created, and how to use it. Those are the subjects of this Part One.

Chapter 1

Creation of Financial Information

A. The Demand for Financial Information

This course is about financial information and how it is used in the practice of law. Specifically, our focus is on financial information as supplied by the accounting systems generally in use today. Before studying these systems, however, it is important to understand **why** we need financial information in the first place. By beginning with the demand for financial information, we can better understand how it is supplied.

Why do we focus on *financial* information? Most financial information relates to businesses operated in pursuit of profits. This is not universally true, however. Trusts and not-for-profit businesses, for example, may not operate in such an entrepreneurial fashion. But we will examine the ordinary profit-seeking business, as that is the source of most of the financial accounting systems we have today.

Any enterprise which makes a profit does so by producing or selling goods or by providing services at a price which exceeds the costs of production, sale or service. While this may seem obvious, it drives much of the demand for financial information. Most of the other uses of financial information are closely related to this profit motive. As you read Problem 1-1 below, consider how this business tries to turn a profit, what other kinds of financial information you would want about the business, and why.

* * *

Problem 1-1

Bill and Ted are recent college graduates. Rather than focusing on the subjects of their majors, they have decided to hang around Collegetown and pursue a most excellent adventure in business. They realized as students that Collegetown needed a good coffee house, and they have therefore founded and now operate The Collegetown Coffeehouse (TCC).

Bill got his hands on some family money, and has invested $75,000 in the business. Ted maxed out his credit cards to the tune of $25,000 to invest in the business. Bill receives 75% of the profits, and Ted receives 25%. Among the people to whom Bill and Ted owe or might owe money are:

- Collegetown National Bank, where the business borrowed $30,000 to purchase appliances and fixtures. The Bank has a lien on the equipment purchased to secure repayment. Fixed payments of $1,500 are due each month.

- Collegetown Bakery Supply, which makes daily deliveries of pastries, cookies and cold drinks. Payments are due on the previous delivery when the next delivery is made.
- Rufus, the master espresso bartender. He is paid weekly based on the amount Bill and Ted can afford.
- Napoleon, the landlord who leases TCC its most resplendent yet charming street-corner on-campus digs. The rent is $3,500 due each month (in advance).
- The Internal Revenue Service, ever hoping, should TCC actually produce triumphant profits, that Bill and Ted will remit taxes due on their shares of those profits. That calculation and payment (if any) is made once each year.
- The State Revenue Department, which collects from The Collegetown Coffeehouse 6 percent of its gross sales. Payments of the sales tax are due each month.

(a) Which of the following events or items do you think would be important to each of the above persons or entities (including Bill and Ted) and why?

(1) TCC's gross sales (before any expenses are subtracted)

(2) TCC's net income (after expenses, including salaries and interest, are subtracted)

(3) TCC's weekly net cash flow

(4) TCC owes $1,000 to a wholesale fruit and vegetable dealer, is late in making payment, and the wholesaler refuses to deal with TCC anymore

(5) A customer fell on TCC's crumbling sidewalk last month and incurred $100,000 in doctor and hospital bills

(6) The value of the furniture and fixtures to an interested buyer

(b) What else might you want to know about TCC? Would it make any difference which of the above persons you are representing?

* * *

Different accounting theories and theorists abound, but much of the financial information sought about any enterprise relates to one of four broad areas:

(1) Description. What is the business? What is General Motors? Is it several hundred thousand employees, lots of large buildings and factories, a bunch of unsold cars, and some other things? If we were more precise about each of these items, would we have a pretty good description? If so, why? If not, why not?

(2) Measurement. How much is there? How much money, inventory, principal left on the mortgage, debt, stock? How many factories, threatened lawsuits, toxic waste dumps? Why do we need to not only describe the entity but measure it as well?

(3) Evaluation. How well is it doing? How much money do we have? How much profit have we made? Compared to last year? Compared to other enterprises in our line of work? How do we provide information which facilitates such evaluations?

(4) Control. How well is the management taking care of the assets entrusted to it? Are they being properly used? Even a profitable business can be run by a self-interested manager who takes more than his or her due. How can we be assured that this isn't happening?

* * *

Problem 1-2

Recall the different types of information listed in Problem 1-1(a). Which is related most closely to description? Measurement? Evaluation? Control? What about the additional items of financial information which you suggested in Problem 1-1(b)?

* * *

B. How Financial Information Is Reported

This section discusses the information traditionally supplied in financial statements. The standards for financial statement presentation are set by bodies whose history and functions we will study in Chapter 3. Although we might differ with the standard-setters, indeed, the previous problem fleshed out some of those differences, they have agreed upon the three financial statements described below: balance sheet, income statement, and statement of cash flows.

1. The Balance Sheet

The primary descriptive financial statement is the balance sheet. It is a listing of the business' assets, and the claims against those assets. A balance sheet is a "snapshot" of an enterprise, or to use another analogy, it "speaks" only as of a specific date. Every balance sheet notes the specific date on which it measures the assets of and claims against an enterprise

Example

General Electric Company and consolidated affiliates presents the following balance sheet (they call it a "Statement of Financial Position") as of December 31, 2019 (all amounts are in millions of dollars). I have simplified it, but only slightly.

Assets		Liabilities and Equity	
Cash	$36,394	Short-term borrowings	$22,072
Investment securities	48,521	Accounts payable	15,926
Current receivables	16,769	Progress collections	20,508
Inventories	14,104	Other current liabilities	15,753
Financing receivables — net	3,134	Long-term borrowings	71,972
Other receivables	7,144	Insurance and annuity benefits	39,826
Property, plant and equipment — net	46,186	Noncurrent compensation	31,867
Intangible assets	37,387	All other liabilities	18,263
All other assets	56,409	**Total Liabilities**	**236,187**
Total Assets	**$266,048**		
		Common stock	702
		Accumulated comprehensive losses	(11,732)
		Other capital	35,956
		Retained earnings	4,935
		Total Equity	**29,861**
		Total Liabilities and Equity	**$266,048**

Consider each of these groups of balance sheet items in turn.

Assets. In general, accounting standards define an asset as something which will probably contribute an economic benefit to the entity.[1] And by convention, assets are listed in several broad categories. Notice that GE has managed to classify over 266 *billion* dollars' worth of assets in just nine categories. Note also that each asset is given a dollar valuation. Obviously, you can imagine that in many instances, a lot of work and even lawyers' time is involved in deciding how much an asset is *worth* and, indeed, whether it even exists at all. One final convention of the balance sheet is that assets are typically listed in order of "usability" or "liquidity" as it is usually called. The more "liquid" an asset is, the more quickly it can be turned

1. Statement of Financial Accounting Concepts No. 6 ¶ 25 (1985). We will describe this type of "Statement" and learn its authoritative weight in Chapter 3.

into money or money's worth. Thus, "cash" is always first, and some things that would be very difficult to sell, intangible assets, for example, are much further down the list.

Claims. On the other side[2] of the balance sheet are listed, in similar fashion, the claims against those assets. It is important to understand that the "real" things of value owned by an entity appear **only** on the asset side of the balance sheet. The other side "mirrors" those assets—it lists who or what claims those things of value. The claims to those assets are divided into two portions—those claims by the creditors of the enterprise, called **liabilities**, and those claims by the owners, called **equity**.[3] Just as accounting standards define assets as probable future economic gains, they define liabilities as probable sacrifices of economic benefits; and equity is simply what is left over after liabilities are subtracted from assets.[4] Thus, the listing of the claims to the assets in GE's balance sheet proceeds in this fashion, and is called "Liabilities and Equity." As the assets are listed with the most liquid or "current" first, so are the liabilities listed with the earliest due first.

The Balance of a Balance Sheet. Thinking of the balance sheet as a listing of assets and claims explains, at least in theory, why it must balance. Assets are valuable and scarce resources. None of the enterprise's assets will go unclaimed, so the assets can never be greater than the claims. And since *all* the assets are presumably listed on the asset side, there is nothing more to be had from the business, and so the assets can never be less than the claims. This is often referred to as the **fundamental accounting equation**:

Assets = Liabilities + Equity

It is reflected in the definition of "equity" stated above: the difference between the assets and liabilities. The balance sheet simply portrays the enterprise in accordance with this fundamental equation.

Problem 1-3

Avon is going into the beauty business selling beauty supplies door-to-door. She began by investing $100 in her business, and using that to purchase $50 worth of beauty supplies (with $50 cash left over). Prepare a balance sheet for Avon after these events. You can use the account titles in Problem 1-4.

---

2. Actually, GE's balance sheet is presented in just one column, so that Assets appear above Liabilities and Equity. I have reformatted it here to demonstrate more clearly the equivalence and balance of the balance sheet.

3. In the case of a corporation, such as GE, there are "accumulated comprehensive losses" and several different lines dealing with shareholder's equity. These are covered in Chapters 4 and 7, respectively.

4. Statement of Financial Accounting Concepts No. 6, *supra* note 1, at ¶¶ 35 (liabilities) and 49 (equity).

Problem 1-4

Avon has the following balance sheet at the end of her first year:

Avon Beauty Consultants — Balance Sheet at end of First Year

Assets		**Liabilities and Equity**	
Cash	$130	Avon, Owner's interest	$180
Beauty supplies	50		
Total Assets	$180	Total Liabilities and Equity	$180

Suppose at the beginning of the second year, Avon borrows $900 from the bank and uses the proceeds to buy a computer to use in her business. What would her balance sheet look like then? How would it be different if Avon still borrowed $900 but the computer only cost $850?

* * *

2. The Income Statement

If we take a "snapshot" of the enterprise today, as we do with a balance sheet, it is bound to be different from the one we took yesterday, since the enterprise is a dynamic institution. Even if it is staid and slow-moving, today's snapshot will certainly be different from last month's or last year's. The income statement describes how we get from one balance sheet to the next, focusing on the "equity" portion of the balance sheet. It is as important as the balance sheet in describing a business.[5]

Example. Wanda sells widgets. She buys them for $10 each. She invested $100 in her business, and purchased 8 widgets. Her initial balance sheet would show $100 in assets ($20 in cash and $80 in widgets) and there would be only one claim: Wanda's claim of ownership of the whole thing, or $100.

Wanda's Widgets — First Balance Sheet

Assets		**Liabilities and Equity**	
Cash	$20	Wanda, Owner's interest	$100
Widgets	80		
Total Assets	$100	Total Liabilities and Equity	$100

5. The balance sheet and the income statement (along with a statement of cash flows) are identified as the basic components of financial information. *See* Statement of Financial Accounting Concepts No. 1 ¶¶ 40–49 (1978).

The balance sheet balances, as it should. Now, the free enterprise system being what it is, suppose Wanda convinces a customer to pay her $12.00 for one of the widgets, even though it only cost Wanda $10.00. If our fundamental accounting equation (and common sense) are correct, someone must have a claim to all of the $102 in assets. That "someone" must be Wanda, since there are no creditors yet.

Wanda's Widgets — Second Balance Sheet

Assets		Liabilities and Equity	
Cash	$32	Wanda, Owner's interest	$102
Widgets	70		
Total Assets	$102	Total Liabilities and Equity	$102

But comparing the First and Second balance sheets doesn't tell us how Wanda came by her extra $2 in equity. Wanda's Second Balance Sheet would look exactly the same if, for example, Wanda:

- had bought a thousand widgets for $10 each, sold them all for $12 each, and withdrawn the $2,000 from the business for her own use; or
- had bought a thousand widgets for $10 each and sold them all for $10.002 each!

Notice that our balance sheets, although providing a good description of Wanda's Widgets, have failed in the other objectives of financial information noted above: measurement, evaluation, and control.

How do we know what happened between the first and second balance sheets? The two transactions are related by explaining, in an income statement, that her revenues were $12 and her expenses were $10. In general, a revenue is any increase in an asset (or decrease in a liability) related to the entity's operations, and an expense is the flip-side, any decrease in an asset (or increase in a liability) related to its operations. Thus, we would have:

Wanda's Widgets — Income Statement for the Period

Revenues — Widget sales	$12
Expenses — Cost of widgets sold	10
Net income	$2

Wanda's net income ($2) is precisely the amount by which her "Owner's interest" increased between the First and Second balance sheets. The income statement explains ***how*** the owners' equity increased (or decreased), which is information not available from the balance sheet alone. ***The net income will be the precise amount by which the equity has increased for the period.*** Conversely, if business has not been good, liabilities will have increased more than assets, and the net loss will be reflected in the decrease in equity for the period.

In this explanation of the income statement, I have introduced to you the fundamental concepts of "revenue" and "expense."

- ***Revenue:*** any increase in an asset (or decrease in a liability) related to the entity's operations.
- ***Expense:*** any decrease in an asset (or increase in a liability) related to the entity's operations.

These definitions are over-simplified; indeed, determining what constitutes revenue or expense is one area where lawyers are often deeply involved in helping with accounting decisions, as we will see in Chapter 4.

The important conceptual point is that the income statement provides a link between successive balance sheets. Together, the income statement and the balance sheet provide the fundamental description of the business, as well as measurement, evaluation, and control of how the management is doing. It works the same way for a large public corporation as it did for Wanda (with a few real-world complications).

Example

Intel Corporation's Consolidated Income Statement for 2019 was as follows (amounts in millions of dollars), slightly simplified:

Net revenue	*$71,965*
Operating expenses:	
Cost of sales	*29,825*
Research and development	*13,362*
Marketing, general and administrative	*6,150*
Other operating expenses	*593*
Total operating expenses	*49,930*
Operating income	*22,035*
Gains on equity investments, net	*1,539*
Interest and other income	*484*
Income before taxes	*24,058*
Provision for taxes	*3,010*
Net income	***$21,048***

As with the balance sheet, the revenue and expense account titles are governed largely by custom and convention. Note that they allow Intel to account for almost $50 billion dollars in expenses in three rather concise categories.

Now, how does this relate to the balance sheet? In a separate "Consolidated Statement of Stockholders' Equity," the company explains that all of this net income is added to the stockholders' equity account as follows (again, in millions of dollars):

Balance, Dec. 29, 2018	*$50,172*
2019 Net income	***21,048***
Repurchase of common stock and rights	*(12,119)*
Cash dividends declared	*(5,578)*
Balance, Dec. 28, 2019	*$53,523*

This demonstrates that the equity, or claim on Intel's assets belonging to Intel stockholders, was increased by $21,048 million — the precise amount of net income. There were distributions to stockholders (repurchases of stock and dividends) which reduced this net claim, so at the end of the year it was only $3,401 million larger than at the beginning.

* * *

Problem 1-5

Here is Wanda's Widgets' Second Balance Sheet from just above:

Assets		Liabilities and Equity	
Cash	$32	Wanda, Owner's interest	$102
Widgets	70		
Total Assets	$102	Total Liabilities and Equity	$102

Wanda purchases two more widgets for $10 each, and sells six for $12 each. (Remember each widget cost Wanda $10.) Prepare Wanda's Third Balance Sheet and an income statement for the period between the Second and Third Balance Sheets.

Problem 1-6

Wilma is also in the widget business. Here is a summary of her first month. On the first day, she contributed $200 to her business. She used this to buy 15 widgets (at $11 each — they are more expensive in Wilma's part of the country) for a total of $165, with $35 left over for other uses. During the month, Wilma sold four widgets for $13 and three for $15. All the customers paid in cash. Wilma also hired an assistant for the month, to whom she paid $50 in cash. Prepare an income statement for Wilma for her first month, and a balance sheet at the end of the first month.

Problem 1-7

George runs a hardware store. His balance sheet at the beginning of the most recent month is as follows:

George's Hardware Store — Balance Sheet at Beginning of Month

Assets		Liabilities and Equity	
Cash	$1,500	Bank loan	$12,000
Supplies	1,000		
Inventory*	12,500		
Furniture and fixtures	20,000	George, Owner's interest**	23,000
Total Assets	$35,000	Total Liabilities and Equity	$35,000

* Refers to the hardware and other materials George sells in the store.

** The owner's interest in an existing business would consist of George's initial investment plus any money he has made but has not withdrawn for personal use.

(a) During the month, George sold all of the inventory for $10,000 and used up $500 worth of supplies in the process. Prepare an income statement for George and a balance sheet at the end of the month. Assume that neither the "Furniture and fixtures" nor the "Bank loan" changes in amount.

(b) At the end of the month, after these statements have been prepared, George is considering (i) paying off $5,000 of the bank loan or (ii) distributing $5,000 to himself as owner. How would either of these affect the income statement or balance sheet you have just prepared? Consider each separately.

* * *

3. The Statement of Cash Flows

"Income" and "cash" may have little to do with each other. In Problems 1-6 and 1-7, you saw businesses with losses but with plenty of cash. Conversely, a business can be "profitable" in the sense that it has a good product and robust sales, but poor cash management will bring an untimely end. Because the amount and flow of cash in a business is a paramount concern to the business' creditors and investors, cash is separately calculated and presented in the Statement of Cash Flows.

The statement of cash flows focuses, as its name indicates, solely on transactions involving cash. The statement then **classifies** every inflow (receipt) or outflow (payment) as one from one of three basic types of business activities: *operations*, *financing* or *investing*.

Financing: transactions with creditors or owners

Investing: purchase or sale of long-term fixed assets

Operations: everything else (normal day-to-day business activities)

Illustration

Recall Wanda's second balance sheet and subsequent events from Problem 1-5:

Assets		Liabilities and Equity	
Cash	$32	Wanda, Owner's interest	$102
Widgets	70		
Total Assets	$102	Total Liabilities and Equity	$102

Wanda purchases two more widgets for $10 each, and sells six for $12 each. Her statement of cash flows would be as follow:

Opening balance	$32
Cash from operations:	52
Ending balance	$84

The $52 is the difference between cash from sales ($72) and the payment for new widgets ($20)

* * *

Problem 1-8

Wilma's Widgets (in Problem 1-6) had the following story. On the first day, she contributed $200 to her business. She used this to buy 15 widgets (at $11 each—they are more expensive in Wilma's part of the country) for a total of $165, with $35 left over for other uses. During the month, Wilma sold four widgets for $13 and three for $15. All the customers paid in cash. Wilma also hired an assistant for the month, to whom she paid $50 in cash.

Prepare a statement of cash flows for Wilma's Widgets for this period. Calculate the amounts and classify each cash flow according to the three-part scheme above.

* * *

Problem 1-9

Return to George's Hardware Store in Problem 1-7. Recall that the business' Cash balance at the beginning of the month was $1,500.

(a) During the month, George sold all of the inventory for $10,000 and used up $500 worth of supplies in the process. Prepare a statement of cash flows for the month.

(b) At the end of the month, after this statement has been prepared, George is considering (i) paying off $5,000 of the bank loan or (ii) distributing $5,000 to himself as owner. How would either of these affect the statement of cash flows you have just prepared? (Consider each separately.) Assume that these two activities are both considered "financing" activities.

(c) George has received an offer to buy some of his furniture and fixtures for $10,000. Assume that the items in question cost George $8,000. What impact would this sale have on the income statement? What impact would it have on the statement of cash flows? Assume that this activity is considered an "investing" activity.

C. How Financial Information Is Generated

So far, we know:

Who wants financial information: owners and creditors

Why they want it: description, measurement, evaluation, and control

What is supplied: balance sheet, income statement, cash flow statement

Now we turn to the **how?** How are these financial statements created from the mass of financial information generated by a business?

In order to understand financial statements, you must understand *generally* how they are prepared. I emphasize the word *generally* because we are about to cover in concentrated form what normally takes much longer in traditional financial and cost accounting courses. But this *general* understanding will be perfect for you as a **lawyer** (not an accountant) to deal with the financial statements you will encounter in practice.

1. Bookkeeping and Its Terminology

The fundamental accounting equation

Assets = Liabilities + Equity

explains the near-universal practice of double-entry bookkeeping. This system of bookkeeping maintains the balance sheet in balance by making sure that whenever a change is made to one item on the balance sheet, a compensating change is made to another item to keep the balance sheet in balance. This double-entry system serves as a running check on the integrity of the accounting system. A balance sheet can be calculated at any time; if it doesn't balance, then a mistake has been made. Of course, there could still be other mistakes; items may have been posted to the wrong accounts. But the double-entry system does assure that when an entry is made, the corresponding impact on the balance sheet has been considered.

What follows is a description of how the double-entry bookkeeping process works. It is the same whether the bookkeeper is a little person with a green eyeshade and quill-and-ink pen or the financial information computers at any large company which may process thousands of transactions every hour. To understand the process, you will need to become familiar with six new terms: **journal, account, debit, credit, ledger, and post**.

a. Journal

The **journal** is the foundation of the bookkeeping system. As its name implies, it is a chronological record of all the financial events of the business. Think of it as you might keep a narrative journal or diary. Everything that happens in the world which affects the financial position of the business is recorded in the journal. This is true whether the "journal" is paper, or virtual, or both.

This simple item has a critical purpose. The journal is the *only* proper way in which information gets into the accounting records. Behind every tidbit of information in a company's financial statements there is a journal entry. The journal is known as the "book of original account" or "original entry" and is a vital part of an accounting and internal control system.

b. Accounts

We have discussed what a journal is, but not what one looks like. Although it is like a diary, it is not a narrative. Because the essence of financial information is that it deals with money or money's worth, the journal records events measured in dollars. In addition, each event is recorded in a standardized format, looking toward the eventual use of the journal information to prepare financial statements and other valuable information. Thus, the dollar amounts are collected in descriptive groups known as accounts. Each item, whether an asset, a liability, an equity, a revenue, or an expense, is recorded in an account.

Account names for external financial reporting are standardized more through custom than detailed proscription of account names and contents. How much detail is provided in each category depends on the purpose of the financial statement. For example, when General Motors reports to its shareholders, it will group billions of dollars worth of steel, plastic, rubber, partially finished cars and trucks, and so forth together as "inventory." When a plant manager or warehouse manager reports internally to her superiors at General Motors, however, simply calling all of it "inventory" is not sufficiently detailed. But because we are learning about general purpose financial reporting to *external* users, the general groupings will do.

Assets are normally grouped together in accounts such as cash, accounts receivable, inventory, equipment, buildings, patents and so forth. All of the billions of dollars of assets of a large corporation may be listed in as few as a half dozen accounts; recall the General Electric balance sheet earlier in this chapter.

Liabilities normally consist of accounts payable, short-term debt and long-term debt. Certain significant specific assets or liabilities may be listed separately.

Equity accounts vary depending upon the type of business entity involved. In a sole proprietorship or partnership, the accounts may simply be the names of each of the owners. In a corporation, equity accounts normally consist of the money originally invested in the business (reflected in "common stock" and "paid in capital" or "contributed capital" accounts) and money made since then and not repaid to the owners (reflected in a "retained earnings" account).

Revenue and expense accounts may also vary according to the type of business. Revenue may simply be recorded as "revenue" or "sales," as we saw in the income statements excerpted above. Expenses and their types vary widely, but typically include the cost of sales (also known as the cost of the goods sold), and administrative expenses.

Illustration

A delivery truck backs up to the loading dock of the local grocery store. The shipper proceeds to unload dozens of cases of different types of canned goods, frozen foods, and the like. When everything is unloaded, the store manager is presented with an invoice. The manager would then give the shipper a check for the invoiced amount, if it is correct. Perhaps our journal would reflect these changes as follows:

July 1, 20xx. Received $115,000 of inventory, paid in cash.

Note that the journal-keeper made some significant decisions and generalizations. First, the inventory was recorded with a *dollar value*. Second, standard *account names* were used; all the groceries were grouped together as "inventory," and the check was called "cash" even though it wasn't currency. These are types of accounts customarily used for external financial reporting. Surely the frozen foods manager is going to want more detail on contents and costs than this one invoice, but those are different reports than the *general purpose financial statements* we are constructing. If we agree with the account titles and classifications, so far this journal has done its job.

This journal looks a lot like a narrative. It would require careful sifting through the day's journal to collect all the financial information. Through the years, accountants have devised a standardized form for recording in journals. Some cynics might say that it is deliberately designed to confuse outsiders and deter them from understanding accounting information. But this is not so, as we are about to see.

c. Debits and Credits

So far our narrative journal seems to serve our purposes pretty well. But it doesn't allow us to determine how the fundamental accounting equation has been affected, and thus to prepare the Balance Sheet, Income Statement and Cash Flow Statement which everyone is expecting.

Recall the fundamental accounting equation:

Assets = Liabilities + Equity

and how it forms the basis for the balance sheet. If necessary, review part B.1 of this chapter to help you recall this information.

Note how the fundamental accounting equation puts assets on "one side" of the equal sign and liabilities and equity on the "other side." Now comes the tricky part: the "one side" [always the left side] is the ***debit*** side, and the "other side" [always the right side] is the ***credit*** side.

WARNING

"Debit" means "left" and "credit" means "right." That is all. Attaching any other meaning to these terms will be hazardous to your understanding of accounting.

It only takes a moment's reflection to see that assets (on the left side) are debit accounts, or accounts which normally carry debit balances. Correspondingly, liability and equity accounts (on the right side) normally carry credit balances. To add to a debit balance (make it larger) we "debit" that account. To reduce a debit balance (make it smaller) we "credit" that account. The reverse is true for accounts with credit balances. This is a critical distinction, so let's practice.

* * *

Problem 1-10

(a) Recall the grocery store example above: "Received $115,000 of inventory, paid in cash." How would you record in a journal the receipt and payment in full for $115,000 of inventory? Both "inventory" and "cash" are assets, which normally carry debit balances. To increase the inventory account, you would [debit/credit] it for $115,000. And to decrease the cash account to reflect the payment, you would [debit/credit] it for $115,000. Do the total debits equal the total credits?

(b) Suppose that, instead of paying for the groceries in the above problem, the shipper agrees to bill the store and the store agrees to pay later when billed. In accounting terms, this is an "account payable," a liability account normally with a credit balance. To increase the inventory account, you would [debit/credit] it for $115,000.

And to increase the accounts payable to reflect the obligation to pay later, you would [debit/credit] it for $115,000. Do the total debits equal the total credits?

(c) Suppose that General Motors sells $1 billion worth of new common stock to investors. The cash received is an asset, an account with a debit balance. To increase the cash account by $1 billion, we would therefore [debit/credit] the cash account for $1 billion. The common stock is an equity, an account with a credit balance. To increase the common stock account by $1 billion, we would therefore [debit/credit] the common stock account for $1 billion. Does the total of debits equal the total of credits?

Problem 1-11

Let's see how things are going with Bill and Ted at The Collegetown Coffeehouse (TCC).

(a) TCC makes a payment of $1,000 in cash to the bank, to be applied to the principal on the bank loan.

> **(i)** To reduce the balance in the "Cash" account, which is an *asset* account with a *debit* balance, we would [debit/credit] that account.
>
> **(ii)** To reduce the balance in the "Bank Loan" account, which is a *liability* account with a *credit* balance, we would [debit/credit] the account.

(b) Collegetown Bakery Supply delivers 20 cases of Jones soda and 20 dozen cookies and scones. TCC agrees to pay $450 next week.

> **(i)** If we record the soda and cookies as "Supplies," this is an [asset/liability/equity] account with a [debit/credit] balance. To increase the amount in the account, we would [debit/credit] that account.
>
> **(ii)** If we record the obligation as an "Account Payable," this is an [asset/liability/equity] account with a [debit/credit] balance. To increase the amount in the account, we would [debit/credit] that account.
>
> **(iii)** Make sure after completing (i) and (ii) that your work makes sense, that is, the appropriate balances have moved in the right directions, and all debits equal credits.

* * *

With this knowledge of debit and credit entries and how you add and subtract from each kind of account, we're ready to prepare a standard journal entry: (1) date, (2) a listing of accounts and amounts debited, with the abbreviation "Dr" (for debit)[6] (3) indented to the right, a listing of accounts and amounts credited, with the abbreviation "Cr" (for credit) and (4) a brief narrative description of the transaction. In

6. This is the accepted abbreviation for "debit," though it is admittedly confusing. It may have originated as an abbreviation for "debtor," although attaching any such meaning to current usage is incorrect, as the above "warning" box makes clear. W. Richard Sherman, *Where's the "R" in Debit?*, 13 Accounting Historians Journal 137, 138 (Fall 1986) ("They simply mean 'left' and 'right.' No more, no less.").

abbreviated form (like accounting textbooks), the date and narrative explanation are often omitted.

Illustration

Recall Wanda's Widgets in the "brief illustration" on p. 1–7. Wanda had invested $100 in her business. She bought eight widgets for $10 each. Assuming this happened on January 1, the proper journal entry would be:

		Dr	Cr
1/1	Dr Widgets (or Inventory)	$80	
	Cr Cash		$80

Purchased widgets for cash.

* * *

Problem 1-12

Using the above format, prepare journal entries for the transactions in Problem 1-10. Assume that each transaction occurred on January 1.

(a) Received $115,000 of inventory, paid in cash.

(b) Received $115,000 of inventory on account (a liability).

(c) Issued $1 billion of common stock (an equity) for cash.

Problem 1-13

Using the above format, prepare journal entries for the transactions in Problem 1-11. Assume that each transaction occurred on January 1.

(a) TCC makes a payment of $1,000 in cash to the bank, to be applied to the principal on the bank loan.

(b) Collegetown Bakery Supply delivers 20 cases of Jones soda and 20 dozen cookies and scones. TCC agrees to pay $450 next week.

Problem 1-14

(a) Suppose a business has the following four transactions on January 2. Prepare journal entries for each. You may use the following account titles: Cash, Accounts Payable, Equipment, Owner's Equity, Bank Loan. Before you begin, be sure you know whether each of these accounts is an asset, liability, or equity.

(1) Borrows $10,000 from the bank

(2) Purchases a new machine for $5,000

(3) Pays off $2,500 of its bills to suppliers

(4) Distributes $1,000 in profits to the owner

(b) If the balance in the Cash account at the beginning of the day was $10,000, and these were the only activities for the day, what is the balance in the Cash account at the end of the day?

* * *

In these journaling exercises, we have dealt with various combinations of entries to three types of accounts: asset, liability, and equity. Consider all the possible types of debits or credits we could enter.

Debit Entries	Credit Entries
• increase an asset	• decrease an asset
• decrease a liability	• increase a liability
• decrease an equity	• increase an equity

Every journal entry will involve at least one debit and one credit entry, illustrated here with three of the possible combinations.

Combination of Entries	Example
• increase (debit) an asset • decrease (credit) an asset	Exchange of one asset for another, such as purchasing equipment or inventory for cash.
• increase (debit) an asset • increase (credit) a liability	Acquisition of an asset "on credit," that is, in exchange for a promise to pay.
• increase (debit) an asset • increase (credit) an equity	A contribution by an owner of cash (or other assets) to the entity.

* * *

Problem 1-15

Describe a transaction which would:

(a) Decrease (credit) an asset and decrease (debit) a liability

(b) Decrease (credit) an asset and decrease (debit) an equity

Problem 1-16

(a) Owner sells today a truck for $5,000 cash. The truck was previously "on the books" at $5,000. Ignore depreciation. What would be the journal entry to record the sale?

(b) When Owner bought the truck, she did so with a loan from Bank. The loan was originally for $5,000, but has been paid down to $4,500. What would be the journal entry when Owner pays off the outstanding amount of the loan?

(c) Suppose that in (a) above, instead of selling the truck for $5000, Owner sold it for $6000? What would be the journal entry?

(d) Suppose that in (a) above, instead of selling the truck for $5000, Owner sold it for $4000? What would be the journal entry?

* * *

Actually, there are still more possibilities, since many transactions involve more than two accounts; but still, the debits must always equal the credits in each journal entry. When such a transaction occurs, it results in a *compound* journal entry.

Illustration

Suppose an entity purchases equipment for $1,000, and pays $500 now and agrees to pay the rest in 30 days. The liability created thereby would normally be called an "Account Payable," and the compound journal entry to record this event would be as follows:

Dr Equipment	1,000	
Cr Cash		500
Cr Accounts Payable		500

The double-entry bookkeeping system works because, for each and every journal entry, debits must equal credits. "The recording of these two aspects is double entry bookkeeping. Everything else in accounting derives from this beginning—it is the big bang of accounting."[7]

d. Ledgers and Posting

In Problem 1-14(b), you were asked to compute the balance in the Cash account after posting four transactions to that account. It was a relatively simple matter to review each journal entry, and add or subtract as you went along whenever "Cash" was involved (the tricky part was keeping the debits and credits straight). But if there were hundreds or thousands of such transactions, the calculation would be a bit more daunting.

The ledger is the place we collect financial information from the journals, classified by account rather than in chronological order. Each account has its own ledger, and the information from the journals is painstakingly ***posted*** to the ledger on a regular basis. Whether done by quill pen or computer, the process of posting is simply to collect all the journal entries to one account in one place.

7. Ted J. Fiflis, Commentary, *Thoughts Evoked by "Accounting and the New Corporate Law,"* 50 Wash. & Lee L. Rev. 959, 971 (1993).

The ledger page (again, whether in a book or on a computer) consists of a debit and a credit side, hence a ledger is often called a "T" account because of the lines separating the top and the two sides:

Account title	
Debit entries	Credit entries

Illustration

In Problem 1-14(b), each of the journal entries would have been posted to the appropriate ledger, and all the entries involving "Cash" would have been posted to the Cash ledger. We were told that the Cash account started with a $10,000 balance, and all the other entries from the four events in Problem 1-14 were:

(1) Borrows $10,000 from the bank

(2) Purchases a new machine for $5,000

(3) Pays off $2,500 of its bills to suppliers

(4) Distributes $1,000 in profits to the owner.

These events would be posted in the cash ledger as follows:

Cash	
10,000	5,000 (2)
10,000 (1)	2,500 (3)
	1,000 (4)
11,500	

Each ledger entry is identified with the number of the journal entry from which it came, so that it is possible to trace every ledger entry back to the journal, the book of original entry. The double line indicates that a balance is being calculated (or "struck").

Notice how much easier it is to compute the balance in the account when all the numbers are in the ledger, as opposed to picking them out of the journal. Admittedly, this is a simplistic step, since this is done automatically in any computerized accounting system. But the concept of a ledger and posting to a ledger is still important in our understanding of how the accounting system works.

* * *

Problem 1-17

Georgia owns and operates a small hardware store. At the end of the day yesterday, her cash balance was $1,000. Today, Georgia: (i) records sales of $1,500, all in cash, (ii) pays off $500 of a $10,000 bank loan she took out last year, and (iii) pays $500 to herself as owner (she has invested over $10,000 in the business). Post each of these events to the "Cash" ledger. What is the balance in that ledger after these transactions?

Problem 1-18

Walter has begun a competing widget business, contributing cash to the business and purchasing assets. After a few days of business, he has generated the ledgers below. As with the previous example, the ledger entries are numbered in reference to the journal entries from which they came.

(a) Prepare journal entries for each transaction reflected by these ledgers; include a description of each transaction.

(b) Prepare a balance sheet for Walter after these transactions.

Cash		Widgets	
(1) 5,000	(4) 750	(1) 5,000	
	(5) 1,000	(3) 1,000	
Office Supplies		**Accounts Payable**	
(2) 500		(4) 750	(2) 500
			(3) 1,000
Bank Loan		**Walter, Owner's Equity**	
(5) 1,000	(1) 5,000		(1) 5,000

* * *

2. Revenue and Expense Accounts

So far, all of the examples in this Section have involved trading among assets, liabilities and equities. Indeed, we noted earlier that *all* financial transactions could be described by changes in these accounts. While this is technically true, that's not the way it's done, for reasons that were explained with Wanda's Widgets when we first met the income statement in section B(2) of this Chapter. You may want to review this material now.

The income statement describes how we get from one balance sheet to the next. In order to create an income statement, we need to have accounts which store information *temporarily* in accounts other than balance sheet accounts. These are the revenue and expense accounts. Increases in assets (or decreases in liabilities) related to the entity's operations (what it's in business for) are called **revenues**, and recorded in revenue accounts. Decreases in assets (or increases in liabilities) related to the entity's operations are called **expenses**, and are recorded in expense accounts.[8]

a. Compiling the Accounts

Now, how do these new revenue and expense accounts fit into the grand scheme of debit and credit accounts and balances? Recall that these accounts exist only temporarily in order to calculate net income, which becomes part of the owner's equity. Since we know that the owners' equity account normally has a credit balance, we therefore know that:

- Revenue accounts (which increase equity) have credit balances.
- Expense accounts (which decrease equity) have debit balances.

Or, to present it graphically with the "T" account of owner's equity:

Owner's Equity	
[Debit entries *decrease* balance]	[Credit entries *increase* balance]
Expenses	Revenues
+ (debit) – (credit)	– (debit) + (credit)

The purpose of these revenue and expense accounts is to collect information *between* balance sheet dates, so that we can prepare an income statement which correctly reflects the activity which occurred between those two balance sheet dates.

Example. Let's return to Wanda's Widgets now that we're experts in journals, ledgers, debits and credits, to see how revenue and expense accounts work.

Recall Wanda's first balance sheet as she began business:

Wanda's Widgets — First Balance Sheet

Assets		**Liabilities and Equity**	
Cash	$20	Wanda, Owner's interest	$100
Widgets	80		
Total Assets	$100	Total Liabilities and Equity	$100

8. Statement of Financial Accounting Concepts No. 6 ¶¶ 78 & 80 (1985).

Next, Wanda sells one of the widgets, which cost her $10, for $12 cash. If we were to record this event in the journal, it might look like this:

Dr Cash	12	
Cr Widgets		10
Cr Owner's equity		2
Sold one widget, cost $10, for $12 cash.		

This would be accurate — the debits equal the credits, the balance sheet balances, and Wanda's ownership equity has increased by $2, reflecting her profit on the sale. But, if we make changes directly to the "Owners' Equity" account, we will not see *how* we got from one balance sheet total to the next.

> **REVENUE AND EXPENSE ACCOUNTS**
>
> We use revenue and expense accounts to **separately** collect the revenues and the expenses. The calculation of profit or loss (and the resulting addition to/subtraction from equity) will wait for a later time.

While this concept may seem unduly formalistic in Wanda's example, consider a more complicated business with costs not clearly related to any particular "widget" sold: office rent, repairs on a widget-making machine, property taxes, and so on. We need to wait a proper amount of time (the "accounting cycle") before collecting all the costs and revenues in order to say we have a good idea of whether the business realized any net income, and if so, how much.[9] The revenue and expense accounts serve as "buckets" to collect this information for the accounting cycle. These buckets are then emptied into an income statement, or, in proper accounting terminology, we "close" the books. That is the title of the next subsection. After closing, the revenue and expense accounts are then ready to begin collecting again in the next accounting cycle.

Here's how it works. Let's record Wanda's transaction properly. We have a sale, and we have a related expense. ***Each is a separate transaction — this is probably counterintuitive to you but is critical to understanding bookkeeping.*** Here's how the accountants do it.

Dr Cash (asset account)	12	
Cr Sales (revenue account)		**12**
Sold one widget for $12		
Dr Cost of goods sold (expense account)	**10**	
Cr Widgets (asset account)		10
One widget sold from inventory, cost $10		

9. The accounting cycle is almost always a calendar year, though it certainly doesn't have to be. For example, companies with publicly-traded securities are required to issue income statements every three months.

The highlighted entries reflect our new revenue and expense accounts. Note that they have the proper balances: credit balance for revenues, debit balances for expenses. **That's it.** This doesn't say that Wanda has any income. Remember, that will wait until it is time to "empty the buckets," or close the revenue and expense accounts into an income statement.

* * *

Problem 1-19

Recall George's hardware store from Problem 1-7. His balance sheet at the beginning of the most recent month is as follows:

George's Hardware Store — Balance Sheet at Beginning of Month

Assets		**Liabilities and Equity**	
Cash	$1,500	Bank loan	$12,000
Supplies	1,000		
Inventory*	12,500		
Furniture and fixtures	20,000	George, Owner's interest	23,000
Total Assets	$35,000	Total Liabilities and Equity	$35,000

* Refers to the hardware and other materials George sells in the store.

(a) During the month, George sold all his inventory for $10,000 and used up $500 worth of supplies in the process. In Problem 1-7, you were asked to prepare an income statement based on these events. Review these problems and your answers now.

(b) Now, with the benefit of using revenue and expense accounts, prepare a journal entry for the store when it sells the inventory for $10,000 cash. Remember, we're not yet concerned with expenses. You would [debit/credit] the cash account [an asset account which has a debit balance] to record the increase in cash. The balancing entry would be to [debit/credit] the "sales" account [a revenue account which has a credit balance] to increase the amount of sales.

(c) Next, recall that George used up $500 worth of supplies during the month. You would [debit/credit] the supplies account [an asset account which has a debit balance] to record the decrease in supplies. The balancing entry would be to [debit/credit] the "supplies expense" account [an expense account which has a debit balance] to increase the amount of supplies expense.

(d) Finally, assume it is the end of the month, and George is prepared to take stock of his inventory. You would [debit/credit] the inventory account [an asset account which has a debit balance] to record the decrease in inventory. The balancing entry would be to [debit/credit] the "cost of sales" or "cost of goods sold" account [an expense account which has a debit balance] to increase the amount of cost of sales/cost of goods sold.

Problem 1-20

Smart opens his law practice. During the first month, Smart:

(1) Deposits $5,000 into a bank account as his initial investment

(2) Purchases $1,000 of office equipment for cash

(3) Buys library books for $500 on credit from East Publishing Co.

(4) Writes a will for Able and is paid a $400 fee in cash

(5) Pays office rent of $300 in cash

(a) Make the appropriate journal entries for each event. You may use these account titles:

Cash	Library books
Accounts payable	Owner's equity
Accounts receivable	Fee income
Office equipment	Rent expense

Be sure to label each account as an asset, liability, equity, revenue, or expense. How did you decide?

(b) What is the cash balance after these transactions have been completed?

* * *

b. Closing the Books

"Closing the books" is how accountants refer to the work done on the journal and ledgers to prepare a balance sheet and income statement.

How do the books look at the end of the period? According to what we've set up so far, there is a journal (or several journals) running every day, and all this information is collected in ledgers, one for each account. By making our journal entries properly, we are assured that debits and credits are equal. Using ledgers allows us to calculate the balance in an account at any time.

There are two basic steps required to turn this day-to-day system of recording into financial statements: calculating a *trial balance*, and separately displaying and totaling the revenue and expense accounts in an income statement.

(1) Trial balance. Once all the journal entries have been made, the accountant or the computer prepares a trial balance. This is simply a listing of all the accounts regardless of type, and the debit or credit balances in each. It is a "trial" balance because in non-computerized systems, it may be the first real check that there are no errors of calculation, transcription, and the like which would prevent debits and credits from being equal.[10]

---

10. *See* Edward Peragallo, *Origin of the Trial Balance*, 31 Accounting Review 389, 390 (1956) (describing early accounting writers' description of "the trial balance as a check on the equality of the debits and credits").

Example. Let's return to Wanda's Widgets. Recall that her first balance sheet, upon organization of the business, was as follows:

Wanda's Widgets—First Balance Sheet

Assets		Liabilities and Equity	
Cash	$20	Wanda, Owner's interest	$100
Widgets	80		
Total Assets	$100	Total Liabilities and Equity	$100

Now Wanda has been in business for a month. During that month, she contributed another $100 to the business, and purchased 10 more widgets at $10 each all paid for in cash. She has sold a total of 16 widgets for $12 each in cash. She also paid $150 cash in rent for retail space. Her trial balance after these events would be as follows:

Wanda's Widgets Trial Balance as of the end of the month

Account	Debit	Credit
Cash	$62	$
Inventory (widgets)	20	
Sales		192
Cost of goods sold	160	
Rent expense	150	
Wanda, Owner's equity	—	200
	$392	**$392**

This is not sleight of hand but the double-entry process in action. You should verify to yourself each of these totals and their places as debit or credit balances from the facts given above. The number $392 at the bottom of each column has little significance in the life or value of the business, What matters is, of course, that it is the *same total* for each column. Debits equal credits.

(2) Closing the income statement accounts. Now that all the accounts are properly prepared, it's time to "empty out" or close the revenue and expense accounts to an income statement, and add the net income to (or subtract the net loss from) the owner's equity. But first, we need to know which account is which.

Example. Using the shorthand

A = asset
L = liability
Q = equity
R = revenue
X = expense,

We would classify Wanda's trial balance as follows:

Wanda's Widgets Trial Balance as of the end of the month

Account	Debit	Credit
Cash [A]	$62	$
Inventory (widgets) [A]	20	
Sales [R]		192
Cost of goods sold [X]	160	
Rent expense [X]	150	
Wanda, Owner's equity [Q]	___	200
	$392	$392

Now it's simply a matter of collecting the revenue and expense accounts in an income statement:

Wanda's Widgets — Income Statement for the month

Revenues		
Sales		$192
Expenses		
Cost of goods sold	160	
Rent	150	310
Net loss		$(118)

And now we have removed the revenue and expense accounts and can prepare a balance sheet. To do so, we add the net income to (or subtract the net loss from) the owner's equity account. The double-entry system has already assured us that our balance sheet will balance. Wanda's equity at the beginning of the month was $200. From that, we subtract the net loss for the month, $118, for a balance at the end of the month of $82.[11]

Wanda's Widgets — Balance sheet at end of month

Assets		Liabilities and Equity	
Cash	$62	Wanda, Owner's equity	$82
Inventory (2 widgets)	20		
Total Assets	$82	Total Liabilities and Equity	$82

11. This step is often referred to as "closing the income statement to the balance sheet" and can be done by way of formal journal entries to temporary reconciling accounts. I have omitted that step to keep it simple. We will see a more formal example in Chapter 7.

The financial statements (save for the statement of cash flows) are complete. Now the revenue and expense accounts are emptied out and ready to begin collecting data for a new accounting period.

* * *

Problem 1-21

Begin with Wanda's balance sheet after the first month in business.

Wanda's Widgets — Balance sheet at end of month

Assets		Liabilities and Equity	
Cash	$62	Wanda, Owner's equity	$82
Inventory	20		
Total Assets	$82	Total Liabilities and Equity	$82

The following events take place during the second month, as Wanda gets a little more aggressive with her business.

(1) Wanda needs cash to expand, and goes to the bank to secure a $100 loan. She also contributes $100 more of her own money to the business. She uses the proceeds of the loan and the investment to purchase 20 widgets for $10 each.

(2) She purchases an ad in a local monthly craft magazine for $50 cash.

(3) She sells six widgets at a craft fair for $13.50 each, paid in cash.

(4) The advertising begins to pay off, and the next weekend she sells ten more widgets for $14 each, paid in cash.

(5) At the end of the month, she pays the bank $1 cash as interest on the loan. She is not yet obligated to make any principal payments.

(a) Prepare journal entries for each of these events. You may use the following account titles, or make up your own (so long as they are reasonably descriptive and consistent).

Cash	Sales	Advertising
Cost of sales	Interest	Bank loan
Wanda, Owner's equity		

Be sure you can identify each as an asset, liability, equity, revenue or expense account.

(b) Prepare a trial balance at of the end of the second month.

(c) Close out the revenue and expense accounts, prepare an income statement for the second month, and add the gain to (or subtract the loss from) the appropriate account.

(d) Prepare a balance sheet as of the end of the second month.

Problem 1-22

Meanwhile, back at George's Hardware Store, he is in his fifth month of business. His balance sheet at the beginning of the fifth month is as follows:

George's Hardware Store Balance Sheet at the Beginning of Month Five			
Assets		**Liabilities and Equity**	
Cash	$500	Accounts payable**	$1,500
Accounts receivable*	800	Bank loan	11,500
Supplies	1,200		
Inventory	15,000		
Furniture & fixtures	20,000	George, Owner's interest	24,500
Total assets	$37,500	Total Liabilities and Equity	$37,500

* Amounts due from customers who have purchased goods on store credit.

** Amounts which George is obligated to pay but has not yet paid. We will learn more about these accounts in the next section.

The following events take place during the fifth month. Prepare journal entries for each, and then a trial balance at the end of the month, an income statement for the month, and a balance sheet at the end of the month.

(1) First week sales: $5,000. Of this amount, $4,500 was paid in cash and $500 on store credit. [Note here that you will credit Sales for $5,000 and debit Cash for $4,500. What will be the remaining debit entry to balance? What asset was received instead of cash?]

(2) Paid $500 of the accounts payable in cash.

(3) Second week sales: $2,500, all paid in cash.

(4) Paid $1,000 in principal on the bank loan, and $100 interest for the month, in cash.

(5) Third week sales: $3,500: $3,000 in cash and $500 on store credit.

(6) Customers pay $750 of their store credit accounts in cash.

(7) Fourth week sales: $4,000: $3,000 in cash and $1,000 on store credit.

(8) End of month counts of inventory: $2,000 of inventory remains on hand. Note that we started with $15,000, and there were no purchases, so $13,000 is therefore expensed as "Cost of Sales." Similarly, $700 of supplies remain, we started with $1,200, and therefore $500 are expensed.

Problem 1-23

Prepare a statement of cash flows for George's Hardware Store for the month just completed in the previous problem. Explain to George why the cash balance has changed. What other account(s) have change substantially during the month? What does this tell you about George's business in this month?

* * *

3. Accrual and Deferral

In the last problem, you first met a business which did not operate entirely on a cash basis. Some of George's customers made purchases on credit, and George made some purchases for his store on credit. You saw a first example of how revenue and expense accounts differ slightly from the flow of cash in and out of a business.

Why is there such a difference? Most people believe they have received income when the cash or check is received, and similarly that they have incurred an expense when the cash or check is given. This system has a simple but important name: **cash basis** accounting. It is probably the way you and I (and some small businesses) keep their books.

But cash basis accounting will not do for a more complex operation, because the receipt and payment of cash don't match up very well with the *accounting cycle*— discussed in the previous section—the period for which we are measuring income. The accounting cycle's income statement must include everything relevant for that period *and nothing else.* This is the fundamental accounting principle of **matching** the economic events of the accounting period.[12]

In order to match events with their economic significance, we will often have to adjust our cash payments to conform to the proper accounting treatment. This adjustment process has a technical name. Recognizing expenses or income when cash hasn't been received or paid is called **accrual**. *Not* recognizing expenses or income *even though* cash has been received or paid is called **deferral**.

	Income/expense recognized?	Cash received/paid?
Accrual	YES	NO
Deferral	NO	YES

The entire system is usually referred to as **accrual basis** accounting, the main alternative to cash basis accounting.

a. Accrual of Income and Expenses

First, consider accrual: recognizing income/expense even though cash has not been received/paid.

12. We will cover the fundamental accounting assumptions in Chapter 3.

i. Accrual of Income

Accrual of income occurs when revenue is recognized even though no cash is received. Because cash is not affected, we need to debit a different account to account for the revenue.

> *Example 1.* George's Hardware Store offers its customers in-store credit. If a customer wishes to make a purchase, the price can be paid within 90 days for no additional charge. Suppose a customer purchases a table saw on July 1 for $250, but takes advantage of the 90-day deferral. George would book the revenue, with a credit to "Sales," a revenue account with a credit balance:
>
> 7/1/xx Cr Sales **(R)** 250
>
> But what would be the offsetting debit entry? It is not to reduce some other liability, because George has no liability to this customer. And it is not to reduce an equity, because we don't make entries to equity accounts directly.[13] It is not to cash, an asset account with a debit balance, because no cash has been received. We will establish another asset for this purpose—the ***accrual*** entry is a debit to "Accounts receivable," also an asset account with a debit balance.[14]
>
> George's accountant would complete the above journal entry as follows:
>
> 7/1/xx Dr Accounts receivable **(A)** 250
> Cr Sales **(R)** 250
> *Sold table saw on store credit.*

Accrual of income results when sales are made "on credit," as in the above example. It also results when income is recognized over time. The main examples of this are in the lending and leasing businesses.

> *Example 2.* Landlord leases shopping center space on July 1 to Tenant for $24,000 per year, $6,000 payable every three months. Suppose Landlord is preparing financial statements at the end of the month. No cash has been received on the lease. Both an accountant and a lawyer would agree that some amount is due the Landlord. If the lease is performed as agreed, that amount would be the prorated lease amount, or $2,000. The Landlord's accountant would assume that this leasing business will continue in its ordinary course, and would journal as follows:
>
> 7/31/xx Cr Rental Income **(R)** 2,000
>
> Income has been recognized, and although an attorney and accountant might disagree over the amount, the recognition is clearly proper. But what

13. Recall this is the purpose of "revenue" and "expense" accounts as described in part C(2) above.

14. The account could have some other title which accurately describes the transaction, such as "Credit sales," "Customer credits," and so on, but "Accounts receivable" is the customary parlance. It is often abbreviated by the shorthand A/R.

would be the corresponding debit entry if no cash is received? As with the hardware store example, it would be a "receivable," an asset account with a debit balance. The Landlord's accountant would complete the journal entry as follows:

7/31/xx	Dr Lease receivable (A)	2,000	
	Cr Rental Income (R)		2,000

Recognized one month's income on lease.

ii. Accrual of Expenses

Accrual of an expense occurs when an expense is recognized even though no cash is paid. The expense is a debit entry, but we need a non-cash balancing entry.

Example 3. A pipe burst on December 1 at George's Hardware Store. George hired a contractor to make repairs the following week for $3,500. The contractor did the work and has billed George for the amount, but George has not paid it yet. It is appropriate to recognize an expense, as the amount has been incurred, so George's accountant would do so as follows:

12/1/xx	Dr Repair expense (X)	3,500

But what is the offsetting credit entry? No other asset has been reduced, as George has not yet paid for the repairs with cash (or tools or anything else). No equity is affected, because we don't make direct entries to equity accounts for this purpose.[15] The balancing entry is to recognize a liability of "Accrued expenses"[16] for the amount to be paid:

12/1/xx	Dr Repair expense (X)	3,500	
	Cr Accrued expenses (L)		3,500

Contractor services to repair burst pipe.

Accrual of income and expenses can be major assets and liabilities on a business' balance sheet.

Example

Walmart, Inc. tallied almost $524 billion in sales during its most recently completed fiscal year. The company notes that it "recognizes sales revenue, net of sales taxes and estimated sales returns, at the time it sells merchandise or services to the customer." That may not require that cash be paid, and the result is that Walmart shows $6.3 billion of "Accounts Receivable" on its Jan. 31, 2020, balance sheet.

15. Recall this is the purpose of "revenue" and "expense" accounts as described in part C(2) above.

16. The account could have some other title which accurately describes the transaction, such as "Repairs on credit" or "Unpaid expenses" and so on, but "Accrued Expenses" is the customary title. If George was making purchases from a supplier or wholesaler with whom the store had an account, the entry would be to "Accounts Payable," again a customary title, often abbreviated by the shorthand A/P.

Similarly, the company has recorded, on that same balance sheet, "Accrued Liabilities" of $22 billion for wages, benefits, taxes, interest, and advertising expenses which have been incurred but not yet paid for.

* * *

Problem 1-24

Bank lends $100,000 to Customer at 10% interest ($10,000) per year. The loan is for ten years, and none of the principal amount is due until maturity. At the end of the first year, it is time to account for the $10,000 in interest. No cash has been paid by Customer or received by Bank.

(a) On Bank's accounts, how would it recognize the $10,000 interest income? It would recognize (accrue) the income to an account titled "Interest revenue," but what would be the corresponding entry?

(b) On Customer's accounts, how would it recognize the $10,000 interest expense? It would recognize (accrue) the expense to an account titled "Interest expense," but what would be the corresponding entry?

* * *

b. Deferral of Income and Expenses

Next, consider deferral: not recognizing (thus "deferring") income/expense even though cash has been received/paid. With deferral, our pen is driven to the ledger by the cash entry, of course, but the difficulty is in determining what should be the balancing account.

i. Deferral of Income

Income is deferred when we don't recognize it right now in a revenue account, even though we've received cash.

> ***Example 4, Part 1.*** George's Hardware Store offers "gift cards" to its customers. A customer may purchase a gift card of a certain amount and a holder of such a card may later redeem some or all of its value for merchandise at the store. Suppose a customer purchases a gift card on September 1 for $300. Obviously, George must recognize the cash by debiting that asset account:
>
> 9/1/xx Dr Cash (A) 300
>
> But what will be the balancing credit entry? George has not earned the right to keep the money yet, so crediting a revenue account is not the right answer. Would you make a credit entry by reducing some other asset? Has George sold anything which was exchanged for the cash received? Not really. And

we would not make a credit entry by directly adjusting equity accounts. The remaining option is that we have created a liability. A complete journal entry would be as follows:

9/1/xx	Dr Cash (A)	300	
	Cr Gift card obligations (L)		300

Sale of gift card.

A prepayment or deposit is the most common form of deferred revenue, whether a general deposit, as in the above example, or payment in advance on a contract, as in the following example.

Example 5, Part 1. Landlord leases shopping center space on July 1 to Tenant for $24,000 per year, payable three months ($6,000) in advance. Landlord also requires a $10,000 security deposit. Tenant writes a check to Landlord for $16,000 on July 1. Again, our recording pen is driven to the ledger by the receipt of cash:

7/1/xx	Dr Cash (A)	16,000	

Again, we search for a credit entry to offset this debit entry. There is no appropriate credit entry to reduce an asset, as there is no other asset surrendered or sold in exchange for this cash. An equity entry is not appropriate because there is no gain or loss. Again, the only possible entry is to recognize a liability. But here we have two types. The prepaid rent is a liability which we expect to be satisfied through lease time, and the security deposit is (with a compliant tenant and ethical landlord), a liability which we would expect to be satisfied with a return of the deposit. So with that minor difference in classification, the Landlord would complete the entry thus:

7/1/xx	Dr Cash (A)	16,000	
	Cr Prepaid Rent (L)		6,000
	Cr Security Deposit (L)		10,000

Receipt of security deposit and first three months' rent in advance.

It is important to complete the story to see how the accrual system works. Following a ***deferral*** of income, which we just illustrated, there will be an ***accrual*** of income, much as we studied in the preceding part. Let's see how each story would conclude.

Example 4, Part 2. George's Hardware Store offers "gift cards" to its customers. A customer comes in to the store on December 27 to purchase a table saw for $250, and tenders as payment a gift card with a $300 balance. Clearly we can journal the sale as follows in the conventional fashion:

12/27/xx	Cr Sales (R)		250

The debit entry, however, is not to cash (to increase an asset) but rather to the gift card liability created earlier (to decrease a liability).

12/27/xx	Dr Gift card obligations (L)	250	
	Cr Sales (R)		250

Sale of table saw with payment by gift card.

Notice two important things about this example. First, the gift card retains its $50 unspent balance, and George's Hardware Store balance sheet will still reflect this $50 liability. Second, the sale has placed the recognition of revenue at the right time. The journal entry in Example 4, Part 1 did not involve any entries to income statement amounts. The journal entry in Example 4, Part 2 recognized the income, but did not involve any entries to the cash account.

> ***Example 5, Part 2.*** Landlord leases shopping center space on July 1 to Tenant for $24,000 per year, payable three months ($6,000) in advance. Tenant wrote a check to Landlord on July 1 to cover the first three months' rent. At the end of July, Landlord wishes to update its financial statements to, among other things, recognize one month's of lease income. Landlord would do so as follows:
>
> | | | | |
> |---|---|---|---|
> | 7/31/xx | Cr Lease revenue (R) | | 2,000 |
>
> The balancing debit entry would be the "payment" for the lease. But it is not a debit to cash (to increase an asset), or to any other asset for that matter. The lease is "paid" by reducing the liability owed to the Tenant, as follows:
>
> | | | | |
> |---|---|---|---|
> | 7/31/xx | Dr Prepaid Rent (L) | 2,000 | |
> | | Cr Lease revenue (R) | | 2,000 |
>
> *To recognize one month prepaid rent as earned.*

Notice two important things about this example. First, the "liability" to the Tenant remains at $4,000, reflecting the initial prepayment of $6,000 (see Example 5, Part 1). This amount will be reduced to zero as this exercise is repeated at the end of August and September. I use the word "liability" in quotes, because the amount may *not* be actually owed back to the Landlord under governing law, but the accountant will treat any unearned income as a liability in this fashion. So the attorney and the accountant may have different views on this matter. Second, the revenue recognition occurs at the proper time. The journal entry in Example 5, Part 1 (on July 1) did not involve any revenue. The revenue recognition occurs only after the revenue is earned (on July 31) in Example 5, Part 2, and did not involve any cash! The accrual system is designed to separate receipt of cash from recognition of income in this way.

In each case, in Parts 2 of Examples 4 and 5, we see that a liability is reduced by a corresponding recognition of revenue. An accountant or business will often speak of "taking liabilities into income" by accrual in this fashion. You can now see the logic in this otherwise confusing statement.

Example

Facebook, Inc. reports, on its Dec. 31, 2019, Balance Sheet, a liability of $269 million for "Deferred Revenue and Deposits." The company explains the entry as follows: "Deferred revenue mostly consists of billings and payments we receive from marketers in advance of revenue recognition.... The increase in the deferred revenue balance for the year ... was driven by cash payments from customers in advance of satisfying our performance obligations...."

* * *

Problem 1-25

Wanda has developed a website to help with her widget sales. On January 1, Year 1, she hired WebMasters, a web development and maintenance company for two years for a total of $5,000. The company demanded up-front payment of the entire amount.

(a) If WebMasters is preparing its books on December 31, Year 1, how should the company account for this payment?

(b) What entry should be made by WebMasters on December 31, Year 2, to account for the expiration of the second year of the contract?

* * *

ii. Deferral of Expenses

An expense is deferred when we don't recognize it right now in an expense account, even though we've paid the cash. Again, as with any deferral, our pen is driven to the ledger by the disbursement of cash, but we have determined *not* to recognize an expense. Therefore, the balancing entry must be to some other account.

> ***Example 6, Part 1.*** Wanda has developed a website to help with her widget sales. On January 1, Year 1, she hired WebMasters, a web development and maintenance company, for two years for a total of $5,000. The company demanded up-front payment of the entire amount. Wanda would obviously journal the payment:
>
> | | | | |
> |---|---|---|---|
> | 1/1/1 | Cr Cash (A) | | 5,000 |
>
> But what would be the balancing debit entry? The value of the contract has not dissipated, that will happen over the next two years. So we would not debit an expense, at least not yet. What other debit entries are possible? We could reduce a liability, but there is none involved here; that's not what Wanda did with the $5,000. We do not want to write directly to the equity account, so the only other possible debit entry is that Wanda has another asset. She would journal thusly:
>
> | | | | |
> |---|---|---|---|
> | 1/1/1 | Dr Prepaid web service contract (A) | 5,000 | |
> | | Cr Cash (A) | | 5,000 |
>
> *Purchased two-year web service contract.*

It may seem odd to think of prepaid expenses as "assets," just is it seemed odd to think of prepaid revenue as a "liability." But just as the prepaid revenue may never be earned, and may need to be refunded, so the prepaid expense may never be actually incurred.

It is important to complete the story to see how the accrual system works. Following a ***deferral*** of an expense, which we just illustrated, there will be an ***accrual*** of the expense, much as we studied in the preceding part on accrual entries.

> ***Example 6, Part 2.*** Wanda has developed a website to help with her widget sales. On January 1, Year 1, she hired WebMasters, a web development and maintenance company for two years for a total of $5,000. In Part 1, we noted that she recognized an asset, "Prepaid web service contract" of $5,000. At the end of Year 1, Wanda will have used up, or consumed if you will, the benefit of one year of a two-year contract. Unless the contract itself specifies some other way to measure its value, an accountant will likely assume the value expires ratably over time, and thus half the value should be considered an expense in Year 1. The journal entry to recognize, or "accrue" that expense, is as follows:
>
> | | | | |
> |---|---|---|---|
> | 12/31/1 | Dr Web maintenance exp (X) | 2,500 | |
> | | Cr Prepaid web service contract (A) | | 2,500 |
>
> *To recognize expense of one year under web service contract.*

As with the deferral of income followed by accrual, there are two important things to note here with the similar treatment of expenses. First, the value of the asset will be reduced to reflect its remaining value. At the end of the second year, the same expense will be accrued, and the value of the asset will be reduced to zero. Second, the expense recognition occurs at the proper time. The journal entry in Example 6, Part 1 (on January 1) did not involve any expense. The expense accrual occurs only after the asset is used in the course of business during Year 1. That recognition, in Example 6, Part 2, and did not involve any cash. The accrual system is designed to separate payment of cash from accrual of expenses in this way.

We also account for other long-term assets in this way. If Wanda purchases a delivery truck for her widget business for $30,000, and it is expected to last several years, she will recognize an asset and reduce its value over those years. The concept of an asset as a prepaid expense may be even clearer in the case of physical assets. We will study this process in detail in Chapter 5, appropriately titled "Assets and Expenses," recognizing this connection.

c. Recap

We have reviewed accrual and deferral of both revenues and expenses. That gives us four possibilities. Remember for *accrual*, there will be entries to revenue/expense accounts but *not* to cash. Accrual is recognizing the income/expense even without cash movement. For *deferral*, there will be entries to cash, but *not* to revenue/expense accounts. Here, there is cash movement, but no recognition of revenue or expense. And as we have seen, an event of deferral is usually followed later by an event of accrual.

	Revenue	Expense
Accrual (no cash)	Dr Liability (if prepaid) Dr Accts. Receivable (if not) **Cr Revenue**	**Dr Expense** Cr Asset (if prepaid) Cr Liability (if not)
Deferral (no revenue or expense)	**Dr Cash** Cr Liability	Dr Asset **Cr Cash**

Accrual is a powerful concept and a key part of accounting's fundamental assumptions—that events should be recognized when they occur. The accrual system also is a prime incubator for fraud, because it separates an objective measure—receipt or payment of cash—from the recognition event. Consider the above table and try to predict where the greatest probability for fraud would exist. Imagine how a devious owner might try to improve the financial position of the company. It would probably be by recognizing as much income as possible and by ignoring as many expenses as possible. Thus, it is those areas, highlighted below, which are the danger zones for financial fraud:

Financial fraud danger zones		
	Revenue	Expense
Accrual (no cash)	Dr Liability (if prepaid) Dr Accts. Receivable (if not) **Cr Revenue**	
Deferral (no revenue or expense)		Dr Asset **Cr Cash**

Accrual of Income

Deferral of Expenses

* * *

Problem 1-26

In Problem 1-20, Smart opened his law practice. Here's a recap of his first month:

(1) Deposits $5,000 into a bank account as his initial investment

(2) Purchases $1,000 of office equipment for cash

(3) Buys library books for $500 on credit from East Publishing Co.

(4) Writes a will for Able and is paid a $400 fee in cash

(5) Pays office rent of $300 in cash

With your knowledge about deferral of expenses and revenues, reexamine each decision you made about the cash paid and received by Smart.

(a) Is the office equipment expenditure all an expense for the month? What about the books?

(b) How would Smart account for item (4) if Able didn't pay cash for the will, but Smart sent Able a bill?

(c) How would Smart account for item (5) if the payment was for next month's rent, which isn't due until the end of next month?

Problem 1-27

Dr. Strangelove is a physician who runs a small private practice, with a nurse and a receptionist. He prepares monthly financial statements. On Tuesday, November 30, he:

(1) paid his nurse her $2,000 salary for November

(2) paid one-half of the November rent. The total rent of $5,000 is due today, but he doesn't have the money.

Make the appropriate journal entries for these events.

Problem 1-28

In each problem below, one month is the relevant accounting period.

(a) Tenant pays Landlord $1,200 for three months' rent beginning January 1. What would be the appropriate entry in Tenant's journal on January 31 to recognize one month of rent expense?

(b) Appliance repair firm sells a one-year maintenance contract for $600 effective January 1. What would be the appropriate entry in the firm's journal on January 31 to recognize one month of revenue?

(c) Landlord hired painters to paint an apartment for $200. The painters began and completed work on January 15, but haven't billed Landlord for their work yet. What would be the appropriate entries in Painter's journal upon completion of the painting work? What would be the appropriate entry when the Landlord pays $200 on February 4?

(d) Landlord bills Tenant each month for the past month's rental. What entry would be made in Tenant's books on January 31 to reflect the fact that one month's rent ($400) is "expensed" and owed? What entry would be made on February 4 to reflect a $400 cash payment to Landlord for the January rent?

Problem 1-29

We continue with Dr. Strangelove. On this same Tuesday, November 30, he:

(1) pays a $250 internet bill received (and expensed) on October 24

(2) noted that his receptionist had worked two days so far this week, but won't be paid until Friday. Her salary is $200 per week.

Make the appropriate journal entries. Hint: what entry was made on October 24? What entry will be made on December 3?

Problem 1-30

Smart billed Baker last year $1,000 for services rendered. This amount was recognized by Smart as income last year by Smart even though Baker made no payment,

Today (in the current year), Smart receives a check from Baker for $1,500 with the following note attached: "Please apply this amount to my bill and the rest as a deposit for your future services." Make the appropriate entry in Smart's journal upon receipt of this check and note.

Problem 1-31

Fran is a local florist. Write journal entries for the following events which occurred in the shop last month.

(1) She purchased flowers from a local grower for $5,000.

(2) She purchased a commercial refrigerator from Appliance World for $7,000, paying with a promissory note to the store. The refrigerator should last for three years.

(3) One of her delivery trucks broke down, and she had to spend $1,000 to rent a replacement while the truck was in the shop.

(4) She sold $1,000 of flower arrangements to customers on credit.

(5) She owes $100 interest on the loan to Appliance World but hasn't paid it yet.

(6) Flowers which cost Fran $500 have remained unsold, are now spoiled and must be composted.

(7) She purchased a franchise for 1-800-Flowers for one year and paid the first month's franchise fee of $1,000. She will owe $1,000 each month for the next eleven months after this one.

(8) She plans to replace the windows in three months. She has signed a contract with a renovation specialist and made a deposit on the contract of $1,000.

* * *

4. Review and Practice

This procedure of generating financial statements is conceptually pretty simple, but it's easy to get lost in the details, so we'll take a little time to practice. In working the following problems, you may despair, with thoughts such as "lawyers don't do bookkeeping/math/etc." While in general this may be true, keep the following in mind.

- Lawyers in the cases we'll read shortly could have kept lots of clients out of trouble if they had understood how journals and ledgers work.
- Lawyers, especially those representing small businesses, may be called on informally to give some general business-type advice.
- An accounting process question may come up in counseling or litigation; the accountants and auditors with whom the lawyer works will analyze issues using bookkeeping terminology, concepts and examples.
- Lawyers do bookkeeping, or they supervise someone who does, because they're all in business themselves.

Problem 1-32

Dr. Strangelove is ready to complete his balance sheet and income statement. He has made journal entries according to your advice from previous problems, and has struck the following trial balance. Prepare an income statement for his practice for the month ended November 30 and a balance sheet as of that same date.

Dr. Strangelove, MD
Trial balance as of November 30

Account	Debit	Credit
Cash		300
Accounts receivable	1,500	
Fees earned		6,500
Salary expense: nurse	2,000	
Salary expense: receptionist	820	
Accrued expenses		40
Rent expense	5,000	
Rent due		2,500
Office equipment	12,000	
Accounts payable (suppliers)		450
Owner's equity: Strangelove	____	12,130
	21,620	21,620

Problem 1-33

Roger's Rovers is an in-house pet grooming service, which Roger started a few years ago. Its balance sheet as of March 1 is as follows:

Cash	250	Accounts payable	500
Grooming supplies	1,000		
Equipment	5,000		
Prepaid liability insurance	100	Owner's equity	5,850
	6,350		**6,350**

The liability insurance runs through April 30, and then an annual premium of $600 is due.

During March, Roger incurs the following cash expenses:

Grooming supplies	2,000
Equipment repair	250

He also used an additional $500 of grooming supplies from his inventory.

He collects revenues of $2500 in cash.

On March 14, Roger is contacted by Shady Acres Retirement Home. The home wants Roger to come in every two weeks on Tuesdays to offer grooming services for its residents' pets. The home will pay Roger $300 for each visit. Roger's first day to provide services under the contract is April 1. Shady Acres made a $300 cash deposit on the contract.

Prepare a balance sheet for Roger's Rovers as of March 31 and an income statement for the month of March.

Problem 1-34

Janice has launched her new food truck venture, "Janice's Jambalaya." The adventure began on June 1 when she took out a second mortgage on her home for $25,000 to invest in the business.

Janice leased a suitable trailer at $24,000 per year payable monthly in advance. She made the June payment on June 1 and the July payment on June 30. She rented a parking space and commissary (for food preparation and storage) for $1000 per month, with the first three months ($3000) paid in advance on June 1.

On June 2, she spent $15,000 to outfit the trailer for preparing and serving food. The fixtures will last (with maintenance) for about five years. On that same day, she purchased food preparation equipment for an additional $3,000.

Additional costs paid in cash in June:

Food	$4500
Service products (plates, cups, utensils, etc.)	$1500
Cleaning and maintenance supplies	$1,000

Janice is too busy preparing for the July 4 holiday to take a June 30 inventory of these items. She assures you that "hardly anything is left sitting around," but she estimates the total value of everything on hand in the above categories on June 30 to be about $1,000.

She hired Jasmine, a chef/assistant, for $800/week. Jasmine works five days per week. Janice paid Jasmine $3200 for the four weeks through June 27. Jasmine also worked on June 30, but wasn't paid until the end of that week (in July). Janice also incurred costs (taxes, benefits) for Jasmine amounting to 10% of salary, but has not paid those amounts to anyone yet.

Janice sells her food for cash and Venmo only. Her receipts through June 30 were $15,000.

Required. Prepare the following statements for Janice's Jambalaya.

(a) an income statement for the month of June

(b) a statement of cash flows for the month of June

(c) a balance sheet as of June 30.

Problem 1-35

Down the street from The Collegetown Coffeehouse, three entrepreneurs have banded together to form The Collegetown Laptop Company to sell laptops and related supplies, and to provide repair and consulting services for the computers they sell. Henry Founder, Collegetown's well-known small appliance repairman, will contribute his existing small warehouse and store valued at $200,000. Jane Whiz, a recent computer science graduate, will make a modest initial contribution of $1000. Henry and Jane agreed to split the profits from the business 90% for Henry (who will take no salary), and 10% for Jane, who will also be paid a $20,000 annual salary. Charlene Cash, a wealthy investor, will lend $200,000 at 10% interest with a fixed repayment schedule. After organizing the business as indicated above, their balance sheet appears as follows.

Collegetown Laptop Company
Balance Sheet — January 1

Assets		Liabilities and Equity	
Cash	$201,000	Loan from Charlene	$200,000
Land & Buildings	200,000	Henry, Owner's equity	200,000
		Jane, Owner's equity	1,000
Total Assets	**$401,000**	**Total Liabs. & Equity**	**$401,000**

At the end of the year they give you the following information, gleaned from scraps of paper and their collective memories.

(1) They purchased laptop computers for sale at a cost of $1,750,000. All purchases were made with cash.

(2) Computers were sold for $2,900,000. In addition, repair and consulting services were performed for $500,000.

(3) Of the total amount of computer sales described in (2), $500,000 was sold on credit. The company offers 90 days' "same as cash" financing. $400,000 of credit sales were collected in cash during the year. All the repair and consulting services were paid for in cash.

(4) The loan agreement with Charlene requires semiannual payments. For the first year, there were two payments. Each payment was $10,000 interest and $5,000 repayment of principal. Both payments were timely made during the year, in cash.

(5) The total of additional expenses related to the sales and service of computers — supplies, wages for personnel, costs of operating and maintaining the building and equipment — was $1,000,000. These expenses were all paid in cash. There was no inventory remaining at the end of the year.

(6) Jane was paid her agreed salary as well as a bonus of 10% of her salary, later agreed upon by all three investors.

Make all appropriate journal entries required by the above events, and prepare an income statement for the year and a balance sheet as of Dec. 31. Ignore depreciation and taxes.

Problem 1-36

Let's look at a month in the life of The Collegetown Coffeehouse, recalling the basic set-up of the business from Problem 1-1:

- Bill invested $75,000 in the business; Ted invested $25,000. Assume both contributions were made in cash.
- TCC borrowed $30,000 from Collegtown National Bank to purchase appliances and fixtures. The first payment on the loan will be due at the end of the month as follows: $490 interest and $10 repayment of the loan.
- TCC bought a total of $50,000 worth of appliances and fixtures, all paid in cash.
- Rufus, the master espresso bartender, is paid weekly based on the amount Bill and Ted can afford. For now, Rufus has agreed to take $300 per week plus a payment of 2% of TCC's receipts at the end of the month.
- TCC signed a lease with Napoleon, owner of TCC's most resplendent yet charming street-corner on-campus digs. The rent is $3,500 due each month on the last day of the month.

We'll start with TCC's balance sheet at the beginning of the month, and we'll derive a balance sheet and income statement after the month's activities. In this simple world we will ignore depreciation and taxes.

(a) Assume the first three bulleted events above happened on August 1. What would the TCC balance sheet look like once the proper journal entries were made?

(b) The following events occurred at TCC during August. Assume payments are cash unless otherwise indicated.

August 1—TCC purchased $5,000 worth of supplies (pastries, cookies and bottled drinks) from Collegetown Bakery Supply "on account."

August 2—TCC takes out an advertisement in the Collegetown Times, to run weekly throughout the month. The cost is $500, which was paid in cash.

August 8—Bill and Ted tally up the first week's receipts, which are $1,000. After a brief air-guitar celebration, they pay Rufus his $300.

August 9—Collegetown Bakery Supply delivers $2,500 worth of supplies. At the same time, TCC pays the $5,000 due from the August 1 delivery.

August 22—Business has been auspiciously good the past two weeks, so much so that Bill and Ted did not have occasion to count their proceeds. They held their breaths (Ted actually passed out, which he described as "awesome") as they added up the total: $4,500 in cash! Rufus was paid $600 for the past two weeks (with a most humble apology for being too busy to make last week's payment).

August 23—Four counter stools were destroyed in an entirely uncool brawl at TCC and had to be replaced. The old stools had cost $50 each, but the new ones cost $75 each and were paid for in cash. Bill and Ted of course had no insurance for such events.

August 27—Collegetown Bakery Supply delivers $5,000 worth of supplies. At the same time, TCC pays the $2,500 due from the August 9 delivery.

August 29—The fourth week's most excellent receipts are tallied: $2,000 in cash, and $500 on customers' "tabs" (which Bill and Ted agreed to begin offering). Rufus is paid his $300 salary.

August 30—Bill reluctantly makes the first required payment on the Bank loan: $490 interest and $10 repayment of the loan.

August 31—Socrates (pron. *So'*-crates), a local accountant, comes in to philosophize and to do the end-of-month bookkeeping for Bill and Ted. He figures the following:

(i) Sales on August 30 and 31 totaled $500 in cash

(ii) A check of the storeroom reveals that $2,500 worth of supplies remains on hand, meaning that the supplies expense for the month is $10,000.

(iii) Rufus will not be paid until the end of the following week (assume Rufus works six days each week and that he worked on both the 30th and 31st).

(iv) He knows that payments are due to Napoleon the landlord and to Rufus for his 2% gross-receipts share, but Bill and Ted have departed with the company checkbook for a most triumphant party. He cannot make the payments, but does account for the expenses.

Write appropriate journal entries for each event. Make sure that everything balances after each entry, and be sure to include any needed end-of-month entries made by Socrates. Use the following account titles:

Cash	Accounts receivable	Furniture & fixtures
Bank loan	Accounts payable	Sales
Supplies	Supplies expense	Casualty expense
Rent expense	Advertising expense	Salary expense
Interest expense	Accrued expenses	
Bill, Owner's interest	Ted, Owner's interest	

(c) Prepare ledgers for each account and calculate the trial balance for TCC as of August 31. Be sure the debits equal the credits.

(d) Next, "close the books" by calculating income (or loss) in an income statement for the month of August. Then add that income to (or subtract that loss from) the equity in the balance sheet. Remember that the income (or loss) is allocated between Bill and Ted according to their agreement: 75% to Bill and 25% to Ted.

(e) Finally, prepare the balance sheet for TCC on August 31. If we've done our work correctly, the balance sheet will balance.

Problem 1-37

Further down the street from The Collegetown Coffeehouse, Sudsy and Rinso have decided to start a self-serve laundry, to be called "Wash-Mart." The following events occurred during the month of August 20xx. Based on these events, prepare

(a) all required journal entries, including end-of-month accrual entries

(b) a balance sheet as of August 31, 20xx, and

(c) an income statement for the month of August 20xx.

Unless otherwise stated, assume that all expenses are paid in cash. This is the calendar for August 20xx.

August 20xx

Su	M	Tu	W	Th	F	Sa
1	2	3	4	5	6	7
8	9	10	11	12	13	14
15	16	17	18	19	20	21
22	23	24	25	26	27	28
29	30	31				

August 1. Sudsy contributes $10,000 to the business. Rinso contributes ten used washers and five used dryers, valued at $10,000.

August 2. Sudsy signs a one-year $18,000 lease for a prime washing location. He pays $1,500 security deposit and the first month's rent of $1,500. Rent is due on the first of each month (but was paid today for August). Rinso obtains a loan from Bluegrass Bank for $30,000, which is used to purchase equipment for the Wash Mart. The loan is for five years, with semi-annual payments of interest due on October 1 and April 1 of each year. The interest rate is 8%, or $200 each month.

August 5. Sudsy buys a website for Washmart for $1000 from a web hosting company. He also agrees to pay $100 month, beginning in September, for website maintenance and tracking of visits, purchases, and data management. Through this website and at the store, The Wash-Mart provides Wash-Cards, stored-value cards which can be used in person or online to pay for machine usage at Wash-Mart.

August 6. Rinso hires Charlene Cheer as a weekday attendant, at a salary of $400 per week. Charlene starts work on Monday, August 9, and is to be paid on Friday of each week. She receives no other benefits.

August 7. Wash Mart has its grand opening, offering free wash and dry for the day. Sudsy and Rinso estimate that they have foregone $200 in revenues.

August 13. The bank reports that Wash-Card sales are $1,500 for the week, which is transferred to the company's bank account. Charlene is paid.

August 15. Sudsy leases a dry-cleaning machine from Industrial Equipment Corp. The monthly lease payments are $500, due on the last day of each month. No down payment or deposit was required. The August lease payment is pro-rated at $250.

August 20. The bank reports that Wash-Card sales are $1,750, which is transferred to the company's bank account. Charlene is paid.

August 22. Unforeseen plumbing and electrical problems require some repair work. After heated arguments with the landlord, Rinso and Sudsy agree to pay and do pay $500 of the total $750 in repairs.

August 27. The bank reports that Wash-Card sales are $1,650 for the week, which is transferred to the company's bank account. Charlene is paid.

August 29. A freshman computer science student hacks into the company's website and gets the machines to provide free wash, dry, and dry cleaning for two days until Rinso gets wind of the problem. The website hosting company agrees to fix the problem for no charge. Rinso and Sudsy estimate the little prank cost them $700 in revenues.

August 31. The bank reports Wash-Card sales of $960 and transfers that amount to the company's bank account. The website hosting company reports that remaining balances on Wash-Card accounts — amounts purchased but not yet used — total $950.

Problem 1-38

Consider each of the following developments at Smart's Law Office.

(a) Smart has completed writing Baker's will, for which he sends Baker a bill for $500. What would be the appropriate journal entry if Smart kept his books

(1) on a cash basis?

(2) on an accrual basis?

(b) Baker sends Smart a check for $500 in payment of his bill. What would be the appropriate journal entry if Smart kept his books

(1) on a cash basis?

(2) on an accrual basis?

(c) Smart purchases for cash $1000 worth of time and billing software from MicroWare. The software is expected to last several years and has no other upkeep or subscription costs. What would be the appropriate journal entry if Smart kept his books

(1) on a cash basis?

(2) on an accrual basis?

(d) Smart interviews Clumsy, agrees to take his slip-and-fall case, and receives Clumsy's payment of a $1000 retainer. What would be the appropriate journal entry if Smart kept his books

(1) on a cash basis?

(2) on an accrual basis?

(e) Smart's office rent of $5000 is due today. What would be the appropriate journal entry if Smart kept his books

(1) on a cash basis?

(2) on an accrual basis?

Problem 1-39

Warren began Wise Webmasters out of his basement in his spare time with his personal computer. This is his first year in business. He brings you the following information.

Expenses (all cash):

Web design software	$3,000 (will last approximately 2 yrs before it is obsolete)
Security software	1,000 (annual subscription)
Advertising (online)	1,000 (covers three months this year and three months next year)
Liability insurance	500 (covers this year)
Office supplies	500 ($100 left over at end of year)

Revenues: He earned $7,000 in cash payments from businesses whose websites he maintains, and he billed for $2,000 more but has not collected on it yet.

(a) Prepare an income statement for the year and a balance sheet at the end of the year.

(b) Warren wants to keep costs down by using cash-basis accounting. Prepare an income statement for the first year and a balance sheet at the end of the year on a cash basis.

Chapter 2

Analysis of Financial Information

Now you have a full understanding of how financial statements are generated. In this chapter, we examine some commonly-used tools for analysis of those statements.

It is important to keep our mission in mind when using these tools: we are preparing, reviewing, and analyzing ***general purpose external financial statements.*** These statements are prepared primarily for two audiences: investors and creditors, and the tools about which we learn in this chapter are relevant primarily to those users. However, investors and creditors do not necessarily have the same goals or information needs. Indeed, sometimes they stand in stark opposition. But these are the people whom most modern financial analysis is intended to benefit.

A. What Is Financial Analysis?

Financial analysis is the process of using financial information to reach or help inform a decision. That decision might be one of hundreds, but our study here is limited to decisions which will involve ***investors or creditors*** and a ***lawyer.*** We will *not* be concerned with identifying a company which might be undervalued or a good investment, as such. That is primarily the concern of financial advisers and others in these markets.[1] Lawyers use financial information and engage in financial analysis to assist their business clients in a myriad of ways. The following are a few examples.

- ***Measures of performance.*** Many legal consequences turn upon how a well a business is being managed. Directors, officers and trustees are held to legal standards of care, which are measured in part by their exercise of reasonable business or fiduciary judgment.
- ***Covenants and compliance.*** Creditors and other contract parties will routinely demand and bargain for covenants or guarantees based on a company's financial and accounting information.[2]
- ***Strategic planning.*** Lawyers are routinely involved in helping set a business client's long-term goals. An important part of strategic planning is identifying objective standards as measures of success. Although this may be a matter pri-

1. We will study the valuation of a business in Chapter 11, but that study is related to a lawyer's work rather than the search for the best investment.

2. This is distinct from the regulation of financial information itself, the topic of Chapter 12.

marily for a business' internal management, if the process is not managed well, it could have legal consequences.[3]

What types of financial analyses will be most relevant in tackling these jobs? They will be in three broad areas.

- ***Risk.*** A lawyer's job includes risk minimization (or at least measurement). Part of a business manager's job is the profitable undertaking of carefully calculated risks. It may already be obvious that these two concepts—profitability and risk—are intimately related, but the nature of that relationship is important to understand.
- ***Profitability.*** As stated at the beginning of Chapter 1, our overall inquiry is financial information from for-profit entities. And calculations or measures of profit will be relevant even for non-profit entities, which still will desire to get the most from their assets. This may also be broadly termed "performance" analysis for this reason.
- ***Comparability.*** Finally, the measures of profitability and risk are not relevant in a vacuum. Consider how a business manager's performance might be measured in a legal setting. Critically relevant would be *comparisons* with how the entity had performed in the past, or how it had performed in relation to similarly situated peers. Thus, we have a need not only to measure profitability and risk but to examine those measures over time and over different entities.

Finally, we need to know about the typical tools of the trade. Introductory financial analysis usually involves using three types of measures.

- ***Ratios.*** Ratio analysis consists of comparison of one financial statement number with another (or a combination of numbers). A good analyst should keep in mind that these figures are the beginning, rather than the end, of the inquiry. Ratio analysis requires an understanding of how the ratio is calculated and the subject company's "economic environment and business strategy."[4] Even so, ratios are only as good as the underlying financial information from which they are derived, and are subject to all the limitations of the accounting process which generated them.[5]
- ***Common-size financial statements.*** Common-size financial statements facilitate comparisons among different financial statements. A common size balance sheet simply lists every item as a percentage of total assets or total liabilities and equity, and a common size income statement normally lists every item as a percentage of gross sales. As with ratio analysis, the use of common-size financial statements is a beginning, rather than an end. "[C]ommon-size statements should not be used simply to provide a scaling factor for standardization, but rather *to develop*

3. Consider, for example, a company which sets improper revenue targets in order to meet aggressive growth forecasts, a scenario we will study in Chapter 4.

4. James M. Wahlen, et al., Financial Reporting, Financial Statement Analysis, and Valuation: A Strategic Perspective 240 (9th ed. 2018).

5. Donald E. Kieso et al., Intermediate Accounting 1437 (16th ed. 2016); see also Wahlen et al., *supra* note 4.

insights into the economic characteristics of different industries and of different firms in the same industry."[6]

Illustration

General Widget Co., Inc.
Balance Sheet Dec. 31, 20xx

Assets		
Cash	$100,000	2.6%
Accounts Receivable	150,000	3.8%
Inventory	1,000,000	26.0%
Plant and Equipment	2,500,000	65.0%
Misc. Assets	100,000	2.6%
Total Assets	**$3,850,000**	**100.0%**

Liabilities and Equity		
Accounts payable	$100,000	2.6%
Current portion of long-term debt	250,000	6.5%
Bonds due Dec. 30, 205x	1,000,000	26.0%
Net worth	2,500,000	64.9%
Total Liabilities and Equity	**$3,850,000**	**100.0%**

This balance sheet makes computation of certain financial ratios straightforward. In addition, it makes General Widget's balance sheet comparable to any other, even if one has total assets of $100,000 and the other $100 billion. General Widget's common-size income statement, shown below, makes clear the company's performance relative to its sales.

General Widget Co., Inc.
Income Statement for the year ended Dec. 31, 20xx

Sales	$3,500,000	100.0%
Cost of goods sold	2,275,000	65.0%
Other operating expenses	527,000	15.1%
Interest expense	100,000	2.9%
Income taxes	273,000	7.8%
Net Income	**$325,000**	**9.2%**

6. Gerald I. White, et al., The Analysis and Use of Financial Statements 202 (1994) (emphasis in original).

- ***Cash flow statements.*** The third measure used in financial analysis is the third of the basic three financial statements from Chapter 1. The Statement of Cash Flows[7] focuses less on accrual accounting's measures of revenues and expenses and specifically on the sources and uses of cash in the business.

So now we need to simply take our tools (ratios, common-size financial statements, and cash flow statements) and see how they are used in the types of financial analysis relevant to lawyers (risk, profitability, and comparability), to help lawyers advise their clients in performance, compliance, and strategic planning.

Financial statement analysis		
Relevant legal decisions	**Types of analysis**	**Measuring tools**
Performance Compliance Strategic planning	Risk Profitability Comparability	Ratios Common size statements Cash flow statements

This chapter proceeds according to the three attributes: risk, profitability, and comparability.

B. Risk and Financial Structure

A business faces risks at every turn. Financial information is used by lawyers to help their clients measure and manage those risks. Conventional financial analysis divides risk into short-term and long-term variants. Each has separate measures and indicators.

1. Short-Term Risk

A business will likely fail in the short-term if it does not have enough cash to meet its current obligations. This is especially common with start-up businesses which underestimate the need for cash, but can also be true with a mature business, otherwise profitable, which finds itself poorly managed and with very few liquid assets. In such a situation, employees will leave, short-term creditors will evaporate, and long-term creditors will threaten foreclosure and bankruptcy. A business short on cash can be brought to a standstill virtually overnight.

7. See Chapter 1(B)(3).

Short-term risk is gauged primarily by two types of ratios. The first measures ***liquidity***— its present ability to pay short-term obligations. The second measures ***activity***— its near-term ability to generate sufficient cash.

a. Liquidity

Liquidity ratios compare liquid assets with short-term obligations.

The **current ratio** is current assets divided by current liabilities. A current asset is one which is expected to be converted into cash during the next year. This usually includes cash, accounts receivable, marketable securities, and inventory.[8] Likewise, a current liability is one which is expected to be paid during the next year. For this purpose, financial statements usually classify the long-term debt into a "current portion" (that amount due within the next year) and the "remaining portion." The current portion is considered a current liability. "Banks, suppliers, and others that extend short-term credit to a firm generally prefer a current ratio in excess of 1.0...."[9]

The **quick ratio** is a similar but more demanding measure, including only the most liquid of current assets — cash, marketable securities, and accounts receivable — in the numerator, divided by current liabilities. "Few businesses can instantaneously convert their inventories into cash. So, the quick ratio does not include inventory.... It therefore provides a measure of *very* immediate liquidity."[10]

Since the current and quick ratios have many accounts in common, they tend to be closely correlated. Both are also subject to year- or period-end "window dressing." Since they include liquid assets in the numerator, a company could quickly create more cash or receivables by, for example, postponing payments on noncurrent liabilities or capital investments or by accelerating billings to create receivables.[11]

---

8. You may rely on this list for the exercises in this chapter. In the future, you, as a lawyer, should ***always*** ask what is included in "current assets" in the analysis you make or one which is presented to you, especially if the term is used in a loan agreement, bond indenture, or other contract. Most books which define the "current ratio" do so by simply stating that it is "current assets divided by current liabilities."

9. Wahlen, et al., *supra* note 4, at 295. The authors caution in the remainder of that sentence that "current ratios should not be evaluated in isolation and should be assessed in the context of other factors affecting a firm's liquidity."

10. Lawrence Revsine, *et al.*, Financial Reporting and Analysis 278 (5th ed. 2012).

11. Wahlen, et al., *supra* note 4, at 364–65.

Problem 2-1

Hometown Groceries has the following balance sheets and income statement.

Hometown Groceries Balance Sheet Jan. 1, 20x1 (in $000)			
Assets		**Liabilities and Equity**	
Cash	$200	Accounts Payable	$500
Accounts Receivable	200	Current portion of Long-term Debt	100
Inventory	700		
Furniture and fixtures	600	Long-term Debt	1,400
Land and building	900	Owner's equity	600
Total	**$2,600**	**Total**	**$2,600**

Hometown Groceries Balance Sheet Dec. 31, 20x1 (in $000)			
Assets		**Liabilities and Equity**	
Cash	$200	Accounts Payable	$700
Accounts Receivable	400	Current portion of Long-term Debt	100
Inventory	700		
Furniture and fixtures	700	Long-term Debt	1,300
Land and building	800	Owner's equity	700
Total	**$2,800**	**Total**	**$2,800**

Hometown Grocery Income Statement for year ending Dec. 31, 20x1 (in $000)	
Sales	$11,000
Cost of goods sold	8,200
Administrative expenses	2,500
Interest	100
Income taxes	100
Net Income	**$100**

(a) What is Hometown's current ratio on Dec. 31, 20x1? Is the company in good shape?

(b) The accounts payable typically include accrued expenses which will be due shortly. Some of those are probably for amounts due employees and short-term suppliers. If the accounts receivable (such as goods sold on credit) are not due until after the end of the month, does this change your conclusion in (a)?

(c) What is Hometown's quick ratio on Dec. 31, 20x1? Is this a better measure of the company's liquidity? Will Hometown generate sufficient cash to pay the current liabilities?

(d) If Hometown were able to borrow $100,000 on Dec. 31, 20x1, how would this change the company's current and quick ratios and your analyses if the debt:

(i) were short-term trade credit due in the next month?

(ii) were a second mortgage on the company's property due in 20 years?

Problem 2-2

Here is sample language for a covenant limiting a borrower's current ratio.

The Company will not permit the ratio of (i) consolidated current assets of the Company and its Subsidiaries to (ii) consolidated current liabilities of the Company and its Subsidiaries at any time to be less than 1.25 to 1. For purposes of this section, ... there shall be excluded from consolidated current assets all cash and cash equivalents and all prepaid expenses and that there shall be excluded from consolidated current liabilities the currently maturing portion of all long-term Indebtedness of the Company and its Subsidiaries and accrued interest expense.[12]

(a) What is Hometown Groceries' current ratio under this covenant language?

(b) Why would a lender exclude "prepaid expenses" from the definition of current assets? Recall from Chapter 1 how these assets arise in the first place.

(c) Why would a lender exclude "accrued interest expense" from the definition of current liabilities? Recall from Chapter 1 how these liabilities arise in the first place.

b. Activity

The ratios described above are static ratios, because they are derived from balance sheet numbers, and the balance sheet is a "snapshot." Activity ratios utilize income statement numbers, and therefore provide a better look at the entity's liquidity over time.[13]

The principal activity ratios used in analyzing liquidity risk relate to inventory, accounts receivable, and accounts payable.

- Inventory turnover = Cost of sales / average inventory[14]
- Receivables turnover = Credit sales[15] / average accounts receivable
- Payables turnover = Purchases[16] / average accounts payable.

---

12. Carolyn E.C. Paris, Drafting for Corporate Finance: Concepts, Deals, and Documents 432 (2d ed. 2014).

13. Cory S. Cagle, *et al.*, *Analyzing Liquidity Using the Cash Conversion Cycle*, 215 J. of Accountancy 44 (No. 5, Spr. 2013), 2013 WLNR 34388733.

14. Note that adjustment that is needed to your ratios when dividing an **income statement** number by a **balance sheet** number. The income statement measures the business over time, and the balance sheet measures the business at an instant, so the two must be made consistent. This is usually done by averaging the beginning and ending balance sheets to compare with the income statement amount for that period. Some ratio calculations specify that the balance sheet number is to be the ending balance. Consistency is critical here; be sure you have "apples to apples" comparisons.

15. Some sources calculate this based on all sales, because credit sales may not be a number presented in the financial statements. Again, consistency is the key.

16. The amount of purchases is not normally disclosed in the financial statements, but it can be approximated by cost of goods sold plus beginning inventory minus ending inventory. Wahlen, *et al.*, *supra* note 4, at 298.

An arithmetic variation of each of these ratios yields the number of days it would normally take the business to clear each of these balance sheet accounts.

- Days' inventory held: 365 / inventory turnover ratio
- Days' receivables outstanding: 365 / receivables turnover ratio
- Days' payables outstanding: 365 / payables turnover ratio.

Looking at the numbers in this fashion, calculating the average number of days involved, allows an analyst to calculate the company's **cash conversion cycle**.

Cash conversion cycle = (days' inventory held) + (days' receivables outstanding) – (days' payables outstanding)

Graphically, it can be illustrated on a timeline, as below, as the time (in days) for which the business needs to have financing for its operations. It is the difference between the time the company pays for its inventory and the time it is paid for that inventory.

The Cash Conversion Cycle: Timeline

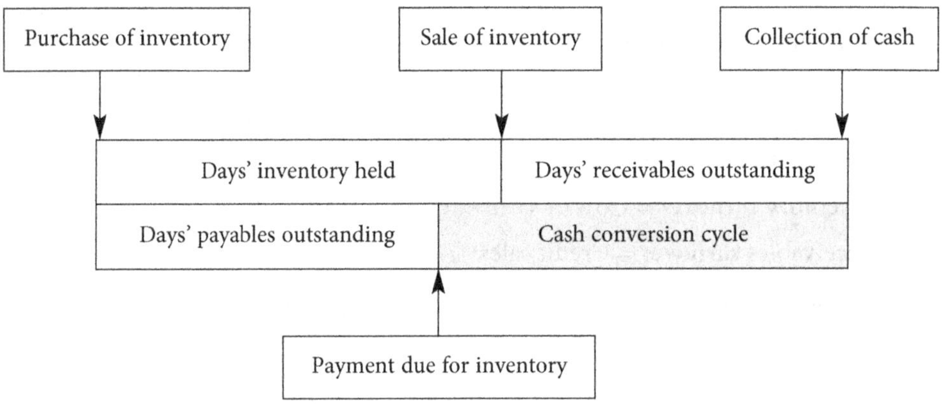

Example

Using the cash conversion cycle formula allows us to calculate the cycle for different businesses.

	Starbucks	Wal-Mart	Nordstrom	Amazon
Days inventory	56	50	88	25
Plus Days receivables	13	3	46	0
Less Days payables	28	34	47	74
Cash conversion cycle	41	19	87	-49

This can tell us something about the business itself, and about the retailing industry. Wal-Mart's conversion cycle is shorter than Starbucks' because it has proportionately fewer receivables (customers who owe Wal-Mart money) and is able to hold more payables (short-term borrowing). Nordstrom presumably owes its longer cycle to having more and slower-moving inventory. Amazon collects its customers' money right away (zero days receivables) and is able to borrow on good terms from its short-term creditors. Amazon's *negative* cycle means that it has substantial positive cash flow from its operations.

Sources: Wahlen, *et al.*, *supra* note 4, at 280; Revsine, *et al.*, *supra* note 10, at 299.

* * *

Problem 2-3

(a) What is Hometown Grocery's inventory turnover for 20x1? Its days' receivables outstanding for 20x1? (Use total sales for the receivables calculation.)

(b) What is Hometown Grocery's cash conversion cycle for 20x1?

* * *

The cash conversion cycle for a business is one aspect of its short-term cash management. The number shows, on average, how many days' of short-term financing a business needs. All other things being equal, of course, a business would prefer a shorter cycle to a longer one. The length of the cycle will affect the borrowing options available to the business, and the business will use an attorney to help select and implement those borrowing options. These can include bank loans, supplier financing, asset-based financing, and factoring.[17] You can provide better legal advice by understanding your client's cash needs.

As the cash conversion cycle becomes longer, there will be fewer options available to the business. Lenders will see the longer cycle as more volatile—more bad things can happen with a longer time horizon.[18] Although it seems non-intuitive, a business with a long cash conversion cycle may well have good liquidity as measured by the static tools (current ratio and quick ratio).[19] A convincing illustration is the case of Circuit City Stores, Inc., which had a current ratio above its competitors, but was forced into bankruptcy in 2008 because of, among other things, its long cash conversion cycle.[20]

Activity ratios can be used to measure other attributes, such as asset turnover, but that is not necessarily a measure of financial health, as such numbers can vary widely

17. Richard Brealy *et al.*, Principles of Corporate Finance 783 (13th ed. 2020); Jose M. Gabilondo *et al.*, Corporate Finance 197–212 (4th ed. 2017).

18. Verlyn D. Richards & Eugene J. Laughlin, *A Cash Conversion Cycle Approach to Liquidity Analysis*, 9 Financial Management 32, 35 (No. 1; Spring 1980).

19. *Id.*

20. Cagle *et al.*, *supra* note 13.

in different industries.[21] The primary use of activity ratios is in short-term financing as described above.

* * *

Problem 2-4

Suppose a company were able to reduce the number of days' payables outstanding, by reducing the amount of short-term borrowing from suppliers.

(a) Recall the cash conversion cycle formula:

Cash conversion cycle = (days' inventory held) + (days' receivables outstanding) – (days' payables outstanding)

If all other measures are held equal, would this increase or reduce the cash conversion cycle?

(b) If all other measures are held equal, how would this reduction in the amount of accounts payable affect the company's current ratio?

(c) If your client were lending to this business, would you want the protective covenants in the loan agreement you write for your client to focus on the current ratio or the cash conversion cycle? Why?

* * *

2. Long-Term Risk

A business which has reliably met its payroll or paid its suppliers has managed its short-term risk. Its long-term risk stems from financial attributes which may make the profits from that business more uncertain in the long run. The main component of long-term risk is the amount of borrowing a business does. First, we will examine the concept of borrowing—or "leverage"—and second, we will turn to how financial analysis measures this risk.

a. Leverage, Risk and Return

"Leverage" refers to the extent to which the money invested by the business is borrowed from creditors rather than contributed by owners. Leverage is important to a business' financial health and profitability because the use of leverage (debt) increases both the financial risks and the potential financial returns.

---

21. Kieso, *et al., supra* note 5, at 575, noting an asset turnover ratio of 0.32 for a utility company, but 2.73 for a retail grocer.

A simple illustration. Suppose you can invest $100,000 in a business which will provide a 3% return. In one year you would make $3,000. Not bad.

Suppose, instead of investing $100,000 of your own money, you invested only $50,000 of your own money, and borrowed $50,000 from someone to whom you had to pay 2% annual interest. At the end of the year, the income would be:

Investment income	$3,000
Interest expense	1,000
Net income	$2,000

The total return to you is lower, of course, but so was your initial investment. The ***return on your investment*** *was $2,000 / $50,000 = 4%.* Much better!

This illustrates how leverage can increase the return on your investment. It can also increase the risk of your investment, because the interest expense is a fixed cost, which must be paid even if the investment is not otherwise profitable.

A simple illustration with bad news. Suppose instead your investment didn't pay 3% but, as it turned out, paid only 1%. If we invested all our own money, we would still have a 1% return on our investment. Not a stellar investment, but we're still ahead. **However,** if we borrowed half the money, again at 2% interest cost, our income would be:

Investment income	$1,000
Interest expense	1,000
Net income	-0-

Ouch! And suppose, even worse, our investment paid out **nothing at all**, we would have made $0 if we invested all our own money, but if we borrowed half the money at 1%, we would still owe the lender $1000. In short, we would be $1000 in the hole! We would have lost **2% on our investment of $50,000**. Double-ouch!

Let's compare our simple examples to see the effect of leverage.

Return on investment if no money is borrowed	3%	1%	0%
Return on investment if one-half the investment is borrowed at a 2% interest cost	4%	0%	-2%

Leverage (borrowing) **increases the return** (from 3% to 4% if the investment is favorable) **and increases the** loss (0% to -2% if the investment is unfavorable). **Risk and return** go inexorably hand-in-hand in efficient financial markets. An investment which is risky will have a higher return, and all other things being equal, leverage increases risk. Many people try to make money in markets which might be temporarily mispriced, and which might therefore let you get a higher return for no higher risk. This is much harder than it looks.

b. Measures of Leverage

How does ratio analysis measure leverage? Usually a ratio states the relative amount of debt a company has incurred. The simplest is the **Debt/Equity ratio**, calculated just as its title says, total debt divided by total equity. **Debt/Total Assets** is another variation. Other ratios measure variations of income or earnings before interest and tax expenses against interest expense or debt charges (including principal) to determine how many times an entity's income "covers" (could pay) its debt charges. For example, a simple **Interest Coverage Ratio** would be the net income for the period divided by the interest expense for the period.

* * *

Problem 2-5

What is Hometown Grocery's debt-to-equity ratio? What is its interest coverage ratio? Does Hometown appear to be over-leveraged?

Problem 2-6

Leveraged Co. borrows $500,000 by issuing bonds at 10% annual interest, due in 10 years, using the funds to purchase equipment. Its Balance Sheet, giving effect to the loan and the purchases, is as follows:

Cash	50,000	Accounts Payable	100,000
Marketable Securities	100,000	Short-term Notes	150,000
Inventory	250,000	10% Bonds due 20xx	500,000
Fixed Assets	1,000,000		
Patents (net)	500,000	Common Stock	250,000
Goodwill (net)	100,000	Contrib. Capital	500,000
		Retained Earnings	500,000
	2,000,000		2,000,000

The lender insists on the following conditions in the loan, violation of any of which is a default under the loan agreement:

- a debt/equity ratio of 1.0 or less;
- net income each year of at least two times the amount of interest due annually on the loan; and
- "working capital" (current assets less current liabilities) of at least $150,000.

(a) On Jan. 1 of the following year, your client wants to buy inventory, financed with short-term notes. Earnings for the year are projected to be $125,000. Which covenant is most likely to pose a problem for this inventory purchase plan?

(b) Suppose that instead of the third covenant above, the lender had insisted upon a current ratio of 1.5, to be met at the end of each fiscal quarter. On March 30, the company has $300,000 in current assets and $225,000 in current liabilities, for a current ratio of 1.33. In order to avoid violating this loan covenant, Wizard, the chief financial officer, plans today to pay off $75,000 of the current liabilities in cash, so that tomorrow (March 31) the current ratio will be $225,000/$150,000, or the required 1.5. Is this chicanery or prudent management?

* * *

3. Cash Flows

Risky businesses are critically short of cash. Short-term cash flow problems can sink an otherwise seaworthy business, and long-term cash flow problems will eventually result in business failure.

In Chapter 1, we saw that accounting income is often very different from those cash flows. Thus, a third important financial statement—along with the balance sheet and income statement—is the Statement of Cash Flows. Although this statement is technically part of the basic financial statements, its purpose is more specific, as indicated by the Financial Accounting Standards Board when it first required the use of this statement.

> The information provided in a statement of cash flows, if used with related disclosures and information in the other financial statements, should help investors, creditors, and others to: (a) assess the enterprise's ability to generate positive future net cash flows; (b) assess the enterprise's ability to meet its obligations, its ability to pay dividends, and its needs for external financing; (c) assess the reasons for differences between net income and associated cash receipts and payments; and (d) assess the effects on an enterprise's financial position of both its cash and noncash investing and financing transactions during the period.[22]

The flow of cash is often evaluated by other means as well. We will discuss each of these in turn. All of these help us develop the legal conclusions we need to reach.

> By and large, lawyers under-use cash flow statements. Yet they are worth understanding because, if one can see the forest through the trees, cash flow statements show us two things of great importance. First, they tell us whether the company is an absorber or a generator of cash. Second, they give us important clues about what management is doing, wants to do, and—in some cases—must do. By revealing what management does with any discretionary

22. Statement of Financial Accounting Standards No. 95, *Statement of Cash Flows* ¶ 5 (Nov. 1987). The Board and its issuance of statements is covered in Chapter 3.

cash, the cash flow statement sends a strong signal regarding the company's strategy.[23]

The statement of cash flows was introduced in Chapter 1—you should review Part B(3) of that chapter to recall the basics. A business which uses accrual accounting may recognize or defer of items of income or expense despite the receipt or lack of receipt of cash. This accrual or deferral, in turn, will result in the creation of various assets or liabilities before the cash receipt or payment and the items of income or expense are reconciled. You may want to review the accrual and deferral process in part (C)(3) of Chapter 1.

a. Calculation of Cash Flows

A business calculates its cash flows from operations[24] using one of two methods. Each is described and evaluated below.

i. The Direct Method

Recall how financial information is recorded for a business, in the journal and with a ledger for each account. It may seem obvious now that preparing a statement of cash flows should be a simple process. "Cash" is one of a business' main assets, and has its own account. There is a ledger in which we record every receipt and expenditure of cash, with a supporting journal entry. It should be a simple matter to present these cash receipts and expenditures in an understandable fashion directly from the Cash ledger book. This conclusion would be correct. It *is* a simple matter to prepare a summary of the Cash ledger and present a Statement of Cash Flows in this manner.

A brief illustration recapitulated. Recall the saga of Wanda's Widgets, familiar to you from Chapter 1. Here is the full story, with a journal entry at each step along the way. First, Wanda invested $100 in her business.

(1) Dr Cash	100
Cr Wanda—Owner's Equity	100

Next, she purchased eight widgets for $10 each.

(2) Dr Widgets	80
Cr Cash	80

Next, Wanda sold one of those widgets for $12. Since we know how to use revenue accounts, we can record just the sale.

(3) Dr Cash	12
Cr Revenue	12

Next, Wanda borrowed $10, giving a promissory note to the lender.

---

23. Robert B. Dickie, Financial Statement Analysis and Business Valuation for the Practical Lawyer 111 (3d ed. 2020).

24. Cash flows from other business activities are discussed in part b immediately following.

(4) Dr Cash	10
Cr Note Payable	10

Now, let's look at Wanda's Cash ledger after these transactions.

Cash	
100 (1)	80 (2)
12 (3)	
10 (4)	
42	

Obviously, the debit entries increase the cash amount, and the credit entries decrease the cash amount. Changing the terminology slightly to comport with the cash flow accounting standards, we will call the former "sources" of cash, and the latter "uses" of cash. With that one change, we could prepare a statement of cash flows as follows.

Wanda's Widgets — Statement of Cash Flows for the Period

Cash balance, beginning of period		$0
Sources of cash:		
Initial investment	$100	
Sales	12	
Borrowing	10	122
Uses of cash:		
Purchase of inventory	$(80)	(80)
Cash balance, end of period		$42

This seems simple and straightforward, taking the cash flows directly from the Cash ledger. Hence the name: the "direct method."

ii. The Indirect Method

You might conclude that the direct method, being easy to understand, would be the method predominantly used in public company Statements of Cash Flows. However, this is not the case, for reasons having to do with politics and with one of the fundamental assumptions of accounting, namely, that providing accounting information has costs, which should always be compared with the benefits to be obtained.

The direct method is simple, but in our example, we dealt with Wanda's Widgets, which had four transactions and a cash balance of never more than $100. Consider a large company such as Wal-Mart Stores, Inc., whose January 31, 2019, financial statements show over $7.7 *billion* in cash as of that date, and almost $28 *billion* in cash flows from operations in the year then ended. According to the annual report, the company serves over 275 million customers each week. Wal-Mart could hardly afford to go through the billions of transactions on their cash ledgers and report them in a comprehensible fashion without an enormous expenditure of resources. Or so large companies argued to the accounting standard-setters in any event.[25]

The compromise reached was to allow another method of calculating cash flows, called the "indirect" method.[26] The "indirect" method begins with the accrual-accounting net income and adjusts it for amounts reported as income or expense which did not involve receipt or outlay of cash. The indirect method does not require substantial investment in collecting and preparing data. Indeed, it can be prepared largely from the other financial statements: an income statement for a period, and balance sheets at the beginning and end of the period.

Example

Wal-Mart Stores, Inc., presents the following calculation of "Cash flows from operating activities" for its fiscal year ended January 31, 2019 (in millions of dollars).

Consolidated net income	$7,179
Adjustments to reconcile net income to net cash:	
Depreciation and amortization*	10,678
Unrealized losses*	8,366
Other operating activities*	1,235
Changes in certain assets and liabilities:†	
Increase in accounts receivable	(368)
Increase in inventories	(1,311)
Increase in accounts payable	1,831
Increase in accrued liabilities	183
Decrease in accrued income taxes	(40)
Net cash provided by operating activities	$27,753

(Footnotes explained in text following.)

25. Most users of financial statements wanted the direct method; it was the preparers of financial statements who protested its costs. *See* Statement of Financial Accounting Standards No. 95, Statement of Cash Flows ¶¶ 111–114 (Nov. 1987), available at http://www.fasb.org/cs/BlobServer?blobcol=urldata&blobtable=MungoBlobs&blobkey=id&blobwhere=1175820920892&blobheader=application%2Fpdf. We will discuss in Chapter 3 accounting standards and how they are set.

26. The compromise was not without controversy. It was adopted only by a 4–3 vote of the accounting standard-setting board, and resulted in an unusual dissenting opinion from the three members who disapproved. *See* SFAS No. 95, *supra* (the dissenting statement appears in the unnumbered paragraphs following ¶ 34); *see also* Kieso, *et al.*, *supra* note 5, at 1352.

Note how Wal-Mart begins with accrual-accounting net income and adjusts it to arrive at "net cash provided by operating activities." Two types of adjustments are made.

(1) Adding back expenses which did not require cash outlays. First, Wal-Mart added to its net income items which were treated as expenses but did *not* require cash outlays. These are denoted by * in the above calculation. Depreciation is ordinarily the largest non-cash expense for a company with significant fixed assets. It is simply a way to allocate past cash expenditures among future periods according to the "useful life" of the asset purchased.[27] So, those amounts: depreciation, and non-cash expenses from "other operating activities" are "added back" to net income to approximate cash flows.

(2) Calculating the cash effects of changes in current assets and liabilities. The second group of adjustments, captioned "Changes in certain assets and liabilities" and denoted by the †, can be a little more daunting to understand. Here we are comparing the balance sheet amounts of current assets and current liabilities from last year and this year.[28]

- If the net amount of a current asset increases, we would consider that to be a ***use*** of cash, much as if we had purchased that net amount of additional assets.
- If the net amount of a current asset decreases, we would consider that to be a ***source*** of cash, much as if we had sold that net amount of additional assets.
- Liabilities are, of course, treated in just the opposite fashion. If the net amount of a current liability increases, we would consider that to be a ***source*** of cash, just as if we had borrowed that net amount of cash.
- If the net amount of a current liability decreases, we would consider that to be a ***use*** of cash, just as if we had repaid that net amount of current liabilities.

To summarize:

	Current Assets	Current Liabilities
Increase	Use of cash	Source of cash
Decrease	Source of cash	Use of cash

The "indirect method" is no harder (and no simpler) than that. To learn more about the "indirect" method is beyond this introductory coverage. However, the ex-

27. Full coverage of depreciation is in Chapter 5(B).

28. A "current" asset is one which is expected to be converted into cash during the next year; likewise, a current liability is one which is expected to be paid during the next year. We do this only with current assets and liabilities, because the other assets and liabilities are treated separately in the calculation of cash flows from other activities, in part b immediately following.

posure at this point is important, as nearly every reporting company uses the indirect method of reporting cash flows in this manner.[29]

b. Classification of Cash Flows

Cash flows are classified into three types of activities.

- *Operating activities:* The normal day-to-day business activities.[30]
- *Financing activities:* Transactions with owners or creditors, such as borrowing or repaying debt, issuing or repurchasing stock, paying dividends.
- *Investing activities:* Purchase or sale of long-term fixed assets, financial investments, other businesses, or any other asset which is not held primarily for sale.

For financing and investing activities, the direct method (discussed in part a(i) above) must be used. This is normally not a burden for most businesses, because the number of transactions which are "financing" and "investing" activities is very few compared to the thousands of "operating" activity transactions done every business day.

* * *

Problem 2-7

How would you characterize the three initial events in the life of The Collegetown Coffeehouse in cash flow statement terminology?

- Bill invested $75,000 in the business; Ted invested $25,000, both in cash.
- TCC borrowed $30,000 from Collegetown National Bank to purchase appliances and fixtures.
- TCC bought a total of $50,000 worth of appliances and fixtures, paid in cash.

Problem 2-8

Indicate whether the events reflected below would affect an entity's cash flows from operations, investing or financing, and whether it would *increase* or *decrease* that amount.

(a) issuance of common stock for cash

(b) payment of trade creditors in cash

---

29. American Institute of Certified Public Accountants, Accounting Trends & Techniques 2010, at 533 (Table 6-2 presenting survey data from 2006–2009). "Companies like the indirect method for three reasons: (1) It is easier to prepare, (2) it focuses on the differences between net income and net cash flow from operations, and (3) it tends to reveal less company information to competitors." Terry D. Warfield, *et al.*, Intermediate Accounting: Principles and Analysis 257 (2nd ed. 2008).

30. In the official accounting standards, "operating activities" are simply defined as any activities which are not either financing or investing activities.

(c) net increase in accounts receivable

(d) sale of operating plant for cash

* * *

C. Profitability

You may be surprised to see profitability given second-billing in financial analysis. But remember, we are looking at the subject as lawyers, not as investors. Liquidity is important to the entity's short-term survival. Profitability remains important because it is key to the entity's long-term survival. In addition, because profit is likely the prime motivator of your *client*'s actions, it is important for the attorney.

One key measure of profitability — net income — has already been studied in Chapter 1. We focus here first on a new measure known as "margin," and then on different measures of return on investment. The purpose of varying standard net income in these ways is to focus on the accounting information which is useful in predicting the company's future income and financial position.

1. Margin

"Margin" literally refers to the difference or distance, such as between these words and the edge of the page. "Margin" in an accounting or business sense refers to the difference between receipts from an activity and the costs of that activity. You can see it is thus similar to net income, but it differs depending on what is included in receipts and costs. There are no standard requirements for margin calculation, so it is important for a lawyer (or any analyst) to know what the presenter is using when a "margin" is listed in a financial statement.

Gross margin (or gross profit) typically refers to the company's revenues from its core products or services, that is, those which are continuing from year to year, less the *direct* or *variable* costs of those goods or services. The term *direct* or *variable* costs usually refers to the costs which vary depending on the amount of the goods or services produced. For example, in the manufacturing process, raw materials, labor costs of manufacture, and supplies would be variable costs; the more units of product manufactured, the greater those costs. By contrast, the costs of plant and equipment would not be considered to be variable; these costs would not change if more (or less) product is manufactured. Costs which are not variable are usually called *fixed, indirect* or *overhead* costs. Whether a cost is variable depends on your time frame.[31] But for our purposes, it would be reasonable to assume that the time

31. If, for example, your time frame is 20–30 years, even the costs of the manufacturing plant and equipment are "variable" because a new one could be constructed. Such a time frame may not be useful, though. British economist John Maynard Keynes famously observed that "in the long run,

period involved to separate the short run from the long run is that of the financial reports, or one year.

The gross margin measures the short-term contribution by the company's core business to the payment of the company's other expenses. If, for example, a company sells its main product for more than it costs to produce, the difference contributes to the company's ability to pay its fixed and non-recurring costs. Such a company may remain in business even though it cannot cover all of its costs, so long as there are eventually changes. However, a company with a very low or negative gross margin is not even covering its direct costs, and will face financial difficulties much sooner.

Illustration

Overboard Co. and Underwater Co. both make and sell pleasure boats. They have the same cost structure, as follows:

Costs per boat:	$10,000 materials
	$10,000 labor.
Costs per month:	$50,000 rent and utilities
	$20,000 interest on loan.

Overboard sold 10 boats during the month for total proceeds of $250,000. A quick calculation indicates Overboard lost $20,000 during the month. However, its proceeds are enough to pay its suppliers and employees ($200,000), so it may be able to continue production next month. It may negotiate with the landlord or the bank for restructuring or forbearance on those payments.

Underwater sold 8 boats during the month for total proceeds of $150,000. Like its competitor, it too lost money, a total of $80,000. But its loss is more severe, because it does not make enough to pay its suppliers and employees ($160,000). If Underwater doesn't change its productivity, pricing, or something else, it will lose its employees and suppliers and be out of business.

Operating margin includes all costs of production, both direct and indirect costs, but not the costs of financing nor taxes. It reflects the total costs of the company's core business and provides a medium-range measure of the profitability of the business.

---

we are all dead." The Collected Writings of John Maynard Keynes, Vol. 4: A Tract on Monetary Reform 65 (Royal Economic Society ed. 1971). His admonition was made in discussing monetary policy, not business planning, but it wisely exhorts us to not extend the planning horizon to an impractical distance in any context.

Illustration

Overboard Co. and Underwater Co. both make and sell pleasure boats. They have the same cost structure, as follows:

Costs per boat: $10,000 materials
$10,000 labor.

Costs per month: $50,000 rent and utilities
$20,000 interest on loan.

Overboard sold 10 boats during the month for total proceeds of $250,000. The margin calculation is as follows:

Gross margin: sales – variable costs = $250,000 – $200,000 = $50,000.

Operating margin: sales – variable <u>and fixed</u> costs = $250,000 – $270,000 = -$20,000.

Underwater sold 8 boats during the month for total proceeds of $150,000. The margin calculation is as follows:

Gross margin: sales – variable costs = $150,000 – $160,000 = -$10,000.

Operating margin: sales – variable <u>and fixed</u> costs = $150,000 – $230,000 = -$80,000.

Note that even Underwater's *gross* margin is negative, indicating, as noted in the previous illustration, that Underwater is not even covering its variable expenses.

Net margin includes all recurring costs of production as well as costs of financing and taxes. The company would thus include its expenses for interest, dividends on preferred or senior securities,[32] and income taxes. The net margin "shows how well a company has done for its owners after taking care of all other claimants, including vendors, employees, lenders, and tax collectors."[33] In contrast to the operating margin, which shows how profitable this particular *business or industry* is, the net margin shows how profitable this particular *company or enterprise* is, taking into account all of its costs.

What is left out of the net margin computation? The only items which are not included in net margin which *are* included in standard net income are non-recurring items, for example, profits or losses from a business which the company has discontinued in the past year, or items which for one reason or another are not expected to recur. "[W]hen the analyst uses measures of past profitability to forecast the firm's

32. The different kinds of stock will be discussed in Chapter 7.

33. Dickie, *supra* note 23, at 134.

future profitability, the emphasis is on those revenues, expenses, gains, and losses that are expected to persist."[34]

Illustration

Consider General Widget, whose income statement we saw at the beginning of the chapter. Using the numbers provided there, we can calculate GW's margins.

General Widget Co., Inc.
Income Statement for the year ended Dec. 31, 20xx

Sales	$3,500,000	
Cost of goods sold	2,275,000	
Gross margin		*$1,225,000*
Other operating expenses	527,000	
Operating margin		*698,000*
Interest expense	100,000	
Income taxes	273,000	
Net margin		*325,000*
Net income	$325,000	

GW has no nonrecurring or other expenses which would make its net margin different from net income.

* * *

Problem 2-9

Calculate Hometown Grocery's gross, operating, and net margins using the income statement from Problem 2-1, reproduced below.

Hometown Grocery Income Statement for year ending Dec. 31, 20x1 (in $000)	
Sales	$11,000
Cost of goods sold	8,200
Administrative expenses	2,500
Interest	100
Income taxes	100
Net income	**$100**

34. Wahlen, *et al.*, supra note 4, at 255.

2. Return on Investment

In the previous part, we learned to calculate margins, or variations on a company's reported net income to isolate that number from non-traditional or non-recurring items, or from the company's financial structure or particular tax position. In this part, we calculate returns by taking those margin numbers and dividing them by various balance sheet measures.

The two most common ratios for profitability are return on assets and return on equity. **Return on assets (ROA)** is net income (before interest expense[35]) divided by the average total assets for the income reporting period. **Return on equity (ROE)** is net income (unadjusted[36]) divided by the average total equity.[37]

Return on Assets (ROA) isolates the business' profitability from its financial structure, just as the operating margin does in contrast to the net margin. ROA represents the profitability of this ***type of business*** independent of its financing mix.

Return on equity (ROE) includes the impact of the business' financing decisions. ROE represents the profitability of ***this particular business financed as it is.*** The difference between the return on the assets and the return to the *owners of those assets*—or return on equity, is explained entirely by leverage.[38]

Recall in Part B(2)(a) of this chapter the effect of leverage was demonstrated. After looking at the return on assets, and the costs of borrowing money, the following table was developed.

Return on investment if no money is borrowed (equals return on **assets**)	3%	1%	0%
Return on **investment** if one-half the investment is borrowed at a 2% interest cost	4%	0%	-2%

The "return on investment" is identical to the return on equity we are measuring here. You can see how borrowing money—leverage—increases the return to the owner (borrower) if the return on the assets is greater than the cost of the borrowed funds. Conversely, leverage decreases the return if the return on the assets is not greater than the cost of the borrowed funds.

35. There is one technical adjustment here: the tax effect of the interest expenses must be eliminated, since interest is a deductible expense.

36. A technical adjustment is necessary here, too. We must subtract any required payments to senior equity holders, usually known as "preferred dividends." These are not considered expenses comparable to interest (and are not deductible) but nonetheless reduce the amount available to the common equity holders, which is what ROE measures.

37. See footnote 14 on comparing balance sheet numbers with income statement numbers.

38. Dickie, *supra* note 23, at 145.

Graphically, leverage can be illustrated as increasing (or "levering") the return to the owners of a business, as follows.

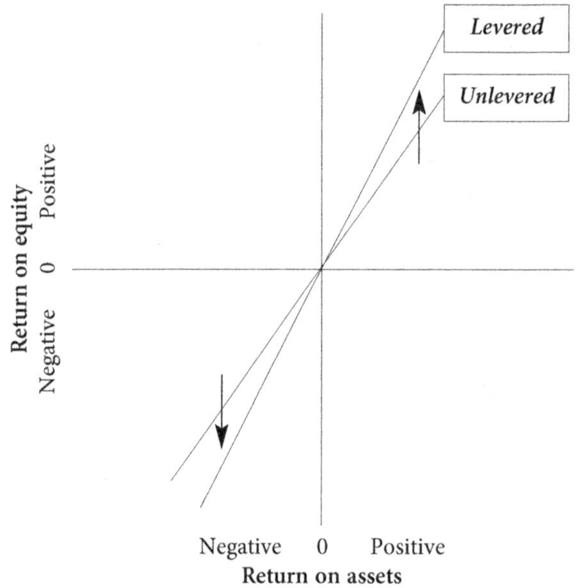

In the top right-hand quadrant, the positive effect of leverage is demonstrated: the return on the equity is higher because of the leverage. In the lower left-hand quadrant, the negative effect of leverage is demonstrated: the return on equity is lower because of the leverage.

Example. Consider the returns for 2018 in the crop production industry. This industry is highly leveraged, as indicated by its debt/equity ratio of 1.36. The table below lists the returns on assets and equity for the top quartile and the bottom quartile of firms in that industry. As we can see, the leverage increases both positive and negative returns.

	25th Percentile	75th Percentile
Return on assets	1.7%	-15.7%
Return on equity	5.3%	-30.0%

Source: Key Business Ratios, www.mergentkbr.com.

Problem 2-10

Hometown Groceries has the following balance sheets and income statement.

Hometown Groceries Balance Sheet Jan. 1, 20x1 (in $000)			
Assets		**Liabilities and Equity**	
Cash	$200	Accounts Payable	$500
Accounts Receivable	200	Current portion of Long-term Debt	100
Inventory	700		
Furniture and fixtures	600	Long-term Debt	1,400
Land and building	900	Owner's equity	600
Total	**$2,600**	**Total**	**$2,600**

Hometown Groceries Balance Sheet Dec. 31, 20x1 (in $000)			
Assets		**Liabilities and Equity**	
Cash	$200	Accounts Payable	$700
Accounts Receivable	400	Current portion of Long-term Debt	100
Inventory	700		
Furniture and fixtures	700	Long-term Debt	1,300
Land and building	800	Owner's equity	700
Total	**$2,800**	**Total**	**$2,800**

Hometown Grocery Income Statement for year ending Dec. 31, 20x1 (in $000)	
Sales	$11,000
Cost of goods sold	8,200
Administrative expenses	2,500
Interest	100
Income taxes	100
Net income	**$100**

(a) What is Hometown Grocery's return on assets for 20x1?

(b) What is Hometown Grocery's return on equity for 20x1? *Note:* when calculating average total equity, do not add the amount which represents net income for the period. That would be double-counting.

(c) What explains the difference between the two measures? *Note:* remember you calculated the company's debt/equity ratio in Problem 2-5.

* * *

D. Comparability

Financial analysis is relevant primarily because it can be compared with something else. This is what the business manager wants to know—how are we doing compared to *X*? And often, that is the lawyer's inquiry as well.

Common-size financial statements are often used to aid in comparisons. Recall the General Widget common-size statements from the introduction, reproduced here for convenience.

General Widget Co., Inc.
Balance Sheet Dec. 31, 20xx

Assets		
Cash	$100,000	2.6%
Accounts Receivable	150,000	3.8%
Inventory	1,000,000	26.0%
Plant and Equipment	2,500,000	65.0%
Misc. Assets	100,000	2.6%
Total Assets	**$3,850,000**	**100.0%**
Liabilities and Equity		
Accounts payable	$100,000	2.6%
Current portion of long-term debt	250,000	6.5%
Bonds due Dec. 30, 205x	1,000,000	26.0%
Net worth	2,500,000	64.9%
Total Liabilities and Equity	**$3,850,000**	**100.0%**

General Widget Co., Inc.
Income Statement for the year ended Dec. 31, 20xx

Sales	$3,500,000	100.0%
Cost of goods sold	2,275,000	65.0%
Other operating expenses	527,000	15.1%
Interest expense	100,000	2.9%
Income taxes	273,000	7.8%
Net income	**$325,000**	**9.2%**

Common-size statements and ratios are designed to eliminate differences among financial statements. Thus, they say very little in isolation. They are more useful for exposing trends or departures from trends, and are usually compared with information from the same company over time, or different companies in a comparable group, usually the same industry. In addition, any ratio or common-size financial statement is useful only when the analyst has carefully identified in advance: (1) what kind of information is being sought, (2) how the planned analysis will provide that information and the theoretical legitimacy of that conclusion, and (3) the integrity of the numbers being analyzed or compared.

Example

The following data are provided by www.bizstats.com on the general purpose machinery manufacturing industry for 2016.

Average Balance Sheets

Cash	7.53%	Accounts Payable	9.42%
Receivables	13.59%	Loans/Notes Payable	8.45%
Inventory	11.27%	Other Current Liabilities	9.97%
Other Current Assets	6.72%	Total Current Liabilities	27.84%
Total Current Assets	39.11%	Other (Long-term) Liabilities	18.58%
Fixed Assets	26.31%	Total Liabilities	48.50%
Other Non-Current Assets	34.58%	Net Worth	51.50%
Total Assets	100.00%	Total Liabilities & Net Worth	100.00%

Industry Income-Expense Statements		Industry Financial Ratios	
Sales	100.00%	Return on Sales	7.19%
Cost of Sales	64.13%	Return on Assets	5.38%
Gross Profit	35.87%	Return on Net Worth	10.48%
Officers Compensation	1.91%		
Salary-Wages	9.27%	Quick Ratio	0.76
Rent	1.32%	Current Ratio	1.40
Taxes	1.74%	Inventory Turnover	6.65
Advertising	0.66%	Assets/Sales	1.34
Benefits — Pension	3.14%	Total Liabilities/Net Worth	0.94
Repairs	0.33%		
Bad Debts	0.12%		
Other SG&A Expense	7.05%		
Amortization & Depreciation	2.89%		
Interest Earned	0.26%		
Interest Expense	1.38%		
Other Income	1.39%		

* * *

Problem 2-11

Assume that the data in the above example from bizstats.com is the best information available to you at the moment and your task is to evaluate the financial position of General Widget Co. (GW), the company in the preceding example.

(a) Compare GW with the industry's current ratio, quick ratio, and debt-assets ratio. What does this indicate about GW's liquidity?

(b) Assume that interest rates have dropped and that GW would like to refinance (pay off and reissue at lower rates) its 205x bonds. Standard covenants in bonds are **(i)** a maximum allowed debt/equity ratio and **(ii)** a minimum "times interest earned" multiple. What are reasonable amounts to propose in GW's debt covenants?

Problem 2-12

Reproduced below are selected items from the common-size financial statements of A Co. and B Co. for the past five years. "Gross profit" and "net income" are expressed as a percentage of revenues, and the other amounts are expressed as a percentage of total assets.

	2xx1	2xx2	2xx3	2xx4	2xx5
A Co.					
Gross profit	10	20	30	30	30
Net income	-5	-25	2	12	10
Cash	1	0.3	0.8	2	2
Accounts receivable	10	10	30	32	30
Inventory	8	8	9	7	9
B Co.					
Gross profit	50	30	55	48	52
Net income	10	-20	12	10	7
Cash	2	5	4	3	2
Accounts receivable	20	22	28	18	7
Inventory	20	20	24	28	33

(a) Which is more likely to be a new company?

(b) Which is more likely to have liquidity problems in the near future?

(c) What is unusual or suspicious, considering the trends about

(i) A Co. in 2xx3?

(ii) in general in 2xx2?

(d) How would it affect your analysis to know that B Co. was ten times the size of A Co.?

Index of Formulas Used in This Chapter

Cash conversion cycle = (days' inventory held) + (days' receivables outstanding) – (days' payables outstanding), p. 58

Current Ratio = Current assets / Current liabilities, p. 55

Days' inventory held = 365 / inventory turnover ratio, p. 58

Days' payables outstanding = 365 / payables turnover ratio, p. 58

Days' receivables outstanding = 365 / receivables turnover ratio, p. 58

Debt/Equity ratio = total debt / total equity, p. 62

Debt/Total Assets = total debt / total assets, p. 62

Gross margin or **gross profit** = core or continuing revenues less the *direct* or *variable* costs of producing those revenues, p. 69

Interest Coverage Ratio = Net income / Interest expense for the period, p. 62

Inventory turnover = Cost of sales / average inventory, p. 57

Net margin = core or continuing revenues less all recurring costs of production as well as costs of financing and taxes, p. 71

Operating margin = core or continuing revenues less all costs of production, both direct and indirect costs, but not the costs of financing nor taxes, p. 70

Payables turnover = Purchases / average accounts payable, p. 57

Quick Ratio = (Cash + Marketable securities + Accounts receivable) / Current liabilities, p. 55

Receivables turnover = Credit sales / average accounts receivable, p. 57

Return on assets (ROA) = net income (before interest expense) / average total assets, p. 73

Return on equity (ROE) = net income (unadjusted) / average total equity, p. 73

Chapter 3

Standardization of Financial Information

It is no accident that there are standard terms, practices, and reports in accounting information. In this chapter, we will see the rich history of these standards. In addition, there is regularly some kind of financial crisis which generates new legislative and regulatory inquiry into the conduct of accounting professionals. So new history is regularly being made. If past is indeed prologue,[1] studying the development of accounting standards is important for your lifetime practice as attorneys working with accountants.

In this chapter, we will learn in Part A how accounting standards come to be made and the philosophical basis of accounting rules. If you believe that there could not be a more arid topic, you may be surprised to learn that this has been a focus of recent legislation and many special studies. In Part B, we will examine the closely related but slightly different world of auditors. Audits are an important part of the standardization of financial information. We will examine who auditors are, where they get their standards, what they do, and what the public thinks of their work.

A. Accounting Standards

Between Problem 1-1, when we looked at what financial information we *might want* about a business, and Part B of that Chapter, when we looked at what is *usually given* us — the balance sheet, income statement, and statement of cash flows — there was a great leap to standardization. These standards may not always be relevant. Sometimes your clients will be satisfied with or demand financial statements prepared under different standards. But you can only learn the variations if you can play the basic theme. Only if you know the standards you can interpret the nonstandard information you are also likely to encounter.

1. The Development of Private Standards

In the United States, the accounting profession, through its main membership group, the American Institute of Certified Public Accountants (AICPA) and its pred-

1. *See* William Shakespeare, *The Tempest*, Act II, Sc. 1. There the words are spoken by Antonio referring to a murder plot. We don't deal with anything that heinous here.

ecessor organizations, promulgated its own standards for many years. In 1973 a small revolution took place, wherein the standard-setting power was given to a body called the Financial Accounting Standards Board (FASB), which still exercises that power today.[2]

The FASB is a private institution founded by five organizations: the AICPA, the American Accounting Association, the Financial Analysts Federation, the Financial Executives Institute, and the National Association of Accountants. The FASB wrote many kinds of statements, but undertook in the early years of the new century to codify *all* existing highest-level accounting authority. In 2009, this ambitious project was completed and the result is the ***Accounting Standards Codification (ASC).*** The ASC is the one authoritative source of ***Generally Accepted Accounting Principles*** or ***GAAP***. GAAP is important in public financial statements because it is the standard by which the auditors, who evaluate the company's statements, measure its work.

There are separate accounting rules applicable to companies which file financial reports with the Securities and Exchange Commission (SEC). These requirements are supplements to GAAP, and not a replacement for it. Although the SEC has the authority under federal law to require certain methods of accounting for businesses subject to its jurisdiction, the SEC determined early in its life to let the private accounting profession lead the way.[3] In the Sarbanes-Oxley Act of 2002, passed in response to Enron and other accounting and auditing scandals, Congress considered replacing the FASB with some other public sector body. However, the consensus reached was to continue to rely on the FASB's work as the primary accounting standard setter. After this Congressional blessing of the SEC-FASB arrangement, the SEC formally reaffirmed its reliance on that arrangement, but with some conditions suggesting more vigilant oversight. The Commission indicated that it expects the FASB to:

- provide timely guidance to companies
- keep investor protection as a fundamental objective
- take steps toward convergence of US and international standards, and
- remain objective in its standard-setting, allowing participation by all affected entities and groups in its standard setting.[4]

---

2. A full discussion of the history and politics of accounting standard-setting is beyond the scope of this introductory text. Good concise summaries of these stories can be found in the following texts: Richard G. Schroeder, *et al.*, Financial Accounting Theory and Analysis 1–19 (12th ed. 2017); Jerry W. Markham, A Financial History of Modern U.S. Corporate Scandals: From Enron to Reform 158–61 (2006); Stephen A. Zeff, *A Chronology of Significant Developments in the Establishment of Accounting Principles in the United States, 1926–1972*, 10 J. Acctg. Res. 217 (1972); James F. Strother, *The Establishment of Generally Accepted Accounting Principles and Generally Accepted Auditing Standards*, 28 Vand. L. Rev. 201, 211–19 (1975). A good critical review of the whole process (with useful sources) can be found in George Mundstock, *The Trouble with FASB*, 28 N.C. Journal of International Law and Commercial Regulation 813 (2003).

3. 11 Fed. Reg. 10,913 (Apr. 25, 1938).

4. Financial Reporting Release No. 70, 68 Fed. Reg. 23,333 (Apr. 25, 2003).

2. Accounting's Fundamental Assumptions

Ever since there have been discussions about accounting standards, there have been discussions about the fundamental nature of those standards. Most GAAP consists of fairly specific rules about how to account for particular events or transactions. There has always been philosophical discussion about what general principles should guide accountants in developing and applying these rules.

There have been many different groups involved in the search for a coherent statement of accounting theory, mostly in the 20th century.[5] In 1978, the FASB became the most recent contributor to this effort, beginning a "Conceptual Framework" providing a theoretical underpinning for all accounting standards. This Framework presently consists of two chapters: one on "the objective of general purpose financial reporting," and a second on "qualitative characteristics of useful financial information."[6] It has provided a useful statement of accounting's fundamental assumptions with the following four elements.

(1) The objective of general purpose financial reporting is "to provide financial information that is useful to existing and potential investors, lenders, and other creditors in making decisions about providing resources to the entity."[7]

(2) Fundamental qualitative characteristics of useful financial information. According to the FASB, there are two:

- **Relevance.** Financial information is relevant if it has predictive value or confirmatory ("feedback") value.[8]
- **Representational faithfulness.** Financial information has representational faithfulness if it is complete, neutral, and free from error.[9]

(3) ***"Enhancing" qualitative characteristics of useful financial information.*** These secondary characteristics "should be maximized to the extent possible," but cannot replace or make up for failings in the fundamental characteristics:[10]

- comparability
- verifiability
- timeliness, and
- understandability.[11]

---

5. For a good overview of the development of accounting theory, see C. Richard Baker, *The Influence of Accounting Theory on the FASB Conceptual Framework*, 44 Acctg. Historians Journal 109 (no. 2, Dec. 2017).

6. The most recent installment is Statement of Financial Accounting Concepts No. 8, *Conceptual Framework for Financial Reporting* (Sept. 2010).

7. *Id.* ¶ OB2. You should at this point compare these statements with your conclusions from Problem 1-1. Who were the main users of the financial information that could be provided about The Collegetown Coffeehouse?

8. *Id.* ¶¶ QC 5–QC 10.

9. *Id.* ¶¶ QC 12–QC 15.

10. *Id.* ¶ QC 33.

11. *Id.* ¶ QC 19.

(4) Cost constraint. Finally, the FASB notes that all of this information "imposes costs, and it is important that those costs are justified by the benefits of reporting that information."[12]

The FASB has thus catalogued most of the underlying assumptions made by accountants in preparing financial information. These might be called the "broad" or "overarching" principles.

Broad Principles

(1) Relevance. The information provided must help in making the decisions for which we turn to the financial statements for guidance. Remember from the FASB's statement of the general objectives of financial reporting this means relevance to *investors* and *creditors.* This includes the FASB's characteristic of "understandability."

(2) Verifiability. The information must have, to use the FASB's terminology, "representational faithfulness." It should be what it purports to be, and it should be stated in such terms that there are ways to check that. This includes the FASB's characteristics of "free from error" and "verifiability."

(3) Completeness. The financial information should present a full picture of the economic events in the life of the entity. Note that this is where we got the idea in Chapter 1 that a "complete" set of financial statements includes a balance sheet, income statement, and a statement of cash flows.

(4) Neutrality. The information should appear the same no matter who is looking at it. If there are interpretations to be made, they should not favor one user of the financial information over another.

(5) Comparability. The information should be prepared in the same fashion over time and among entities.

(6) Timeliness. The information should be sufficiently easy to collect that it is useful to users (management, owners, and creditors) in making their decisions.

There are, in addition, more discrete ideas or principles, which I list below with the *caveat* that any such summary reflects some of the value judgments of its author, and like any summary runs the risk of simplification in the hope of providing some overall understanding.[13] These principles should be applied with the goal of furthering

12. *Id.* ¶ QC 35.

13. You can find similar lists in many other places. For example, Donald E. Kieso, et al., Intermediate Accounting 40–52 (16th ed. 2016), breaks down the FASB's Conceptual Framework into "Fundamental Concepts" from the FASB Conceptual Framework stated above, and then into nine subsidiary "Recognition and Measurement Concepts," corresponding roughly to the principles I present here. *Accord.* Schroeder *et al., supra* note 2 at 40 (Fig. 2.1).

one or more of the broader principles. For example, there is the principle (below) of the "accounting entity." This should help assure that the information is *relevant* to the creditor of or investor in the entity whose financial information is presented. This is specifically the focus of Problem 3-1(a) below.

Narrower Principles

(1) **Accounting entity.** The accounting information is presented for a discrete economic unit, and all such units are combined and presented together when that is the most useful way to do it.

(2) **Monetary unit.** All information must be reduced to dollars (or other fungible monetary units) which can be mathematically manipulated.

(3) **Periodicity.** The accounting information relates to a particular cycle. We must provide information as it is needed, and not just wait, for example, until the liquidation of the business to evaluate its financial performance.

(4) **"Going concern."** The information assumes that the entity will continue in existence and will not be liquidated or otherwise terminated.

(5) **Accrual and deferral.** The receipt and expenditure of cash is not necessarily the best measure of timing of the creation of assets, liabilities, equity, revenue, or expenses.

(6) **Approximation and judgment.** Because all events must be measured in monetary units (see no. 2 above), some adjustments are required to present uncertain and somewhat unquantifiable business events in monetary units.

(7) **Materiality.** This is related to no. 6 above. The financial information is prepared with the particular users in mind (owners, investors, creditors). Some information may simply not be sufficiently helpful to these users to be worth the cost of collection and preparation of that information.

(8) **Conservatism.** The second qualitative characteristic — faithfulness — has components of neutrality and freedom from error. These may drive accountants to be conservative in their evaluations, often so much so that this may overshadow the first qualitative characteristic — relevance.

(9) **Substance over form.** Any combination of accounting rules should not yield a result which, although technically correct, does not properly represent the transaction.

* * *

Problem 3-1

Consider each of the accounting problems below. Which accounting assumptions are involved in deciding each problem? Based on those assumptions, what accounting treatment do you think should be required in each instance?

(a) Sub Corporation is a small manufacturer whose common stock is publicly traded, although 55% is owned by Parent Corporation. Whose financial statements would best present the position of Sub Corporation?

(b) Southern Airlines, Inc. began a "frequent flyer" program in its year just ended. Its records show that program members have amassed mileage permitting them to take approximately 400 free coach-fare trips or take 600 upgrades to first-class at regular coach fares. Southern's current coach fares for its various routes vary from $150 to $950. Should any account be taken of these frequent flyer miles? How much? When?

(c) General Submarine, Inc. has just received a contract from the government to build a nuclear submarine. It is to be delivered in three years, at which time the government will pay General $300 million. General estimates that it will spend $50 million this year and $100 million in each of the next two years to build the submarine. How and when should General account for its expenses and for the revenues from the government?

(d) Smalltown Bank has invested some of its assets in collateralized debt obligations (CDOs), which were issued by various securities firms as packages of various mortgages and other obligations of individual borrowers. The CDOs are carried on Smalltown's books at their acquisition costs of $250 million, but the issuers are all currently in bankruptcy, and these securities could likely be sold for no more than $225 million. Should any account be taken of this decline in value? If so, how should it be presented?

* * *

3. Principles or Rules?

A philosophical debate of sorts is charting the future of accounting standards. Should accounting standards consist of broad principles to be applied (with judgment) in every situation, or should they be a collection of narrower rules (more mechanical, with fewer judgment calls) tailored for every situation?

The lawyers. We appreciate narrow rules. You celebrate when you find a case, statute, or rule "on point." On the other hand, when there is no such precise guide, it is helpful to have some kind of theoretical grounding, so that we can extrapolate from the specific rules we *see* to the general rule we *want*.

In your answers to Problem 3-1, you (perhaps unconsciously) recognized this dichotomy in determining answers to specific questions. It seems in some cases that a general rule should be followed, or in others that it was prudent for an exception to be made. And you tried, in each case, to remain consistent as best you could.

All this is familiar to a lawyer or even a veteran law student such as yourself. We have principles and we have rules. Some are general principles from judicial decisions,[14] others in statutes.[15] Some are specific rules for many situations, be it the Rule Against Perpetuities, the Federal Sentencing Guidelines, or the useful life of fixed assets for federal income tax purposes. And, most perplexing of all, we know that even specific rules have exceptions, sometimes only implicitly stated (if at all).

The accountants. Lawyers are comfortable with this analysis because we have a grounding in common law or some other fundamental set of legal rules — malleable though they may be. But the accounting profession comes relatively late to this game. Accountants were concerned about an overall "theory" only since about the early part of the last century.[16] The whole transformation of standard-setting from the AICPA (practitioners) to the FASB (independent organization intent on developing a conceptual theory) is an important part of this change, too.[17]

> ***"Well, it may be all right in practice, but it will never work in theory."***
>
> (Warren Buffett, CEO of Berkshire Hathaway, Inc., on how the academic community regards his investment approach.)
>
> ***"In theory, there is no difference between theory and practice, but, in practice, there is."***
>
> (Attributed to Yogi Berra.)

The Enron scandal was perhaps the height of the triumph of rules over principles. Enron took advantage of accounting rules to create fictitious profits by self-dealing transactions with entities which it controlled but which, by the technical accounting rules, were treated as independent. The day of reckoning came with massive financial corrections, the bankruptcy of Enron, the demise of its auditor Arthur Andersen, investigations, and indictments. Following the rules was not a credible defense. GAAP provides specific rules, hundreds of them, for many specific transactions.

> Admits a former Enron accountant[,] "All the rules create all these opportunities. We got to where we did because we exploited that weakness." Here's how another former [Enron] employee describes the process: "Say you have a dog, but you need to create a duck on the financial statements. Fortunately, there are specific accounting rules for what constitutes a duck: yellow feet, white covering, orange beak. So you take the dog and paint its feet yellow and its fur white and you paste an orange plastic beak on its nose, and then you say to your accountants, 'This is a duck! Don't you agree that it's a duck?'

---

14. Recall the famous statement from *Marbury v. Madison*: "It is emphatically the province and duty of the judicial department to say what the law is. Those who apply the rule to particular cases, must of necessity expound and interpret that rule. If two laws conflict with each other, the courts must decide on the operation of each." Marbury v. Madison, 5 U.S. (1 Cranch) 137, 177 (1803). Note, appropriately for our discussion, this is a meta-rule about general rules applicable to specific situations.

15. For example, "[e]very person is bound, without contract, to abstain from injuring the person or property of another, or infringing upon any of his or her rights." Cal. Civ. Code § 1708.

16. Schroeder *et al.*, *supra* note 2, at 4–5. For a good overview of the development of accounting theory, see C. Richard Baker, *The Influence of Accounting Theory on the FASB Conceptual Framework*, 44 Acctg. Historians Journal 109 (no. 2, Dec. 2017).

17. See the first paragraph of subsection (A)(1) of this Chapter.

> And the accountants say, 'Yes, according to the rules, this is a duck.' Everybody knows that it's a dog, not a duck, but that doesn't matter, because you've met the rules for calling it a duck."[18]

The regulators. Thanks in part to the Enron debacle, the timeless debate of "rules versus principles" was rekindled once again. In Section 108(d) of the Sarbanes-Oxley Act, Congress directed the SEC to prepare a "Study and Report on Adopting Principles-Based Accounting."[19] The resulting study[20] concluded that "rules-based" and "principles-based" accounting were not exclusive alternatives, but rather ends of a continuum. Rules based standards "can provide a roadmap to avoidance of the accounting objectives inherent in the standards." However, "[a]t the other extreme, a principles-only approach (which some have suggested as the meaning of the term principles-based accounting standards) typically provides insufficient guidance to make the standards reliably operational." The SEC staff concluded the best standards are on a middle ground, and coined the term "***objectives-oriented accounting***" for the recommended approach. It was explained as follows:

> [A]n optimal standard involves a concise statement of substantive accounting principle where the accounting objective has been included at an appropriate level of specificity as an integral part of the standard and where few, if any, exceptions or conceptual inconsistencies are included in the standard. Further, such a standard should provide an appropriate amount of implementation guidance given the nature of the class of transactions or events and should be devoid of bright-line tests. Finally, such a standard should be consistent with, and derive from, a coherent conceptual framework of financial reporting.[21]

The FASB, in response to the SEC, noted that the change to different types of standards will require significant changes in the way accountants and auditors behave. Accountants like detailed rules and bright lines in part because of a "fear of 'second guessing' by enforcement agencies and the trial bar."[22] Notwithstanding that rather pessimistic observation, the FASB has embraced the idea of objectives-oriented accounting standards development, without using that same term.[23]

* * *

18. Bethany McLean & Peter Elkind, The Smartest Guys in the Room: The Amazing Rise and Scandalous Fall of Enron 142–43 (2003).

19. Pub. L. No. 107-204, Title I, § 108, 116 Stat. 745, 769 (2003).

20. Study Pursuant to Section 108(d) of the Sarbanes-Oxley Act of 2002 on the Adoption by the United States Financial Reporting System of a Principles-Based Accounting System, available at www.sec.gov/news/studies/principlesbasedstand.htm (Jul. 25, 2003).

21. *Id.* (Executive Summary).

22. FASB Response to SEC Study on the Adoption of a Principles-Based Accounting System 6–7 (July 2004).

23. Schroeder *et al.*, *supra* note 2, at 54–55.

Problem 3-2

A Case Study: Rules, Principles, and Leases

A good example of rules v. principles in action is the recent development of accounting standards governing leases. A leases a $200,000 warehouse for her completed widgets. She pays $1000/month on a month-to-month lease. B, with an identical widget warehouse next door, purchased her warehouse, borrowing $200,000 and paying $1000/month on her 15-year 4.75% loan,

(a) If all other things are equal, how will A's balance sheet compare to B's?

(b) B has an existing loan (taken out before buying the warehouse) which requires her to maintain a debt/equity ratio of 1.0. How will that ratio be affected by her purchase of the warehouse?

(c) C wants to acquire an identical warehouse. C has a clever accountant who would like C to have the same accounting treatment as A (the lessor) but wants a similar economic bargain as B (the purchaser). So C leases her warehouse for 30 years, for lease payments of $1000/month.

(i) Does C have a "lease"? Shouldn't it therefore be accounted for just like A's lease?

(ii) Is C's lease the economic equivalent of a purchase with borrowed money?

Suppose you are the writer of accounting standards. You want to make sure that leases are accounted for as leases, and purchases as purchases. Consider the following proposed rules.[24]

> ***Standard #1***. A lease will be accounted for as a lease unless one of the following is true, in which case it shall be accounted for as a purchase (known as a "capital lease"):
>
> - Ownership is transferred to the lessor at the end of the lease;
> - The lease contains a bargain purchase option;
> - The least term is equal to 75% or more of the estimated economic life of the property; or
> - The present value of the minimum lease payments is at least 90% of the fair market value of the leased asset.

24. I have taken this summary of the rules from Denton L. Collins, *et al.*, *Financial Reporting Outcomes under Rules-Based and Principles-Based Accounting Standards*, 26 Accounting Horizons 681, 705 (2012).

Standard #2. A lease will be accounted for as a lease unless one of the following is true, in which case it shall be accounted for as a purchase:

- Ownership is transferred to the lessor at the end of the lease;
- The lease contains a bargain purchase option, and it is reasonably certain that the option will be exercisable;
- The lease term is for the major part of the economic life of the leased asset;
- The present value of the minimum lease payments is at least equal to substantially all of the fair value of the leased asset; or
- The leased assets are of a specialized nature such that only the lessee can use them without major modifications being made.
- Other factors that suggest a lease might properly be accounted for as a purchase:
- If the lessee can cancel, the lessor's losses associated with the cancellation are borne by the lessee.
- Gains or losses in the fair market value of the leased asset will accrue to the lessee.
- The lessee has the ability to continue the lease for a supplemental term at below-market rent.

(d) Which standard is "rules based"? Which standard is "principles based"?

(e) If none of the four conditions in Standard #1 is satisfied, can you be sure your client's lease will be accounted for as an operating lease under Standard #1? Even if you miss by only a trivial amount, for example, if the lease term is 74% of the estimated useful life? Would you expect to see a lot of "operating leases" at the 74% useful life level? Can you be as confident about your advice under Standard #2? Which rule would make it easier to create a duck out of a dog?

* * *

Advantages and disadvantages. You can see from the above problem that rules-based standards have much to recommend them. They are certain, easy to apply, and have consistent and predictable outcomes. On the other hand, they can be easily manipulated.

You can see from the above problem that principles-based standards have much to recommend them. They are more comprehensive and will yield more comparable results across entities. On the other hand, they require much more judgment by the accountant, auditor (or lawyer), and may result in inconsistent treatment.

The evidence on leases. So let's fact-check these above two paragraphs with two recent studies on the standards we looked at in Problem 3-2. We can do that because (until recently) these *were* the applicable standards. Standard #1 was GAAP as promulgated by the FASB, and Standard #2 was the international rule, promulgated by the International Accounting Standards Board (IASB).[25] In two different studies, one of corporate financial officers and one of actual disclosures, researchers concluded that:

- the more-precise Standard #1 resulted in the kind of aggressive decision making we would expect with rules-based Standards,
- the less-precise Standard #2 did not encourage a wider range of responses in application by reporting companies.[26]

The rest of the story. Both the FASB and the IASB changed their rules, effective in most cases in 2019, to require *all* leases longer than 12 months to be accounted for as capital leases.[27] This basically rendered moot all the sound and fury directed at distinguishing between Standard #1 and Standard #2!

Professor Donald Weidner, reviewing the entire almost decade-long process resulting in the new coordinated standards, concluded that the new rules "reflect and reinforce the trend away from formalism toward economic substance" and "a further shift away from a rules-based approach and toward the IASB's principles based approach."[28] Do you agree with this assessment?

* * *

Problem 3-3

The new standards for lease accounting apply an asset-liability requirement to all leases beyond twelve months. This was considered by the rule makers to be an exception for short-term leases, recognizing that, in such cases, the benefit of the additional information did not exceed the costs inherent in making the valuations required.

(a) Could a company wanting to avoid placing an asset and liability on its books for a ten-year lease simply negotiate a one-year lease which is renewable for nine years?

(b) The FASB recognized this possibility, but "concluded that there are significant economic disincentives to both parties to entering into a series of short-term leases in place of longer-term leases such that there is not a significant structuring risk throughout the system. For example, lessees may have to pay a premium rental price

25. The IASB functions and is organized analogously to the FASB, but its full story is beyond our coverage here. For details, see www.iasb.org.

26. Christopher P. Agoglia, Timothy S. Doupnik, & George T. Tsakumis, *Principles-Based versus Rules-Based Accounting Standards: The Influence of Standard Precision and Audit Committee Strength on Financial Reporting Decisions*, 86 The Accounting Review 747 (2011), and Collins, *et al.*, *supra* note 24.

27. Background information on the new FASB rule is at http://www.fasb.org/jsp/FASB/FASBContent_C/NewsPage&cid=1176167901466. The new FASB rule, reflected in ASC Part 842, still divides leases into "operating" and "capital" leases, but, regardless of that title, all leases for longer than twelve months must follow asset-and-liability booking rules. Background information on the new IASC rule is available at www.ifrs.org/issued-standards/list-of-standards/ifrs-16-leases/.

28. Donald J. Weidner, *New FASB Rules on Accounting for Leases: A Sarbanes-Oxley Promise Delivered*, 72 Bus. Law. 367, 404 n. 210 (2017).

to compensate the lessor for its increased residual asset risk, and some lessors will be unable to enter into short-term leases depending on the terms of the financing they obtained to acquire the underlying asset."[29] Are you convinced?

* * *

Rules or Principles? Or Ethics? Other writers have noted that the whole set-up of a dichotomy between "rules" and "principles" is a false one. "The SEC correctly concludes the question is one of objectives," writes Professor Lawrence Cunningham,[30] and makes the further distinction that the push to "[p]rinciples-based regulation may be a call to *ethical* principles."[31] So as the debate between "rules" and "principles" continues, remember that the real point may be about something else: the accountant's ability and willingness to exercise professional judgment. You, as an attorney, will have much experience to bring to the table here. You can help your client and your client's accountant make the tough calls and do so correctly and defensibly.

B. Auditing and Auditing Standards

1. The Need for Audits

Standardized financial reporting, as discussed above, is necessary at least in some instances. For The Collegetown Coffeehouse, Bill and Ted may be happy with their own rough-and-ready approximations of how the business is doing, and TCC's creditors may be happy with their own evaluations of the business. But for a business of significant size, standardized financial statements, prepared according to GAAP, are a necessity. Sophisticated creditors, absentee owners (such as shareholders) and others who need the business information but are not intimately familiar with the business, will require that financial information be presented in standardized form.

But who prepares those standardized financial reports? Even if everyone agreed on exactly what GAAP requires in every instance, it is the *business management* who prepares those financial statements. And it is that same management who is reporting to the external users of those financial statements on its performance. Eventually, those external users began to require third-party verification of management's work, and the auditing profession was born.

> An independent audit is necessary because of the inherent potential conflict between the entity's management and the users of its financial information. Since financial statements are one of the means used to evaluate management's performance in operating the entity, management could have an incentive to bias the measurement. The bias could range from unconsciously presenting performance in a better light to outright misrepresentation.

29. Accounting Standards Update 2016-02, *Leases*, ¶ BC 381.

30. Lawrence A. Cunningham, *A Prescription to Retire the Rhetoric of "Principles-Based Systems" in Corporate Law, Securities Regulation, and Accounting*, 60 Vand. L. Rev. 1411, 1470 (2007).

31. *Id.* at 1477.

> This does not suggest, however, that managements are not honest. Rather there is an inherent *potential* conflict between management and users of financial statements. Often an audit can help to protect management against accusations that financial statements have been presented in a biased manner. Management has discretion in the preparation of financial information and in the use of assets in conducting the business. Audits have a restraining influence on management's activities in both areas.
>
> ....
>
> The accounting system and the controls over it are designed to produce proper recording of performance and accountability for the assets entrusted to the entity. Users of financial statements need assurance that management has fulfilled its stewardship responsibility by establishing and supervising a system that adequately protects corporate assets. An audit provides reasonable assurance that management has fulfilled its responsibility.[32]

Modern auditing dates from the emergence of large industrial corporations and the corresponding growth of creditors and owners from roughly 1850 to the early 1900s. It resulted initially from demands of creditors and owners — still the principal users of audited financial reports today. Audits are demanded in private transactions by creditors or owners, but came also to be standard in the public securities markets. The New York Stock Exchange first required audits in 1932 for all companies whose stock was listed there for trading, and audits were required under the federal securities laws beginning the following year.[33]

As we saw in the first part of this chapter dealing with accounting information, decision-makers are looking for *relevant* and *reliable* financial information. Making that information *relevant* is the job of *accounting* standards, which we examined in Part A. Making that information *reliable* is the job of the auditor.[34]

2. The Development of Standards

There are auditing standards and standard-setters, just as there are accounting standards and standard-setters. Auditing standards have been in the legal and political spotlight even more than accounting standards, however.

Unlike accounting standards, which have been created by a variety of standard-setters, auditing standards have always been developed by a committee of the AICPA,

---

32. The Commission on Auditors' Responsibilities: Report, Conclusions, and Recommendations 5 (1978). This Commission, also known as the "Cohen Commission" for its chair, former SEC Chairman Manuel F. Cohen, was established by the AICPA with the charge to "develop conclusions and recommendations regarding the appropriate responsibilities of independent auditors." *Id.* at xi. *See also* Daniel R. Fischel, *The Regulation of Accounting: Some Economic Issues*, 52 Brooklyn L. Rev. 1051, 1051–52 (1987).

33. *See* Securities Act of 1933, Schedule A, 48 Stat. 88, 15 U.S.C. §77aa.

34. Don M. Pallais, Audits and Other Accountants' Services: A Handbook for Lawyers 2 (Am. Bar Ass'n 2010).

the Auditing Standards Board (ASB).[35] The ASB promulgates Statements on Auditing Standards, or SASs. These SASs are binding on every AICPA member auditor. Together they comprise ***generally accepted auditing standards***, or ***GAAS***. And as they did with GAAP, the SEC has traditionally relied for the most part on private auditing standard-setters for GAAS.

The financial crises of 2001–02 and the Sarbanes-Oxley Act changed auditing standard-setting, probably more dramatically than accounting standard-setting. The Act created a new private entity, the Public Company Accounting Oversight Board, or PCAOB, to oversee the accounting profession. The PCAOB is required to inspect and register all accounting firms that audit the books of companies whose shares are publicly-traded, hence the PCAOB's name.

In addition, and more importantly for our purposes, Sarbanes-Oxley "fired" the private auditing standard setters for public companies. The Act *mandates* that the PCAOB approve auditing standards. The PCAOB was given the option to initially rely on the ASB (or some other private body) for promulgation of standards,[36] but it declined this invitation. The pre-Act standards were adopted on a transitional basis, and in 2015 the PCAOB "blended" its own standards in with the private-sector standards it adopted so that the whole is now one integrated work.[37]

The SEC generally oversees the PCAOB. The Sarbanes-Oxley Act modeled the SEC's oversight of the PCAOB on the SEC's existing oversight of self-regulatory organizations such as the New York Stock Exchange. Board members are appointed and can be censured or removed by the SEC, and the board's rules and budget (among other things) must be approved by the SEC as well. In many respects the SEC's oversight goes beyond that provided for oversight of private self-regulatory organizations, and the arrangement presented a host of unique constitutional and administrative law issues.[38] In *Free Enterprise Fund v. Public Company Accounting Oversight Board*,[39] the U.S. Supreme Court confronted the provision in the Act which permits removal of PCAOB members only "for cause." This, combined with the fact that the President may remove members of the SEC only "for cause"[40] created the following issue, summarized and answered by Chief Justice Roberts, delivering the Court's opinion.

35. For a brief history of the development of the auditing standard-setters, see James F. Strother, *The Establishment of Generally Accepted Accounting Principles and Generally Accepted Auditing Standards*, 28 Vand. L. Rev. 201, 218–19 (1975).

36. Recall that the SEC was given this same choice with accounting standards as well, and decided to continue to rely on the FASB; *see* supra note 4 and accompanying text.

37. *See* PCAOB Release No. 2015-002 (March 31, 2015), https://pcaobus.org/Rulemaking/Docket040/Release_2015_002_Reorganization.pdf. All the standards are available at http://pcaobus.org/STANDARDS/Pages/default.aspx. The PCAOB has also issued standards-related rules, and ethics and independence rules (more on these below).

38. For a full discussion, see Donna M. Nagy, *Playing Peekaboo with Constitutional Law: The PCAOB and its Public/Private Status*, 80 Notre Dame L. Rev. 975 (2005).

39. 561 U.S. 477 (2010).

40. So agreed by all parties under the authority of *Humphrey's Executor v. United States*, 295 U.S. 602 (1935); *see Free Enterprise Fund*, 561 U.S. at 487.

> The question is whether these separate layers of protection may be combined. May the President be restricted in his ability to remove a principal officer, who is in turn restricted in his ability to remove an inferior officer, even though that inferior officer determines the policy and enforces the laws of the United States?
>
> We hold that such multilevel protection from removal is contrary to Article II's vesting of the executive power in the President. The President cannot "take Care that the Laws be faithfully executed" if he cannot oversee the faithfulness of the officers who execute them.[41]

After this decision, the SEC issued a statement indicating that it interpreted the Court's decision to effectively excise the offensive provision but leave the act otherwise intact. The SEC thus concluded that "the members of the PCAOB [are] subject to removal by the [SEC] without restriction."[42] There has not been to date any contrary interpretation.

The PCAOB is the standard-setter for *public* company audits. It promulgates Auditing Standards, which are referred to and cited here as "PCAOB AS xxxx." The ASB, of course, retains its role as standard-setter for *private* company audits, and in areas which the PCAOB chooses not to address. "While not identical, GAAS and PCAOB standards tend to be similar. Standards issued by one body are largely adopted by the other, although there are often lags as the bodies catch up to each other."[43] The ASB's work, Statements on Auditing Standards, have also been recently codified and "clarified" to be more readable and consistent with international standards. These rules are referred to and cited here as "AU-C § xxx.xx."[44]

3. The Auditor's Work

We now know why there are auditors and the broad standards overlying their work. But what exactly *does* an auditor do? "Auditing is a systematic process of objectively obtaining and evaluating evidence regarding assertions about economic actions and events to ascertain the degree of correspondence between those assertions and established criteria and communicating the results to interested users."[45] This is a very broad definition, prepared by accountants, but each phrase was carefully chosen and adds importantly to the definition.

It is difficult to describe in detail what goes on in an audit, for two major reasons. First, each audit is unique to the entity in question. Remember, part of the reason for audits in the first place was that users of financial statements don't know very

41. *Free Enterprise Fund*, 561 U.S. at 483–84.

42. SEC News Digest 2010-119 (June 28, 2010), 2010 WL 2561434.

43. Pallais, *supra* note 34, at 17.

44. For background on the clarification project, see https://www.aicpa.org/research/standards/auditattest/clarifiedsas.html.

45. American Accounting Association, Report of the Committee on Basic Auditing Concepts, 47 (Supp.) Accounting Review 18 (1972).

much about the entity's operations. It is the auditor's job to become familiar with those operations, and this each audit is unto itself. An audit of The Collegetown Coffeehouse is different from an audit of General Motors, needless to say. Second, auditors are professionals; auditing involves professional judgment based on the unique circumstances of each audit.

We can provide a general idea, however. Auditing standards require that the auditor:

- Assess the risks of material misstatement and plan procedures responsive to those assessed risks;[46] and
- Design procedures to obtain "sufficient appropriate audit evidence."[47]

Together, these standards structure the auditor's work.[48] Consider each part.

a. Risk Assessment

This is probably the most difficult area for an audit newcomer to understand. The client presumably already has an accounting system in operation. In general, an auditor can significantly limit the scope of testing, evaluation and so on which must be done (in the next step) if the auditor can be assured that, for each assessed material risk of inaccuracy, the entity has a reliably functioning control system.[49] We discuss accounting control systems in Chapter 9.

Illustration

Suppose we were to audit Wanda's Widgets' financial statements, beginning with the inventory. If the auditor observes and tests Wanda's inventory recording system (purchases, invoices, storage, control, and so forth) the auditor may reduce or even eliminate the need to physically count all or part of Wanda's inventory in order to be satisfied that the inventory amount is accurate.

* * *

46. AU-C §§ 315–330.

47. *Id.* § 500.

48. For additional succinct summaries of the work of an audit, see some of the following: Karla M. Johnstone, *et al.*, Auditing: A Risk-Based Approach 6–8 (11th ed. 2019); Pallais, *supra* note 34, Chs. 2–4; David A. Jaffe, *The Allocation of Fault in Auditor Liability Lawsuits Brought by Sophisticated Third Party Users of Financial Statements — A Plea for Proportionate Liability*, 54 U. Pitt. L. Rev. 1051, 1054–56 (1993); Bily v. Arthur Young & Co., 834 P.2d 745, 749–51 (Cal. 1992); Samuel S. Paschall, *Liability to Non-clients: The Accountant's Role and Responsibility*, 53 Mo. L. Rev. 693, 698–703 (1988); Willis W. Hagen II, *Certified Public Accountant's Liability for Malpractice: Effect of Compliance with GAAP and GAAS*, 13 J. Contemp. L. 65, 66–69 (1987); T.J. Fiflis, *Current Problems of Accountants' Responsibilities to Third Parties*, 28 Vand. L. Rev. 31, 35–40 (1975).

49. AU-C §§ 315.05–13.

Problem 3-4

Wilbur's Widgets is a competing widget retailer. Wilbur has a fairly large ($10 million in sales) operation, and a lot of inventory. Explain what features you would expect to see in Wilbur's inventory control system. You would first identify the **risks** of financial misstatement in the system, and only then can you devise controls to mitigate those risks. Once you have identified the controls, how will you determine whether the controls are operating properly?

* * *

b. Evidence Collection

The auditor's objective here is "to design and perform audit procedures that enable the auditor to obtain sufficient appropriate audit evidence to be able to draw reasonable conclusions on which to base the auditor's opinion."[50] Both of the auditing standard-setters have issued guidelines for this important task, summarized below.

- ***Quantity:*** How much evidence is needed? A "sufficient" amount, depending on the assertions made and the auditor's judgment about risk.
- ***Quality:*** The evidence must be *relevant* and *reliable.*
  - ***Relevant:*** We need to test the assertion or control directly (does it measure or control?) and test for overstatement or understatement.
  - ***Reliable:*** This is measured by standards probably familiar to lawyers with a background in evaluating evidence: direct observations, computations, and inspections are more reliable than evidence obtained indirectly, and external evidence is probably more reliable than internally-generated evidence.[51] The control system (see above) is also relevant in determining whether evidence is reliable.
- ***Evidence of what?*** There are five different kinds of assertions made in financial statements.[52]

Existence or occurrence—Assets or liabilities of the company exist at a given date, and recorded transactions have occurred during a given period.

Completeness—All transactions and accounts that should be presented in the financial statements are so included.

Valuation or allocation—Asset, liability, equity, revenue, and expense components have been included in the financial statements at appropriate amounts.

50. *Id.* § 500.04.

51. PCAOB AS 1105.08; AU-C §§ 500.27–.32; *accord*, Pallais, *supra* note 34, at 56.

52. PCAOB AS 1105.11; AU-C § 501.03.

Rights and obligations—The company holds or controls rights to the assets, and liabilities are obligations of the company at a given date.

Presentation and disclosure—The components of the financial statements are properly classified, described, and disclosed

- *How do we test?* By inspection, observation, inquiry, confirmation, recalculation, reperformance, and analytical procedures (data analysis).[53]
- *How do we select the test population?*
  - Random samples
  - "Stratified" amounts (for example, all transactions in the population over a certain dollar amount) or all items which meet specific criteria (for example, insider transactions, or those which were troublesome the prior audit)
  - For some low-volume high-importance (or high-value) populations, all transactions will be examined.

Illustration: Accounts Receivable

One text suggests the following tests for a company's accounts receivable:

1. Obtain an understanding of the internal controls over sales and accounts receivable. Update last year's analysis, walk-through to determine controls are operative.
2. Compare accounts receivable balance and the ratio of accounts receivable to sales to last year's data.
3. Obtain an aged trial balance, confirm amounts with the general ledger, test accuracy of aging by confirming with invoice amounts and dates
4. Obtain third-party confirmation of selected accounts, reconcile differences between confirmations and recorded balances.
5. Test adequacy of allowance for uncollectible accounts [Ed.: covered in Chapter 5(C)] by comparison to last year, analysis of ratio of allowance to bad debt expense, and by comparison to the aging categories above. Inquire about collection problems regarding specific customers or products.
6. Scan the sales journal for unusual or large transactions just before or just after year-end. Review credits issued after year-end and determine whether they should be accrued to prior year. Reconcile large-account collections after year-end to deposit slips.

Source: Don M. Palais, Audits and Other Accountants' Services: A Handbook for Lawyers 61 (2010).

53. PCAOB AS 1105.15–.21; AU-C §§500.A10–.A26; Pallais, *supra* note 34, at 55–65.

Illustration: Inventory

The Auditing Standards Board offers the following example for inventory auditing:

- Attend physical inventory counting and:
  - Evaluate management's instructions and procedures;
  - Observe the counts
  - Inspect the inventory
  - Perform test counts
- Review final inventory records to determine whether they reflect inventory count results
- If count is taken at a date other than that of the financial statements, perform procedures to determine if changes were properly recorded

If inventory is in control of a third party, confirmation and inspection should be undertaken.

Source: AU-C §§501.11–.15.

* * *

Problem 3-5

We are not training to be accountants or auditors, of course, but a lawyer or law student should be a good judge generally of the types of evidence needed to support an assertion. Assume that you are preparing for an audit of The Collegetown Coffeehouse financial statements prepared at the end of Problem 1-37. Review your work and assume that you have been presented with the income statement and balance sheet from that problem.

(a) You notice that there is a large loan from Collegetown National Bank. Bill confirms the loan, the payment dates, remaining balance and associated details (Ted finds such details unbefitting a rock star and "most uncool"). What steps might you take to confirm the details of the bank loan?

(b) You notice that, although TCC has a most resplendent location, that there is no item on the balance sheet reflecting "Land and Buildings." Ted brings in Napoleon, the landlord, who confirms that TCC leases the property from him at $3,500 per month in advance. Are you satisfied?

(c) Bill and Ted reviewed with you their weekly procedure for counting proceeds from sales (except for those few weeks when they were too busy to do so). Is this a sufficient method for accounting for the sales made at TCC? How would you assure yourself that their procedures are accurate?

* * *

To get an appreciation for how audit testing works in the real world, consider the following SEC proceeding concerning a famous inventory fraud which took place in the 1970s. What kinds of judgments did the auditors make regarding collection of "sufficient appropriate audit evidence"?

In the Matter of Seidman & Seidman

Securities and Exchange Commission, 1976
46 S.E.C. 524

OPINION AND ORDER PURSUANT TO RULE 102(e) OF THE COMMISSION'S RULES OF PRACTICE[54]

....

CENCO INCORPORATED

Cenco is a Delaware corporation with its principal offices in Chicago, Illinois. It is a diversified company with sales of almost $300 million for its fiscal year ended April 30, 1975. At that time through numerous divisions and subsidiaries, Cenco engaged in the manufacture and distribution of products and services in five general areas: health care, education, water pollution abatement, technology and nursing homes. Its common stock is listed for trading (although trading is currently halted) on the New York and Pacific stock exchanges. Seidman & Seidman, through its Chicago office, was the independent auditor of Cenco for approximately 15 years. During that time Cenco grew to be one of the largest of Seidman & Seidman's accounts. Since February 1976, Seidman & Seidman has ceased to act as independent auditors for Cenco.

An investigation conducted by the Commission staff has revealed false financial reporting by Cenco of substantial proportions with respect to its audited annual financial statements from about 1970 to 1974.[55] Throughout that period Seidman & Seidman issued unqualified reports with respect to Cenco's annual financial statements. The staff's investigation indicates that the false financial reporting was the result of a calculated scheme directed and conducted by certain officers of Cenco and its subsidiaries and others. During 1975 substantial changes were made in the management and board of directors of Cenco. Under its new management, Cenco is in the process of divesting itself of its health care and certain other businesses.

Cenco's false financial reporting was accomplished in large part through manipulations of the financial statements of certain subsidiaries in its Health Care Group. Predominant among these was Cenco Medical Health/Supply Corporation ("CMH").

---

54. [Ed.] Under the SEC's Rules of Practice, the Commission may, in an administrative proceeding (before an administrative law judge, who is an agency employee but independent from the rest of the agency), censure, suspend or bar any professional from practicing before the Commission who is found to be unqualified, lacking in character or integrity, or to have willfully violated or aided and abetted a violation of the securities laws.

55. Some details of the scheme were brought to light in part through the cooperation of Seidman & Seidman during the staff's investigation.

During the years 1973 and 1974, CMH was primarily in the business of distributing health and medical products to hospitals and other institutional customers through a network of approximately 20 branch warehouses and marketing facilities located throughout the United States. The reported sales of CMH, included in the consolidated financial statements, were approximately $32.8 million and $41.8 million for the fiscal years ended April 30, 1973 and April 30, 1974, respectively. The reported inventory of CMH as included in the Cenco consolidated financial statements was approximately $32.1 million and $39.0 million for the fiscal years ended April 30, 1973 and April 30, 1974, respectively.

The staff's investigation ... indicates that intentional inflation of inventory quantities and values was among the means used to accomplish the fraud.... This was carried out by Cenco management assisted by lower level employees, primarily by altering the quantities recorded on the prenumbered, two-part inventory tags used by CMH in counting the inventory; by altering quantities reflected on computer listings prepared to compile the physical count of inventory; and by creating inventory tags to record quantities of nonexistent inventory.

The staff's investigation reveals that Cenco personnel at various levels and in various operational areas engaged in certain activities for the apparent purpose of concealing the falsification of the financial statements from Seidman & Seidman. Notwithstanding such concealment, the remedial sanctions described below are based in part on our findings that in conducting its audits of Cenco's ... financial statements, Seidman & Seidman failed to comply with applicable professional standards with respect to obtaining sufficient, competent evidence to afford a reasonable basis for its opinions and failed to take adequate measures to assure appropriate supervision of professional staff conducting the field work.

....

For the fiscal year ended April 30, 1973 Cenco reported pretax income of $27.3 million. Consolidated inventory valued at $104.4 million represented about 33% of total assets at fiscal year end. The valuation of year end inventory and cost of goods sold was based primarily on a physical inventory taken in May 1973. It appears that about 50% of the $32.1 million reported CMH portion of year end inventory was in fact non-existent. This overstatement of inventory substantially inflated Cenco's consolidated pre-tax income.

During the ... audit of CMH, Seidman & Seidman reached two significant audit conclusions which pertained to the CMH inventory accounting system. The first was that the CMH internal controls over inventory continued to be inadequate. The second was that as in prior years, CMH did not have reliable general ledger inventory balances or perpetual inventory systems. The auditors therefore believed that CMH was forced to rely almost entirely on the results of the physical inventory. In our opinion, the conditions as they believed them to exist required extensive audit testing of inventory. It is our judgment that Seidman & Seidman did not give adequate audit effect to the clear requirements of these conclusions. Under the circumstances, the

Commission also believes that the audit program for CMH inventory should have expressly noted these internal control deficiencies and included appropriately detailed instructions concerning the nature and scope of audit tests.

....

As a part of its audit procedures, Seidman & Seidman observed the physical inventory count at nine of the twenty CMH warehouses, representing about 65% of the total CMH inventory. The engagement instructions transmitted from the Chicago office of Seidman & Seidman to the auditors conducting the observations directed the observing auditors to use their discretion with regard to the extent of audit testing during the observation. These instructions did not inform the field auditors of inadequacies in CMH internal controls or the reliance by CMH on the results of the physical count. As a result, most of the observing auditors were required and permitted to exercise discretion over the extent of testing without being informed of all relevant information bearing on the extent of testing appropriate in the circumstances.

The Seidman & Seidman instructions to the auditors observing the inventory count required the auditor to either obtain or prepare a document for control of the inventory tags used, unused or voided. The program also required that after completion of the counting, the document be tested for accuracy. However, Seidman & Seidman did not obtain or prepare tag control documents at four of the nine branches observed. It is our judgment that in failing to comply with its own audit requirements at four of the nine branches, the auditors did not properly assure themselves that control of the inventory tags was adequate and that the conclusion reached by Seidman & Seidman that tags had been properly controlled did not reflect an objective review of the results of that audit work.

As a part of the observation of the physical count of inventory, Seidman & Seidman auditors checked the accuracy of the CMH counting procedures by test counting the results recorded by CMH personnel. Seidman & Seidman recorded certain of these test counts on schedules which were included in the observation workpapers. The purpose of recording these test counts was to provide evidential matter upon which the auditors could reach a conclusion on the reliability of the CMH representations of the quantities reflected in the computer listings.

In regard to quantities of inventory, our investigation indicates that Seidman & Seidman generated evidential matter from two principal sources. These sources were the procedures pertaining to control of the inventory tags and the comparison of recorded test counts taken during the observation to the final computer listings. As previously concluded, Seidman & Seidman did not generate sufficient evidential matter to conclude that inventory tags had been adequately controlled. Therefore the principal source of evidential matter which provided a reasonable basis for concluding that CMH was reliably representing its inventory quantities, was the comparison of test counts to inventory listings. It is our opinion that Seidman & Seidman unreasonably relied on this procedure and that the results of this procedure in fact provided substantial indications that CMH was not accurately stating its inventory quantities.

The comparison of recorded test counts to the computer listings in the nine warehouse locations in which the inventory count was observed indicated error rates ranging from .9% to 38.8% of the test counts, with error rates in excess of 10% in several locations. It is our opinion that the number and percentage of test count differences warranted additional procedures to determine the reasons for the differences and the possible effect on the inventory computations. This is particularly so in light of the large number of tags used to count the inventory. Seidman & Seidman did attempt to ascertain the reasons for the differences in the Miami comparisons, following discovery that the bulk of the differences were uniformly an increase by a multiple of ten. A similar pattern also appeared in another comparison. The auditors first demanded an explanation from Cenco management and were informed by the former director of CMH operations that the pattern of differences was attributable to errors made by a key-punch operator. The auditors then asked to see the inventory tags, but the same CMH official stated that the tags had been destroyed. Seidman & Seidman did not ascertain the extent to which such "keypunch errors" might have affected the untested portion of the inventory listing. The Seidman & Seidman workpapers do not contain any reference to this investigation. Without attempting any further procedures, the auditors apparently accepted management's explanation and concluded that no adjustments to the bulk of the Miami inventory were required.[56]

....

Seidman & Seidman prepared a schedule which set forth the comparative inventory balances at April 30, 1972 and April 30, 1973 for a number of the CMH branches. This schedule reflected significant increases from the prior year. A CMH financial officer wrote on this schedule management's explanations for the increases in inventory amounts.[57] Seidman & Seidman did not attempt to determine the reasonableness or credibility of these explanations.[58] It is our opinion that Seidman & Seidman unduly relied on these explanations and did not take those steps necessary under the circumstances to verify their reasonableness. This is particularly so in light of the fact that the amount of increase in inventory was substantially greater than the corresponding increase in sales.

....

The deficiencies in the ... audits of Cenco appear to have been caused in large part by a lack of appropriate audit planning and failure to adequately consider the potential for misstatement inherent in the CMH inventory. There were extreme

56. It is the view of Seidman & Seidman that nothing short of a recount would have provided substantial additional assurance that the Miami inventory was fairly stated and that the degree of uncertainty did not warrant so drastic a measure.

57. For example, an increase of 80% (about $400,000) was explained by "larger warehouse." An increase of 35% amounting to $400,000 was explained by "poor purchasing." An increase of more than 50% amounting to $350,000 was explained by "new warehouse". An increase of more than 100% amounting to $550,000 was explained by "volume doubled ($625,000 increase)."

58. In the auditors' view the credibility of the management explanations was enhanced by the belief that the financial officer's responsibilities were not in the area of inventories.

delays in receiving key documents necessary to perform important aspects of the audit work which resulted in the need to perform substantial work, particularly with respect to inventory, during the last weeks of the engagements. Efficient audit procedures are often dependent in large part on early production of required documents by the client. A delay in document production should not in itself be the cause of a reduction in the scope or completeness of an accountant's examination and should not cause a deviation from established procedures. We do not think that Seidman & Seidman approached the audits of the CMH inventory with the skeptical attitude necessary to properly achieve the purposes of the audits.

Notes and Questions

1. How did this attempted fraud work to the advantage of Cenco? How does overstating the inventory help the company look better? Consider the impact on the income statement.

2. How did Seidman & Seidman's audit plan compare to the recommended steps for inventory audit from the auditing standards board (preceding Problem 3-5)?

3. Why did the Commission fault Seidman & Seidman for its failure to have a "skeptical attitude necessary to properly achieve the purposes of the audits"? Is an auditor not supposed to believe *anything* she sees or reads? If you were Cenco's auditors, at what point would you become less likely to believe your client's responses?

* * *

Problem 3-6

Able, Baker & Co. (AB), an accounting firm, was engaged to audit the financial statements of General Widget Corp. (GWC).

Out of a total of $500 million in assets, GWC lists $200 million accounts receivable on its balance sheet for the year just ended. During its audit, AB reviewed the list of receivables, confirmed 10% of the receivables directly with customers in writing, confirmed 50% of all receivables over 90 days old (which constituted 25% of all receivables by number and 15% by amount), observed GWC's invoicing and billing procedures, and (with a computer consultant) reviewed the programs used for billing.

Nonetheless, GWC was able to hide approximately $40 million of worthless and fictitious receivables from AB. The news became public thanks to a former executive vice-president with a grudge. Was AB's audit work satisfactory?

* * *

4. The Auditor's Opinion

The culmination of this audit work is the opinion of the auditor on the client's financial statements. Those who demand audits (creditors, absentee owners, federal regulators) want the auditor's assurance that the financial statements comply with GAAP. The vehicle for this assurance is the auditor's opinion. Although that opinion is brief, it is almost a foreign language, for each word has a special meaning and significance.[59] The novice reader of an auditor's opinion would be tempted to dismiss all the language as just so much boilerplate. In fact, there has been significant controversy over the form and content of the auditor's opinion through the years.

Example

The following is from the 2018 Annual Report of Apple, Inc.

Report of Independent Registered Public Accounting Firm

To the Shareholders and the Board of Directors of Apple Inc.

We have audited the accompanying consolidated balance sheets of Apple Inc. as of September 29, 2018 and September 30, 2017, and the related consolidated statements of operations, comprehensive income, shareholders' equity and cash flows for each of the three years in the period ended September 29, 2018, and the related notes (collectively referred to as the "financial statements").

In our opinion, the financial statements present fairly, in all material respects, the financial position of Apple Inc. at September 29, 2018 and September 30, 2017, and the results of its operations and its cash flows for each of the three years in the period ended September 29, 2018, in conformity with U.S. generally accepted accounting principles.

These financial statements are the responsibility of Apple Inc.'s management. Our responsibility is to express an opinion on Apple Inc.'s financial statements based on our audits.

We conducted our audits in accordance with the standards of the PCAOB. Those standards require that we plan and perform the audit to obtain reasonable assurance about whether the financial statements are free of material misstatement, whether due to error or fraud. Our audits included performing procedures to assess the risks of material misstatement of the financial statements, whether due to error or fraud, and performing procedures that respond to those risks. Such procedures included examining, on a test basis, evidence regarding the amounts and disclosures in the financial statements. Our audits also included evaluating the accounting principles used and significant estimates made by management, as well as evaluating the overall presentation of the financial statements. We believe that our audits provide a reasonable basis for our opinion.

/s/ Ernst & Young LLP

We have served as Apple Inc.'s auditor since 2009.

San Jose, California
November 5, 2018

59. In the example which follows, the portion of the auditor's opinion concerning "internal controls" has been omitted. It will be the subject of our study in Chapter 9.

In 1988, the Auditing Standards Board first wrote comprehensive rules for auditor's opinions. Most of the above language in Ernst & Young's opinion comes from these and subsequent rules, including:

- A title that includes the word *independent*
- A statement that the financial statements identified in the report were audited
- A statement that the financial statements are the responsibility of the Company's management and that the auditor's responsibility is to express an opinion on the financial statements based on his or her audit
- A statement that the audit was conducted in accordance with generally accepted auditing standards and an identification of the United States of America as the country of origin of those standards (for example, auditing standards generally accepted in the United States of America or U.S. generally accepted auditing standards)
- A statement that those standards require that the auditor plan and perform the audit to obtain reasonable assurance about whether the financial statements are free of material misstatement
- A statement that an audit includes:

  Examining, on a test basis, evidence supporting the amounts and disclosures in the financial statements;

  Assessing the accounting principles used and significant estimates made by management; and

  Evaluating the overall financial statement presentation.
- A statement that the auditor believes that his or her audit provides a reasonable basis for his or her opinion
- An opinion as to whether the financial statements present fairly, in all material respects, the financial position of the Company as of the balance sheet date and the results of its operations and its cash flows for the period then ended in conformity with generally accepted accounting principles. The opinion should include an identification of the United States of America as the country of origin of those accounting principles (for example, accounting principles generally accepted in the United States of America or U.S. generally accepted accounting principles)
- The manual or printed signature of the auditor's firm
- The date of the audit report.[60]

The auditor's report has been modified over the years to correct many misinterpretations which the reading public has had about these opinions, including:

- that the financial statements are prepared by the auditor;

60. PCAOB AS 3101.06 to .10.

- that the auditor reviews and approves everything in the company's financial reports; or
- that the financial statements are free from error or fraud.

The difference between what the auditor's work involves and what the public *thinks* it involves has become known as the "expectations gap," and we will have more to say about it in the next section.

The opinion given above by Ernst & Young on Apple's financial statements is known as an "unqualified" opinion, or colloquially as a "clean" opinion, as the auditor declares its opinion that the company's financial statements "present fairly" the company's financial position in accord with GAAP. There are four other types of opinions which might be offered, however:

• an ***unqualified opinion with explanatory language*** added; often this describes a change in GAAP which has occurred since the previous opinion was given.[61]

Example

KPMG LLP, gave an unqualified opinion on the financial statements presented Apple, Inc.'s 2008 Annual Report. After the opinion was presented, the following *explanation* was added:

> *As discussed in note 1, the consolidated financial statements for the year ended September 27, 2008 have been restated to give effect to the retrospective adoption of the Financial Accounting Standards Board's amended accounting standards related to revenue recognition for arrangements with multiple deliverables and arrangements that include software elements.*

Other common explanations include a variety of items from the innocuous to the critically important, such as: a reference to the work of other auditors, a justified departure from GAAP, or doubts about the entity's ability to continue as a going concern.[62]

• a ***qualified opinion***, which identifies one of two problems: either the lack of sufficient appropriate audit evidence (either because it does not exist, cannot be found, or the auditor is denied access[63]); or there is an actual departure from GAAP. The

61. *See* AU-C § 708.

62. Johnstone, *et al.*, *supra* note 48, at 804–11, Kieso, *supra* note 13, at 1423–26.

63. In this specific instance—management-imposed limitations—the auditor is to withdraw from the representation if practicable. *See* AU-C § 705.13.

auditor's opinion can be qualified only if these problems are not material enough or pervasive enough to require a more severe opinion (below).[64]

• a ***disclaimer of opinion***, which states that no opinion can be expressed. Such a disclaimer would be appropriate when the above problems are so pervasive and material that a qualified opinion is not appropriate.

• an ***adverse opinion***, which states the opposite of an unqualified or qualified opinion, namely, that the company's financial statements do ***not*** fairly present the company's financial condition in accordance with GAAP. Such an opinion would be appropriate when a departure from GAAP is so pervasive or material that a qualified opinion is not appropriate.

Qualified, disclaimed, and adverse opinions are infrequently seen. They are not acceptable in publicly-filed financial statements, and even in private transactions, companies are likely to do what is necessary to avoid such a result.

5. Public Perceptions of Auditing

We are now familiar with why there are audits, what auditors do, how they do it, and the nature of the opinions they give on the financial statements which they audit. This is knowledge which much of the general public does not have. The distance between what auditors actually do and what the public thinks they do has been an enduring problem. With the knowledge you have from the rest of this chapter, you can begin to appreciate the "perception" problem which auditors have. And this is not a new problem; indeed, it is a testament to the difficulty of the auditor's public relationship that a crisis erupts at least once each decade. Following is a brief survey of fifty years of attempts to deal with misconceptions about auditors and their role.

The 1970s. Concerns about "bribes" paid by U.S. companies overseas and other issues[65] prompted the AICPA to study the needs of users of financial statements and compare them with the industry's standards. The resulting body commissioned to study those needs, established in 1974, is commonly known as the "Cohen Commission" for its chair, former SEC Chairman Manuel F. Cohen. The main conclusions of this report were:

1978 Cohen Commission Report

- The standardization of the auditor's report (since 1933) has changed its character. It is no longer as descriptive of the entity as it once was.
- The standard language tends not to be read carefully, but is considered "boilerplate."

---

64. For a complete description of qualified, disclaimed, and adverse opinions, see PCAOB AS 3105.

65. For a good review, see Douglas W. Hawes, *Truth in Financial Statements: An Introduction*, 28 Vand. L. Rev. 1, 1–12 (1975). He identifies the "pioneering" work in the field as Homer Kripke, *The SEC, The Accountants, Some Myths and Some Realities*, 45 N.Y.U. L. Rev. 1151 (1970).

- Some messages are not explicit, for example, that the financial statements are those of the company's management, or that the auditor must exercise professional judgment in reaching an opinion.
- Technical terminology may not be meaningful to lay readers, such as the auditor's tests of accounting records or the ultimate language that the financial statements "present fairly" the condition of the company.[66]

1987 Treadway Commission Report

The 1980s. Despite the Cohen Commission's recommendations, the problem persisted and even got worse. The problem was popularly known as the "Expectations Gap," referring to the difference between what most users believed that the auditor's report meant and what the auditors actually meant. In the mid- to late-1980s, the spectacular meltdown of the savings and loan industry exposed many questionable accounting practices. There were congressional hearings, and more special oversight commissions. The most important of these was the National Commission on Fraudulent Financial Reporting, known as the "Treadway Commission," after its Chair, former SEC Commissioner James C. Treadway, Jr. The Treadway Commission addressed the audit profession's inability to address fraud in financial statements.[67] There was a watershed response from the Auditing Standards Board, in an unprecedented flurry of standards published in April 1988. The ASB published nine new standards addressing many of the subjects which the public had formerly believed auditors took as part of their responsibility, most notably the obligation to search out and find errors and fraud in the financial statements. Many of these standards did not broker enduring solutions and have been amended or replaced in large part since then.

1995 Litigation Reform and "Auditing for Fraud"

The 1990s. Next on the scene in the 1990s was a political compromise between the large accounting firms, which were facing ever-increasing liability in private lawsuits, and the Congress, which sought extraction from the auditing profession of some responsibility to detect and report on fraud. In the Private Securities Litigation Reform Act (PSLRA) of 1995,[68] the deal was struck. Auditing firms received relief from liability by making a defendant "liable solely for the portion of the judgment that corresponds to the percentage of responsibility of that ... person."[69] In addition, the PSLRA modified the procedures to be followed in securities class-action lawsuits, by specifying a "lead" plaintiff appointed by the court in certain instances, heightened pleading standards, and limitations on the calculation of damages in actions involving securities traded in an active market.[70] The *quid pro quo* was a requirement that audits required under the

66. The Commission on Auditors' Responsibilities: Report, Conclusions and Recommendations 71–75 (1978).

67. We will study the Treadway Commission's work in detail in Chapter 9 on Internal Controls, as much of the Commission's work deals with internal controls.

68. Pub. L. 104-67, 109 Stat. 737 (1995).

69. Securities Exchange Act § 21D(g)(2)(B).

70. *Id.* § 21D(a)–(e), Securities Act §27.

federal securities laws include, among other things, "procedures designed to provide reasonable assurance of detecting illegal acts," and requires the auditor to report any such acts discovered to management with further notice given to the SEC.[71]

2002
Sarbanes-
Oxley Act

The 2000s. The Sarbanes-Oxley Act, passed in 2002 in response to the Enron and WorldCom failures, added many rules concerning the relationship between a company and its auditors. We have discussed in detail earlier in this chapter the fundamental misunderstandings between management and its auditors which allowed these spectacular frauds to occur. Among other things, the Act

- established standards for the audit committee of a corporation's board of directors
- made the audit committee explicitly responsible for hiring the auditor and approving all audit and non-audit functions
- required certain specific reports to be made by the auditor to the audit committee, and
- required that auditors of public companies may not engage in any other work for that audit client.[72]

2010
Treasury
Dept. Report
2019
"Critical
Audit
Matters"
requirement

The 2010s. The economic problems of the financial crisis of 2008–10 were in part the result of more spectacular failures of financial firms such as AIG and Lehman Brothers. Again, policy makers were concerned with the role of auditors in examining these companies' financial statements. In 2008, the Treasury Department commissioned an "Advisory Committee on the Auditing Profession" which examined not only the structure and concentration in the industry but, again, the "expectations gap" and "confusion about auditor responsibility to detect fraud."[73] In response to this report, the PCAOB announced in June 2011 a wide-ranging "concept release" on various aspects of the auditor's report,[74] which was concluded last year. Most significantly, the PCAOB has addressed the "expectations gap" by requiring that the auditor's report be amended to include a separate report on "determination of critical audit matters," and how those matters were resolved.[75] The release notes ominously that "[t]he Board expects that, in most audits to which the requirement to communicate critical audit matters applies, the auditor will determine that at least one matter involved

71. Securities Exchange Act § 10A(a)–(b).

72. *See generally* Securities Exchange Act § 10A(g)–(m).

73. Department of the Treasury, Advisory Committee on the Auditing Profession: Final Report VII:17 (Oct. 2008), available at http://www.treasury.gov/about/organizational-structure/offices/Documents/final-report.pdf.

74. PCAOB, Concept Release on Possible Revisions to PCAOB Standards Related to Reports on Audited Financial Statements (June 2011), available at http://pcaobus.org/Rules/Rulemaking/Docket 034/Concept_Release.pdf.

75. PCAOB AS 3101.11 to .17.

especially challenging, subjective, or complex auditor judgment."[76] In 2019, the Auditing Standards Board made conforming changes to the GAAS rules.[77]

The problems we have identified with public expectations of auditors' work are more than an image problem for the profession. They form the basis for determination of auditors' liability, which we study in Chapter 12.

76. PCAOB, The Auditor's Report on an Audit of Financial Statements When the Auditor Expresses an Unqualified Opinion, PCAOB Release No. 2017 001 at 37 (June 1, 2017).

77. Ken Tysiac, *ASB Enhances Communication in Auditors Reports*, Journal of Accountancy (May 2019), available at https://www.journalofaccountancy.com/news/2019/may/asb-enhances-communication-in-auditors-reports-201921143.html; Statement on Auditing Standards No. 134 (May 2019) at https://www.aicpa.org/content/dam/aicpa/research/standards/auditattest/downloadable documents/sas-134.pdf.

Part Two

Accounting Issues That Become Legal Questions

Now you are experts in financial statement generation and analysis. It is time to dive in depth into the murky waters of accounting issues which become "irregularities" and ultimately legal problems. The following five chapters canvass the landscape of accounting issues in which lawyers are routinely intimately involved.

Chapter 4

Revenues

Willie Sutton was a notorious twentieth-century bank robber. He is famously credited with saying that he robbed banks "because that's where the money is."[1] This quote has become famous as "Sutton's Law:" that you should look for answers in the most obvious places.[2]

Sutton's Law applies with full force to a business' revenue recognition policies. Of all the items in the income statement, the revenue line will probably be the largest. We would expect that management, ever eager to show a good face to investors and creditors, would be tempted to engage in improper revenue recognition practices first and foremost. Our expectation is borne out by four important recent studies.

- In the first study, Congress directed the Government Accountability Office (GAO) to examine "restatements" or "corrections" of financial statements.[3] The GAO found that, in the 1997–2002 period, 38% of restatements were required by improper revenue recognition policies. In a 2002–2005 follow-up study, revenue recognition as a reason for restatements had slipped to second place, but was still significant at 20%.[4]
- In the second study, also of restatements, but this time in the 2003–12 period, researchers noted a downward trend in revenue problems, due primarily to regulatory changes instituted by the SEC after "technology bubble" ended in 2000. Although revenue restatements were on the decline, the author of this study noted the enduring importance of revenues.

    This downward trend is good news for investors—who are typically more concerned about revenue restatements than restatements of other

1. When asked about the quote, Sutton remarked: "I never said it. The credit belongs to some enterprising reporter who apparently felt a need to fill out his copy.... If anybody had asked me, I'd have probably said it. That's what almost anybody would say.... Why did I rob banks? Because I enjoyed it. I loved it." Willie Sutton & Edward Linn, Where the Money Was: The Memoirs of a Bank Robber 161 (1976).

2. See *id.* at 159. The law, as stated in a medical journal in 1961, "recommends proceeding immediately to the diagnostic test most likely to provide a diagnosis." Tsung O. Cheng, Editorial, *William Dock, Willie Sutton and Sutton's Law*, 141 Int'l J. Cardiology 209 (2010). For further interesting background, see Steve Cocheo, *The Bank Robber, THE QUOTE, and the Final Irony*, ABA Banking Journal 71 (Vol. 89, No. 3) (March 1997).

3. We will examine the standards governing restatement of financial statements in Chapter 12.

4. U.S. Government Accountability Office, Financial Restatements: Update of Public Company Trends, Market Impacts, and Regulatory Enforcement Activities 17 (2006), available at www.gao.gov/cgi-bin/getrpt?GAO-06-678.

accounts — and for companies, because they are more likely to be sued over revenue restatements.[5]

- In the third study, this one of Securities and Exchange Commission accounting-related enforcement proceedings from 1998 to 2007, improper revenue recognition was present in 61% of the cases brought.[6]
- In the fourth study, revenue recognition returned to the top of the charts as the leading cause of restatements. In a review of financial statements in the 2000–19 period, researchers identified revenue recognition problems in 17% of restatements.[7]

Obviously, we have found where the money is. Or, in the words of one lawyer and analyst perusing these same statistics,

> Lawyers are not trained as accountants and are not expected to function as accountants. Nevertheless, it is worth noting that approximately 50% of all securities fraud cases involve revenue recognition — i.e., the incorrect and typically premature recording of revenue.... Hence, a heads up concerning the problems that may be lurking will help a lawyer advise his or her client in many situations, such as negotiating or documenting an acquisition or financing.[8]

We begin, in Part A, with an understanding of the basic principles of revenue recognition and how they might be led astray. Part B then covers special types of income and their reporting and presentation in the financial statements.

A. General Principles of Recognition

The FASB recently concluded a long project on this topic, and the new rules below were adopted in 2014, but are fully effective for all entities in 2020. Although this rewrite fundamentally changes the terminology used by accountants for their decisions about revenue recognition, many of the core issues faced by lawyers will remain the same. We look first at how the concept is presented by the current accounting standards, and then compare the new rules with the older ones more familiar to most practitioners.

---

5. Susan Scholz, Financial Restatement Trends in the United States: 2003–12, at 7 (Center for Audit Quality, 2014), available at www.thecaq.org/financial-restatement-trends-united-states-2003-2012.

6. Committee of Sponsoring Organizations of the Treadway Commission, Fraudulent Financial Reporting 1998–2007, at 17 (2010), available at https://www.coso.org/documents/coso-fraud-study-2010-001.pdf.

7. Don Whalen *et al.*, 2019 Financial Restatements: A Nineteen Year Comparison, *Audit Analytics* Report No. 2022-07-22, at 23 (July 2020), available at www.auditanalytics.com.

8. Robert B. Dickie, Financial Statement Analysis and Business Valuation for the Practical Lawyer 11 (3d ed. 2020).

1. The Contract-Based Standards

Accounting Standards Codification Topic 606, *Revenue from Contracts with Customers*, states the new GAAP in this area. The bedrock principle is that

> [A]n entity recognizes revenue to depict the transfer of promised goods or services to customers in an amount that reflects the consideration to which the entity expects to be entitled in exchange for those goods or services.[9]

This principle, in turn, yields the following steps.[10]

The Five Steps of Revenue Recognition

1. Identify the contract(s) with the customer.
2. Identify the performance obligation(s) in the contract.
3. Determine the transaction price.
4. Allocate the transaction price to the performance obligations.
5. Recognize revenue when (or as) a performance obligation is satisfied.

The lawyer's work here will involve primarily steps 1, 2 and 5. Because the language is contracts-based, we already have a good idea of how this will work.

Revenue recognition when there is a contract. First, we need to determine whether there is a contract. Fortunately, GAAP says this is a matter of law,[11] so the rules will be familiar.

- Contracts create (or result from) enforceable rights and obligations.[12]
- Contract terms can be implied or variable.[13]
- Wholly executory contracts do not require an accounting because they are not enforceable.[14]

Once we know a contract exists, we can apply these rules.

Note: The Joy of Reading Original GAAP. I have included lightly edited but otherwise unfiltered standards language here for two reasons.

1. As lawyers, you will become used to reading original language and making inferences or summaries of it. Much of the law is given to you in unfiltered

9. ASC 606-10-05-3.
10. ASC 606-10-05-4.
11. ASC 606-10-25-2.
12. *Id.*
13. ASC 606 10 25 3
14. ASC 606-10-25-4.

form (such as the many cases you have read) and you must make your own analysis.

2. As people working with accountants, you should have an appreciation of what your colleagues have to work with when they seek grounding in the universal principles of their craft.

The language can be difficult to decipher, true. The only other place in this book I have reproduced original FASB language for you to read is in Chapter 6 on Contingent Liabilities, where we will read GAAP which lawyers use on a regular basis.

Accounting Standards Codification

Topic 606—Revenue from Contracts with Customers
Subtopic 10—Recognition

25-1. An entity shall account for a contract with a customer … only when all of the following criteria are met:

a. The parties to the contract have approved the contract (in writing, orally, or in accord with other customary business practices) and are committed to perform their respective obligations.

b. The entity can identify each party's rights regarding the goods or services to be transferred.

c. The entity can identify the payment terms for the goods or services to be transferred.

d. The contract has commercial substance (that is, the risk, timing, or amount of the entity's future cash flows is expected to change as a result of the contract).

e. It is probable that the entity will collect substantially all of the consideration to which it will be entitled in the exchange for the goods or services that will be transferred to the customer.… In evaluating whether collectability of an amount of consideration is probable, an entity shall consider only the customer's ability and intention to pay the amount of consideration when it is due.

25-14. At contract inception, an entity shall assess the goods or services promised in a contract with a customer and shall identify as a performance obligation each promise to transfer to the customer either:

a. A good or service (or a bundle of goods or services) that is distinct

b. A series of distinct goods or services that are substantially the same and that have the same pattern of transfer to the customer.

25-23. An entity shall recognize revenue when (or as) the entity satisfies a performance obligation by transferring a promised good or service (that is, an asset) to a customer. An asset is transferred when a customer obtains control of that asset.

Performance Obligations Satisfied Over Time

25-27. An entity transfers control of a good or service over time and, therefore ... recognizes revenue over time, if one of the following criteria is met:

a. The customer simultaneously receives and consumes the benefits provided by the entity's performance as the entity performs ...

b. The entity's performance creates or enhances an asset ... that the customer controls as the asset is created or enhanced ...

c. The entity's performance does not create an asset with an alternative use to the entity ... and the entity has an enforceable right to payment for performance completed to date....

Performance Obligations Satisfied at a Point in Time

25-30. ... To determine the point in time at which a customer obtains control of a promised asset ... an entity shall consider indicators of the transfer of control which include, but are not limited to, the following:

a. The entity has a present right to payment for the asset....

b. The customer has legal title to the asset....

c. The entity has transferred physical possession of the asset....

d. The customer has the significant risks and rewards of ownership of the asset....

e. The customer has accepted the asset....

Revenue recognition when there is not a contract. There may be some understanding between the parties short of a contract. A lawyer might call this an implied contract, or *quantum meruit* recovery, or even prevention of unjust enrichment. The accounting standard (ASC 606-10) goes on to discuss recognition in these situations.

25-7. When a contract with a customer does not meet the criteria in paragraph [25-1] and an entity receives consideration from the customer, the entity shall recognize the consideration received as revenue only when one or more of the following events have occurred:

a. The entity has no remaining obligations to transfer goods or services to the customer, and all, or substantially all, of the consideration promised by the customer has been received by the entity and is nonrefundable.

b. The contract has been terminated, and the consideration received from the customer is nonrefundable.

c. The entity has transferred control of the goods or services to which the consideration that has been received relates, the entity has stopped transferring goods or services to the customer (if applicable) and has no obligation under the contract to transfer additional goods or services, and the consideration received from the customer is nonrefundable.

25-8. An entity shall recognize the consideration received from a customer as a liability until one of the events in the [above] paragraph occurs or until the criteria in [the first] paragraph ... are subsequently met.

* * *

Problem 4-1

You are counsel for American Ambulance Corp (AAC). Six months ago, AAC signed a contract with Commonwealth Hospitals Inc. (CHI), which owns hospitals in a six-state region, to purchase 55 ambulances. AAC was required to construct a prototype which would be tested by CHI before CHI was required to accept delivery of ambulances manufactured by AAC. Ultimately, the prototype was accepted and AAC began production under the contract. The first five ambulances were recently delivered. However, those ambulances had other defects. CHI refused to accept delivery and told AAC not to deliver any more until the defects were remedied.

AAC management wants to show this profit for the current fiscal year, which ends in two weeks, and seeks your advice on the following plan.

AAC and a local dealer will sign a purchase order for the 55 ambulances. The completed ambulances will be removed to the dealer's lot and the dealer will confirm the existence of the account receivable due from the dealer with the auditors when they examine the year-end financial statements. The dealer would then resell the ambulances to CHI, but the dealer was not obligated under the purchase order to pay AAC until it received payment from CHI. What is your advice to management?

Problem 4-2[15]

Midwest Air Conditioning Corp. (MAC) has signed a contract with a local hospital to design, build and install heating, ventilating and air-conditioning (HVAC) units at the hospital. MAC will build and install the units, and will provide spare parts for the units. The hospital has requested that MAC keep possession of the spare parts, because there is no room for them at the hospital and MAC's facilities are nearby. MAC keeps the parts separate in its factory, identifies them as belonging to the hospital, and cannot sell the parts to anyone else. At the signing of the contract, MAC

15. Adapted from ASC 606-10-55-409 to -412 (Example 63).

expects to keep the spare parts for two to four years. Discuss the revenue-recognition significance of the following events.

(a) The contract is signed, and a nonrefundable down-payment is made by the hospital so that MAC can begin its design work.

(b) The HVAC units are installed, and title of the spare parts is transferred to the hospital even though the parts remain at MAC

(c) The spare parts are delivered as needed over the next two years to the hospital.

Problem 4-3[16]

Meadow Ridge Condominiums, Inc. (MRCI) is building and selling units in a new residential complex downtown. Customers sign contracts for specific units under construction. Each has the same or similar floor plan, but the units differ in other respects (such as location within the complex). Advise MRCI on the revenue implications of these alternative contracts.

Contract I. Customer makes a 10% down-payment to MRCI on signing the contract. The balance is due upon completion and transfer of title of the unit to the customer. If the customer defaults, MRCI retains the deposit.

Contract II. Customer makes a 20% initial payment and four 20% "progress payments" at specified phases of completion. If customer defaults, MRCI has the option to complete construction and to demand full payment, or it may transfer title to the unit as completed to date and retain the progress payments made so far.

* * *

2. Comparing the Old and New Rules

ASC 606 is sweeping in its impact. It has replaced existing well-established GAAP on revenue recognition with new terminology. It requires accountants (and lawyers) to make decisions under this new regime without the benefit of experience or precedent.

The rules before ASC 606 had two primary sources: GAAP statements generally describing rules of revenue recognition, and SEC guidance which was pretty well recognized as authoritative. A summary of each is presented below.

FASB, ASC 605-10-25-1
Revenue Recognition (superseded)

The recognition of revenue and gains of an entity during a period involves consideration of the following two factors, with sometimes one and sometimes the other being the more important consideration:

16. Adapted from ASC 606-10-55-173 to -179 (Example 17).

a. **Being realized or realizable.** Revenue and gains generally are not recognized until realized or realizable. [R]evenue and gains are *realized* when products (goods or services), merchandise, or other assets are exchanged for cash or claims to cash. [R]evenue and gains are *realizable* when related assets received or held are readily convertible to known amounts of cash or claims to cash.

b. **Being earned.** [R]evenue is not recognized until earned. [A]n entity's revenue-earning activities involve delivering or producing goods, rendering services, or other activities that constitute its ongoing major or central operations, and revenues are considered to have been earned when the entity has substantially accomplished what it must do to be entitled to the benefits represented by the revenues. [G]ains commonly result from transactions and other events that involve no earning process, and for recognizing gains, being earned is generally less significant than being realized or realizable.

SEC, Codification of Staff Accounting Bulletins, Topic 13, *Revenue*

[The staff first summarizes the GAAP standards above and continues as follows.]

The staff believes that revenue generally is realized or realizable and earned when all of the following criteria are met:

- Persuasive evidence of an arrangement exists,
- Delivery has occurred or services have been rendered,
- The seller's price to the buyer is fixed or determinable, and
- Collectability is reasonably assured.

Officially, all of this old learning has been swept away. When ASC 606 becomes fully effective, all of ASC 605 will be obsolete. Similarly, the SEC has stated that the adoption of ASC 606 "eliminates the need for Topic 13," so presumably that agency will not be providing informal guidance either.

Because of ASC 606, accountants and auditors are grappling with a major change in their practices. Lawyers can expect to see new cases involving revenue recognition, and the courts will make decisions based on the new standards. However, existing legal precedent is still based on the old standards, of course. We now review two cases which are good studies of the existing common law on revenue recognition.

Background: The following case is excerpted in Chapters 4 and 5 to illustrate each accounting issue as it arises. The case is an administrative proceeding by the Securities and Exchange Commission (SEC) against Arthur Andersen & Co., formerly one of the largest accounting firms in the U.S. This proceeding is under the SEC's "Rules of Practice" to determine if Andersen should be sanctioned for not meeting standards of professional conduct applicable to auditors practicing before the SEC. The relevant conduct involved Andersen's audit of Mattel, Inc., a famous toy maker, for its fiscal year ended Jan. 31, 1971. Through the SEC's description of the case, we see and can evaluate the conduct of officials and employees at Mattel which created the accounting problems, as well as the conduct of the partners at Arthur Andersen in making the accounting and auditing judgments involved.

In the Matter of Arthur Andersen & Co.

Securities and Exchange Commission, 1981
47 S.E.C. 565

I. BACKGROUND

Mattel, a Delaware Corporation with its principal offices in Hawthorne, California was at all relevant times the largest manufacturer of toys in the United States.

By January 1970, Mattel had achieved five years of record sales and earnings and its common stock was selling at approximately 35 times earnings. In the Fall of 1970 Mattel was projecting earnings of approximately $1.20 per share. Mattel's management had arbitrarily set targets for various operations in order to meet its predetermined growth objectives. As the end of fiscal 1971 (January 30, 1971) approached, Mattel's management was keenly aware that its financial objectives would not be met without extraordinary efforts. It had miscalculated the market for "hot wheels" and "sizzlers", products which had accounted for 25 percent of 1970 sales. Saturation of the market had forced Mattel to offer substantial credits, known in the trade as "inventory relief" or "help money," to retailers with excess inventory.

II. SUMMARY OF FALSE AND MISLEADING FINANCIAL STATEMENTS AND ACCOUNTANTS' REPORTS

Through false financial reporting which was part of a calculated scheme directed by certain officers and directors of Mattel and others, Mattel substantially overstated its pre-tax income for fiscal 1971 and substantially overstated its pre-tax loss for fiscal 1972. This scheme involved, directly or indirectly, a large number of Mattel officers and employees from the most senior executives to clerical personnel. The fraud was perpetrated by, among other things, the preparation of forged or falsified records and accounting entries, and a pattern of false representations and responses by Mattel personnel which misled AA & Co. Ultimately, several of the senior executives of Mattel were indicted for and convicted of criminal offenses in connection with this scheme.[17]

Background: SEC financial fraud investigations

This case is typical of SEC financial fraud investigations, which normally begin with an investigation of the issuer (Mattel in this case). If the investigation reveals culpable wrongdoing, typically the issuer consents to an injunction, and agrees to various measures imposed by the Commission designed to prevent the fraud in the future. Occasionally, especially egregious conduct is referred by the SEC to the Department of Justice, which may decide to prosecute the individuals involved, as it did here, see the footnote reference below to *U.S. v. Handler,* criminal proceedings against Mattel management. In any event, the investigation typically continues to determine the involvement of the issuer's auditors. Frequently the "other shoe" in these investigations, following action against the issuer, is a proceeding against the issuer's auditors. Recall the prior case involving the firm of Seidman & Seidman and the inventory fraud at Cenco, Inc., discussed in Chapter 3.

III. IMPROPER RECORDING OF SALES

A. Mattel's Practices

To maintain the momentum of a sixth straight year of record sales and earnings, in January 1971 Mattel's management, among other things, initiated a program designed to give the appearance of substantially increased sales and earnings for fiscal 1971. Under this program, approximately $14.7 million was falsely recorded as sales in January 1971, causing fiscal 1971 pre-tax earnings to be overstated by approximately $7.8 million.

The activities underlying the improper recording of sales were generally referred to by Mattel personnel as the "bill and hold" program.[18] It involved 35 customers and 156 invoices. Under this program, Mattel contacted certain of its customers, generated invoices and recorded them as sales in January 1971, even though they did not qualify as sales for, among others, the following reasons:

---

17. U.S. v. Handler (No. CR. 78-148 RMT) (C.D. Cal. 1978), CCH Fed. Sec. L. Rep. ¶ 96,519.

18. "Bill and hold" generally is a practice whereby a customer agrees to purchase the goods but the seller retains physical possession until the customer requests shipment to designated locations. Before January 1971, Mattel's bill and hold transactions had been limited to a few, large, national retail customers; had been evidenced by written agreements with the customers; and apparently had required Mattel to segregate merchandise subject to the agreements. Beginning in January 1971, Mattel prepared shipping documents which falsely represented that merchandise had been shipped.

1. The merchandise was not shipped as of January 30, 1971.
2. The customer did not have to make any payments until the goods were accepted and received by him.
3. The merchandise was not physically segregated from Mattel's inventory nor labeled as the property of the customer.
4. The customer could cancel the order without penalty at any time prior to his receipt and acceptance of the merchandise.
5. The risks of ownership remained with Mattel, including the risk of loss due to damage, theft or destruction of the merchandise.
6. In many instances the invoices were prepared without prior consultation with, or participation by, the customer as to the content of the order.

In effect, Mattel made participation in the bill and hold program riskless for the customer. Its customers merely received the equivalent of an option to purchase the merchandise included on bill and hold invoices. In short, no sale had taken place.[19]

The paperwork generated by Mattel in support of the "bill and hold sales" consisted of customers' orders, sales invoices and bills of lading and required several departures from Mattel's standard procedures. For example, all of the above documents generally carried the special notation "Bill and Hold" or "B & H." The bills of lading, which normally provided evidence of shipping, were signed and dated by a Mattel employee in the signature box where the common carrier would normally sign. The above documents were processed through Mattel's accounting system in the usual manner, normally within one day, so that the purported sales would be recorded in fiscal 1971.[20]

Mattel adjusted its inventory records by reducing recorded inventory quantities for the "bill and hold" invoices, even though the merchandise had not been shipped or physically segregated. As a result, serious recordkeeping problems grew out of the bill and hold program. Mattel found that its inventory records were unreliable. Mattel employees could not tell how much inventory was physically on hand and available to be matched against shipping instructions. When merchandise was shipped, it became cumbersome for its employees to process the shipment and to determine whether it represented a fiscal 1972 sale or a previously recorded "bill and hold sale."

---

19. Under generally accepted accounting practices for manufacturers of merchandise, a sale is generally not recognized until the seller has completed all of his obligations to the buyer and the risk of ownership has transferred to the buyer.

20. All "bill and hold" invoices utilized in January 1971 bore dates of its last eleven days (January 20–30) and included 41 large invoices ranging from $100,000 to $787,575 and aggregating approximately $12.4 million. Eight of these large invoices were dated January 30, 1971, the last day of the fiscal year, and totalled approximately $3.2 million. In addition, 52 smaller invoices, also dated January 30, brought the total sales recorded on that day to approximately $3.8 million. Both the numbers and dollar amounts were high in relation to Mattel's normal volumes.

These difficulties and others prompted Mattel to reverse the "bill and hold sales" on its books and records and to record such sales only as they were actually shipped. During fiscal 1972 Mattel "cancelled" approximately 85 percent of the improperly recorded "bill and hold sales." The first reversal, which occurred in May 1971, totalled $12.9 million ($6.3 million of "bill and hold" sales improperly recorded in January 1971 and $6.6 million improperly recorded during the first quarter of fiscal 1972). This reversal was recorded in Mattel's accounts receivable subsidiary accounts as well as in Mattel's general ledger accounts receivable and sales control accounts and immediately created another unusual situation. Because Mattel's May 1971 reversals exceeded its actual sales for the month, Mattel's general ledger sales account and several of its internal sales reports showed negative sales and shipments for the month of May 1971.

To offset the negative sales and thereby conceal this situation, Mattel recorded a journal entry for an $11.1 million fictitious sale in May 1971. The fictitious sale was posted to the general ledger sales and accounts receivable control accounts but not to the accounts receivable subsidiary accounts. The entry resulted in a difference of $11.1 million between Mattel's accounts receivable subsidiary records and the accounts receivable general ledger control account at the end of May, June, July and August 1971. The subsidiary accounts receivable trial balances for these months all showed a "reconciling item" of $11.1 million labeled "May shipping."

In August 1971, Mattel had enough sales to absorb additional reversals and, in that month, $6.9 million in sales and accounts receivable were reversed from both the subsidiary and general ledger control accounts. The $6.9 million reversal was composed of $6.2 million of the January 1971 "bill and hold sales" and $700,000 of "bill and hold sales" which had been improperly recorded in the first quarter of fiscal 1972. It was not until September 1971 that normal sales were able to absorb the cancellation of the $11.1 million May 1971 fictitious sales entry. At that point, Mattel reversed the fictitious entry in its control accounts. As a result, sales were understated by approximately $14.7 million and the pre-tax loss was overstated by approximately $7.1 million for fiscal 1972.

Notes and Questions

1. Which components of revenue recognition, as established by ASC 606, were absent in this case? Consider this guidance in ASC 606-10-55-83:

> In addition to applying the guidance in paragraph 606-10-25-30 [Ed: reprinted on in Section A(1), above], for a customer to have obtained control of a product in a bill-and-hold arrangement, all of the following criteria must be met:
>
> a. The reason for the bill-and-hold arrangement must be substantive (for example, the customer has requested the arrangement).
>
> b. The product must be identified separately as belonging to the customer.

c. The product currently must be ready for physical delivery to the customer.

d. The entity cannot have the ability to use the product or to direct it to another customer.

2. The financial manipulation involved in this case is hardly sophisticated. Why do you suppose senior officers at a relatively large and prestigious corporation were persuaded to engage in such chicanery? What was the environment like at Mattel in the early 1970s? Was there pressure to produce results? How might any pressure be avoided? Consider the following analysis of the psychology of "insider incentives and heuristics" in the Enron case by Prof. Larry Ribstein.

> Actors' judgment biases may depend somewhat on their self-esteem, in the sense that those with the highest self-esteem are the most likely to misjudge their control and skill.... Since insiders are convinced that they are doing the right thing in defending their company's value from destruction by misguided markets, they are ... not subject to a significant moral constraint.
>
> As soon as insiders begin engaging in fraud, their incentives change. At this point, insiders risk of loss of wealth and even personal freedom unless they continue the cover-up. Indeed, the consequences of discovery may be so severe that even a small chance of success might lead a rational actor to cover up.[21]

Herzfeld v. Laventhol, Krekstein, Horwath & Horwath

United States Court of Appeals, Second Circuit, 1976
540 F.2d 27

MOORE, Circuit Judge:

Laventhol, Krekstein, Horwath & Horwath, a firm of certified public accountants ("Laventhol"), appeals from an amended judgment for the amount of $153,000, entered against it and in favor of plaintiff, Gerald L. Herzfeld ("Herzfeld") after a trial to the Court.

....

FGL was a California company engaged principally in the business of purchasing real estate and thereafter syndicating or reselling it. In November 1969, FGL planned to raise $7,500,000 by the private [sale of FGL debt and equity securities]....

Through friends, Herzfeld became interested in the venture. A purchase agreement, entitled "Note and Stock Purchase Agreement", dated November 10, 1969, was delivered to Herzfeld by FGL with an accompanying letter which advised him that the closing date for the sale of the notes would be December 16, 1969, "to permit the preparation of audited financial statements, as at and for the eleven months ended November 30, 1969, copies of which will be delivered to you." The letter added that these "audited statements will serve as the basis for confirming the unau-

21. Larry E. Ribstein, *Market vs. Regulatory Responses to Corporate Fraud. A Critique of the Sarbanes-Oxley Act of 2002*, 28 J. Corp. L. 1, 20, 22 (2002).

dited Projected Financial Statements annexed to the Note and Stock Purchase Agreement as Exhibit B."

Exhibit B was a balance sheet and income statement. It portrayed FGL as a strikingly profitable corporation with over $20 million in assets, a net worth of close to a million dollars, sales of over $17 million, deferred income of $2.7 million and an after-tax income of $315,000. FGL warranted that it fairly presented its financial condition as at November 30, 1969.

Herzfeld read the entire income statement and the balance sheet and noted that it represented FGL as being very profitable, with earnings of approximately $2 a share for the period ending November 30, 1969. He then signed the agreement to purchase two units thereunder.

To prepare the promised audit (to be as of November 30, 1969), FGL retained Laventhol as the accountants for the task....

The spotlight of Herzfeld's claim of a materially misleading audit, knowingly made with admitted awareness of the facts, focuses upon Laventhol's accounting treatment of two real estate transactions in which FGL allegedly engaged in late November 1969, referred to herein as the FGL-Monterey purchase and the FGL-Continental sale. Purporting to reflect these transactions are two agreements. Each agreement is on an identical printed form entitled "AGREEMENT FOR SALE OF REAL ESTATE" and certain typewritten provisions have been inserted therein. The first is dated November 22, 1969 and is between Monterey Nursing Inns, Inc. ("Monterey") as seller and FGL as buyer. The transaction was subject to two conditions: (1) the buyer's approval of a preliminary title report and CC&R's[22] of Record on each property (there is no evidence that any such documents were ever prepared, delivered or approved); and (2) execution of a lease per terms of "Exhibit D attached hereto" (no such exhibit appears to have been attached). Twenty-three (23) nursing homes were the subject of the sale "as per Exhibit 'A' attached hereto" (no such exhibit appears to have been attached). The purchase price is stated as $13,362,500, $5,000 of which was payable before November 30, 1969 (*i.e.,* upon the signing of the contract).

On an identical printed form with almost identical typewritten inserts is an agreement by FGL as seller to sell to Continental Recreation Company, Ltd. ("Continental") as buyer. Again, there is no Exhibit A listing the properties. The purchase price is stated as $15,393,000 with $25,000 as a down payment, other payments to be made in 1970 and thereafter.

This purchase and sale of nursing homes, if ever consummated, would have been the largest single transaction in the history of FGL. Placing these two purported agreements side by side, if the obligations therein were ever fulfilled in the future, FGL would have bought Monterey for $13,362,500 and sold it for $15,393,000, thus producing a profit, when, as and if the transactions were consummated, of $2,030,500, no part of which was even contemplated as having been received prior to November

22. Covenants, Conditions and Restrictions.

30, 1969, and only payments of $5000 by FGL to Monterey and $25,000 from Continental to FGL may have been made.

A comparison of the financial condition of FGL with and without these transactions demonstrates the importance of them to FGL:

	Monterey Included	Monterey Excluded
Sales	$22,132,607	$6,739,607
Total Current Assets	6,290,987	1,300,737
Net Income	66,000	(169,000)
Deferred Profit	1,795,000	-0-
Earnings/Share	0.10	(0.25)

Thus, the accounting treatment of these transactions determined the health of FGL's financial picture. Laventhol knew this was so. By this treatment, namely, immediate recognition of a so-called profit, Laventhol notes, dated November 30, 1969, reveal the conversion of estimated $772,108 losses into a $1,257,892 gain by the addition of the $2,030,500 "profit"....

Little wonder that when at the outset a Laventhol partner was discussing the situation from an accounting standpoint, he referred to it as a "fictitious or proposed or artificial transaction." Appendix ("App.") p. 887. But Laventhol undertook the task, albeit it had to engage in considerable soul-searching during it. Laventhol also learned that Monterey transactions were nowhere recorded in the FGL books and that there were no corporate minutes or resolutions approving or even adverting to the transactions. The absence was remedied by Laventhol, who prepared adjusting entries and ordered the FGL controller to enter them in the FGL books. Illustrative is the letter from Laventhol's audit manager to FGL's controller enclosing "the journal entries which *we generated* for the financial statements at November 30" (emphasis added). These very entries were prepared by Laventhol as if the transaction had been consummated: yet the agreements on their face showed that no profits could result therefrom until long after November 30.

....

The November 22 and 26 contracts came to Laventhol's attention on or about December 1st through its partners, Chazen and Lipkin, and Schwabb, the audit manager. Schwabb sought Lipkin's advice about the proper way to report the transactions in the audit. Lipkin sought to gather the pertinent information by meeting with Scott, a FGL vice-president, and Firestone. Scott told him that FGL was busy acquiring the necessary documentation. Firestone said that the agreements were legitimate and described Continental's principal, Max Ruderian, as an experienced real estate operator and a wealthy individual. Laventhol learned that Continental had a net worth of $100,000 and that its assets consisted of "miniature golf courses plus other assets." Ruderian's business practice was to "buy and resell prior to final payment on his sales contracts."

Lipkin also examined the sales contracts. He was an attorney but had only practiced one year. He concluded that the contracts were legally enforceable. He consulted another Laventhol partner who assured him that there need be no concern about Ruderian. Ruderian's references concurred in the appraisal.

Lipkin also consulted over the telephone with a Los Angeles attorney. The attorney did not see the contracts, nor were the contracts in their entirety read to him, despite the fact that his offices were only one-half hour away by cab. Nevertheless, the attorney gave a telephone opinion that they were valid and enforceable.

The first tangible results of Laventhol's accounting efforts appear in its audit enclosed in its letter to FGL, dated December 6, 1969. In the consolidated balance sheet as of November 30, 1969, the amount of $1,795,500 was recorded "as unrealized gross profit." The same characterization was given to this assumed profit in the income statement with a reference to an explanatory Note 4. This Note only explained the $1,795,500 by stating that "because of the circumstances and nature of the transactions, $1,795,500 of the gross profit thereon will be considered realized when the January 30, 1970 payment is received." The $1,795,500 was apparently arrived at by first adding the $25,000 paid upon execution of the Continental agreement, the $25,000 not yet due (until January 2, 1970) and $185,000 a liquidated damage figure for non-performance. These amounts totalled $235,000. They were apparently considered as received and were deducted from the then fictitious profit of $2,030,500, resulting in the figure of $1,795,500. This first December 6, 1969 report is marked "Withdrawn & Superseded."

The reason for the withdrawal is found in the testimony that FGL wanted the audit to reflect the entire amount of $2,030,500 as pre-November 30, 1969, income resulting from a sale by FGL to Continental. On December 4, 1969, Chazen and Lipkin met with FGL officers. Firestone objected to the tentative accounting treatment of the Monterey transactions, and FGL threatened to withdraw its account and sue Laventhol if the private financing did not go through.

A second report (also dated December 6, 1969) was then submitted by Laventhol. In the income statement "unrealized gross profits (Note 4)" was changed to "Deferred gross profit (Note 4)" and Note 4, itself to read: "Of the total gross profit of $2,030,500, $235,000 is included in the Consolidated Income Statement and the balance $1,795,500 will be considered realized when the January 30, 1970 payment is received. The latter amount is included in deferred income in the consolidated balance sheet." It was this second report which was distributed to the investors, including Herzfeld.

Unlike the initial report, the opinion letter accompanying this second and final report was qualified. It stated: "In our opinion, subject to collectibility of the balance receivable on the contract of sale (see Note 4 of Notes to Financial Statements) the accompanying consolidated balance sheet and related consolidated statements of income and retained earnings present fairly the financial position of (FGL)...."

....

Neither the Monterey nor the Continental transactions were consummated and somewhat over a year later FGL filed a petition under Chapter XI of the Bankruptcy

Act. [Herzfeld suffered a loss of most of his investment,] ... for which, by this suit, he claims that Laventhol, because of its materially misleading audit, is responsible.

The Trial Court first considered Herzfeld's claim under § 10(b) of the Securities Exchange Act of 1934, and Rule 10b-5 thereunder.[23] The Court found that "Laventhol knew that its audited report was required for the FGL private placement and that investors would be relying on the financial statements;" that Laventhol had access to information concerning FGL which was not available to investors. As to Laventhol's legal duty, the Court held that it was the policy of the securities laws that investors be provided "with all the facts needed to make intelligent investment decisions (which) can only be accomplished if financial statements fully and fairly portray the actual financial condition of the company."

After analyzing the facts, the Court concluded that "the Laventhol report was materially misleading." The Court found that Note 4, claimed by Laventhol to be fully explanatory, was misleading: (1) in not disclosing that Continental, obligated to pay almost $5,000,000, had assets of only some $100,000; (2) in affirmatively stating that FGL had "acquired" the nursing homes (when it had not); (3) in reporting that $1,795,500 was deferred income; and (4) in stating that there was a lease back (when apparently no such lease existed). The Court's conclusion was that "the inclusion of the Monterey transaction in sales and income was misleading without a full disclosure by Laventhol of all the material facts about the transactions."

....

The issue here is not one of negligence, but of the "materially misleading" treatment of facts known to Laventhol in its submitted audit.

The function of an accountant is not merely to verify the correctness of the addition and subtraction of the company's bookkeepers. Nor does it take a fiscal wizard to appreciate the elemental and universal accounting principle that revenue should not be recognized until the "earning process is complete or virtually complete," and "an exchange has taken place." Insofar as FGL's interest in the Monterey transactions is concerned, the earning process had hardly commenced, let alone neared completion. As of November 30, 1969, FGL had paid only $5,000 cash out of $13.2 million dollar purchase price and accepted a $25,000 "deposit" under a $15.3 million contract. Conditions for closing were unsatisfied. There remained the consummation of its purchase from Monterey, the furnishing to Continental of current title reports, and the delivery of the CC&R's and a copy of a lease. By the close of November 30, 1969, title had not passed. Nor was this the exceptional instance of a conditional sale or a long-term lease with purchase option, where the retention of title does not vitiate the economic reality of a consummated exchange.

....

23. [Ed.] Rule 10b-5 makes it unlawful "to make any untrue statement of a material fact or to omit to state a material fact necessary in order to make the statements made, in the light of the circumstances under which they were made, not misleading ... in connection with the purchase or sale of any security."

Laventhol knew that the issuance of FGL securities depended upon a correct ascertainment of [the company's financial] condition. It is undisputed that, without the Monterey-Continental transactions, for the eleven months preceding November 30, FGL had sustained a loss of $772,108. Query: by what accounting legerdemain was this figure converted into a substantial profit? The Monterey purchase added nothing to the FGL till. To the contrary, it reduced it by $5,000 (if the check was honored). The Continental sale produced a down payment of $25,000 (if made) but no profit. In fact, if the hoped-for profit of $2,030,500 were ever to be realized, it could only come after the transactions had been consummated and consummation was never even contemplated before the audit date, November 30, 1969.

Laventhol points to the Trial Court's finding that the Monterey-Continental transactions were not "phony". This finding, however, only implies that there were signed agreements between the parties. By no stretch of the imagination does it imply that profits of $2,030,500 were realized therefrom before November 30, 1969, or would be at any time until consummation. In fact, both agreements showed on their face that the principal payments were to be made in 1970.

In such circumstances, the recognition of Monterey transactions was a materially misleading statement which, once included at the top of the income statement as a sale, resulted in, or necessitated, compensating adjustments which distorted all the financial figures which followed. A reasonable man in Herzfeld's position might well have acted otherwise than to purchase the FGL securities, had the truth been told and the Monterey transactions not been misleadingly represented as a consummated purchase and sale.

This misleading impression was aggravated by Laventhol's labelling of the $1,795,500 as "deferred" as opposed to "unrealized" gross profit. Such nomenclature conveyed the erroneous impression that all that profit was so much cash in hand and would be recognized periodically *in futuro* just as if it were prepaid interest or management fees. But as Laventhol well knew, net cash had increased only $20,000, and the transaction was still in doubt.

....

Laventhol did not provide a clear explanation of the reasons for the qualification [of its opinion]. A simple note would have sufficed saying in substance:

> Agreements for the purchase of Monterey Nursing Inns, Inc. for $13,362,500 and the sale thereof to Continental Recreation, Inc. for $15,393,000, have been executed. When, as and if these transactions are consummated, FGL expects to realize a profit of $2,030,500.

Instead, Laventhol chose to delete from its first so-called explanatory Note 4, the sentence "Because of the circumstances and nature of the transaction, $1,795,500 of the gross profit therein will be considered realized when the January 30, 1970 payment is received" and substituted therefor the sentence "Of the total gross profit of $2,030,500, $235,000 is included in the Consolidated Income Statement and the balance, $1,795,500 will be considered realized when the January 30, [1970] payment is received." The substituted note also changed "unrealized gross profit" to "deferred income". Even in the first Note, there is no explanation of what were the circumstances and nature of the transaction or, in the second Note, how or why $235,000 could qualify as gross profit or income as of November 30, 1969.

From the very outset of the audit, the danger signals were flashing.

> (1) Even if Laventhol accepted the agreements as not "phony", on the face of the Monterey agreement were two conditions to be performed, *i.e.*, approval by FGL of a title search and a lease back. There was no proof that they were performed or that Laventhol made any effort to verify these facts.
>
> (2) Normally on transactions of such magnitude and vital importance, corporate minutes, resolutions and other corporate papers authenticating the transaction would be examined. No proof of such examination was presented.
>
> (3) Laventhol demonstrated an awareness that the legality of the agreement with Continental might be important. However, a telephone call to an attorney who did not even see or read the agreement and who only heard such excerpts as Laventhol's partner chose to read to him, scarcely qualifies as a legal opinion as to enforceability.
>
> (4) As for Continental, Laventhol knew that it had contractually committed itself to pay $15,300,000 to FGL and that Continental had assets of only some $100,000, consisting mostly of miniature golf courses. Laventhol was aware that Max Ruderian was a well-known, successful, and wealthy real estate operator and had signed the Continental agreement but there is no document which evidences that Ruderian's wealth was in any way committed to the Continental purchase.
>
> (5) The absence of entries of the transactions on FGL's books and the necessity for Laventhol to create journal entries thereof.
>
> (6) Laventhol, whose duty it was to reveal the truth rather than be subservient to the dictates of its clients, FGL, should have taken warning from FGL's pressurizing tactics to change "unrealized profits" to "deferred".

In sum, we affirm the result reached by the Trial Court in holding that the Laventhol report contained materially misleading omissions and misrepresentations....

....

The judgment in favor of Herzfeld against Laventhol ... is affirmed....

Notes and Questions

1. Can you identify factual similarities surrounding FGL's desire to recognize the Monterey transaction in *Laventhol* and Mattel's desire to recognize revenue from slow-moving "hot wheels" and "sizzlers"?

2. If you were counsel for Mattel or FGL at the time these transactions were contemplated, what would be your advice? Could your client proceed with the transactions

as proposed? Would you propose modifications to the transaction? Would additional disclosures solve the problems?

* * *

Problem 4-4

Midwestern Scientific Glass, Inc. (MSGI) is a small high-tech company, whose scientists have developed what they believe is a practical technology for mass production of solar panels. MSGI does not plan to engage in production for retail sale, but rather will sell the technology and manufacturing plants to interested companies who will, in turn, hope to profit by production and sale of the solar panels.

MSGI management has been negotiating with Earthlux Group, a partnership of investors and producers of industrial glass. Earthlux has agreed to purchase a solar cell processing facility from MSGI for $6 million. The terms of the agreement are that a $1.8 million "downpayment" will be made when MSGI delivers specifications, operating instructions, and technical "know-how" sufficient for Earthlux to operate the facility, and the remainder of the purchase price when the facility is completed.

These negotiations are being completed in marathon sessions, since management would like to "close the deal" before the end of MSGI's fiscal year in nine days. Management would also like to recognize revenue on the project; they note, in "rough calculations," that recognition of $1.8 million in revenue would result in MSGI's first profitable year ever, and in it being the first company to ever show a profit in solar cell mass production technology. This news would likely mean that MSGI would be able to make a public offering of its stock next year as well as be favorably considered for U.S. Department of Energy and Environmental Protection Agency grants and contracts.

MSGI has prepared several binders of documents constituting the specifications, plans, and instructions for the plant, and has delivered them to Earthlux. MSGI then recognizes $1.8 million in revenue, creating a corresponding receivable on its books for the fiscal year about to end.

(a) Has MSGI complied with GAAP? If not, what else would you advise could be done within the next few days in order to properly recognize the revenue?

(b) Suppose it is now after the fiscal year end. MSGI's auditors are preparing to do their work on MSGI's books for the year just ended. They request that MSGI send a letter to Earthlux confirming the existence of the receivable. The auditors receive the following response:

> Earthlux confirms a $1.8 million receivable to MSGI and receipt of technical specifications and know-how. Our payment has been delayed due to difficulties arranging for a performance bond by MSGI. The contracts are proceeding as planned and we expect the bond should be resolved within the next 30 days.

With this information, may the auditors deliver an unqualified opinion on MSGI's financial statements?

(c) Regardless of your answer in (b), assume the auditors delay issuing the opinion until the details of the receivable are resolved. MSGI receives a $500,000 payment from an account in the name of Earthlux's lawyer. It turns out that Earthlux is not willing to pay the remaining $1.3 million unless MSGI guarantees its performance under the contract and provides a bank guarantee for the $1.3 million. How do these developments affect your answer in (b)?

(d) If your decisions in (a)–(c) above were based on the pre-ASC 606 standards, review your decisions using ASC 606 standards. If you initially used ASC 606, review your answers using the old standards. Identify the differences, if any.

* * *

So why have new standards if the answers and reasoning seem very similar? We need to look outside the small world of contracts for a one-time delivery of goods or services. That "small world" is the one on which most of the legal precedent is focused. The new standards were developed to address two main issues:

- Much of business today consists of trade in services, rather than goods, or in "bundled" sales of goods, or a mix of goods and services. The "delivery" of a service may be difficult to pinpoint and to measure.
- GAAP was becoming littered with specific industry guidance on revenue recognition. The FASB was determined to move from a "rules-based" approach to a "principles-based" approach,[24] and to create an enduring set of rules that apply to all circumstances and all companies. In addition, this was an opportunity to harmonize US GAAP with the international accounting standards.

Yes, It's Accounting, But ASC 606 Could Have a Huge Impact on Your Company

Tien Tzuo

Forbes guest blog, Aug. 10, 2017

The new standards are based on one overarching principle: companies must recognize revenue when goods and services are transferred to the customer, in an amount that is proportionate to what has been delivered at that point.

That's pretty easy to do when you're selling widgets, but poses problems in the digital economy, where service relationships can change drastically over time.

In my company's experience, every subscription contract undergoes an average of four mid-term changes. These changes can make the most basic compliance obligation — identifying a contract — a matter of some debate. In some circum-

24. Recall the discussion about "rules-based" versus "principles-based" accounting standards in Chapter 3 and the story of the dog who became a duck.

stances, contract changes are handled as a modification to the existing contract, while in other situations, a separate contract is created.

Additionally, subscriptions are complex and rolled out over time. The handling of common subscription characteristics (e.g., evergreen subscriptions, nonrefundable upfront fees) becomes tricky when companies have to decide whether to recognize revenue right away or defer it.

[R]evenue recognition standards need to change to keep pace with the global explosion of digital services. Today's accounting rules were written for the 15th century, and they simply don't apply to the modern world of recurring digital services. Today, the requirements for reporting recurring revenue—a critical metric for evaluating a company's financial performance—vary across all sorts of different industries and markets. These new regulations are intended to level the playing field.

www.forbes.com/sites/groupthink/2017/08/10/asc-606-is-the-biggest-business-story-youve-never-heard-how-it-will-affect-your-company/#740d50581d52

B. Specific Components of Income

We now understand the general rule of revenue recognition, and applications of that rule. We now consider the inevitable exceptions.

1. Investment Securities

One of the assets any business may have is investments in other businesses. Ordinarily, we would expect an investment in stock or bonds of another company to be treated like any other asset. Gain or loss would be recognized when the asset is sold, and income from that investment (dividends or interest) would be recognized as income when it is received. But because of the nature of these assets and the markets for their purchase and sale, GAAP rules favor more immediate measurement of gain or loss.

a. Recognition without Realization

Investment securities must be reported at their current "fair value"[25] at the end of each reporting period, and the increase or decrease for the period included in calculation of income. The only exception is if the security is a debt security for which the reporting entity has the positive intent and ability to hold the debt until it matures.

25. "Fair value" means the price at which the securities could be sold in an orderly transaction between market participants at the measurement date. Accounting Standards Codification (ASC) ¶¶ 320-10-20 and 321-10-20.

So we must, in the vernacular, "mark to market" our investment securities—that is, at the end of the reporting period, we check the market quote and book the gain or loss (from last period) as income or loss,

Illustration

If a business purchased X Corp. stock for $100,000 on Jan. 1, it would journal:

1/1	Dr Investment securities	100,000	
	Cr Cash		100,000

When the end of the year comes, and the market price of X Corp. stock has increased to $105,000, the business would journal as follows:

12/31	Dr Investment securities	5,000	
	Cr Investment income		5,000

The GAAP rules assume that there is a market price through which to determine "fair value" for all debt securities and for most equity securities. If there is no market for equity securities,[26] GAAP requires that the holder value the security at cost and carry it at that value, subject to two modifications:

- If there are "orderly transactions" in an "identical or similar investment of the same issuer," then the value of the investment should be changed to reflect that transaction price.[27]
- If the value of the security is "impaired" by, among other things, deterioration of: the issuer's earnings, credit, or assets; regulatory, economic, or technological environment; or general market conditions, then that impairment must be recognized and taken as a loss in that reporting period.[28]

---

26. These are technically known as equity securities "without a readily determinable fair value." ASC ¶ 321-10-35-2.

27. *Id.* "Orderly transactions" is defined as a market in which a security is openly offered for sale, as opposed to being quickly disposed of at distressed prices. ASC ¶ 321-10-20.

28. ASC ¶ 321-10-35-3. Impairment is not separately accounted for in the other classifications. In securities which are revalued according to a trading market, presumably the market price measures and values any such decline in value. Held-to-maturity debt securities are not subject to a market revaluation *per se*, but financial problems of the debtor may force the holder to conclude it no longer has the ability to hold the debt security to maturity. It would then change the classification from held-to-maturity to one of the other debt categories (available-for-sale or trading) where market value loss is measured and recognized. ASC ¶ 320-10-35-5.

Any gains or losses *actually realized* from sales are recognized, of course. In addition, any interest or dividend income actually received by or credited to the owner of any investment security is recognized as income when it is received or credited.[29]

Illustration (continued)

On Jan. 1, a business owns X Corp. stock valued at $105,000. On Feb. 1, X Corp. pays a dividend on its shares. The amount received by the business is $2,500. The business would journal:

Dr Cash	2,500	
Cr Investment Income (revenue)		2,500
Receipt of cash dividends on X Corp. stock.		

On July 1, the business decides to sell the X Corp. stock for $110,000, it would journal:

Dr Cash	110,000	
Cr Investment Income		5,000
Cr Investment securities		105,000
Sale of X Corp. stock.		

b. The "Equity Method" of Accounting for Stock

The second exception relates only to equity securities (stock) of another company. Since equity securities represent ownership and therefore control of a company, the accounting treatment reflects whether ownership of stock of another company results in "control" of that company. If it does, then the financial statements of the two entities are consolidated.[30] Short of control, but more than just an indifferent investor's interest, is the ability to "significantly influence" a company's activities through investment in its equity securities. If there is such "significant influence," then the investment can accounted for according to the "equity method."

What is "significant influence"? GAAP rules presume that ownership of 20 percent or more of the entity's voting stock provides the owner with significant influence. That presumption may be rebutted by showing facts which indicate control actually resides firmly elsewhere, such as

- a majority owner which exercises control without consulting any other owners
- an agreement by the minority owner to *not* exercise any such influence

---

29. ASC ¶ 320-10-35-4 (debt securities); ASC ¶ 321-10-35-6 (equity securities).
30. Consolidations are covered in Chapter 8.

- attempts by the minority owner to exercise control which are rebuffed by the entity (such as requests for information or attempts to seek representation on the board of directors) or others (such as through litigation or resort to government regulators).[31]

Conversely, ownership of *less* than 20 percent of the entity's voting stock might yield "significant influence" if the owner has the ability to exercise some control over the company's operating and investment decisions.[32] In sum, the 20% presumption is a beginning point for evaluating facts and circumstances.[33]

What is the equity method of accounting? This is a much easier question to answer. If there *is* the ability to "significantly influence," then the investor may use the following method to account for its investment. The investment is initially recorded at cost, as always, but:

- The investor *adds* to its carrying value its proportionate share of the company's net income (or subtracts a loss) each period,[34] and
- The investor *reduces* its carrying value to reflect any dividends paid by the company in which it invests.[35]

Illustration

Overboard Industries LLC owns 350,000 shares (35%) of the common stock of Underwater Company. It purchased the stock on Jan. 1 for $500,000. Upon the purchase, it journalled as follows:

1/1	Dr Underwater Co. common stock	500,000	
	Cr Cash		500,000

On Dec. 31, Underwater Co. concludes its fiscal year, and reports on its financial statements net income of $100,000. Overboard, if using the "equity" method, would recognize its proportionate share (35%) of that income.

12/31	Dr Underwater Co. common stock	35,000	
	Cr Investment income (revenue)		35,000

On Feb. 1 of the next year, Underwater declares a one cent per share cash dividend. Because Overboard has now "realized" some of its investment, it would reduce the carrying value accordingly.

2/1	Dr Cash	3,500	
	Cr Underwater Co. common stock		3,500

31. ASC ¶ 323-10-15-10.
32. ASC ¶ 323-10-15-6.
33. ASC ¶ 323-10-15-7.
34. ASC ¶ 323-10-35-4.
35. ASC ¶ 323-10-35-17.

In addition to the above entries, the investor must recognize impairment of the investment of there are other than temporary losses suffered by the entity which are not reflected in losses otherwise taken into account under the equity method.[36]

The following table summarizes these rules.

Amount of voting securities owned	Less than 20% *and ALL debt securities*	20% to 50% "significant influence"	More than 50% "control"
Accounting treatment	**(1) Debt held-to-maturity;** <u>**Cost method**</u> - carry at historical cost **(2) All other debt and all equity securities:** <u>**Fair value method**</u> - ***recognize*** unrealized gain/loss in net income - different rules for computing gain/loss for equities which are not market-traded **(3) *All* investment securities** - recognize interest or dividend income	<u>**Equity method**</u> - record investment at cost - accrue proportionate share of net income when reported by investee - reduce book value by dividends received from investee	**Consolidation** is required (with a few exceptions)
Main authority	ASC Topic 320 (debt) ASC Topic 321 (equity)	ASC Topic 323	This book Ch. 8; ASC Topic 810

Example

Berkshire Hathaway, Inc. is, for the most part, an insurance company, and therefore has lots of investment securities. The company's 2019 annual report indicates the following with respect to the valuation rules we just covered:

> *We classify investments in fixed maturity securities at the acquisition date and re-evaluate the classification at each balance sheet date. Securities classified as held-to-maturity are carried at amortized cost, reflecting the ability and intent to hold the securities to maturity. Securities classified as trading are acquired with the intent to sell in the near term and are carried at fair value with changes in fair value reported in earnings. All other securities are classified as available-for-sale and are carried at fair value with net unrealized gains or losses reported in accumulated other comprehensive income. As of December 31, 2019, substantially all of our investments in fixed maturity securities were classified as available-for-sale.*

36. ASC 323-10-35-31.

We carry substantially all of our investments in equity securities at fair value and record the subsequent changes in fair values in the Consolidated Statement of Earnings as a component of investment gains/losses.

We utilize the equity method to account for investments when we possess the ability to exercise significant influence, but not control, over the operating and financial policies of the investee. The ability to exercise significant influence is presumed when the investor possesses more than 20% of the voting interests of the investee. This presumption may be overcome based on specific facts and circumstances that demonstrate that the ability to exercise significant influence is restricted. We apply the equity method to investments in common stock and to other investments when such other investments possess substantially identical subordinated interests to common stock. In applying the equity method, we record the investment at cost and subsequently increase or decrease the carrying amount of the investment by our proportionate share of the net earnings or losses and other comprehensive income of the investee. We record dividends or other equity distributions as reductions in the carrying value of the investment.

Notice how this disclosure follows almost identically the GAAP rules discussed in this chapter.

* * *

Problem 4-5

(a) A Corp. owns 100,000 shares of the common stock of B Corp. What questions do you need answered in order to determine the proper accounting treatment of this investment on A Corp.'s books?

(b) Suppose instead that A Corp. owned $1 million face value of B Corp. 6% bonds, due in ten years. Now what questions need to be asked?

Problem 4-6

Sonny's Inns Inc. operates approximately 500 family restaurants in 12 states. Most of the restaurants are franchised to independent owners, but many are owned and operated by Sonny's. What would be the appropriate treatment of each of the following financial assets on Sonny's financial statements?

(a) Sonny's lent $1 million to Travel Host Corp. to help finance that company's purchase of land and buildings for six Sonny's Inns. Sonny's received Travel Host 7.5% bonds due in ten years. Sonny's owns no stock in Travel Host. Regrettably, Travel Host's locations were not favorable, and the company lapsed into desperate financial straits during the last year, and missed the most recent semiannual interest payment on the bonds. Several banks and investors have offered to buy the Travel Host bonds for prices averaging about $700,000. Despite these offers, Sonny's plans to hold the bonds to maturity, believing that if Travel Host downsizes and trims its expenses, it can return to profitability, make up the missed payment, and meet all required future payments including repayment of the principal on the due date.

(b) Sonny's owns 25% of the common stock of Central Delivery Corp., created last year by Sonny's and two other companies to make deliveries of food and supplies to Sonny's Inns. Another food chain manager owns 24% of Central Delivery stock, and 51% is owned by Central Trucking Corp. Although Sonny's 25% ownership would entitle it to elect one of Central Delivery's four directors according to applicable state law, Sonny's has agreed to let Central Trucking vote Sonny's shares and exercise day-to-day control over all of Central Delivery's operations. Central Delivery's net income for its fiscal year (ended last week) was $400,000, and it paid no dividends.

(c) Sonny's owns 200,000 shares of General Motors, Inc. common stock. Last week's closing price for GM was $65 per share; a year ago it was $70 per share.

* * *

2. Comprehensive Income

We saw in the above section that, in the case of "available for sale" debt securities, gain or loss would be recognized even though not realized, *and* would be reported as a direct charge or credit to the owner's equity account. This makes the income statement less useful as a guide to "articulation" or what goes on between the dates of two different balance sheets. This gain or loss would not be reflected in the income statement at all!

The FASB determined in the late 1990s to remedy this lack of transparency by requiring *all* changes to owner's equity to be separately stated in one financial statement. However, since some of these items (see above) were determined not to be appropriately included in the *income statement*, what could we call this additional statement? The FASB settled on the term ***comprehensive income***, which includes net income (traditionally calculated) ***and*** all the other changes made to the equity accounts during the year. The FASB described its reasoning as follows.

> Historically, issues about income reporting were characterized broadly in terms of a contrast between the so-called current operating performance (or dirty surplus) and the all-inclusive (or clean surplus) income concepts. Under the current operating performance income concept, extraordinary and nonrecurring gains and losses are excluded from income. Under the all-inclusive income concept, all revenues, expenses, gains, and losses recognized during the period are included in income, regardless of whether they are considered to be results of operations of the period....
>
> Some users of financial statement information expressed concerns about the increasing number of comprehensive income items that bypass the income statement. Currently, an enterprise is required to report the accumulated balances of those items in equity. However, because of the considerable diversity as to how those balances and changes in them are presented in financial state-

> ments, some of those users urged the Board to implement the concept of comprehensive income that was introduced in FASB [Concepts Statements].
>
> As a first step in implementing the concept of comprehensive income, this Statement requires that all items that meet the definition of components of comprehensive income be reported in a financial statement for the period in which they are recognized....[37]

The comprehensive income rule requires *all* changes in equity—whether from net income or from other changes which "bypass" the income statement—to be displayed together in one statement. The FASB recommends that this statement be called "Comprehensive Income," although the term is not required.[38] The following table summarizes the different types of gain or loss reported in each category.

Items of Net Income	Items of Comprehensive Income *outside* of Net Income
• Net Income from continuing operations • Net Income from discontinued operations • Net Income from unusual items[39]	• Unrealized gains and losses on available-for-sale debt securities[40] • Foreign currency translations and transactions • Some derivative instruments classified as "cash flow hedges" • Some pension costs related primarily to past obligations

Example

Pfizer, Inc. is a large bio-pharmaceutical company. For the year ended Dec. 31, 2018, Pfizer reports $53,647 million of sales, resulting in $11,188 million of net income. That number is further changed in the company's "Statement of Comprehensive Income" as follows (amounts in millions):

Net Income	$11,188
Foreign currency translation adjustments	(821)
Unrealized holding gains (losses) on derivatives	247
Unrealized holding gains (losses) on available-for-sale securities	(522)
Benefit plans: actuarial losses	(153)
Benefit plans: prior service credits and other	(207)
Tax effect of comprehensive losses	(518)
Comprehensive Income	**$9,214**

37. Statement of Financial Accounting Standards No. 130, Reporting Comprehensive Income ¶¶ 2, 4–5 (FASB June 1997).

38. *See generally* ASC 220-10-45 on reporting and presenting comprehensive income.

39. "Unusual" or "infrequent" items (both as defined in ASC 225-20-45) should be presented as a separate item in the income statement; see ASC 225-20-45-16.

40. Available-for-sale securities were discussed in part 1(a) above.

As we studied earlier, the entire $11,188 million of net income is added to the "stockholders' equity" section of Pfizer's balance sheet. The difference between "Net Income" and "Comprehensive Income" of $1,974 million is reserved in a separate equity account in the balance sheet entitled "Other Comprehensive Loss" which has a cumulative total on Dec. 31, 2018 of $11,275 million, or about 7.1% of Pfizer's total assets.

* * *

Problem 4-7

(a) Jumpy Co. has $100,000 in owner's equity on January 1, 20x1. During 20x1, its debt securities classified as "trading" increase $12,000 in value, and its debt securities classified as "available-for-sale" decrease $15,000 in value. If Jumpy has $15,000 income from its operations not including any of the above amounts, prepare an appropriate display for Jumpy's net income and comprehensive income for 20x1.

(b) In 20x2, Jumpy's "trading" debt securities increase $50,000 in value, but its "available-for-sale" debt securities do not change. Jumpy also is fortunate to have a refund from its pension fund of $25,000 and a favorable adjustment on the currency translations for its first foreign operations of $10,000. If Jumpy's 20x2 operations have otherwise generated a $20,000 loss, prepare an appropriate display for Jumpy's net income and comprehensive income for 20x2.

Problem 4-8

Waterhouse, Inc. is a regional producer and bottler of "premium" spring, distilled and flavored waters. Waterhouse has invested some spare cash in debt securities which it has presently classified as "available for sale." It is the last week of Waterhouse's fiscal year, and the net income numbers are not coming in as well as management had hoped. They have asked you if it would be permissible to reclassify some of the "available for sale" securities which have unrealized gains as "trading" securities. Would this give Waterhouse's income the year-end boost which management desires? Is it legal? The following GAAP may assist you.

ASC ¶ 320-10-20

"Trading" means an activity involving securities sold in the near term and held for only a short period of time. The term trading contemplates a holding period generally measured in hours and days rather than months or years.

ASC ¶ 320-10-35-12

Given the nature of a trading security, transfers into or from the trading category should be rare.

ASC ¶ 320-10-35-13

Available-for-sale securities shall not be automatically transferred to the trading category because the passage of time has caused the maturity date to be within one year or because management intends to sell the security within one year.

Chapter 5

Assets and Expenses

Now that we are experts on revenues, it's time to turn to the rest of the income statement. After the revenues, the next-largest items on a company's income statement will typically be the major expenses (the "cost of sales" or "cost of goods sold" for a manufacturing or retailing entity).

We can apply Sutton's Law here too, because financial statement problems related to expenses are on the rise. The most recent study of restatements (corrections) of financial statements pegs various expense accounting issues, taken together, as the cause of about half of all restatements over the 2000–19 period.[1]

If the title of this chapter seems confusing, recall from Chapter 1 the intimate connection between assets and expenses. Each major expense is often associated with one or more assets. We are already experts in the basic rules of ***revenue*** recognition from our study in the preceding chapter. GAAP provides three theoretical options for ***expense*** recognition:[2]

- ***matching*** with revenues, so that costs are recognized when the associated revenues are recognized. Accountants and economists call these associated costs *direct* costs or *variable* costs.
- ***systematic allocation*** to future periods expected to be benefited by the expenditure. If this allocation involves a long-lived asset used in production, it is called ***depreciation***. If it involves using up purchased oil or minerals in the ground, it is called ***depletion***. If it involves any other asset or a prepaid expense, such as a trademark or five-year insurance policy, it is called ***amortization***. But all three names are describing a method of allocating costs expected to benefit future periods to those future periods.
- ***recognition when expenditures are made***, if the costs cannot be "matched" with revenue or allocated over future periods. These expenses are commonly called *indirect* costs, *fixed* costs, or *overhead*, because they do not specifically relate to any product or revenue or vary with production. Selling and administrative expenses are a common example.

* * *

1. Don Whalen *et al.*, 2019 Financial Restatements: A Nineteen Year Comparison, *Audit Analytics* Report No. 2022-07-22, at 23 (July 2020), available at www.auditanalytics.com. As noted in the introduction to Chapter 4, revenue recognition remains at the top of the list in this study, but expense-related issues, taken together, account for a higher percentage of restatements.

2. Statement of Financial Accounting Concepts No. 5, *Recognition and Measurement in Financial Statements of Business Enterprises* ¶ 86 (Dec. 1984).

Problem 5-1

Which of the above cost-recognition principles should be applied in each of the following situations involving Northwest Department Stores, Inc.?

(a) The company engages in a special seasonal advertising campaign.

(b) The company buys inventory for sale in the various departments of its stores.

(c) Some of the company's products require expenditures for special displays and trained sales personnel.

* * *

In the rest of this chapter, we will apply these basic rules of GAAP cost allocation in the two main areas of a business' expenses: inventories (Part A) and long-lived assets (Part B). In addition, we will look separately at the rules for recognizing impairment of those assets (Part C). In each area, we will examine the accounting for *both* the asset and its related expenses. In this fashion, as with the revenues, we will have found "where the money is," or at least where it went.

A. Inventories and Cost of Sales

In most manufacturing, wholesaling or retailing businesses, inventory is a major asset and its sale the major cost of doing business. Questions about allocation of cost to inventory fall into two major areas: (1) how does inventory move from being held for sale to being sold, and (2) what *does* the inventory "cost" anyway? Each of these is examined in turn below.

1. Inventory Flows

In a business of any size, keeping track of the items held for sale can be a daunting task. In order to determine what is in inventory, the accountants make some assumptions about how the items held for sale flow through a business and therefore what is left in a closing inventory. There are three widely used inventory methods: perpetual, periodic, and retail.

Perpetual inventory. Under the perpetual method, an entity takes inventory constantly. For example, each item may be identified by a bar code or similar marking so that the accounting information system can identify an item sold immediately.

Periodic inventory. Under the periodic method, an entity counts its inventories for valuation purposes at the close of the accounting cycle. Every unit that is not present in the closing inventory is considered a cost of sales, as calculated by this formula:

Periodic Inventory Formula
Beginning Inventory + Purchases – Ending Inventory = Cost of Sales

Example. Wilma's Widgets balance in "Inventory" at the beginning of the year is $10,000. During the year, she purchases more widgets for $100,000 cash. At the end of the year, she takes an inventory count in the warehouse and determines she has $15,000 worth of widgets on hand. Wilma's cost of goods sold for the year is:

$10,000 + $100,000 – $15,000 = $95,000.

* * *

Problem 5-2

Shoreline Service Station has the following records of its purchases and sales of tires for the month of January.

Date	No. of tires	Unit cost	Total cost
Jan. 1—beginning inventory	50	$10	$500
Jan. 3—sales	4	$10	$40
Jan. 19—sales	8	$10	$80
Jan. 21—purchases	15	$10	$150
Jan. 31—ending inventory	53	$10	$530

The sale on Jan. 3 was at $24 per tire, and the sale on Jan. 19 was at $22 per tire. What are the required journal entries on each date if Shoreline used the:

(a) perpetual inventory method?

(b) periodic inventory method (with a count taken on Jan. 31)?

* * *

Under either method of taking inventory, we will have a record of the number of units of inventory sold and the number remaining in inventory. It is a simple matter to convert units into costs if the cost per unit is uniform and unchanging. Such was the case at the Shoreline Service Station in the problem you just completed. But most businesses are not so lucky. And even a perpetual inventory system normally keeps track only of units, but not the costs of each unit. To cope with this problem, ac countants use several different inventory flow assumptions, each being an alternative under GAAP. The most common are: first-in-first-out (FIFO), last-in-first-out (LIFO), and average cost.[3]

Illustration

Wanda's Widgets purchased 100 widgets last year. Her records indicate that she purchased

25 widgets @ $8 each in January

3. See Accounting Standards Codification (ASC) ¶¶ 330-10-30-9 through -12.

50 widgets @ $9 each in April; and

25 widgets @ $10 each in October.

Her warehouse contained 10 widgets with a cost of $7 each on January 1, and it contained 20 widgets on December 31. What is the value of the 20 widgets remaining on December 31? The above inventory flow assumptions yield the following results.

FIFO. First-in-first-out means last-in-still-here. Thus the 20 widgets in the warehouse are assumed to be the ones purchased in October for $10 each, so the inventory value is $200.

LIFO. Just the opposite. Thus, we assume that, of the 20 widgets in the warehouse, 10 were purchased in January for $8 each, and 10 were from the original inventory at $7 each, so the inventory value is $150.

Average Cost. Wanda had available for sale 110 widgets at a total cost of $970, so each widget has a value of $970/11 = $8.82. Thus, the 20 widgets in the warehouse are assumed to be worth $176.40.

* * *

Problem 5-3

(a) In the above example, calculate Wanda's Cost of Goods Sold under each of the three inventory flow assumptions. What does this tell you about the impact of LIFO in times of rising prices, as was the case with Wanda?

(b) Wanda's Sales account shows the following for the year: 15 widgets @ $9, 42 widgets @ $10 and 28 widgets @ $12, for a total of 85 widgets sold for $891. What is Wanda's gross profit (sales less cost of goods sold) under each inventory flow assumption?

(c) Wanda had 110 widgets available for sale, 85 were sold, and 20 remain in inventory. What happened to the other five widgets? Would it make a difference if Wanda used a perpetual inventory system?

* * *

Should your business use the perpetual or periodic inventory method? Each has its benefits, but a mature business will usually have the assets to invest in a perpetual system. The periodic inventory method is most practical for businesses that cannot afford the cost of an inventory tracking system.

> If your business is small, or if you do not have extra money to invest, periodic inventory management may be a better choice for you because you can get by with just a cash register and a simple accounting procedure. If you sell

services rather than products, you may not need an inventory management system unless you own a restaurant or you are in the hospitality business.

As your business grows, you may want to switch over to a perpetual inventory management system as it allows you to know the balance in your inventory account at any point in time. Large businesses typically have perpetual inventory systems rather than periodic inventory systems since the rest of their financial and accounting systems are computerized.[4]

In practice, all three inventory flow assumptions are used widely by businesses. And within the same business, different groups of inventory may be valued under different assumptions.

Retail inventory. GAAP also allows you not to count your inventory at all, through the "retail inventory" or "reverse mark-up" inventory method.[5] This combines the inventory count and valuation by using value of inventory as a proxy for its amount. To do this, the entity calculates its sales, subtracts the "normal" profit margin, and the remainder is cost of goods sold. The profit margin is calculated based on the ratio of the total cost of goods available for sale (beginning inventory plus purchases) to the retail value of that same inventory.

Illustration

Galactic Stores, Inc. has the following records for its inventory for the year.

	Cost	Retail value
Beginning inventory	$10,000	$15,000
Purchases	300,000	400,000
Total goods available for sale	310,000	415,000
Ratio of costs to sales	310,000 / 415,000 = 0.75	
Less Sales		350,000
Ending inventory at retail (Total goods available for sale — sales)		$65,000
Ending inventory at cost (Retail value times cost ratio)	$48,750	

This method allows Galactic to quickly value its inventory without a physical count.

4. Rosemary Peavler, *Periodic or Perpetual Inventory: Which Should Your Company Use?*, www.thebalance.com/choosing periodic or perpetual inventory-system-392936 (updated June 6, 2018).

5. ASC ¶ 330-10-30-13.

The retail inventory method is customarily used, as its name suggests, in the retail industry. Inventory in these businesses is widely varied and fast moving. If a perpetual inventory system is not used, taking a periodic inventory is considered to be simply too cumbersome and costly to be worth the additional information. In addition, this method allows these companies to quickly value their inventory for quarterly reports and for insurance purposes. This method can also be done on a "LIFO" basis, using the cost ratios for the earliest purchases to value the ending inventory, according to the relative values of each.

Example

Macy's, Inc. provides the following disclosure in its February 1, 2020 financial statements about how it accounts for its $5.2 billion in merchandise inventory.

> *Merchandise inventories are valued at lower of cost or market using the last-in, first-out ("LIFO") retail inventory method. Under the retail inventory method, inventory is segregated into departments of merchandise having similar characteristics, and is stated at its current retail selling value. Inventory retail values are converted to a cost basis by applying specific average cost factors for each merchandise department. Cost factors represent the average cost-to-retail ratio for each merchandise department based on beginning inventory and the annual purchase activity.... The retail inventory method inherently requires management judgments and estimates, such as the amount and timing of permanent markdowns to clear unproductive or slow-moving inventory, which may impact the ending inventory valuation as well as gross margins.*
>
> *Permanent markdowns designated for clearance activity are recorded when the utility of the inventory has diminished. Factors considered in the determination of permanent markdowns include current and anticipated demand, customer preferences, age of the merchandise and fashion trends. When a decision is made to permanently markdown merchandise, the resulting gross margin reduction is recognized in the period the markdown is recorded.*
>
> *Physical inventories are generally taken within each merchandise department annually, and inventory records are adjusted accordingly, resulting in the recording of actual shrinkage. Physical inventories are taken at all store locations for substantially all merchandise categories approximately three weeks before the end of the year. Shrinkage is estimated as a percentage of sales at interim periods and for this approximate three-week period, based on historical shrinkage rates. While it is not possible to*

> *quantify the impact from each cause of shrinkage, the Company has loss prevention programs and policies that are intended to minimize shrinkage, including the use of radio frequency identification cycle counts and interim inventories to keep the Company's merchandise files accurate.*

Obviously, the retail inventory method requires careful management of inventory prices and costs and meticulous attention by management to the assumptions it has made about past and future sales. For example, if management has lowered prices in order to boost sales, then the usual profit margin assumptions for inventory calculation may be improper, as Macy's indicated in the above excerpt.[6]

Regardless of the inventory accounting method used, businesses usually take a physical inventory count periodically to avoid unsatisfied customer orders, and to account for costs due to spoilage, loss, and theft. This inventory will also serve as a check on the accounting records.

Financial impact of the choice of inventory method. GAAP permits an entity to choose freely among permitted inventory accounting methods. In fact, one method might be used for one type of inventory and another for some other type.

The choice of inventory flow assumptions can have a significant effect on the value of assets and the net income reported in an entity's financial statements. Because prices have historically been rising (though the rate of change has varied over the years), companies may like to report on a FIFO basis to their shareholders. This is because FIFO puts the older, low-cost inventory into costs of goods sold, thus increasing net income. When reporting for taxes, however, companies would prefer reporting on a LIFO basis, because LIFO has the opposite effect of making net income (and thus the income tax) lower.[7]

The tax, securities, and accounting authorities have addressed these areas in great detail in recent years. In general, the income tax law requires that if a taxpayer uses LIFO on its tax returns, it must use LIFO in its external financial reports.[8] From there, however, the issues become very complicated regarding how LIFO must be calculated and the extent to which supplemental disclosure is required regarding what the inventory values and net income would be if another method were used.[9]

---

6. *See* Robbins v. The Gitano Group, Inc., 1992 WL 276837 (S.D.N.Y. 1992) (denying motion to dismiss a securities fraud complaint on this ground).

7. Review your answers to Problem 5-3(a). Note that the prices in that example were rising.

8. *See* Internal Revenue Code § 472(c). Changes of accounting method for tax purposes must normally be approved by the IRS. See Rev. Proc. 2015-13 (general procedures) and Rev. Proc. 2021-34 (most recent update).

9. See the SEC's accounting rule, 17 C.F.R. § 201.5-02(6)(c).

Example

The Sherwin-Williams Company reports $1.7 billion net income and $1.8 billion of inventories in its December 31, 2017 financial statements. The notes indicate the company's methods for valuation of that inventory and the effect on the financial statements:

> *Inventories were principally stated at the lower of cost or market with cost determined on the last-in, first-out (LIFO) method. The following presents the effect on inventories [and] net income ... had the Company used the first-in, first-out (FIFO) inventory valuation method adjusted for income taxes at the statutory rate in effect at each reporting date and assuming no other adjustments. Management believes that the use of LIFO results in a better matching of costs and revenues. This information is presented to enable the reader to make comparisons with companies using the FIFO method of inventory valuation....*

($ millions)	*2017*	*2016*
Percentage of total inventories on LIFO	*66%*	*79%*
Excess of FIFO over LIFO inventory value	*$287*	*$253*
Decrease in net income due to LIFO	*$21*	*$1.4*

Source: The use of Sherwin-Williams as an example is taken from the Bloom & Cenker article, *supra* note 9. The figures are updated.

Problem 5-4

Global Petroleum Corp. accounts for its crude oil reserves on a LIFO basis. It does so because this reduces the company's income tax expense. Recently, oil production has been severely curtailed due to insurgencies in the Middle East and South America, where Global extracts most of its oil. As a result, Global has dramatically reduced inventories, with the result that the older, low-cost "layers" of LIFO inventory have been reported as cost of goods sold. In addition, the retail price of Global's products and all other associated costs has been rising because of the reduced supply.

Explain to a concerned shareholder, legislator, or investigator how this "technical" accounting has increased Global's profits to levels which the shareholder might call "artificial," the legislator "obscene," or the investigator "illegal."

Problem 5-5

You are counsel to Dime Store Supply Corp. (DSSC), a small novelty toy retailer. DSSC's two current hot products are Gizmos and Gadgets. Gizmos are a new "trendy" toy, and all of DSSC's purchases from manufacturers have been very recent, and all at prices from $5–$6 each. Gadgets, on the other hand, have been a staple item for DSSC, and it has been purchasing them from manufacturers for the last 10 years. Although Gadgets were cheaper in years past, the current purchase price for Gadgets, like Gizmos, is about $5–$6 each.

DSSC accounts for its inventory on a LIFO basis, with Gizmos and Gadgets pooled together in the same group. Gonzo, DSSC's Chief Financial Officer, has come to you with the following data and plan.

DSSC's inventory as of December 31, 20x7, was $1,500,000. Gonzo's calculations from DSSC's internal records shows that this is made up of:

200,000 Gizmos @ av. cost of $5.50 = $1,100,000
200,000 Gadgets @ av. cost of $2.00 = $400,000.

For financial accounting purposes, however, each toy sold is reported at the average cost of all inventory and purchases for the year. Thus, if a Gizmo or a Gadget were sold from this inventory, the related cost would be $3.75 ($1,500,000/400,000 units).

Gonzo sees an opportunity in recent market trends, which show that the demand for Gizmos is slowing, while the demand for Gadgets is remaining strong. He believes that DSSC will be able to satisfy the demand for Gizmos with inventory and available purchases, but sales of Gadgets will severely deplete if not eliminate DSSC's inventory. He would like to report the cost of Gadgets sold at $2 each instead of the average cost of $3.75 each, since the retail price is holding and may even increase a bit. This would give a significant boost to DSSC's net income.

Gonzo wants to separate Gizmos and Gadgets into individual inventory pools, thus reaching the "old" LIFO layer of $2 Gadgets, thus increasing earnings.

If Gonzo's plan is adopted by DSSC, what additional disclosures would you recommend in the financial statements to make sure they are not misleading?

* * *

2. Inventory Costs

We are now experts at determining which products have been sold. We must solve a second problem in order to account for inventory. How much did the item "cost" anyway? These two questions (inventory *flow* and inventory *cost*) need to be answered each time inventory calculation is an issue.

Determining and tracking inventory costs can be very complicated, and normally constitutes a separate branch of accounting, known (not surprisingly) as "cost accounting" or "managerial accounting." It is distinct from the financial accounting we have been studying so far because it doesn't involve *external* reporting to owners, creditors, and the like. Rather, the information is used by management to determine the profitability of an item, efficiency of a plant, and the like. Nonetheless, the entity's cost accounting decisions do factor in to the external financial statements, as either costs of goods sold or costs of inventory remaining unsold.

The important new inventory cost concept is this: ***almost all of the costs associated with production are collected with, move with, and are displayed as costs of the product itself.***[10] The following illustration works through an example of how costs involved in furniture manufacturing are incorporated into the product's cost, and hence to the inventory and costs of goods sold.

Illustration

Western Furniture manufactures residential furniture. It buys wood and other products, and fashions items for sale in its factory, which are then placed in a warehouse for eventual distribution to retailers.

As with most manufacturers, Western divides its inventory into three classifications: raw materials, work in process, and finished goods. Many companies combine these first two categories, but we will treat them separately for this example. The inventory physically moves through these three classifications on its way out the door. But as it does so, there are two important accounting tasks.

Let's see how this works as Western turns lumber into dining room tables.

> **First:** the costs of inventory are calculated and added to each item of inventory;
>
> **Second:** an inventory flow assumption is made (FIFO, LIFO, or average cost) to determine which units of inventory move on to the next step.

(1) **Raw materials**. Western purchases lumber from mills and dealers. Also included in the cost of the lumber is the cost of freight, insurance, even the costs of building and operating the lumber warehouse, to the extent those costs can be specifically identified and allocated appropriately. That is where the cost accountants come in. Once they have identified the costs, we would journal as follows:

Dr Raw materials	$100,000	
Cr Cash		$100,000

To record purchase of lumber and freight costs.

The costs involved in inventory accounting are of three fundamental types.

- **Variable (or direct) costs** are those which vary according to the amount or number of goods manufactured, such as raw material or labor costs directly associated

10. *See* ASC ¶ 330-10-05-3.

with the manufacture of that item. It also includes some "overhead" items, such as utility costs (electricity, water, gas, waste disposal) which change based on production levels.

- **Fixed (or indirect) costs** are those which remain constant regardless of the amount of production. For example, the cost incurred to build and maintain the manufacturing plant would be fixed costs, as they are the same whether Western makes enough furniture to fill your living room or the Pentagon. GAAP requires that all such costs be allocated to inventory, which is ordinarily based on the firm's "normal" production capacity.
- **Nonproduction costs** are those which are not about production at all. Whether fixed (such as administrative overhead) or variable (selling expenses), these costs are not part of inventory, and are generally expensed as incurred.

Cost allocation where each cost center (product or service) is unique is referred to as "job costing." Cost allocation where each cost center is a group of fungible products is referred to "process costing." Each job may have a combination of the two types, as we do here. *See* Charles T. Horngren, *et al.*, Cost Accounting: A Managerial Emphasis 100–101 (14th ed. 2012).

The cash was actually paid to the lumber yard, the trucker, and the warehouse guard, but it is reflected on Western's books in Raw materials. The business will refer to this as the expenses being "charged to raw materials."

(2) **Work in process**. When the time comes to begin manufacture of dining room tables, the machines and specialized implements are made ready in the factory, and the lumber is brought in from the warehouse. We must make an inventory flow assumption (FIFO, LIFO, average cost, etc.) if only some of the boards in a cost pool or group are used. We include in the costs of each board-becoming-table the costs of the woodworker's salary/benefits, the use of machines, tools, glues, coatings, fasteners, and the like, so long as each cost can be measured and identified to the product. This is where the cost accountants really do their job. We would then journal:

Dr Work in process	$200,000	
Cr Cash		$100,000
Cr Raw materials		$100,000

To record move of lumber to factory and associated costs of production.

Here again, the cash was actually paid to a woodworker, or as part of the cost of a machine, or to the electric company, but the cost is "charged to work in process."

(3) **Finished goods**. Finally, the work is completed and we have a group of dining room tables. They are physically moved from the factory floor to the finished goods (or "inventory") warehouse, to await sale and shipment to local furniture retailers. We make an inventory flow assumption (FIFO, LIFO, average cost, etc.) to determine costs if only some tables are ready for sale. To the cost of each table, we now add packing, shipping, storage costs for the finished goods warehouse as we did for the

lumber warehouse. The cost accountants do their magic and tell us how much to include, and we journal:

Dr Finished goods	$250,000	
Cr Cash		$50,000
Cr Work in process		$200,000

To record move of finished tables into warehouse for sale.

Again, the work of the loader, packager, pallet mover, and so on, would be paid to that person in cash, but "charged to finished goods."

(4) Out the door. The sales staff reports that they have sold this lot of tables to a local furniture store. As the tables leave the finished goods warehouse, we again make some inventory flow assumptions (FIFO, LIFO, average cost) and journal:

Dr Cost of goods sold	$250,000	
Cr Finished goods		$250,000

To record sale of one lot of dining room tables.

Note the important change here for accounting purposes. All of these costs have now moved from being an ***asset*** (inventory) to being an ***expense*** (cost of goods sold).

This is, in very simplified form, how costs move through a **manufacturing** entity. Recall that there are three basic types of businesses (especially for inventory accounting purposes): manufacturing, retailing, and service. In a **retailing** entity, it is much easier to follow costs to finished products, because it has no manufacturing costs to track. However, the retailer does have freight, warehousing, and labor costs. To the extent that these can be tracked and assigned to inventory, those costs are included with the inventory in the same fashion as with the manufacturing illustration above. In a **service** entity, there are little or no inventory costs to track.

Examples

Manufacturing. Ford Motor Co. reported $10.8 billion of inventories on its December 31, 2019, balance sheet. These were divided into $4.4 billion in "raw materials, work-in-process and supplies" and $6.4 billion in "finished products." Ford has approximately 190,000 employees worldwide but reports no separate expense on its income statement for this labor. "Automotive sales" were reported for the year at $144 billion, with "Cost of sales" at $135 billion.

Retail. Macy's, Inc. reports $5.2 billion of "merchandise inventories" on its February 1, 2020, balance sheet. The company has about 123,000 employees, but, as with Ford, no separate labor expense. Macy's reported $24.5 billion of sales with $15.2 billion in cost of sales for the year.

Service. Alphabet, Inc. (Google's parent company) reports $276 billion of assets on its December 31, 2019, balance sheet, but only $1 billion in inventories. Until just recently, the company reported no inventory at all. Its largest single asset is $101 billion of marketable securities. The company has 119,000 employees. For the year ended on that date, Google reports $162 billion in revenues and $72 billion in "Cost of revenues," which consist, according to the notes to the financial statements, of:

- "[Traffic acquisition costs] which are the amounts paid to Google Network Members primarily for ads displayed on their properties and amounts paid to our distribution partners who make available our search access points and services. Our distribution partners include browser providers, mobile carriers, original equipment manufacturers, and software developers.
- Content acquisition costs primarily related to payments to content providers from whom we license video and other content for distribution on YouTube and Google Play (we pay fees to these content providers based on revenues generated or a flat fee);
- Expenses associated with our data centers and other operations (including bandwidth, compensation expense (including SBC), depreciation, energy, and other equipment costs); and
- Inventory related costs for hardware we sell."

* * *

Problem 5-6

Midtown Steel Finishing Co. produces rolled and finished steel products. Its records for the month of March include the following costs for each item of its inventory.

	Raw Materials	Work-in-Process	Finished Goods
Inventory 3/1	$100,000	$100,000	$100,000
Direct purchases	200,000	200,000	200,000
Labor costs		1,000,000	100,000
Other allocated costs	50,000	500,000	50,000
Inventory 3/31	$100,000	$100,000	$50,000

Calculate Midtown's Cost of Sales for the month of March. Use the periodic inventory method and the ending inventory values given.

* * *

B. Long-Lived Assets

Leaving the universe of costs matched with revenues, we turn to the others. Concepts Statement No. 5, summarized at the beginning of this Chapter, provides for two other ways to allocate costs: when expenditures are made, or by systematic allocation to future periods. Thus, the question arises upon an expenditure, if it should all be "expensed" in this accounting period or allocated to future periods (usually referred to as "capitalized").

General rule. GAAP generally requires that an amount spent be "capitalized" if it will provide some "future economic benefit" beyond the current accounting period. That benefit should be spread over future periods "until the underlying the asset is partly or wholly used or lost."[11]

We consider first the factors which help determine whether an amount should be capitalized or expensed. Second, if the amount is capitalized, we consider the various ways the amount can be allocated to future periods.

1. The Decision to Defer

In Re Chambers Development Securities Litigation

United States District Court, Western District of Pennsylvania, 1994
848 F. Supp. 602

LEE, District Judge.

Before the Court are multiple motions to dismiss plaintiffs' Amended Consolidated Class Action Complaint (Document No. 44) (the "Amended Complaint") for various reasons, including plaintiffs' purported failure to state a claim upon which relief can be granted, pursuant to Fed.R.Civ.P. 12(b)(6)....

After consideration of the various motions and responses, the memoranda in support and in opposition and the oral presentations of counsel, these motions to dismiss will be denied.

....

The Defendant

Chambers, a Delaware corporation having its principal executive offices in Pittsburgh, Pennsylvania, is in the business of solid waste management and provides services to its commercial, residential and business customers for the collection, hauling and disposal of solid waste. Chambers also engineers, constructs, manages and operates solid waste sanitary landfills and, through a subsidiary, provides security and investigative services.

Chambers is sued as primary violator of section 10(b) of the Exchange Act, and SEC Rule 10b-5 and as an issuer under section 11 of the Securities Act, as to three

11. Statement of Financial Accounting Concepts No. 6, *Elements of Financial Statements*, ¶ 141 (1985).

public securities offerings accompanied by Registration Statements and Prospectae, namely: the "1989 Debenture Offering," the $110,000,000.00 Convertible Debenture Offering of September 21, 1989; the "1989 Stock Offering" of 2,850,000 shares of Chambers' Class A common stock at $25.00 per share, dated April 19, 1989; and the "1991 Stock Offering" of 6,100,000 shares of Chambers Class A common stock at $24.875 per share, dated June 13, 1991.

....

The Allegedly Improper Accounting Policy and Practices

Plaintiffs claim Chambers' management "cooked" their books from at least 1985 through 1992.... The chief offending accounting policy, capitalizing millions of dollars of indirect expenses of landfill development as assets instead of as operating expenses charged against income in the year incurred, is said to be unique and completely inappropriate to the landfill/solid waste disposal industry and to have artificially enhanced Chambers' financial picture, and the market value of its securities. These indirect expenses included executive salaries, portions of general overhead and public relations costs. Several other accounting practices are also challenged as being well outside the acceptable norms of the accounting profession, including the failure to treat as expenses substantial amounts of interest expense when Chambers restated its 1991 financial statements on March 17, 1992, and duplicating (double counting) deferrals and capitalizations of certain landfill development costs for several years, both of which practices further overstated earnings and inflated net worth.

....

In letters to shareholders attached to annual and quarterly reports and in other public announcements during the class period, J. Rangos, Sr. [Chambers' CEO], allegedly touted the substantial financial achievements of Chambers and its status as "one of the fastest growing solid waste companies in America," and raved about Chambers' "record" sales and profits, "substantial financial growth," and rosy predictions about the "outstanding results" and "significant growth" expected in the coming years.

Plaintiffs allege the Chambers defendants knew or recklessly disregarded that its unique accounting policy regarding capitalization of indirect landfill development expenses and other accounting practices and policies violated GAAP.... Furthermore, capitalization of such indirect costs to landfill and other developmental activities was not supported by contemporaneous time sheets or other supporting material, as required by GAAP, and the amount of capitalized interest which was based on the amount of capitalized costs was excessive under GAAP.

Plaintiffs identify the GAAP violations with references to specific Accounting Principles Board Statements and Financial Accounting Standards Board Statements. One of the major GAAP transgressions claimed is the failure of Chambers ... to disclose that the unique accounting policy regarding landfill expense capitalization, even if arguably proper, was adopted and applied, even though

> the virtually universal industry practice was to expense and not to capitalize such indirect costs. Consequently, capitalizing such costs *without disclosing*

> *such accounting practice confused and deceived the investing public.* Among other things, that nondisclosure was materially misleading with respect to the profitability of Chambers compared with its major competitors. The failure to disclose that Chambers had adopted such an accounting policy violated Opinion No. 22 of the Accounting Principles Board, "Disclosure of Accounting Policies." APB No. 22 states that "a description of all significant accounting policies of the reporting entity should be included as an integral part of the financial statements." It further states:
>
> Disclosure of accounting policies should identify and describe the accounting principles followed by the reporting entity and the methods of applying those principles that materially affect the determination of the financial position, changes in financial position, or results of operations. In general, the *disclosure should encompass important judgments as to appropriateness of principles relating to recognition of revenue and allocation of asset costs to current and future periods....*

Amended Complaint, § 137(f) (emphasis added).

Disclosure should include "existing acceptable alternatives," the principles and methods "peculiar to the industry even if such principles and methods are predominantly followed in that industry," and any "unusual or innovative applications" of GAAP. *Id.*

....

St. Patrick's Day 1992 and its Aftermath

On March 17, 1992, Chambers publicly announced "it revised its 1991 after-tax earnings downward to $1.6 million (or 3 cents per share) from the previously reported after-tax earnings for 1991 of $49.9 million (or 83 cents per share)." Plaintiffs suggest this announcement resulted from the refusal of the new team of ... auditors ... "to sign off on Chambers' 1991 financial statements." This revision was made to properly record the indirect landfill development expenses as costs rather than capitalizing them, and included a charge to 1991 earnings to reflect the effect on reported earnings from 1985 forward. Chambers, however, stated that it was adopting the change in its accounting practices "to recognize ever increasing operational aspects of its business ... [and that] because of its growth, identification and allocation of these indirect expenses had become increasingly complex."

Following this announcement, the bottom fell out of the market for Chambers' Class A common stock, the price of which dropped from $30 1/2 on March 17, to a closing price of $11 1/2 per share on March 18, 1992. On April 13, 1992, Chambers issued another press release stating that its revised 1991 earnings reported on March 17, 1992 ($.03 per share) had been overstated and Chambers no longer believed that its 1991 earnings would "be as much as the $.03 per share previously announced." Eventually, Chambers' "accounting adjustments" as of October 1992 necessitated a $362 million charge against its accumulated earnings for 1991 and prior years.

....

The Chambers Defendants frame their arguments to dismiss around the "spin" they place on the Amended Complaint, characterizing plaintiffs' claims as little more than a disagreement over the choice made between reasonable accounting practices. These defendants state plaintiffs' "fraud claims are based on nothing more than the allegation that Chambers restated its 1989 and 1990 financial statements and that its ... results for year-end December 1991 are materially different than indicated in prior announcements," which does not support an allegation of scienter sufficient to state a claim of fraud. Chambers Defendants' Memorandum of Law, at 1–2. This is an extraordinarily constricted reading of a complaint which asserts much more than a decision to make "accounting adjustments" of some $362 million and includes the requisite allegations that these defendants knowingly or recklessly engaged in a deceptive accounting practice that was designed, maintained and concealed in order to artificially enhance Chambers' profits, its financial picture and financial projections, especially in comparison to those of its competitors, none of whom followed this unique and undisclosed accounting method.

While a [fraud] claim is not made out where a representor merely changes its mind or its accounting practice, or where a plaintiff merely alleges corporate mismanagement in the accuracy of accounting practices, plaintiffs have alleged that these defendants had actual knowledge or recklessly disregarded the truth that Chambers' accounting practices were improper, inflated earnings and net worth over several years, violated GAAP and were unique to the industry, from the inception of each defendants' participation in the deceptive scheme, and made material misrepresentations or omissions regarding Chambers' accounting practices, its yearly earnings and its net worth and its future financial projections in financial statements, SEC filings and public announcements upon which plaintiffs relied. The thrust of plaintiffs' section 10(b) claim is that these defendants deliberately or recklessly hid expenses in order to artificially enhance the market value of Chambers' securities.

The Amended Complaint quite plainly alleges the requisite scienter as to material misrepresentations in Chambers' financial projections made without a genuine belief or reasonable basis, and as to material misrepresentations and omissions made in financial statements and SEC filings with regard to auditing and accounting practices. *See Bradford-White Corp. v. Ernst & Whinney*, 872 F.2d 1153 (3d Cir.) *cert. denied*, 493 U.S. 993, 110 S.Ct. 542, 107 L.Ed.2d 539 (1989) (upholding jury finding that auditor who claimed to comply with GAAS but did not was liable under section 10(b)) *cited in [In re] Westinghouse Sec. Litig.*, 832 F.Supp. at 971 (Westinghouse defendants' argument that plaintiffs were "merely quibbling over one of at least two proper methods of establishing loan loss reserves ... under GAAP ... loses some force under the combined weight of standards promulgated by the American Institute of Certified Public Accountants and ... *Bradford-White Corp.*... and would be a matter more properly raised on a motion for summary judgment").... The motion to dismiss under Rule 12(b)(6) for failure to plead scienter must fail.

The Chambers Defendants vigorously argue the Amended Complaint necessarily *contradicts* an inference of scienter, given the "technical nature of the various accounting standards Chambers supposedly violated, coupled with the consistent string of unqualified audit opinions from a major accounting firm [Grant Thornton]." Memorandum of Law at 19. It is obvious however, that these defendants' *lack* of scienter is not "the only inference that can be drawn from the Complaint," as they suggest, *id.*, although it *may* be *one* of the permissible inferences that are plausible. Equally plausible is the inference that the Chambers Defendants acted ... to hide expenses and inflate net worth by "creative" accounting practices. In light of the Rule 12(b)(6) standards for determining whether a complaint has stated a claim, the "inherent contradiction" argument is without merit, although the Chambers Defendants are entitled to put this argument to a jury.

....

WORLDCOM

The Saga of WorldCom, Inc.

Perhaps the most famous of all decisions to defer is that made by WorldCom, Inc. As described in one opinion from the many court cases which resulted from the company's bankruptcy in 2002, the company deferred almost $4 *billion* in costs:

> With a decline in its revenue, and further prompted by the failure of its attempt to acquire Sprint, WorldCom began a new accounting fraud, no later than 2000, in connection with its single largest operating expense: line costs. WorldCom had entered into long-term lease agreements with other telecommunications companies for the use of their networks. Pursuant to these leases, WorldCom was obligated to make fixed monthly payments for the use of the networks, or lines, regardless of whether WorldCom or its customers in fact used the leased lines. When demand did not grow as WorldCom had hoped, the company found itself with substantial fixed line costs for networks that were not generating any income.
>
> Under GAAP, line costs must be reported as an expense. In October 2000, and without any justification in fact or under GAAP, [WorldCom management] instructed ... WorldCom's accounting department [staff] to make journal entries crediting WorldCom's line cost expense accounts, and instructed [them] to make corresponding reductions in various reserve accounts so that the general ledger would balance.

> In 2001, WorldCom changed its method for disguising the impact of line costs on its revenues. [Management] directed that line costs simply be reclassified as capital expenditures that could be depreciated over time. The effect of the reclassification was to inflate WorldCom's reported earnings.
>
> ....
>
> On June 25, 2002, WorldCom announced that it had improperly treated more than $3.8 billion in ordinary costs as capital expenditures in violation of generally accepted accounting principles ("GAAP") and would have to restate its publicly-reported financial results for 2001 and the first quarter of 2002. WorldCom later announced that its reported earnings for 1999 through the first quarter of 2002 had been affected by manipulation of various reserves and had overstated earnings by $3.3 billion. WorldCom also announced that it would likely write off goodwill of $50 billion. The impact of those disclosures on the price of WorldCom shares and the value of its notes was catastrophic. Its common stock dropped from a high of $65 per share to pennies.

In re WorldCom, Inc. Securities Litigation, 294 F. Supp. 2d 392, 400–01 (S.D.N.Y. 2003).

* * *

Problem 5-7

With the benefit of perfect hindsight, would you recommend that Chambers have disclosed the following facts in its financial statements? If so, draft appropriate language to be added to the financial statement notes. If not, defend your refusal to require disclosure.

(1) The dollar amount of deferred landfill costs

(2) What those deferred costs were (acquisition, development, salaries, advertising)

(3) Nobody else in the industry does this

(4) The dollar effect on net income if the deferred costs were treated as an expense.

Problem 5-8

American Biscuit Company (ABC) is taking a calculated risk, and they want your input. ABC has developed a new line of sustainably-harvested, free-range, snack products packaged in biodegradable containers, to be known as "American Naturals." Significant investments have been required in the production lines for these new products, so that they may be certified as meeting the requirements for these package designations, and in development of new packaging and branding for the product line.

These types of snacks have not been marketed by any major national snack product company, but ABC's own research and management savvy suggest that they could be a huge success. ABC management candidly notes that the products could be a huge flop as well. ABC's past experience with new products shows generally a 75% success rate, although results have varied widely among products and over time.

ABC has had an otherwise dismal year, reporting a large net loss for the first time in 25 years. ABC's management believes that, since "American Naturals" is untested and its value unproven, it would be appropriate to expense the entire production, packaging set-up and brand costs this year. Coincidentally, you note, this would simply add more bad news to a terrible year, and would free up earnings in future years if the product line turns out to be a success.

Has ABC's management devised an acceptable method of cost allocation, or is it manipulating the company's financial records?

* * *

2. Allocation to Future Periods

Assuming that we've resolved the question of whether to capitalize certain costs and spread them over future periods, the question arises: How do we do that? GAAP requires a "systematic and rational" method of allocation. The methods and terminology used vary with the type of asset whose cost is being allocated to future periods.

a. Fixed Assets—Depreciation

The most common use of systematic allocation is depreciation: allocating the costs of fixed assets designed to be used for several years over those years. This can be a significant bookkeeping issue, but conceptually depreciation is very simple: we need know only three things about the asset in order to determine the depreciation expense:

(1) the total cost to be allocated;

(2) the number of years over which the cost is to be allocated; and

(3) the method of allocation to be used.

The total cost includes all the direct or related costs of purchase, transportation, installation and improvement, but not repairs. In addition, the asset's "salvage value" at the end of its useful life is not depreciated. The number of years—the asset's "useful life"—depends of course on the durability of the asset and the technology in the trade or industry. The method of allocation to be used can be either "straight line"—the total cost divided by the number of years of life, charged equally in each year—

or one of a variety of "accelerated" methods, which allocate a greater portion of the expense to the earlier years of the asset's useful life.[12]

Illustration

George's Hardware Store has furniture and store fixtures which he uses in his business. Suppose the furniture and fixtures cost George $20,000 when new, and he has determined they will have a useful life of 5 years and, when used up, a salvage value of $5,000. If George chooses to depreciate his furniture using the "straight line" method, each year he would recognize an expense by journaling as follows:

Dr Depreciation expense (X)	3,000	
Cr Furniture and fixtures (A)		3,000

To recognize one year's depreciation on the furniture.

And at the end of the first year, the balance sheet for George's Hardware Store would reflect this change as follows:

Furniture and fixtures (less accumulated depreciation of 3,000)	17,000

Alternatively, the assets could be carried always at historical cost, and the accumulated depreciation carried in a separate account titled "accumulated depreciation" as follows:

Furniture and fixtures, at cost		20,000
Accumulated depreciation	(3,000)	17,000

Either method is acceptable so long as the total of accumulated depreciation is displayed and the historical cost can be calculated if not separately displayed. In using the second method, we refer to the "Accumulated depreciation" account as a ***contra-asset*** account. It is titled "contra" because it will have the opposite balance of the account it accompanies. It follows the asset account around as its shadow, displayed with it in each case. If the contra-asset account is used, George's first journal entry would be as follows.

Dr Depreciation expense (X)	3,000	
Cr Furniture and fixtures: Accumulated depreciation (C-A)		3,000

To recognize one year's depreciation on the furniture.

If George chooses to use a different method of depreciation, he can choose from several types of ***accelerated depreciation***, which will allocate a larger portion of

---

12. *See generally* ASC ¶¶ 360-10-35-2 to -10.

the depreciation expense to the earlier years of the asset's useful life. This may be appropriate "if the expected productivity … of the asset is relatively greater during the earlier years of its life, or maintenance charges tend to increase during later years."[13]

Example

Ford Motor Co. reports on its December 31, 2018 balance sheet $25.7 billion in "Net property." We learn in the notes to the financial statements that this amount is comprised of property with a $56.7 billion historical cost and $31 billion of accumulated depreciation. Ford also discloses generally its depreciation policies:

> *Net property is reported at cost, net of accumulated depreciation, which includes impairments. We capitalize new assets when we expect to use the asset for more than one year. Routine maintenance and repair costs are expensed when incurred.*
>
> *Property and equipment are depreciated primarily using the straight-line method over the estimated useful life of the asset. Useful lives range from 3 years to 36 years. The estimated useful lives generally are 14.5 years for machinery and equipment, 8 years for software, 30 years for land improvements, and 36 years for buildings....*

b. Intangible Assets—Amortization

Intangible assets are copyrights, patents, trademarks, licenses, customer lists, and other separate identifiable items that have value even without a physical existence.

Notice even that the deferred costs we just finished studying could be considered as one specific type of intangible asset. If we have some costs that can be deferred and spread over future periods, then we have created a type of intangible asset. It is an ***asset***: something for which cash or some other asset was exchanged, and it will have value over future accounting periods. But it is ***intangible***: not a physical asset. The allocation of value in the case of intangible assets is known as amortization. In addition, amortization can be used for physical assets without meaningful limited useful lives.

13. ASC ¶ 360-10-35-7.

Examples

Ford Motor Co. also reports in its Dec. 31, 2019, balance sheet $10.8 million in "Tooling, net of amortization." Tooling (molds, dies, specific assembly and fabrication items) is a physical asset, but its useful life is not limited so much by the physical life of the tooling as the utility of what is produced by the tooling. Ford discloses that "[t]ooling generally is amortized over the expected life of a product program using a straight-line method."

Alphabet, Inc. (Google's parent company) reports on its Dec. 31, 2019, balance sheet intangible assets consisting of (1) patents and other developed technologies, (2) customer relationships and (3) trade names and other intangible assets. These have a total historical cost of $5.9 billion and accumulated amortization of $3.9 billion. Alphabet discloses that "[p]atents and developed technology, customer relationships, and trade names and other have weighted-average remaining useful lives of 2.3 years, 5.6 years, and 3.0 years, respectively."

Before deciding what the "useful life" of an intangible asset is, we must first decide if it has a limited life at all. Because intangible assets are not physical, their lives are not inherently limited.

> If no legal, regulatory, contractual, competitive, economic, or other factors limit the useful life of an intangible asset to a reporting entity, the useful life of the asset shall be considered to be indefinite. The term *indefinite* does not mean the same as infinite or indeterminate. The useful life of an intangible asset is indefinite if that life extends beyond the foreseeable horizon—that is, there is no foreseeable limit on the period of time over which it is expected to contribute to the cash flows of the reporting entity. Such intangible assets might be airport route authorities, certain trademarks, and taxicab medallions.[14]

An intangible asset with an indefinite useful life is not subject to any amortization. However, it is evaluated "each reporting period to determine whether events and circumstances continue to support an indefinite useful life."[15]

If an intangible asset does not have an indefinite useful life, the length of its finite useful life is determined by the following factors:

- expected use;
- expected useful life of related assets

14. ASC ¶ 350-30-35-4.

15. ASC ¶ 350-30-35-16. Conversely, an intangible asset with a limited useful life may find itself "immortalized," that is, with an indefinite useful life, at which time amortization should cease. *Id.* ¶ 350-30-35-10.

- legal, regulatory or contractual provisions
- the entity's historical experience in renewing or extending similar arrangements, consistent with the intended use of the asset
- effects of obsolescence, demand, competition, and other economic factors (such as the stability of the industry, known technological advances, or legislation)
- required maintenance expenditures (high expenditures may suggest a very limited useful life).[16]

Amortization is ordinarily done on a straight-line basis, unless some other method is obviously more useful.[17] Intangible assets must also be tested regularly to see if the assumptions underlying their values and useful lives remain accurate. If the useful life is changed, the remaining carrying value is spread over the new remaining useful life.[18] If the value is reduced without a change in the useful life, the reduction is taken as a current period expense and the remaining carrying amount is reduced accordingly.[19]

c. Oil, Gas and Minerals — Depletion

Land ordinarily cannot be depreciated. Presumably, this is because it never loses its value over time because of being consumed. It may lose or gain value based on market conditions, but that's another matter.[20] If however, the land *is* consumed — as is the case with things taken out of it — we need to allocate the costs of acquisition over future periods as the land is used up. This special type of cost allocation is called "depletion." Accounting in the oil and gas industry raises other significant issues of cost allocation, which are beyond our introductory study here. But we can understand the broad outlines of the accounting and disclosure.

Example

Consider the following disclosures provided by ExxonMobil in its 2018 Annual Report, in excerpts from the note to the financial statements in which the company describes its general accounting policies for its $247 billion of property, plant and equipment.

16. ASC ¶ 350-30-35-3.

17. For example, if a company buys for $1 million the right to put a valuable trademark or brand name on products it sells for the next five years, a charge of $200,000 each year might be appropriate. But if the right is limited to 100,000 units of product, charges based on $10 per unit might be more appropriate.

18. ASC ¶ 350-30-35-9.

19. This is called testing for "impairment" of the asset and is discussed in Part C(2) below.

20. This would be a good place to review your knowledge of GAAP's general rules here. The land, if it has appreciated in value, cannot be "written up" unless sold in a transaction meeting the requirements for recognition of revenue in Chapter 4 (recall the *Herzfeld* case). Notwithstanding that rule, the land must be "written down" and a current period expense recognized if it meets the impairment requirements discussed below.

Property, Plant and Equipment

Cost Basis. *The Corporation uses the "successful efforts" method to account for its exploration and production activities. Under this method, costs are accumulated on a field-by-field basis. Costs incurred to purchase, lease, or otherwise acquire a property (whether unproved or proved) are capitalized when incurred. Exploratory well costs are carried as an asset when the well has found a sufficient quantity of reserves to justify its completion as a producing well and where the Corporation is making sufficient progress assessing the reserves and the economic and operating viability of the project. Exploratory well costs not meeting these criteria are charged to expense. Other exploratory expenditures, including geophysical costs and annual lease rentals, are expensed as incurred. Development costs, including costs of productive wells and development dry holes, are capitalized.*

Depreciation, Depletion and Amortization. *Depreciation, depletion and amortization are primarily determined under either the unit-of-production method or the straight-line method, which is based on estimated asset service life taking obsolescence into consideration.*

Acquisition costs of proved properties are amortized using a unit-of-production method, computed on the basis of total proved oil and gas reserves. Capitalized exploratory drilling and development costs associated with productive depletable extractive properties are amortized using the unit-of-production rates based on the amount of proved developed reserves of oil and gas that are estimated to be recoverable from existing facilities using current operating methods. Under the unit-of-production method, oil and gas volumes are considered produced once they have been measured through meters at custody transfer or sales transaction points at the outlet valve on the lease or field storage tank. The straight-line method is used in limited situations where the expected life of the asset does not reasonably correlate with that of the underlying reserves. For example, certain assets used in the production of oil and natural gas have a shorter life than the reserves, and as such, the Corporation uses straight-line depreciation to ensure the asset is fully depreciated by the end of its useful life....

Investments in refinery, chemical process, and ... manufacturing equipment are generally depreciated on a straight-line basis over a 25-year life. Service station buildings and fixed improvements generally are depreciated over a 20-year life. Maintenance and repairs, including planned major maintenance, are expensed as incurred. Major renewals and improvements are capitalized and the assets replaced are retired.

Questions

1. The first paragraph of this disclosure outlines ExxonMobil's policies regarding deferral versus capitalization. How does it compare with what was done in *Chambers*?

2. ExxonMobil has purchased a drilling and capping machine for an oil field. It has an estimated useful life of 10 years. The fields are forecasted to be produce oil for 20 years. Would ExxonMobil use the units-of-production method or straight-line method for this machine?

3. Under the units-of-production method, when does ExxonMobil recognize a barrel of oil as "produced" so that its associated costs should be recognized?

3. Contract Assets

When we learned the rules for revenue recognition in Chapter 4, we found that sometimes the result is that a business activity does not result in recognition of revenue. When that happens, we know that receipts which would otherwise be recorded as revenue must instead be recorded as liabilities, and expenditures which would normally be considered costs of sales must remain as assets. This could be inventory (as in the first part of the chapter), a fixed asset, as was attempted in *Chambers Development*, or some other bundle of incurred costs known as a "contract asset."

Illustration

Wanda is creating a large, expensive widget for a customer. It will require two years to complete and produce. It does not meet the ASC 606 standards for revenue recognition this year. If she had spent $1000 creating the widget so far, she would journal:

	Dr	Cr
Dr Contract Asset	1,000	
Cr Cash (or other assets)		1,000

To recognize costs incurred in widget production before sale is completed.

Example

Verizon Communications, Inc. delivers contracted services to its customers over time in a bundle of goods and services. Maybe you're familiar with this process as a cell phone customer. Under ASC 606, this creates complicated revenue-recognition decisions. Verizon reports about $1.1 billion in "contract assets" in its December 31, 2019 financial statements and provides the following description:

> *Contract assets primarily relate to our rights to consideration for goods or services provided to customers but for which we do not have an unconditional right at the reporting date. Under a fixed-term plan, total*

> *contract revenue is allocated between wireless service and equipment revenues.... In conjunction with these arrangements, a contract asset is created, which represents the difference between the amount of equipment revenue recognized upon sale and the amount of consideration received from the customer when the performance obligation related to the transfer of control of the equipment is satisfied. The contract asset is reclassified to accounts receivable as wireless services are provided and billed. We have the right to bill the customer as service is provided over time, which results in our right to the payment being unconditional. The contract asset balances are presented in our consolidated balance sheet as Prepaid expenses and other and Other assets. We assess our contract assets for impairment on a quarterly basis and will recognize an impairment charge to the extent their carrying amount is not recoverable.*

GAAP provides that costs may be capitalized (presented as an asset rather than an expense) if they were incurred to ***obtain*** a contract and the costs (i) would not have been incurred if the contract were not obtained, and (ii) are expected to be recovered.[21] Costs to ***fulfill*** a contract may be capitalized if: (i) the costs involve performance under the contract, (ii) the costs create additional resources for the company to use in the future, and (iii) the costs are expected to be recovered.[22] Contract fulfillment costs which may be capitalized include payments for labor or materials used in providing the contract services to the customer.[23] Contract fulfillment costs which should be expensed when incurred include general administrative costs (unless the customer has agreed to pay them) or costs related to contracts whose revenues have already been recognized.[24]

* * *

Problem 5-9[25]

Continental Software, Inc. (CSI) is finalizing a contract to manage the website and data center for the Metropolitan Public Library System in the city of Metropolis. It will be a four-year contract, under which CSI will earn a base rate plus additional fees depending on the level of usage and service. CSI estimates it will incur the following costs if the contract is signed.

- A sales commission of $10,000, included in the contract price
- $120,000 for an internal "interface" between CSI's equipment and the Library's computers. This belongs to CSI but would be used to deliver the contract services.

21. ASC 340-40-25-1.
22. ASC 340-40-25-5.
23. ASC 340-40-25-7.
24. ASC 340-40-25-8.
25. Adapted from ASC 340-40-55-5 to -9.

- $180,000 for additional hardware and software, which belongs to CSI and may be used for other purposes both during and after the Library contract.

CSI would like to know if any of these expenses will create new assets for CSI rather than being current expenses. What is your advice?

* * *

C. Impairment

Regardless of which of the three expense-recognition rules we follow—matching, allocation, or current recognition—GAAP has a rule overarching each of these options requiring recognition of an expense regardless of the above timing rules. If "it becomes evident that previously recognized future economic benefits of an asset have been reduced or eliminated," then an expense must be recognized at that time, *regardless* of the presence or absence of any related revenue or other benefit.[26]

Illustration

A patent becomes useless due to the invention of a new product. The remaining book value of that patent must be recognized in the year it becomes worthless, despite the fact it still had a remaining "legal life" of many years. If an existing asset is impaired, we would journal as follows:

Dr Patent Obsolescence Expense (X)	100	
Cr Patent (A)		100
To retire obsolete patent.		

The rules about asset impairment are simply specific applications of the general impairment rule quoted at the beginning of this section. The particulars vary by the type of asset involved. We discuss below each type of asset for which impairment is a common issue.

1. Inventory

Inventory valuation follows the "lower of cost or market" rule. If the value of inventory is lower than its cost (calculated under whatever method—FIFO, LIFO, etc.—is appropriate), then the value of the inventory must be reduced and that re-

26. Statement of Financial Accounting Concepts No. 5, *Recognition and Measurement in Financial Statements of Business Enterprises* ¶ 87 (Dec. 1984).

duction shown as a current expense.[27] "Value" for purposes of this rule is defined differently for different methods.[28]

Illustration

Suppose Wanda has purchased 20 widgets for $10 each, planning to sell them for $12 each at the next flea market. However, a glut of cheap imported widgets has depressed the current price to $9 each. Even before Wanda sells any of the widgets, she should recognize an expense as follows:

Dr Inventory obsolescence (X)	20	
Cr Widget inventory (A)		
-or-		
Cr Inventory valuation (C-A)		20

To recognize reduction in market value of widgets below cost.

Because this is a current-period expense, an entity should compare its carrying value for its inventory at least once each accounting period.[29] It is an expense in the current period because the decline in value happens then, even though the sale will occur later. If a valuation contra-account is used, it should be closed when the inventory is sold, as with the Accumulated Depreciation illustration, p. 167.

Example

Xerox Corp. reports $576 million of finished goods inventory on its Dec. 31, 2019, balance sheet and added the following disclosures about its Inventory accounting.

> *Inventories are carried at the lower of average cost or net realizable value. Inventories also include equipment that is returned at the end of the lease term. Returned equipment is recorded at the lower of remaining net book value or salvage value, which is normally not significant. We regularly review inventory quantities and record a provision for excess and/or ob-*

27. ASC ¶ 330-10-35-1B to -2.

28. ASC ¶¶ 330-10-35-1B and 1C. The general rule is that "value" means "net realizable value," which is the expected sale price reduced by costs of completion. But for LIFO and retail-method users, "value" means "market" (replacement) value. The separate rule for these two methods, according to the FASB, is because retail-method entities already approximate "realizable value" in that valuation process, and because LIFO entities already have lower cost items in inventory (assuming prices are rising generally). *See* Accounting Standards Update No. 2015-11, ¶¶ BC6–BC7.

29. ASC ¶ 330-10-35-9 ("The purpose of reducing inventory to market [value] is to reflect fairly the income of the period.").

solete inventory based primarily on our estimated forecast of product demand, production requirements and servicing commitments. Several factors may influence the realizability of our inventories, including our decision to exit a product line, technological changes and new product development. The provision for excess and/or obsolete raw materials and equipment inventories is based primarily on near term forecasts of product demand and include consideration of new product introductions, as well as changes in remanufacturing strategies. The provision for excess and/ or obsolete service parts inventory is based primarily on projected servicing requirements over the life of the related equipment populations.

In the Matter of Arthur Andersen & Co.

Securities and Exchange Commission, 1981
47 S.E.C. 565

[For background on this case, refer to pp. 122–23.]

IV. INVENTORY OBSOLESCENCE

A. Mattel's Practice

Mattel understated its provision for inventory obsolescence by approximately $4 million for fiscal 1971 and approximately $800,000 for fiscal 1972. Mattel calculated its inventory obsolescence through essentially a two step procedure. First, it determined its "excess inventory"—inventories of finished goods, component parts and raw materials which exceeded forecasted sales or usage. The excess inventory computation flagged those goods and raw materials to which a reserve for obsolescence could be applicable. The lower the excess inventory figure, the lower the starting point for inventory obsolescence.[30] Mattel then determined the appropriate amount of its inventory obsolescence by scheduling those items on which its costs were greater than realizable value and charging the total excess cost over realizable value to inventory obsolescence.

Comparison to GAAP. How does Mattel's or Xerox's "excess inventory" estimation square with GAAP's "lower of cost or value" rule?

Some understanding of the toy business is prerequisite to assessing how realistic a particular sales forecast might be. The toy industry is extremely competitive and the market highly volatile.[31] At best, the sales life of a successful toy

30. Forecasts were critically important in this process. The higher the forecast, the lower the excess inventory. Ordinarily a computer generated inventory-versus-requirements report, known as a "CIM" Report, compared inventory with sales forecasts and usage and was used for this purpose.

31. The reliability of forecasting in the toy industry is influenced by the competitiveness and volatility of that industry.

may be only a few years. Major business risks are involved in attempting to anticipate, months in advance, the market for toys in general and how well particular toys will sell. Guessing too low on the production of a toy can mean unfilled orders and lost sales; guessing too high, excess finished goods and component parts.

In 1969, Mattel had restructured its toy section into four separate divisions—wheels, toys, dolls, and games—in a manner which tended to foster over-enthusiastic sales forecasts and unrealistic quotas. Each new division had to compete for top management's support on the basis of its sales quotas, which in turn were based upon its sales forecasts. The higher its sales forecast, the more impressive the division would appear and the higher its quota would be. Unrealistic quotas contributed to the creation of excess inventory.

To make matters worse, Mattel had guessed too high on "hot wheels" and, as described above, was already offering its customers an "inventory relief" program. Top management's approach to the problem of Mattel's excess inventory was first to not recognize it and then to try to hide it in order that it not interfere with Mattel's predetermined structured growth rate.

Mattel had set a $700,000 target for inventory obsolescence for 1971. However, the initial run of its CIM Report for 1971 showed excess inventory of approximately $21 million, a figure which would have made highly unrealistic only $700,000 of obsolescence. Through successive "adjustments" Mattel reduced its 1971 excess inventory figure from $21 million to approximately $4.6 million and booked $700,000 for inventory obsolescence. Similarly, for 1972, Mattel reduced its excess inventory of approximately $13.4 million to approximately $3.8 million and booked $850,000 for inventory obsolescence. After adjustments, "excess" inventories reflected on the final CIM Report were transferred to manually prepared obsolescence schedules, an item-by-item estimate was made of net realizable values and inventory obsolescence was determined.

Mattel was able to reduce its excess inventory by arbitrarily increasing its sales forecasts to the point where they were greater than quantities shown in Mattel's weekly sales analyses[32] for approximately 800 toys or 40 percent of its finished toys in fiscal 1971 and approximately 370 toys or 30 percent of its finished toys in fiscal 1972.

Mattel represented that much of its finished toys could be sold in close-outs at a reduced price, but still at some profit. It also included anticipated close-outs, at greatly reduced selling prices, as forecasted sales to be made at regular prices. For example, during the latter part of 1971 (fiscal 1972), a major oil company proposed to purchase approximately 16 million hot wheel units at a close-out price which was about $1.6

---

32. Mattel's sales analyses, which were updated weekly, contained cumulative sales information by product from the beginning of each calendar year as well as current estimates of future sales for each product.

million below Mattel's standard cost. Instead of increasing obsolescence by $1.6 million to reflect the realizable value of this inventory, Mattel entered the proposed close-out as a forecasted sale and it was not even included in excess inventory. In addition, 5.6 million hot wheel cars carried at approximately $1.2 million were sold to the oil company for about $700,000 and shipped in January, 1972, the last month of the fiscal year. Mattel recorded the items as inventory in fiscal 1972 and did not record the loss until fiscal 1973.[33]

Mattel further reduced its excess inventory by finding, without justification, that component parts of certain obsolete finished goods were interchangeable with component parts of toys in current production. In many instances, requirements for such component parts already had been entered on the CIM Report, but without any reference to a finished goods product as normally would have been appropriate.

Despite the large inventory relief program already aimed at customers with too many hot wheels on hand after Christmas 1970, a large part of Mattel's inventory was eliminated from the excess category simply by representing to AA & Co. that it would be able to sell 1.5 million units of each "hot wheels" model in the year of introduction and 50,000 to 100,000 units per year per model thereafter.

* * *

Problem 5-10

National Shoe, Inc. (NSI) had $250 million in inventory at the beginning of the most recent fiscal year. At the end of the year, the inventory value has increased to $400 million. Management determined to leave its reserve for obsolescence unchanged at $150,000. The company's inventory previous policy required writing off inventory if it meets any one of the following three requirements: (1) shoe styles and types with only four pairs or less, (2) shoes and apparel selling for less than cost, and (3) items that had not been sold in the previous twelve months.

This year, management determined to omit the third requirement, and as a result, leave the reserve for obsolescence unchanged. Is this change in accord with GAAP?

2. Receivables

When an entity makes a sale without receipt of cash, it recognizes an "account receivable" as a current asset. In addition, should an entity such as a bank lend money it will record the loan as a separate asset.[34] A sad fact of life is that some receivables or loans will not be collected. Of course, if the business knew at the

---

33. These maneuvers caused the Mattel, Inc. Vice-President who normally explained Mattel's inventory to AA & Co. [Mattel's auditors] to refuse to do so in 1972.

34. As far as the bank is concerned, the loan a customer took out is an *asset* and the deposit the customer made is a *liability*. It is, of course, just the opposite on the bank customer's books.

time of the credit extension that it would not be collectible, the credit would be refused.

The fundamental accounting principle of matching expenses with revenues requires a business to accrue as a current expense the accounts which will, at some point in the future, be uncollectible. The expense must be accrued if it is "expected."[35] In making this decision, a business should look at past and present events and "reasonable and supportable forecasts," including external as well as internal information, but only if it is "reasonably available without undue cost and effort."[36]

Illustration

Wanda has been selling widgets for years now. She allows her customers to buy widgets on 60-days' same-as-cash store credit. Over the years, Wanda has kept careful records and knows that, on the average, 10% of the amount charged on credit will not be collected. If she made $1000 in credit sales during the relevant period, she would make the following entry in order to accrue this cost.

	Dr	Cr
Dr Bad debt expense (X)	100	
Cr Allowance for doubtful accounts (C-A)		100

Note that this allowance is another "contra-asset" account like the accumulated depreciation account we met on page 5-23.

Wanda does not know exactly *which* account will be uncollectible. Remember, if she did, she would not have extended credit to that customer in the first place. If she ultimately concludes that John Smith's credit account of $75 is uncollectible, she will go into the Accounts Receivable specific account for Smith and journal as follows.

	Dr	Cr
Dr Allowance for doubtful accounts (C-A)	75	
Cr Accounts Receivable — Smith (A)		75

Notice that this entry does not affect the income statement for the period in which the actual account is "written off."

Over time, of course, there should be more charged to the allowance account than the actual accounts written off, so the allowance account should always have a credit balance.

35. ASC ¶ 326-20-30-1. This is new GAAP effective beginning in 2019. Until then, the rules to be applied are those we study in Chapter 6: the loss must be probable and be capable of reasonable estimation.

36. ASC ¶ 326-20-30-7. This standard is intended to be more inclusive than the old "probable and estimable" standard mentioned in the preceding note. The FASB made the change in light of the financial crises in 2008–09, believing that a lower standard should be applied to recognizing likely losses in financial assets. See Accounting Standards Update 2016-13, ¶ BC7.

Example

Bank of America Corporation reports the following reconciliation of its allowance for loan and lease losses (in millions of dollars). I have simplified it slightly.

Balance, Jan. 1, 2019	**$9,601**
Loans and leases charged off	(3,648)
Provision for loan and lease losses	3,463
Balance, Dec. 31, 2019	**$9,416**

The first entry is the actual write off (or charge off) of loans which actually became worthless, for which estimates were made in previous years. The second entry, provision for loan and lease losses, is the addition to this allowance based on the company's estimate of the new loans written in 2019 which will ultimately prove uncollectible. This provision is an expense on Bank of America's 2019 income statement. (If $9.4 billion of loan losses seems like a lot, keep in mind that the company has about $1 *trillion* of loans outstanding.)

In the cases of both Wanda's Widgets and Bank of America, the company had past reliable experience from which it could forecast the anticipated credit losses from current period extensions of credit. Indeed, an entity must have the ability to make reasonable estimates in order to use this method of cost accrual.[37]

What if the entity does not have such reliable experience? Recall one of the requirements of revenue recognition (from Chapter 4) is that "the entity will collect substantially all of the consideration to which it will be entitled.[38] This means that it is probable that the consideration will be collected when the contract is performed by the entity.[39] Otherwise, the recognition of revenue should be delayed until there is full performance of a distinct portion of the contract.[40]

* * *

Problem 5-11

Second National Bank's loan-loss experiences indicate that 2.75% of its loans outstanding at the end of the year will ultimately prove uncollectible. At the beginning of the year, the balance in the allowance for loan loss account was $1.25 million. At

---

37. See text accompanying note 36. Past reliable experience is not perfect, however. In the previous example, Bank of America's loan write-offs of $3,648 million is a net figure, comprised of $5,646 million of new write-offs and reduced by $1,998 million of amounts recovered which were previously written off.

38. ASC ¶ 606-10-25-1(e); see p. 118.

39. ASC ¶ 606-10-55-3A. "Probable" means "likely to occur." *Id.* ¶ 606-10-20.

40. ASC ¶ 606-10-25-7, see pp. 119–20: the entity must have provided the goods or performed the services, and the consideration is fully paid and nonrefundable.

the end of the year, the bank had $50 million in loans outstanding. What is the amount of expense which the bank must recognize for the year?

Problem 5-12

Bill and Ted have been in business only one month but have determined that ultimate coolness demands that they give their best customers the ability to buy food and beverages on store credit. Because they have no experience in their actual ability to collect on these accounts, how should the first $1000 of credit sales be recorded, if the goods sold cost $850?

* * *

3. Long-Lived Assets

Declines in asset value which are not temporary must be recognized in the period in which the decline occurs. The converse (regarding increases in value) is generally *not* true, except for marketable securities as discussed in Chapter 4(B).

What is "value"? In contrast to inventory valuation, which is done by reference to "market value," long-lived assets are ordinarily measured for impairment by comparing the current carrying value with undiscounted cash flows expected from the use and eventual disposition of the asset.[41] If cash flows cannot be determined, an "expected present value" method can be used.[42] If the carrying value exceeds the expected cash flows or present value, the difference must be recognized as an impairment loss (current-period expense) and the carrying value of the asset reduced accordingly.

Note that impairment exists if the carrying value is less than the *undiscounted* cash flows. This means that we are to treat a dollar received ten years from now the same as a dollar received tomorrow. Does this make sense? We will discuss in greater detail in Chapter 11 why modern finance theory does *not* think this makes sense. The FASB concluded in adopting this approach that it "is consistent with the definition of an impairment as the inability to fully recover the carrying amount of an asset and with a basic presumption underlying a statement of financial position that the reported carrying amounts of assets should, at a minimum, be recoverable."[43]

How are assets valued? Assets are grouped together for this valuation purpose at the smallest group of assets for which identifiable cash flows can be determined.[44]

---

41. ASC ¶ 360-10-35-17.

42. ASC ¶ 360-10-35-36.

43. Statement of Financial Accounting Standards No. 121, *Accounting for the Impairment of Long-Lived Assets and for Long-Lived Assets to be Disposed Of* (March 1995) at ¶ 65.

44. ASC ¶ 360-10-35-23.

When are assets valued? Assets are valued under this method to determine if there is an impairment loss in the following circumstances:

- significant decrease in market price
- significant adverse change in the way an asset is being used, or in the asset's physical condition
- significant adverse change in legal factors or business climate that could affect value, including adverse action or assessment by a regulator
- accumulation of costs significantly in excess of the amount originally expected for the acquisition or construction of the asset
- current-period operating or cash-flow loss, combined with a history of such losses, or a projection or forecast demonstrating continuing losses
- current expectation that, more likely than not, the asset will be sold or disposed of significantly before the end of its previously-estimated useful life.[45]

Example

Wal-Mart Stores, Inc. discloses the following about the valuation of its $105 billion of property, plant, and equipment in its 2019 Annual Report:

> *Long-lived assets are stated at cost. Management reviews long-lived assets for indicators of impairment whenever events or changes in circumstances indicate that the carrying amount may not be recoverable. The evaluation is performed at the lowest level of identifiable cash flows, which is at the individual store or club level. Undiscounted cash flows expected to be generated by the related assets are estimated over the assets' useful lives based on updated projections. If the evaluation indicates that the carrying amount of the assets may not be recoverable, any potential impairment is measured based upon the fair value of the related asset or asset group as determined by an appropriate market appraisal or other valuation technique.*

The same rules generally apply to intangible assets,[46] except that intangible assets with indefinite useful lives[47] are tested at least annually for impairment.[48]

45. ASC ¶ 360-10-35-21.
46. ASC ¶ 350-30-35-14.
47. These are described and discussed under "amortization" p. 168.
48. ASC ¶ 350-30-35-18.

Example

General Mills, Inc. reports approximately $6.8 billion of brands and other indefinite-lived intangible assets on its May 27, 2018 balance sheet. The disclosures to the balance sheet indicate where they have had valuation questions related to those brands.

> *Our annual ... indefinite-lived intangible assets test was performed on the first day of the second quarter of fiscal 2018. As of the assessment date, we determined there was no impairment of our intangible assets as their related fair values were substantially in excess of the carrying values, except for the Yoki and Progresso brand intangible assets and the Latin America reporting unit.*
>
> ....
>
> *During the fourth quarter of fiscal 2018, we executed our fiscal 2019 planning process and preliminary long-range planning process, which resulted in lower future sales and profitability projections in our plans for the businesses supporting our Yoki, Mountain High, and Immaculate Baking brand intangible assets. As a result of this triggering event, we performed an interim impairment assessment of these assets as of May 27, 2018, and determined that the fair value of these brand assets no longer exceeded the carrying values of the respective assets. Significant assumptions used in that assessment included our updated long-range cash flow projections for the businesses, royalty rates, weighted average cost of capital rates, and tax rates. We recorded a $96.9 million impairment charge in the fourth quarter of fiscal 2018 related to these assets as follows:*

(in Millions)	*Impairment Charge*	*Carrying Value as of May 27, 2018*
Yoki	*$65.0*	*$63.6*
Mountain High	*$20,0*	*$15.4*
Immaculate Baking	*$11.9*	—
Total	*$96.9*	*$79.0*

* * *

Problem 5-13

BioWidgets, Inc. (BWI) has developed a widget fortification process which makes its widgets impervious to decay and therefore a competitively superior product.

Management anticipates that the process can be kept secret from competitors and used productively as long as BWI continues to manufacture widgets. It has no present intention to discontinue the widget business. How should the costs of the fortification process be allocated to widget production? How would your answers be affected by the following developments?

(a) BWI received a patent for this process with a legal life of 20 years. Thereafter, the fortification process will be available to the company's competitors.

(b) BWI estimates that the competitive advantage of the fortification process will last between 10–20 years, at which time other superior protections will likely be developed.

(c) After three years, an unfortunate incident of corporate espionage has resulted in a leak of the process to one of BWI's competitors. Although the company has identified the guilty parties, recovery from them is unlikely to be substantial.

Problem 5-14

FirstRate Drug Stores, Inc. has been expanding the number of its company-owned retail stores over the past several years. As a result, the company has incurred several million dollars of costs to plan the construction of new stores (design and architectural fees, land zoning and planning fees and related expenses). The company has capitalized these expenses and has added each to the cost of each new store as completed, and included them in the depreciable cost of each store.

A downturn in the company's performance and cash flow has resulted in management's decision to cancel the expansion program. There remain substantial capitalized costs related to acquisition and construction of future stores. Management has now decided to amortize those expenses ratably at $150,000 year. How would you help your client to justify this treatment?

Chapter 6

Contingent Liabilities

In Chapter 5(C), we learned about impairment of assets. The source of this rule was Statement of Financial Accounting Concepts No. 5, Paragraph 87, which states:

> An expense or loss is recognized if it becomes evident that previously recognized future economic benefits of an asset have been reduced or eliminated, or that a liability has been incurred or increased, without associated economic benefits.

In this chapter we deal with the second of those possibilities, that a *liability has been incurred or increased.* Incurring a liability—with a current period expense to boot—is a discomforting event for a business. When the liability is uncertain, or contingent, the problems become even more difficult.

These contingent liabilities are of great concern to lawyers for at least three reasons.

- First, when they arise, they are usually quite material in comparison to other financial events in the company's life. Therefore, the prospect for litigation or other legal problems is good.
- Second, the contingencies themselves usually arise from legal issues or proceedings: things which lawyers are uniquely qualified (and usually asked) to help evaluate.
- Finally, there is the delicate problem of how to handle the auditor's request for information about these contingent liabilities, in order to satisfy the auditor's need for confirmation while not compromising the client's legal status.

We begin the chapter with a careful and critical study of the GAAP of contingent liabilities, and then discuss the treatment of auditors' requests for information and the related topic of privilege and waiver for both the attorney and the accountant.

A. Accounting for Contingent Liabilities

The authoritative GAAP on contingent liabilities is language with which many lawyers are familiar. Because it relates so closely to the lawyer's stock in trade, you are likely to encounter these rules several times in your legal career.[1]

---

1. The Accounting Standards Codification is presented below, but many lawyers and accountants will probably continue for some time to refer to this GAAP by its pre-ASC citation as Statement of Financial Accounting Standards No. 5 or "Statement 5" or "FAS 5" for short.

Accounting Standards Codification

Topic 450 — Contingencies
Subtopic 20 — Loss Contingencies

05. Overview and background

05-5. This Subtopic deals with uncertainty by requiring a probability threshold for recognition of a loss contingency and that the amount of the loss be reasonably estimable. When both of those recognition criteria are met, and the reasonably estimable loss is a range, it requires accrual of the amount that appears to be a better estimate than any other estimate within the range, or accrual of the minimum amount in the range if no amount within the range is a better estimate than any other amount.

Accruals of Loss Contingencies Do Not Provide Financial Protection

05-8. Accrual of a loss related to a contingency does not create or set aside funds to lessen the possible financial impact of a loss. Confusion exists between accounting accruals (sometimes referred to as accounting reserves) and the reserving or setting aside of specific assets to be used for a particular purpose or contingency. Accounting accruals are simply a method of allocating costs among accounting periods and have no effect on an entity's cash flow. Those accruals in no way protect the assets available to replace or repair uninsured property that may be lost or damaged, or to satisfy claims that are not covered by insurance, or, in the case of insurance entities, to satisfy the claims of insured parties. Accrual, in and of itself, provides no financial protection that is not available in the absence of accrual.

25. Recognition

General Rule

25-1. When a loss contingency exists, the likelihood that the future event or events will confirm the loss or impairment of an asset or the incurrence of a liability can range from probable to remote. [This] Topic uses the terms probable, reasonably possible, and remote to identify three areas within that range.[2]

25-2. An estimated loss from a loss contingency shall be accrued by a charge to income if both of the following conditions are met:

a. Information available before the financial statements are issued indicates that it is probable that an asset had been impaired or a liability had been incurred at the date of the financial statements. It is implicit in this condition that it must be probable that one or more future events will occur confirming the fact of the loss.

b. The amount of loss can be reasonably estimated.

---

2. [Ed.] The following definitions are provided in the glossary.
Probable: The future event or events are likely to occur.
Reasonably possible: The chance of the future event or events occurring is more than remote but less than likely.
Remote: The chance of the future event or events occurring is slight.

The purpose of those conditions is to require accrual of losses when they are reasonably estimable and relate to the current or a prior period. Paragraphs 450-20-55-1 through 55-17 and Examples 1–2 (see paragraphs 450-20-55-18 through 55-35) illustrate the application of the conditions....

Assessing Probability of Incurrence of a Loss

25-3. The conditions in the preceding paragraph are not intended to be so rigid that they require virtual certainty before a loss is accrued. Instead, the condition in (a) in the preceding paragraph is intended to proscribe accrual of losses that relate to future periods.

Assessing Whether a Loss Is Reasonably Estimable

25-4. The condition in paragraph 450-20-25-2(b) is intended to prevent accrual in the financial statements of amounts so uncertain as to impair the integrity of those statements.

25-5. That requirement shall not delay accrual of a loss until only a single amount can be reasonably estimated. To the contrary, when the condition in paragraph 450-20-25-2(a) is met and information available indicates that the estimated amount of loss is within a range of amounts, it follows that some amount of loss has occurred and can be reasonably estimated....

Business Risks

25-8. General or unspecified business risks do not meet the conditions for accrual in paragraph 450-20-25-2, and no accrual for loss shall be made.

30. Initial Measurement

30-1. If some amount within a range of loss appears at the time to be a better estimate than any other amount within the range, that amount shall be accrued. When no amount within the range is a better estimate than any other amount, however, the minimum amount in the range shall be accrued. Even though the minimum amount in the range is not necessarily the amount of loss that will be ultimately determined, it is not likely that the ultimate loss will be less than the minimum amount. Examples 1–2 (see paragraphs 450-20-55-18 through 55-35) illustrate the application of these initial measurement standards.

50. Disclosure

Accruals for Loss Contingencies

50-1. Disclosure of the nature of an accrual made pursuant to the provisions of paragraph 450-20-25-2, and in some circumstances the amount accrued, may be necessary for the financial statements not to be misleading. Terminology used shall be descriptive of the nature of the accrual, such as estimated liability or liability of an estimated amount. The term reserve shall not be used for an accrual made pursuant to paragraph 450-20-25-2....

Unrecognized Contingencies

50-3. Disclosure of the contingency shall be made if there is at least a reasonable possibility that a loss or an additional loss may have been incurred and either of the following conditions exists:

a. An accrual is not made for loss contingency because any of the conditions in paragraph 450-20-25-2 are not met.

b. An exposure to loss exists in excess of the amount accrued pursuant to the provisions of paragraph 450-20-30-1.

Examples 1-3 (see paragraphs 450-20-55-18 through 55-37) illustrate the application of these disclosure standards.

50-4. The disclosure in the preceding paragraph shall include both of the following:

a. The nature of the contingency

b. An estimate of the possible loss or range of loss or a statement that such an estimate cannot be made.

50-5. Disclosure is preferable to accrual when a reasonable estimate of loss cannot be made. For example, disclosure shall be made of any loss contingency that meets the condition in paragraph 450-20-25-2(a) but that is not accrued because the amount of loss cannot be reasonably estimated (the condition in paragraph 450-20-25-2(b). Disclosure also shall be made of some loss contingencies that do not meet the condition in paragraph 450-20-25-2(a) — namely, those contingencies for which there is a reasonable possibility that a loss may have been incurred even though information may not indicate that it is probable that an asset had been impaired or a liability had been incurred at the date of the financial statements.

50-6. Disclosure is not required of a loss contingency involving an unasserted claim or assessment if there has been no manifestation by a potential claimant of an awareness of a possible claim or assessment unless both of the following conditions are met:

a. It is considered probable that a claim will be asserted.

b. There is a reasonable possibility that the outcome will be unfavorable.

50-8. No disclosure about general or unspecified business risks is required by this Subtopic....

55. Implementation Guidance and Illustrations

Implementation Guidance

(a) Injury or Damage Caused by Products Sold

55-2. If it is probable that a claim resulting from injury or damage caused by a product defect will arise with respect to products or services that have been sold, accrual for losses may be appropriate. The condition in paragraph 450-20-25-2(a) would be met, for instance, with respect to a drug product or toys that have been sold if a health or safety hazard related to those products is discovered and as a result it is considered probable that liabilities have been incurred. The condition in paragraph 450-20-25-

2(b) would be met if experience or other information enables the entity to make a reasonable estimate of the loss with respect to the drug product or the toys.

(b) Risk of Loss or Damage of Property

55-3. At the date of an entity's financial statements, it may not be insured against risk of future loss or damage to its property by fire, explosion, or other hazards. Some risks, for all practical purposes, may be noninsurable, and the self-assumption of those risks is mandatory.

55-5. The absence of insurance does not mean that an asset has been impaired or a liability has been incurred at the date of an entity's financial statements. Fires, explosions, and other similar events that may cause loss or damage of an entity's property are random in their occurrence. With respect to events of that type, the condition in paragraph 450-20-25-2(a) is not satisfied prior to the occurrence of the event because until that time there is no diminution in the value of the property....

(c) Risk of Loss from Future Events

55-6. An entity may choose not to purchase insurance against risk of loss that may result from injury to others, damage to the property of others, or interruption of its business operations....

55-7. Mere exposure to risks of those types, however, does not mean that an asset has been impaired or a liability has been incurred.... Thus, for example, an entity with a fleet of vehicles should not accrue for injury to others or damage to the property of others that might be caused by those vehicles in the future even if the amount of those losses may be reasonably estimable.

(d) Litigation, Claims, and Assessments

Assessing Probability of the Incurrence of a Loss

55-12. If the underlying cause of the litigation, claim, or assessment is an event occurring before the date of an entity's financial statements, the probability of an outcome unfavorable to the entity must be assessed to determine whether the condition in paragraph 450-20-25-2(a) is met. Among the factors that should be considered are the following:

a. The nature of the litigation, claim, or assessment

b. The progress of the case (including progress after the date of the financial statements but before those statements are issued or are available to be issued)

c. The opinions or views of legal counsel and other advisers, although, the fact that legal counsel is unable to express an opinion that the outcome will be favorable to the entity should not necessarily be interpreted to mean that the condition in paragraph 450-20-25-2(a) is met

d. The experience of the entity in similar cases

e. The experience of other entities

f. Any decision of the entity's management as to how the entity intends to respond to the lawsuit, claim, or assessment (for example, a decision to contest the case vigorously or a decision to seek an out-of-court settlement).

55-13. The filing of a suit or formal assertion of a claim or assessment does not automatically indicate that accrual of a loss may be appropriate. The degree of probability of an unfavorable outcome must be assessed. The condition in paragraph 450-20-25-2(a) would be met if an unfavorable outcome is determined to be probable. Accrual would be inappropriate, but disclosure would be required, if an unfavorable outcome is determined to be reasonably possible but not probable, or if the amount of loss cannot be reasonably estimated.

55-14. With respect to unasserted claims and assessments, an entity must determine the degree of probability that a suit may be filed or a claim or assessment may be asserted and the possibility of an unfavorable outcome. If an unfavorable outcome is probable and the amount of loss can be reasonably estimated, accrual of a loss is required by paragraph 450-20-25-2. For example:

a. A catastrophe, accident, or other similar physical occurrence predictably engenders claims for redress, and in such circumstances their assertion may be probable.

b. An investigation of an entity by a governmental agency, if enforcement proceedings have been or are likely to be instituted, is often followed by private claims for redress, and the probability of their assertion and the possibility of loss should be considered in each case.

c. An entity may believe there is a possibility that it has infringed on another entity's patent rights, but the entity owning the patent rights has not indicated an intention to take any action and has not even indicated an awareness of the possible infringement. In that case, a judgment must first be made as to whether the assertion of a claim is probable.

55-15. If the judgment is that assertion is not probable, no accrual or disclosure would be required. On the other hand, if the judgment is that assertion is probable, then a second judgment must be made as to the degree of probability of an unfavorable outcome. The disclosures described in 450-20-50-3 through 50-8 would be required in either of the following circumstances:

a. An unfavorable outcome is probable but the amount of loss cannot be reasonably estimated.

b. An unfavorable outcome is reasonably possible but not probable.

Assessing Whether a Loss is Reasonably Estimable

55-16. As a condition for accrual of a loss contingency, the condition in paragraph 450-20-25-2(b) requires that the amount of loss can be reasonably estimated. In some cases, it may be determined that a loss was incurred because an unfavorable outcome of the litigation, claim, or assessment is probable (thus satisfying the condition in paragraph 450-20-25-2[a]), but the range of possible loss is wide. Examples 1 and 3 (see paragraphs 450-20-55-18 and 450-20-55-36) illustrate the application of the standards in this Subtopic when the range of possible loss is wide.

Illustrations

Example 1: Litigation Open to Considerable Interpretation

55-18. An entity may be litigating a dispute with another party. In preparation for the trial, it may determine that, based on recent developments involving one aspect of the litigation, it is probable that it will have to pay $2 million to settle the litigation. Another aspect of the litigation may, however, be open to considerable interpretation, and depending on the interpretation by the court the entity may have to pay an additional $8 million over and above the $2 million.

55-19. In that case, paragraph 450-20-25-2 requires accrual of the $2 million if that is considered a reasonable estimate of the loss.

55-20. Paragraphs 450-20-50-1 through 50-2 require disclosure of the nature of the accrual, and depending on the circumstances, may require disclosure of the $2 million that was accrued.

55-21. Paragraphs 450-20-50-3 through 50-8 require disclosure of the additional exposure to loss if there is a reasonable possibility that the additional amounts will be paid.

Example 2: Multiple Case Litigation Example

55-22. The following Cases illustrate application of the accrual and disclosure requirements in the following stages of litigation:

a. The trial is complete but the damages are undetermined (Case A).

b. The trial is incomplete but an unfavorable outcome is probable (Case B).

c. The trial is incomplete and unfavorable outcome is reasonably possible (Case C).

d. There is a range of loss and one amount is a better estimate than any other (Case D).

Case A: Trial Is Complete but Damages Are Undetermined

55-23. An entity is involved in litigation at the close of its fiscal year and information available indicates that an unfavorable outcome is probable. Subsequently, after a trial on the issues, a verdict unfavorable to the entity is handed down, but the amount of damages remains unresolved at the time the financial statements are issued or are available to be issued. Although the entity is unable to estimate the exact amount of loss, its reasonable estimate at the time is that the judgment will be for not less than $3 million or more than $9 million. No amount in that range appears at the time to be a better estimate than any other amount.

55-24. In this Case, paragraph 450-20-30-1 requires accrual of the $3 million (the minimum of the range) at the close of the fiscal year.

55-25. Paragraphs 450-20-50-1 through 50-2 require disclosure of the nature of the contingency and, depending on the circumstances, may require disclosure of the amount of the accrual.

55-26. Paragraphs 450-20-50-3 through 50-8 require disclosure of the exposure to an additional amount of loss of up to $6 million.

Case B: Trial Is Incomplete but Unfavorable Outcome Is Probable

55-27. Assume the same facts as in Case A, except it is probable that a verdict will be unfavorable and the trial has not been completed before the financial statements are issued or are available to be issued. In that situation, the condition in 450-20-25-2(a) would be met because information available to the entity indicates that an unfavorable verdict is probable. An assessment that the range of loss is between $3 million and $9 million would meet the condition in 450-20-25-2(b).

55-28. In this Case, if no single amount in that range is a better estimate than any other amount, paragraph 450-20-30-1 requires accrual of $3 million (the minimum of the range) at the close of the fiscal year.

55-29. Paragraphs 450-20-50-1 through 50-2 require disclosure of the nature of the contingency and, depending on the circumstances, may require disclosure of the amount of the accrual.

55-30. Paragraphs 450-20-50-3 through 50-8 require disclosure of the exposure to an additional amount of loss of up to $6 million.

Case C: Trial Is Incomplete and Unfavorable Outcome Is Reasonably Possible

55-31. Assume the same facts as in Case B, except the entity had assessed the verdict differently (for example, that an unfavorable verdict was not probable but was only reasonably possible). The condition in paragraph 450-20-25-2(a) would not have been met and no amount of loss would be accrued. Paragraphs 450-20-50-3 through 50-8 require disclosure of the nature of the contingency and any amount of loss that is reasonably possible.

Case D: Range of Loss and One Amount Is a Better Estimate than Any Other

55-32. Assume that in Case A and Case B the condition in paragraph 450-20-25-2(a) has been met and a reasonable estimate of loss is a range between $3 million and $9 million but a loss of $4 million is a better estimate than any other amount in that range.

55-33. In this Case, paragraph 450-20-30-1 requires accrual of $4 million.

55-34. Paragraphs 450-20-50-1 through 50-2 require disclosure of the nature of the contingency and, depending on the circumstances, may require disclosure of the amount of the accrual.

55-35. Paragraphs 450-20-50-3 through 50-8 require disclosure of the exposure to an additional amount of loss of up to $5 million.

Example 3: Illustrative Disclosure

55-36. Entity A is the defendant in litigation involving a major competitor claiming patent infringement (Entity B). The suit claims damages of $200 million. Discovery has been completed, and Entity A is engaged in settlement discussions with the plaintiff. Entity A has made an offer of $5 million to settle the case, which offer was rejected by the plaintiff; the plaintiff has made an offer of $35 million to settle the case, which offer was rejected by Entity A. Based on the expressed willingness of the plaintiff to settle the case along with information revealed during discovery and the likely cost and risk to both sides of litigating, Entity A believes that it is probable the case will not come to trial. Accordingly, Entity A has determined that it is probable that it has some liability. Entity A's reasonable estimate of this liability is a range between $10 million and $35 million, with no amount within that range a better estimate than any other amount; accordingly, $10 million was accrued.

55-37. Entity A provides the following disclosure in accordance with Section 450-20-50.

> On March 15, 19X1, Entity B filed a suit against the company claiming patent infringement. While the company believes it has meritorious defenses against the suit, the ultimate resolution of the matter, which is expected to occur within one year, could result in a loss of up to $25 million in excess of the amount accrued.

Consider how the above rules have been applied by the following companies.

Example

Owens-Illinois, Inc. produced fiberglass pipe insulation in the mid-20th century and is still paying the price. Following is the disclosure from the Company's 2018 Annual Report.

> The Company conducts an annual comprehensive legal review of its asbestos-related liabilities and costs in connection with finalizing and reporting its annual results of operations, unless significant changes in trends or new developments warrant an earlier review. As part of its annual comprehensive legal review, the Company provides historical Asbestos Claims' data to a third party with expertise in determining the impact of disease incidence and mortality on future filing trends to develop information to assist the Company in estimating the total number of future Asbestos Claims likely to be asserted against the Company. The Company uses this estimate, along with an estimation of disposition costs and related legal costs, as inputs to develop its best estimate of its total probable liability. If the results of the annual comprehensive legal review indicate that the existing amount of the accrued liability is lower (higher) than its reasonably estimable asbestos-related costs, then the Company will record an appropriate charge (credit) to the Company's results of operations to increase (decrease) the accrued liability.
>
> ... In the fourth quarter of 2018, the Company determined that it was advantageous to accelerate the disposition of certain claims in light

of additional information the Company obtained about higher estimated future claim volumes and values in certain of the affected discrete streams of potential liability. Factors impacting the increased likelihood of these additional losses included changes in the law, procedure, the expansion of judicial resources in certain jurisdictions, and renewed attention to dockets of non-mesothelioma cases. The Company also obtained new information about other Asbestos Claims, which had the effect of reducing its asbestos-related liability. The combined effect of these items resulted in a change in estimate of the Company's asbestos-related liability.

The Company believes that it is reasonably possible that it will incur a loss for its asbestos-related liabilities in excess of the amount currently recognized, which was $602 million as of December 31, 2018. The Company estimated that reasonably possible losses could result in asbestos-related liabilities of approximately $722 million. This estimate of additional reasonably possible loss reflects a qualitative judgment regarding the nature of contingencies that could impact future Asbestos Claims and legal costs, which include, but are not limited to, successful attempts by plaintiffs to challenge existing legal barriers to entry, enact plaintiff-oriented procedural rules or liability or damage-related legislation, establish new theories of liability, revive long-dormant inventories of non-mesothelioma cases, or leverage changing jurisdictional dynamics and a changing litigation environment to increase the volume of Asbestos Claims presented or per-claim indemnity values. However, it is also possible that the ultimate amount of asbestos-related liabilities could be above this estimate.

Example

Volkswagen AG has had a problem with irregularities in its diesel engine emissions levels in testing compared to actual road conditions. The company's 2018 annual report contains six pages discussing civil, criminal and administrative actions from courts and agencies around the world relating to the "diesel issue." This narrative discussion comes to a financial conclusion as follows:

Risk assessment regarding the diesel issue

An amount of around €2.4 billion has been included in the provisions for litigation and legal risks as of December 31, 2018 to protect against the currently known legal risks related to the diesel issue based on existing information and current assessments. Insofar as these can be adequately measured at this stage, contingent liabilities relating to the

> diesel issue were disclosed in the notes in an aggregate amount of €5.4 billion.... The provisions recognized and the contingent liabilities disclosed as well as the other latent legal risks in the context of diesel issue are in part subject to substantial estimation risks given that the fact finding efforts have not yet been concluded, the complexity of the individual relevant factors and the ongoing coordination with the authorities. Should these legal or estimation risks materialize, this could result in further considerable financial charges.

* * *

Problem 6-1

What would be the proper treatment of the following events?

(a) Your client is involved in litigation at the close of its fiscal year.

(1) An unfavorable verdict has been returned, but the amount of damages remains unresolved. Management believes that liability will be between $3 million and $9 million, and it has no reason to believe that one number in this range is more likely than any other to be correct.

(2) Although the trial is not complete at the end of the fiscal year, management still believes that its liability is possible, and in the range set forth in (1) above.

(3) The same facts as in (2) except that management believes liability is very uncertain, and that there is a small chance could be exonerated completely.

(4) How will investors react if the company's disclosure is more favorable to the company than the ultimate results in the litigation? And what will result from that? Should this be a factor in your decisions in (1)–(3)?

(b) Your client has been given notice by the Environmental Protection Agency of potential liability of up to $10 million for cleanup of toxic chemicals at a manufacturing plant still owned but no longer operated by the company. Under relevant law, your client's status as a former operator is a sufficient basis for liability.

(1) Management has no current knowledge of whether there are any toxic chemicals at all on the site, or what any cleanup costs might be.

(2) Management estimates cleanup costs at $5 million, but this figure is "very fluid," they say (like the chemicals involved).

(3) Management believes that cleanup costs will be at least $5 million, and could be as much as $15 million. However, the operator of the plant and a prior owner (both separate unaffiliated parties) are potentially liable along with your client.

Under relevant law, each would bear proportionate liability for the total costs. Management believes its share would be between 30 and 40 percent.

(4) Same facts as in (3), but management also has an environmental liability insurance policy which will pay up to $3 million.

(c) Your client has just purchased substantial real estate in central Wyoming, for purposes of mining coal. No mining has begun yet. Under current law, your client will be responsible for reclamation and recovery of the land when the mining is completed. Management estimates that these expenses will total approximately $10 million, to be incurred when the work is completed.

Problem 6-2[3]

Your client's SEC annual report is due in a month. In your review of the company's intellectual property, you have found that another company has a patent on a process your client had used for many years. Your preliminary research suggests that the other company would be successful in a lawsuit and that the damages would be catastrophic. No one else has reviewed this information as far as you can tell. Your research also indicates that the statute of limitations on a patent action will expire in two months.

It is a federal crime under the securities laws to (1) willfully to fail to file a required report or to file it late or (2) "willfully and knowingly" to make or cause any statement in a required report that is "false or misleading with respect to any *material* fact." There could also be enormous civil liability for any misstatement.

Consider the options in this dilemma.

(a) Should you lie? This can yield personal civil and criminal liability.

(b) Should you disclose? It is a short-term risk, but the magnitude is enormous.

(c) Can you remain silent because it's not "material"? The magnitude is high, but are the potential plaintiffs sleeping on their rights?

(d) Do you even know if the potential plaintiffs know of their rights?

* * *

We have seen companies wanting to defer costs to make their income larger. But why would a company ever want to *accelerate* recognition of costs? Consider former SEC Chairman Levitt's remarks and the motives afoot in the case following, and review Problem 5-8, on p. 165.

---

3. Adapted from Louis Loss, Fundamentals of Securities Regulation 1071–72 (2d ed. 1988).

Remarks by Chairman Arthur Levitt, Securities and Exchange Commission "The Numbers Game"

NYU Center for Law and Business
Sept. 28, 1998

[T]oday, I'd like to talk to you about another widespread, but too little-challenged custom: earnings management. This process has evolved over the years into what can best be characterized as a game among market participants. A game that, if not addressed soon, will have adverse consequences for America's financial reporting system. A game that runs counter to the very principles behind our market's strength and success.

Increasingly, I have become concerned that the motivation to meet Wall Street earnings expectations may be overriding common sense business practices. Too many corporate managers, auditors, and analysts are participants in a game of nods and winks. In the zeal to satisfy consensus earnings estimates and project a smooth earnings path, wishful thinking may be winning the day over faithful representation.

As a result, I fear that we are witnessing an erosion in the quality of earnings, and therefore, the quality of financial reporting. Managing may be giving way to manipulation; Integrity may be losing out to illusion.

....

Miscellaneous "Cookie Jar Reserves"

A[n] ... illusion played by some companies is using unrealistic assumptions to estimate liabilities for such items as sales returns, loan losses or warranty costs. In doing so, they stash accruals in cookie jars during the good times and reach into them when needed in the bad times.

I'm reminded of one U.S. company who took a large one-time loss to earnings to reimburse franchisees for equipment. That equipment, however, which included literally the kitchen sink, had yet to be bought. And, at the same time, they announced that future earnings would grow an impressive 15 percent per year.

....

Numbers in the abstract are just that—numbers. But relying on the numbers in a financial report are livelihoods, interests and ultimately, stories: a single mother who works two jobs so she can save enough to give her kids a good education; a father who labored at the same company for his entire adult life and now just wants to enjoy time with his grandchildren; a young couple who dreams of starting their own business. These are the stories of American investors.

....

In the Matter of Microsoft Corporation

Securities and Exchange Commission, June 3, 2002
Accounting and Auditing Enforcement Release No. 1563
https://www.sec.gov/litigation/admin/34-46017.htm

ORDER INSTITUTING PUBLIC ADMINISTRATIVE PROCEEDINGS PURSUANT TO SECTION 21C OF THE SECURITIES EXCHANGE ACT OF 1934, MAKING FINDINGS AND IMPOSING CEASE-AND-DESIST ORDER

IV.
FINDINGS

On the basis of this Order and the Offer of Settlement submitted by Respondent, the Commission finds that:

> Note: **Section 21C** of the Securities Exchange Act, added in 1990, allows the SEC to proceed administratively against a company whose shares are registered for trading under the Act.

A. Respondent

Microsoft Corporation is a Washington corporation with its principal place of business in Redmond, Washington. Since its initial public offering in 1986, Microsoft's common stock has been registered with the Commission pursuant to Section 12(g) of the Exchange Act and is listed on the NASDAQ Stock Market, Inc. At all times relevant herein, Microsoft was required to make and file certain periodic reports with the Commission. Microsoft's principal lines of business consist of providing software for personal computers, office systems and the Internet.

[B]. Facts

1. Summary

During Microsoft's fiscal years ended June 30, 1995, June 30, 1996, June 30, 1997 and June 30, 1998 (the "relevant period"), Microsoft maintained undisclosed reserves, accruals, allowances and liability accounts (collectively "reserves" or "reserve accounts") that (a) were not in conformity with generally accepted accounting principles ("GAAP") to a material extent, and/or (b) lacked properly documented support and substantiation, as required by the federal securities laws. Moreover, Microsoft failed to maintain internal controls that were adequate under the federal securities laws. Specifically, during the relevant period, Microsoft maintained between approximately $200 million and $900 million in unsupported and undisclosed reserves, a significant portion of which did not comply with GAAP, which resulted in material inaccuracies in filings made by Microsoft with the Commission.

....

4. Reserves Maintained or Used Without Proper Support or Basis

a. Cyclical Accrual for Marketing Expenses

Marketing expenses represented the largest expense item on Microsoft's statement of operations. For management purposes, Microsoft established budgets for marketing expenses for each fiscal quarter and fiscal year. Management generally determined these budgets as a percentage of forecasted revenue.

Microsoft typically recorded budgeted marketing expenses as its reported marketing expenses when preparing its quarterly reports filed with the Commission, even though it did not have a documented factual basis for believing that its marketing budget was a reasonable estimation of its marketing expenses. In order to account for the difference between the marketing expenses recorded in its books and records, and its budgeted marketing expenses, Microsoft maintained a "marketing accrual," to which these differences were recorded. Microsoft generally budgeted quarterly marketing expenses as a substantially constant percentage of revenue and the effect of this practice was to depict marketing expense as a substantially constant percentage of revenue on a quarterly basis throughout the year.... Because Microsoft had insufficient support for recording its marketing expenses as the budgeted amount, this practice did not satisfy the requirement of GAAP that marketing expenses be recorded as and when they are actually incurred.

Microsoft's marketing accrual (i.e., the account containing the difference between recorded expenses and its budgeted marketing expenses) tended to increase during the first three fiscal quarters because, during each of these quarters, the difference between recorded and budgeted marketing expenses would be added into reported expenses. At the end of each fiscal year, Microsoft reversed the marketing accrual and released it into income.[4] The following chart shows the quarterly balances of the marketing accrual.

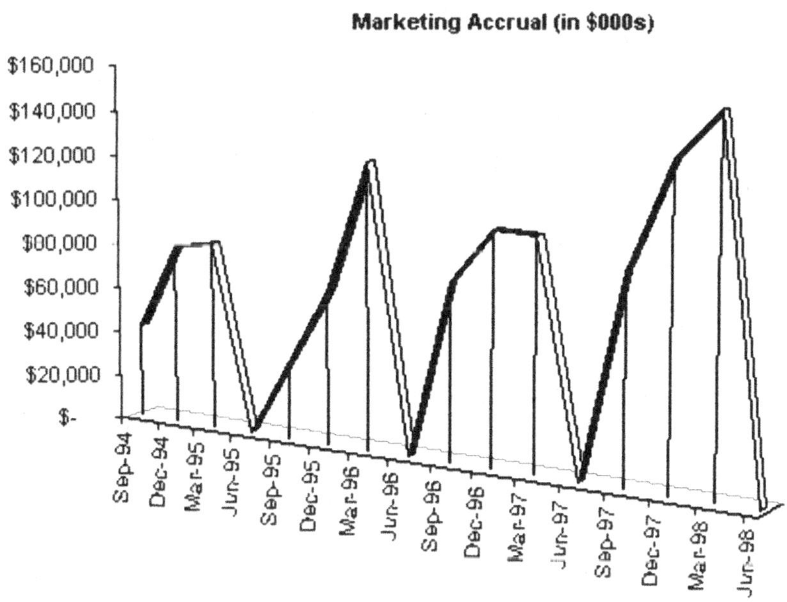

4. As a consequence of this reversal, the marketing accrual did not affect fiscal year-end results.

The marketing accrual was not documented as required by the federal securities laws and, to a significant extent, was not in conformity with GAAP. Because Microsoft did not analyze and document the use of budgeted amounts as a proxy for actual marketing expenditures, its quarterly financial statements filed with the Commission during the first three quarters of its fiscal years 1995, 1996, 1997 and 1998 did not comply with the requirements of the federal securities laws.

[b]. Non-Cyclical Reserves

In addition to the annual cyclical accrual for marketing expenses, Microsoft maintained six other reserve accounts that failed to comply with the federal securities laws. These reserve accounts, along with the marketing accrual discussed above, were not in conformity with GAAP to a material extent and/or lacked properly documented support and substantiation as required by the federal securities laws.

iii. Inventory Obsolescence

[ASC 450-20] requires that certain conditions exist before loss contingencies representing liabilities or asset impairments may be determined and the amount of a reserve accrued. The loss must be probable as of the balance sheet date and reasonably estimable; significantly, the loss must have occurred prior to the creation of the loss contingency and must not be in the future. Furthermore, [ASC 450-20] prohibits the accrual of reserves for general or unspecified risks. As discussed below, Microsoft did not comply with [ASC 450-20] because the company's senior financial personnel did not properly assess whether inventory losses had occurred and made no effort to reasonably estimate the losses.

Microsoft maintained a corporate level reserve account for inventory obsolescence that supplemented the inventory obsolescence reserve accounts determined at the operating level. Microsoft maintained factually supported inventory reserve accounts at the operating level, where operations personnel evaluated and documented the need for such accounts. The corporate level inventory obsolescence reserve had no substantiated basis, as required by [ASC 450-20]. This corporate reserve was not associated with any specific inventory nor was it supported by any statistical or documented analysis....

iv. Impaired Long Term Assets

Microsoft maintained a corporate reserve account for the valuation of financial assets. According to internal documents, the reserve's purpose was to "allow for potential losses, upon disposition, of Microsoft's financial assets." These financial assets consisted of equity investments made in various technology companies. Microsoft amortized the cost of these financial assets with monthly charges to income without any basis for the charges. The appropriate treatment under GAAP would have been to carry the assets at cost or write down the assets to their fair value in the event that the assets had suffered other than temporary declines in fair value....

The cumulative balance of the six non-cyclical reserve accounts discussed above is depicted in the chart below:

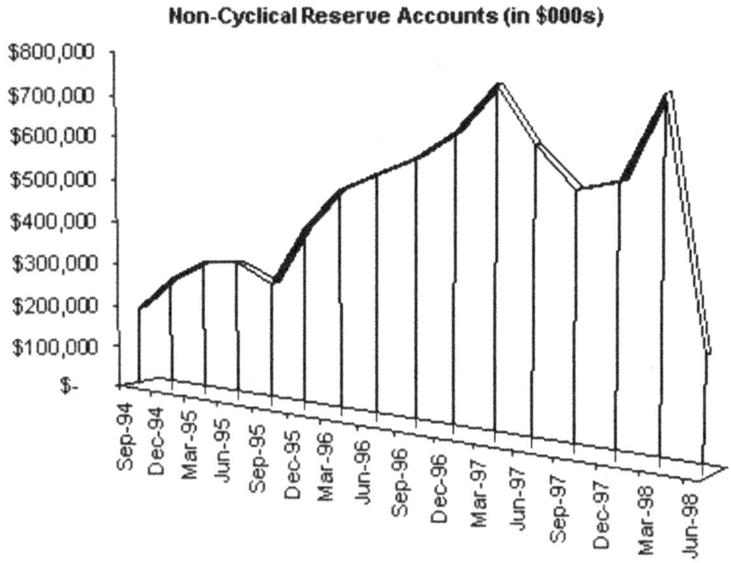

....

VIII.
ORDER

ACCORDINGLY, IT IS HEREBY ORDERED THAT, pursuant to Section 21C of the Exchange Act, Microsoft cease-and-desist from committing or causing any violations of, and committing or causing any future violations of, Sections 13(a), 13(b)(2)(A), and 13(b)(2)(B) of the Exchange Act, and Rules 12b-20, 13a-1, and 13a-13 promulgated thereunder.

* * *

Problem 6-3

Fabulous Computers, Inc. ("Fabcom") has a bonus and profit sharing plan for its employees. In 20X7, the Compensation Committee of Fabcom's board of directors decided on a bonus/profit sharing payout for the year that was less than the accrual the company had created to fund the payout. How should Fabcom account for this change to the plan payout?

Problem 6-4

DataVault, Inc. has a proprietary data storage and retrieval system which it sells at retail and to manufacturers to be installed on hardware. DataVault's main manufacturing customer is Cobalt Computers, Inc., whose orders currently account for about 20% of DataValut's revenue.

DataVault has just been informed that Cobalt has acquired a DataVault competitor, and the orders from Cobalt will be ending soon. Management has contacted several other manufacturers and is in serious negotiations with each.

Management is confident that it will conclude a new sales contract successfully and that the new contract will allow DataVault to continue its record revenue growth. Indeed, the current fiscal year is shaping up to be a record-breaker, thanks to what will be the last of the Cobalt sales. Management wants to ask Cobalt to delay some payments until next fiscal year, so that any disruption in DataVault's revenues will be muted. If that is not possible, management is considering booking some of the Cobalt payments as a "deferred revenue" liability. What is your advice?

* * *

B. Auditors' Letters

We know that GAAP requires, in certain circumstances, contingent liabilities to be disclosed in, or even accrued on, the financial statements. We also know that GAAS requires auditors to obtain "sufficient appropriate audit evidence" to justify their conclusions. When it comes to contingent liabilities, the auditor will ask the lawyer if there are any undisclosed contingent liabilities, much as the auditor might ask a creditor to confirm the existence of a debt. Suppose your client has failed to disclose to its auditor a material contingent liability?

- Should you say you are aware of no undisclosed contingent liabilities? That would be a lie, unethical (even if your client commanded silence) and likely fraudulent as well.
- Should you disclose the contingent liability? Your client likely did not authorize you to do so, which makes the disclosure unethical. And you have now probably cost your client some money, as the auditor will demand that the contingent liability be disclosed on the financial statements.
- Can you say that you are aware of a contingent liability and refuse to say more because of your duty to maintain client confidences? You have been (more) ethical here, but the auditor will then likely qualify the audit opinion, making it unusable for securities law filings and for many other purposes.[5]

This dilemma was solved in the mid-1970s with authoritative pronouncements from both professions, dubbed the "treaty." Both parts of the treaty are presented below.

---

5. *See* T.J. Fiflis, *Current Problems of Accountants' Responsibilities to Third Parties*, 28 Vand. L. Rev. 31, 78 (1975).

Codification of Statements on Auditing Standards

Section 501

Audit Evidence—Specific Consideration for Selected Items

Litigation, Claims, and Assessments

.16 The auditor should design and perform audit procedures to identify litigation, claims, and assessments involving the entity that may give rise risk of material misstatement, including:

a. inquiring of management and, when applicable, others within the entity, including in-house legal counsel;

b. obtaining from management a description and evaluation of litigation,claims, and assessments that existed at the date of the financial statements being reported on and during the period from the date of the financial statements to the date the information is furnished, including an identification of those matters referred to legal counsel;

c. reviewing minutes of meetings of those charged with governance; documents obtained from management concerning litigation, claims, and assessments; and correspondence between the entity and its external legal counsel; and

d. reviewing legal expense accounts and invoices from external legal counsel.

.17 For actual or potential litigation, claims, and assessments identified based on the audit procedures required in paragraph .16, the auditor should obtain audit evidence relevant to the following factors:

a. The period in which the underlying cause for legal action occurred

b. The degree of probability of an unfavorable outcome

c. The amount or range of potential loss

Communication With the Entity's Legal Counsel

.18 Unless the audit procedures required by paragraph .16 indicate that no actual or potential litigation, claims, or assessments that may give rise to a risk of material misstatement exist, the auditor should ... seek direct communication with the entity's external legal counsel. The auditor should do so through a letter of inquiry prepared by management and sent by the auditor requesting the entity's external legal counsel to communicate directly with the auditor.

.21 The auditor should request management to authorize the entity's legal counsel to discuss applicable matters with the auditor.

.22 [T]he auditor should request, through letter(s) of inquiry, the entity's legal counsel to inform the auditor of any litigation, claims, assessments, and unasserted claims that the counsel is aware of, together with an assessment of the outcome of the litigation, claims, and assessments, and an estimate of the financial implications, including costs involved. Each letter of inquiry should include, but not be limited to, the following matters:

a. Identification of the entity, including subsidiaries, and the date of the audit

b. A list prepared by management (or a request by management that the legal counsel prepare a list) that describes and evaluates pending or threatened litigation, claims, and assessments with respect to which the legal counsel has been engaged and to which the legal counsel has devoted substantive attention on behalf of the company in the form of legal consultation or representation

c. A list prepared by management that describes and evaluates unasserted claims and assessments that management considers to be probable of assertion and that, if asserted, would have at least a reasonable possibility of an unfavorable outcome with respect to which the legal counsel has been engaged and to which the legal counsel has devoted substantive attention on behalf of the entity in the form of legal consultation or representation

d. Regarding each matter listed in item *b*, a request that the legal counsel either provide the following information or comment on those matters on which the legal counsel's views may differ from those stated by management, as appropriate:

   i. A description of the nature of the matter, the progress of the case to date, and the action that the entity intends to take (for example, to contest the matter vigorously or to seek an out-of-court settlement)

   ii. An evaluation of the likelihood of an unfavorable outcome and an estimate, if one can be made, of the amount or range of potential loss

   iii. With respect to a list prepared by management (or by the legal counsel at management's request), an identification of the omission of any pending or threatened litigation, claims, and assessments or a statement that the list of such matters is complete

e. Regarding each matter listed in item *c*, a request that the legal counsel comment on those matters on which the legal counsel's views concerning the description or evaluation of the matter may differ from those stated by management

f. A statement that management understands that whenever, in the course of performing legal services for the entity with respect to a matter recognized to involve an unasserted possible claim or assessment that may call for financial statement disclosure, the legal counsel has formed a professional conclusion that the entity should disclose or consider disclosure concerning such possible claim or assessment, the legal counsel, as a matter of professional responsibility to the entity, will so advise the entity and will consult with the entity concerning the question of such disclosure and the requirements of the applicable financial reporting framework (for example; the requirements of Financial Accounting Standards Board [FASB] *Accounting Standards Codification* [ASC] 450, *Contingencies*)

g. A request that the legal counsel confirm whether the understanding described in item *f* is correct

h. A request that the legal counsel specifically identify the nature of, and reasons for, any limitation on the response

i. A request that the legal. counsel specify the effective date of the response

Application and other Explanatory Material

Communication with the Entity's Legal Counsel

.A48 The American Bar Association (ABA) has approved *Statement of Policy Regarding Lawyers' Responses to Auditors' Requests for Information* (the ABA statement), which explains the concerns of the legal counsel and the nature of the limitations that an auditor is likely to encounter in connection with seeking direct communication with the entity's legal counsel about litigation, claims, assessments, and unasserted claims.

.A51 An external legal counsel's response to a letter of inquiry and the procedures set forth in paragraphs .16–.17 provide the auditor with sufficient appropriate audit evidence concerning the accounting for, and reporting of, pending and threatened litigation, claims, and assessments.

.A58 An external legal counsel's refusal to furnish the information requested in an inquiry letter either in writing or orally may cause a scope limitation of the audit sufficient to preclude an unmodified opinion.

Statement of Policy Regarding Lawyers' Responses to Auditors' Requests For Information

American Bar Association, December 1975
31 BUSINESS LAWYER 1709–26 (1976)[6]

Preamble

The public interest in protecting the confidentiality of lawyer-client communications is fundamental. The American legal, political and economic systems depend heavily upon voluntary compliance with the law and upon ready access to a respected body of professionals able to interpret and advise on the law. The expanding complexity of our laws and governmental regulations increases the need for prompt, specific and unhampered lawyer-client communication. The benefits of such communication and early consultation underlie the strict statutory and ethical obligations of the lawyer to preserve the confidences and secrets of the client, as well as the long-recognized testimonial privilege for lawyer-client communication.

Both the Code of Professional Responsibility and the cases applying the evidentiary privilege recognize that the privilege against disclosure can be knowingly and voluntarily waived by the client. It is equally clear that disclosure to a third party may result in loss of the "confidentiality" essential to maintain the privilege. Dis-

6. Copyright by *The Business Lawyer*. Reprinted with permission.

closure to a third party of the lawyer-client communication on a particular subject may also destroy the privilege as to other communications on that subject. Thus, the mere disclosure by the lawyer to the outside auditor, with due client consent, of the substance of communications between the lawyer and client may significantly impair the client's ability in other contexts to maintain the confidentiality of such communications.

....

It is also recognized that our legal, political and economic systems depend to an important extent on public confidence in published financial statements. To meet this need the accounting profession must adopt and adhere to standards and procedures that will command confidence in the auditing process. It is not, however, believed necessary, or sound public policy, to intrude upon the confidentiality of the lawyer-client relationship in order to command such confidence....

Statement of Policy

NOW, THEREFORE, BE IT RESOLVED that it is desirable and in the public interest that this Association adopt the following Statement of Policy regarding the appropriate scope of the lawyer's response to the auditor's request, made by the client at the request of the auditor, for information concerning matters referred to the lawyer during the course of his representation of the client:

(1) *Client Consent to Response.* The lawyer may properly respond to the auditor's requests for information concerning loss contingencies (the term and concept established by [ASC 450-20]), to the extent hereinafter set forth, subject to the following:

(a) Assuming that the client's initial letter requesting the lawyer to provide information to the auditor is signed by an agent of the client having apparent authority to make such a request, the lawyer may provide to the auditor information requested, without further consent, unless such information discloses a confidence or a secret or requires an evaluation of a claim.

(b) In the normal case, the initial request letter does not provide the necessary consent to the disclosure of a confidence or secret or to the evaluation of a claim since that consent may only be given after full disclosure to the client of the legal consequences of such action.

(c) Lawyers should bear in mind, in evaluating claims, that an adverse party may assert that any evaluation of potential liability is an admission.

(d) In securing the client's consent to the disclosure of confidences or secrets, or the evaluation of claims, the lawyer may wish to have a draft of his letter reviewed and approved by the client before releasing it to the auditor; in such cases, additional explanation would in all probability be necessary so that the legal consequences of the consent are fully disclosed to the client.

....

(3) *Response may be Limited to Material Items.* In response to an auditor's request for disclosure of loss contingencies of a client, it is appropriate for the lawyer's response

to indicate that the response is limited to items which are considered individually or collectively material to the presentation of the client's financial statements.

(4) *Limited Responses.* Where the lawyer is limiting his response in accordance with this Statement of Policy, his response should so indicate (see Paragraph 8). If in any other respect the lawyer is not undertaking to respond to or comment on particular aspects of the inquiry when responding to the auditor, he should consider advising the auditor that his response is limited, in order to avoid any inference that the lawyer has responded to all aspects; otherwise, he may be assuming a responsibility which he does not intend.

(5) *Loss Contingencies.* When properly requested by the client, it is appropriate for the lawyer to furnish to the auditor information concerning the following matters if the lawyer has been engaged by the client to represent or advise the client professionally with respect thereto and he has devoted substantive attention to them in the form of legal representation or consultation:

> (a) *overtly threatened or pending litigation,* whether or not specified by the client;
>
> (b) *a contractually assumed obligation* which the client has specifically identified and upon which the client has specifically requested, in the inquiry letter or a supplement thereto, comment to the auditor;
>
> (c) *an unasserted possible claim or assessment* which the client has specifically identified and upon which the client has specifically requested, in the inquiry letter or a supplement thereto, comment to the auditor.

With respect to clause (a), overtly threatened litigation means that a potential claimant has manifested to the client an awareness of and present intention to assert a possible claim or assessment unless the likelihood of litigation (or of settlement when litigation would normally be avoided) is considered remote. With respect to clause (c), where there has been no manifestation by a potential claimant of an awareness of and present intention to assert a possible claim or assessment, ... the client should request the lawyer to furnish information to the auditor only if the client has determined that it is probable that a possible claim will be asserted, that there is a reasonable possibility that the outcome (assuming such assertion) will be unfavorable, and that the resulting liability would be material to the financial condition of the client.

> Notice that this paragraph is directed to the ***client*** and what the client should ask the lawyer to disclose. Curious advice in a document from the ABA intended to be read by the ***lawyer***. Why do you suppose that is so? Who do you suppose writes the letter from the client to the client's lawyer?

Examples of such situations might (depending in each case upon the particular circumstances) include the following: (i) a catastrophe, accident or other similar physical occurrence in which the client's involvement is open and notorious, or (ii) an investigation by a government agency where enforcement proceedings have been instituted or where the likelihood that they will not be instituted is remote, under circumstances where assertion of one or more private claims for redress would normally be expected, or (iii) a public disclosure by the client acknowledging (and thus focusing attention upon) the existence of one or more probable claims arising out of an event or circumstance. In assessing whether or not the assertion of a possible claim is probable, it is expected that the client would normally employ, by reason of the inherent uncertainties involved and insufficiency of available data, concepts parallel to those used by the lawyer (discussed below) in assessing whether or not an unfavorable outcome is probable; thus, assertion of a possible claim would be considered probable only when the prospects of its being asserted seem reasonably certain (i.e., supported by extrinsic evidence strong enough to establish a presumption that it will happen) and the prospects of non-assertion seem slight.

It would not be appropriate, however, for the lawyer to be requested to furnish information in response to an inquiry letter or supplement thereto if it appears that (a) the client has been required to specify unasserted possible claims without regard to the standard suggested in the preceding paragraph, or (b) the client has been required to specify all or substantially all unasserted possible claims as to which legal advice may have been obtained, since, in either case, such a request would be in substance a general inquiry and would be inconsistent with the intent of this Statement of Policy.

The information that lawyers may properly give to the auditor concerning the foregoing matters would include (to the extent appropriate) an identification of the proceedings or matter, the stage of proceedings, the claim(s) asserted, and the position taken by the client.

In view of the inherent uncertainties, the lawyer should normally refrain from expressing judgments as to outcome except in those relatively few clear cases where it appears to the lawyer that an unfavorable outcome is either "probable" or "remote;" for purposes of any such judgment it is appropriate to use the following meanings:

> (i) *probable*: an unfavorable outcome for the client is probable if the prospects of the claimant not succeeding are judged to be extremely doubtful and the prospects for success by the client in its defense are judged to be slight.
>
> (ii) *remote*: an unfavorable outcome is remote if the prospects for the client not succeeding in its defense are judged to be extremely doubtful and the prospects of success by the claimant—are judged to be slight.

If, in the opinion of the lawyer, considerations within the province of his professional judgment bear on a particular loss contingency to the degree necessary to make an informed judgment, he may in appropriate circumstances communicate to the auditor his view that an unfavorable outcome is "probable" or "remote," applying the above meanings. No inference should be drawn, from the absence of such a judgment, that the client will not prevail.

The lawyer also may be asked to estimate, in dollar terms, the potential amount of loss or range of loss in the event that an unfavorable outcome is not viewed to be "remote." In such a case, the amount or range of potential loss will normally be as inherently impossible to ascertain, with any degree of certainty, as the outcome of the litigation. Therefore, it is appropriate for the lawyer to provide an estimate of the amount or range of potential loss (if the outcome should be unfavorable) only if he believes that the probability of inaccuracy of the estimate of the amount or range of potential loss is slight.

The considerations bearing upon the difficulty in estimating loss (or range of loss) where pending litigation is concerned are obviously even more compelling in the case of unasserted possible claims. In most cases, the lawyer will not be able to provide any such estimate to the auditor.

As indicated in Paragraph 4 hereof, the auditor may assume that all loss contingencies specified by the client in the manner specified in clauses (b) and (c) above have received comment in the response, unless otherwise therein indicated. The lawyer should not be asked, nor need the lawyer undertake, to furnish information to the auditor concerning loss contingencies except as contemplated by this Paragraph 5.

(6) *Lawyer's Professional Responsibility.* Independent of the scope of his response to the auditor's request for information, the lawyer, depending upon the nature of the matters as to which he is engaged, may have as part of his professional responsibility to his client an obligation to advise the client concerning the need for or advisability of public disclosure of a wide range of events and circumstances. The lawyer has an obligation not knowingly to participate in any violation by the client of the disclosure requirements of the securities laws. The lawyer also may be required under the Code of Professional Responsibility to resign his engagement if his advice concerning disclosures is disregarded by the client. The auditor may properly assume that whenever, in the course of performing legal services for the client with respect to a matter recognized to involve an unasserted possible claim or assessment which may call for financial statement disclosure, the lawyer has formed a professional conclusion that the client must disclose or consider disclosure concerning such possible claim or assessment, the lawyer, as a matter of professional responsibility to the client, will so advise the client and will consult with the client concerning the question of such disclosure and the applicable requirements of [ASC 450-20].

Commentary

[Following is a portion of the commentary relating to the duties stated in paragraph 5.]

The Lawyer's Response

Concepts of probability inherent in the usage of terms like "probable" or "reasonably possible" or "remote" mean different things in different contexts.... Lawyers do not generally quantify for clients the "odds" in numerical terms; if they do, the quantification is generally only undertaken in an effort to make meaningful, for limited purposes, a whole host of judgmental factors applicable at a particular time, without any intention to depict "probability" in any statistical, scientific or empirically-grounded sense. Thus, for example, statements that litigation is being defended vigorously and that the client has meritorious defenses do not, and do not purport to, make a statement about the probability of outcome in any measurable sense.

Likewise, the "amount" of loss—that is, the total of costs and damages that ultimately might be assessed against a client—will in most litigation, be a subject of wide possible variance at most stages; it is the rare case where the amount is precise and where the question is whether the client against which claim is made is liable either for all of it or none of it.

In light of the foregoing considerations, it must be concluded that, as a general rule, it should not be anticipated that meaningful quantifications of "probability" of outcome or amount of damages can be given by lawyers in assessing litigation. To provide content to the definitions set forth in Paragraph 5 of the Statement of Policy, this Commentary amplifies the meanings of the terms under discussion, as follows:

"probable"— An unfavorable outcome is normally "probable" if, but only if, investigation, preparation (including development of the factual data and legal research) and progress of the matter have reached a stage where a judgment can be made, taking all relevant factors into account which may affect the outcome, that it is extremely doubtful that the client will prevail.

"remote"— The prospect for an unfavorable outcome appears, at the time, to be slight; i.e., it is extremely doubtful that the client will not prevail. Normally, this would entail the ability to make an unqualified judgment, taking into account all relevant factors which may affect the outcome, that the client may confidently expect to prevail on a motion for summary judgment on all issues due to the clarity of the facts and the law.

In other words, for purposes of the lawyer's response to the request to advise auditors about litigation, an unfavorable outcome will be "probable" only if the chances of the client prevailing appear slight and of the claimant losing appear extremely doubtful; it will be "remote" when the client's chances of losing appear slight and of not winning appear extremely doubtful. It is, therefore, to be anticipated that, in most situations, an unfavorable outcome will be neither "probable" nor "remote" as defined in the Statement of Policy.

* * *

Problem 6-5

1. Would you be required to respond to a letter from your client which requested your opinion on an attached list (which the client prepared) listing all major injuries relating to the client's products during the past fiscal year?

2. Your client has requested your commentary to the auditor with respect to an unasserted claim of the type in Problem 6-2 (patent infringement). Should you do so?

3. Your client has requested your commentary to the auditor with respect to all contracts signed by the client in the last fiscal year with consideration paid by the client in excess of $1 million. Should you respond?

4. One of your client's oil tankers ran aground two weeks ago. Your client has not investigated the circumstances of the accident, and does not have any idea whose fault the accident might have been, nor if any oil was spilled. Your client has mailed you the standard request to respond to the auditor, and this accident is not identified by your client in that letter. What are your obligations before responding?

5. In 4, suppose your client suspects that there is a large spill, yet refuses to allow you to release any information to the auditors. What should you do?

Chapter 7

Owners' Equity

We turn in this chapter to the lower right-hand side of the balance sheet, a province which has escaped close scrutiny so far. We learned in Chapter 1 that the purpose of an income statement was to prevent routine changes to the owners' equity accounts in accounting for profits and losses. In this chapter we study the *transactions with owners* which do result in changes to those accounts. Those transactions come in four basic types:

- contributions by the owners of assets to the entity
- allocation of profits and losses to those owners
- distribution by the entity of assets to the owners
- redemption (repurchase) of the owner's interest.

Each of these is considered in turn.

A. Contributions

In Chapter 1, we learned the basics of accounting for the initial contribution to an entity. We now delve into the details by dividing our coverage between the simple rules applicable to non-corporate entities, and the more complicated rules applicable to corporations.

1. Non-Corporate Entities

George might organize his hardware store as a sole proprietorship. If George contributes $10,000 in cash to his Hardware Store in exchange for the entire ownership interest, we would journal:

Dr Cash	10,000	
Cr George — Owner's Equity		10,000
Investment of 10,000 cash in business.		

Similarly, if George and Fred each invested $10,000 in the partnership or limited liability company (LLC) known as George's Hardware Store, we would journal:

Dr Cash	20,000	
Cr George — Capital account		10,000
Cr Fred — Capital account		10,000
Investment of 20,000 cash in partnership.		

The difference is in nomenclature only. We have two equity accounts instead of one, and we have titled them "capital accounts" to conform to the generally accepted titles for those accounts.[1]

2. Corporations

The accounting for contributions to a corporation is complicated by old legal nomenclature dividing the contributions among different owners' equity accounts. Corporations normally issue equity interests called "common stock."[2] Any other type of stock is normally called "preferred stock" because it will have different (usually superior) rights to payment from the corporation. Preferred stock presents rare and different accounting problems, so we will stick to the common stock.

The main accounting aspect of common stock to concern us is *par value*. In olden times (a century ago), "par value" was a dollar value which bore some faint resemblance to the amount of money or property that shareholders contributed or agreed to contribute to the corporation in exchange for their shares. The theory was that creditors relied on a balance sheet showing how much the investors invested in the corporation, so that they could be sure it had real assets.[3] This reliance theory had two important legal consequences, both of which endure in some fashion today. First, if a shareholder did not pay par value for the shares received, payment could be demanded upon the corporation's insolvency.[4] Second, the par value served as a limitation on the amount of assets the corporation could distribute to its shareholders.[5]

---

1. *See, e.g.*, Revised Uniform Partnership Act § 401(a) (deeming an "account" to exist for each partner); Treas. Reg. § 1.704-1(b)(2)(iv) (rules for maintenance of capital accounts for partnership tax purposes, applicable to partnerships or other entities, such as LLCs which opt to be taxed as partnerships).

2. For example, Model Bus. Corp. Act § 6.01(b) provides:

> The articles of incorporation must authorize (1) one or more classes of shares that together have unlimited voting rights, and (2) one or more classes of shares (which may be the same class or classes as those with voting rights) that together are entitled to receive the net assets of the corporation upon dissolution.

3. With the accounting knowledge you have acquired so far, you know that it is folly to rely on the accounts on the right-hand side to represent any "value."

> Whether the concept of legal capital was ever relied on ... by a substantial number of creditors and, if so, for how long a period of American business history, are elusive historical questions. But it is fairly clear that the original concept was understood in the way described and that it stopped being of much possible utility to creditors many decades ago.

Robert C. Clark, Corporate Law 612 (1986). Of course, most creditors do not expect the corporation to liquidate, but rather rely on earnings to provide the cash for repayment. But this "distorted" model nonetheless serves as the basis for our current statutes. Bayless Manning & James J. Hanks, Jr., Legal Capital 23 (4th ed. 2013).

4. *See* Manning & Hanks, *supra* note 3, at 31–32. For an example, see Del. Gen. Corp. Law §§ 152, 153(a), and 162.

5. *See generally* Manning & Hanks, *supra* note 3, at 39–49. This concept is developed more fully in part B below.

Now that you know the ancient history, put it far from your mind; it will only serve to confuse you.[6] Par value is still around today only because the unenlightened corporation laws of many states require it, or punish the corporation in some fashion if it has stock with no par value. The modern definition of par value is simplistic, like our definition of debits and credits.

Par value is par value. Period.

Par value is the amount, expressed in dollars (usually cents, actually), assigned to each share of stock as its par value.

Because par value has legal significance, as described above, we need to keep track of it. Hence, accountants accommodate par value when keeping track of a corporation's transactions in its own stock. When common stock is issued, the par value is normally collected in a separate account entitled "common stock." The remainder of the amount paid for the stock is collected in another account entitled, appropriately, "capital contributed in excess of par" or "contributed capital" for short.

Illustration. Wanda is incorporating Wanda's Widgets, Inc. After the legal formalities are followed, and she has created a corporation, she wants to vest it with assets, so that it can go into business and make more money. As with our very first example, let's suppose Wanda invested $100 in her corporation. If this investment was reflected in 10 shares of common stock with a par value of $1 each, we would journal as follows:

Dr Cash	100
Cr Common stock, $1 par	10
Cr Contributed capital in excess of par	90

To record payment of $100 for 10 shares of common stock, $1 par value.

But why 10 shares? The division into a number of shares is wholly arbitrary, especially for a closely-held corporation.[7] And we will discuss how to set the par value shortly.

---

6. "In large degree, ... it is an error to attempt a precise reconstruction of the way in which the nineteenth century looked at such matters [of corporate finance]. The truth is that there simply was no coherent view of these matters in the nineteenth century." *Id.* at 27. However, the rules of the previous paragraph in the text are still the law in most states today.

7. By contrast, publicly-traded corporations like to adjust the number of shares outstanding to keep the trading price per share in two digits, on the theory that investors would consider $5 stock "too cheap" and $105 stock "too expensive." Expensive stock is also more difficult to trade because of the tradition of market trading in 100 share minimum "lots." *See* Robert W. Hamilton & Richard A. Booth, Business Basics for Law Students § 11.34 (4th ed. 2006).

This is how the contributed capital is accounted for. These two accounts make up (except for a few oddities) the entire amount of a corporation's contributed capital.

B. Allocations

1. Non-Corporate Entities

As a sole proprietorship recognizes gain or loss, the amount of gain or loss is added to or subtracted from the Owner's Equity account. The allocation of profits and losses among multiple owners is a matter for the entity's owners to agree upon amongst themselves.[8] In the Collegetown Coffeehouse, Bill and Ted agreed to split the profits 75%–25%. When we calculated the net income for the business, we "closed the income statement" by allocating (crediting) 75% of the amount to Bill's Owner's Equity account, and 25% to Ted's. If there should be actual distributions or redemptions (see parts B and C below), those would reduce the Owner's Equity account accordingly. The allocation of losses is also a matter for agreement among the owners.[9] These partnership rules will probably govern other entities, such as limited liability companies. Nearly everything that is not a corporation is accounted for as if it were a partnership.

Illustration. The process of "allocation" consists of "closing the income statement to the balance sheet." This was covered in Chapter 1(C)(2)(b), "Closing the books." We there decided to dispense with formal journal entries, but let's now see how they would work. Wanda's income statement at the end of the month is as follows:

Wanda's Widgets — Income Statement for the month

Revenues		
Sales		$250
Expenses		
Cost of goods sold	150	
Rent	50	200
Net income		$50

Each account represents the ending balance in a revenue or expense item. When we *allocate* this amount to Wanda's owner's equity account, the remaining balance sheet accounts will balance. This step would be formally described in the following

8. If they do not agree, state partnership law default rules specify equal sharing of profits. *See* Revised Uniform Partnership Act § 401(b).

9. If they fail to agree about losses, state partnership law default rules will allocate the losses as they agreed to allocate the profits. *Id.*

pair of journal entries, first creating the "income" as a transitory account, and second, transferring it to the balance sheet.

Dr Sales [R]	250	
Cr Cost of goods sold [X]		150
Cr Rent expense [X]		50
Cr Net income		50
To calculate net income for the period.		
Dr Net income	50	
Cr Wanda — Owner's Equity [Q]		50
To transfer income to owner's equity account.		

2. Corporations

When a corporation records net income or loss for the year, the amount is added to or subtracted from a separate account, normally called "retained earnings." Thus, we have three accounts — common stock (par value), contributed capital in excess of par, and retained earnings — which account for the bulk of corporate equity. This tripartite division of corporate capital, as distinct from the other entities' equity accounting, is due to state corporation laws which we previewed above and will study in detail in the next section.

Example

Xerox Corporation reports, on its December 31, 2018, balance sheet, the following amounts of shareholders' equity:

- 232 million shares of common stock with a $1 par value, for a total in the "Common Stock" account of $232 million.
- $3.266 billion of "Additional Paid-in Capital" for that common stock (what we have termed "contributed capital"). This means, on the average, that each purchaser of *new* Xerox common stock from the company paid about $15.087 per share.
- $5.072 billion of "Retained earnings," which is profit made by Xerox not distributed to its shareholders.
- -$3.565 billion of "Accumulated other comprehensive loss." This latter amount should be familiar to you from Chapter 4; it is the total net unrealized losses from certain securities and derivatives trading, foreign currency translation losses, and net pension plan costs.

Illustration. To "close the income statement to the balance sheet" in a corporation, we would make the same initial journal entry as in the example above with Wanda's Widgets. The second closing entry would be as follows:

Dr Net income	50	
Cr Retained Earnings [Q]		50

This calculation is set forth in a report titled "Statement of Changes in Stockholders' Equity," where the net income (or loss) is added to (or subtracted from) retained earnings. See the example of Intel Corporation on p. 10.

* * *

Problem 7-1

Franz and Gregor are starting a new pest control business.

(a) Franz and Gregor each invest $10,000 cash. Make the required journal entries if:

(1) the entity is a partnership.

(2) the entity is a corporation and Franz and Gregor each receive 100 shares of $1 par value common stock in exchange for their cash investments.

(3) the entity is a corporation and Franz and Gregor each receive 100 shares of $100 par value common stock in exchange for their cash investments.

(b) The business makes $10,000 profit its first year. Make the required changes to equity accounts if:

(1) the entity is a partnership and the profits are shared equally.

(2) the entity is a partnership and Franz is allocated 75% of the profits and Gregor is allocated 25% of the profits.

(3) the entity is a corporation and Franz and Gregor each own common stock.

(c) Gregor is flustered with the pest control business and sells his interest in the business to his mother for $25,000. Make the required journal entries if:

(1) the entity is a partnership.

(2) the entity is a corporation.

* * *

C. Distributions

There are basically two ways for an owner to get money out of a business. First, an owner could receive a distribution in his or her capacity as owner. And second, the owner could have her interest in the business (or part of it) redeemed or repurchased by the business.[10] Again, we will discuss each in turn, this part concerning

10. The other way to get money "out of the business" is to sell the ownership interest to a third party. But as you probably now recognize from Problem 7-1(c), a third-party transaction presents few (if any) accounting issues.

payments to the owner and the next Part D concerning repurchases by the entity of the owner's interest.

1. Non-Corporate Entities

The simplest way to withdraw money is to remove assets and debit (reduce) the equity account. This is a transaction we looked at in general in Chapter 1. A withdrawal by a sole proprietor or partner of $100 would result in the following journal entry.

Dr Owner's equity—[name]	100	
Cr Cash		100
To record distribution to owner.		

2. Corporations

If the entity in question is a corporation, we know from the previous portion of this chapter that the capital accounts are more complicated. There are two accounts (common stock and contributed capital) which record the amounts originally paid for the stock, and a third account (retained earnings) which records the accumulated undistributed profit. There are further complications created by the fact that a corporation's equity exists in the form of "stock," which itself could be distributed to shareholders. We will discuss separately below (a) distribution of assets and (b) distribution of a corporation's stock.

a. Distribution of Assets

A distribution to a corporate shareholder which is *not* a redemption (discussed in the next part) is nearly always characterized as a ***dividend***. A dividend must be uniform across all like shares of stock. If George is the sole shareholder at George's Hardware Store, Inc., he could pay himself a dividend with the following journal entry:

Dr Retained Earnings	100	
Cr Cash		100
Payment of dividend to common stockholder.		

* * *

Problem 7-2

Franz and Gregor (from Problem 7-1) have been in their pest control business for several years. Prepare journal entries for a distribution by the business of $1,000 each to Franz and Gregor under each of the following arrangements. Calculate the balance in each owner's equity account after the transactions.

(a) The business is a partnership. Each partner's equity account has a balance of $15,000.

(b) The business is a corporation, in which Franz and Gregor each own 100 shares of $1 par value stock. The corporation's capital accounts appear as follows:

Common stock $1 par value	200
Contributed capital in excess of par	19,800
Retained earnings	10,000

* * *

In the case of a corporate dividend, the debit entry is to retained earnings. We could say, therefore, that the change in the retained earnings account "measures" the amount of the dividend. Indeed, some attorneys (or even statutes, as we will see below) speak of paying a dividend "out of" retained earnings. You know that this terminology is inaccurate — the only things that can be distributed are on the *left-hand* side of the balance sheet.

The use of corporation capital accounts to "measure" the distribution of assets is incorporated into state laws which limit distributions. Before reading the statutes, however, we need to translate the accounting terms into their outmoded counterparts usually present in state corporation laws.

Accounting term	Term in most state laws
Common stock (par value)	Stated capital
Contributed capital in excess of par	Capital surplus *or* Paid-in capital
Retained earnings	Earned surplus

Accountants agreed long ago that calling these equity accounts "surplus" was archaic, but the law persists.

Because the original idea was that amounts in these first two equity accounts constituted money available for creditors, state law requires that par value be paid in by stock purchasers, and restricts payment of corporate assets to shareholders by measuring the payments by these accounts. Consider how the following statutes use these accounting concepts. We will read the Delaware statute, because of that state's status as the home of incorporation for many large public companies, and the Model Business Corporation Act, as it is the basis for many state's corporate laws.

Delaware General Corporation Law

§ 170. Dividends; payment; wasting asset corporations.

(a) The directors of every corporation ... may declare and pay dividends upon the shares of its capital stock either (1) out of its surplus, as defined and computed in accordance with ... § 154 of this title, or (2) in case there shall be no such surplus, out of its net profits for the fiscal year in which the dividend is declared and/or the preceding fiscal year.

....

§ 154. Determination of amount of capital; capital, surplus and net assets defined.

Any corporation may, by resolution of its board of directors, determine that only a part of the consideration which shall be received by the corporation for any of the shares of its capital stock ... shall be capital; but, in case any of the shares issued shall be shares having a par value, the amount of the part of such consideration so determined to be capital shall be in excess of the aggregate par value of the shares.... The excess, if any, at any given time, of the net assets of the corporation over the amount so determined to be capital shall be surplus. Net assets means the amount by which total assets exceed total liabilities. Capital and surplus are not liabilities for this purpose.

Model Business Corporation Act

§ 6.40. Distributions to Shareholders

(a) A board of directors may authorize and the corporation may make distributions to its shareholders subject to restriction by the articles of incorporation and the limitation in subsection § 6.40(c).

....

(c) No distribution may be made if, after giving it effect:

(1) the corporation would not be able to pay its debts as they become due in the usual course of business; or

(2) the corporation's total assets would be less than the sum of its total liabilities plus (unless the articles of incorporation permit otherwise) the amount that would be needed, if the corporation were to be dissolved at the time of the distribution, to satisfy the preferential rights upon dissolution of shareholders whose preferential rights are superior to those receiving the distribution.

Summary of the Statutory Requirements

The general structure of each of these statutes is similar. The statutes place two different kinds of limits on the ability of a corporation to pay dividends.

Balance sheet test. The first limitation is known as the "balance sheet" insolvency test. This test looks at the fundamental accounting equation and requires, that creditors are still protected after the distribution.

• Under Del. Gen. Corp. Law § 170(a)(1), "surplus" is the measure of permitted dividends. Under § 154, surplus is defined as every corporate equity account *other* than "par value." So the amount equal to par value serves as a "cushion" for the protection of creditors.

• Under MBCA § 6.40, the corporation may pay out the *entire amount* represented by *all* the corporation's capital accounts, except for the liquidation preference on the corporation's preferred stock, if any. The capital accounts in an MBCA jurisdiction do not serve to protect creditors.[11]

The above statutes are summarized graphically below. The first two columns list the accounts on the "liabilities and equity" side of the balance sheet, using first their accounting and then their state law terminology.[12] Then follows a summary of each statute.

Accounting terminology	State law terminology	Available for distribution[13] in:	
		Delaware	MBCA
Liabilities	Liabilities	No	No
Common stock (par value)	Capital stock	No	Yes
Contributed capital in excess of par	Capital surplus	Yes	Yes
Retained earnings	Earned surplus	Yes	Yes

A common method of avoiding limitations on distributions based on the par value of shares is to set the par value very low. It is, after all, an arbitrary amount.[14] Most corporations set the par value at pennies per share or less. Setting it at zero may not be advisable, because there can be other statutes which "deem" a zero par value to be some higher amount.[15]

Cash flow based test. The second limitation is also known as the "equity insolvency test." This is yet another use of the term "equity," not in the balance sheet sense, but more in the judicial "equitable" sense.[16] In any event, this test applies, even if a distribution could be made under the balance sheet test, if it would leave the corporation unable to pay its debts. MBCA § 6.40(c)(1) adds "in the usual course of business."

The equity insolvency test is important as a second check on the ability of a corporation to make a distribution, and a further protection of creditors. If, for example, the corporation has been profitable but has invested the assets in machines, inventory, or real estate, it may have substantial equity in the accounting sense, but have very

11. This is not an oversight; *see supra* note 3.

12. From the chart on page 220.

13. Note that, in referring to these equity accounts as "available for distribution," we have used the typical lawyer's terminology, which suggests that these accounts represent anything of value. They, of course, do not; rather, what they do is measure the amount of assets which can be distributed.

14. Manning & Hanks, *supra* note 3, at 44.

15. *See, e.g.*, 8 Del. Code Ann. § 503(a) (annual franchise tax based on par value, but deemed to be $100/share if no par value is stated). Two can play this game, however. Minn. Stat. Ann. § 302A.401(2)(c) provides that shares in Minnesota corporations shall be deemed to have a par value of one cent per share "solely for the purpose of a statute or rule imposing a tax or fee based upon the capitalization of a corporation."

16. *See* Manning & Hanks, *supra* note 3, at 68, tracing the origin of the concept to the English chancery (equity) courts.

little cash flow. The corporation is "wealthy," but may be driven to insolvency or bankruptcy because it cannot make required debt service payments.

Delaware uses a quite different income-based test. Del. Gen Corp. Law § 170(a)(2) is known as the "nimble dividends" test.[17] It permits a corporation to pay a dividend "out of surplus," or, "in case there shall be no such surplus, out of its net profits for the fiscal year in which the dividend is declared and/or the preceding fiscal year." This short clause raises a host of interpretive questions.

> Given the importance of Delaware as a leading state of incorporation, it might be thought that its legal capital provisions would be elegantly sophisticated in their drafting. Regrettably, the situation is otherwise.... [T]he interpretational questions set out below ... are representative of the range of issues arising out of Delaware's Delphic provision on "nimble dividends."
>
> ... *Accounting questions:* What is intended by "net profits"? Same as "earnings"? Why "net"? Assuming that the imprecise term "out of surplus" means "charged against surplus," what does it mean as an accounting matter to have dividends "charged against net profits"?
>
> *Substantive questions:* The provision purports to make the "net profits" avenue available as an option if but only if there is no surplus. But suppose the corporation has a $1 surplus and net profits of $20? How much can be distributed? Is it permissible to distribute $1 first and then, since no surplus is left, pay out the $20 in a second distribution? Or $19?...
>
> *Timing questions:* Is the reference to the fiscal year to be taken literally (*i.e.* as meaning a full year), so that the corporation may not, at six months into the year, pay dividends "out of" the "net profits" of the first six months? On the other hand, if the corporation has its income statement for Year N, it also has the balance sheet for Year N, so the earnings in year N are already reflected on the balance sheet; if both surplus *and* earnings for that year can be used, does that not double count? Or does "net profits" mean "as taken into the balance sheet?" Or, if not, then does $1 in a dividend from "net profits" reduce by $1 the surplus available for further dividends? And what is the "preceding year"? Preceding what?... And what is the timing relationship implied in the reference to separate dates of declaration and payment?
>
> *Miscellaneous question:* What could be intended by the inviting but puzzling "and/or" in the statutory text?[18]

17. This means "in essence that directors must be nimble in declaring dividends before the earnings are transferred to offset deficits." James D. Cox & Thomas Lee Hazen, Corporations § 20:17 n.3 (3d ed. 2020) (citing *Recent Cases, Corporations — Dividends — Virginia Statute Construed to Allow Dividends from Current Profits Despite Capital Deficit*, 62 Harv. L. Rev. 130 (1948)).

18. Manning & Hanks, *supra* note 3, at 84–85 & n.47.

Despite these interpretive problems, "nimble dividends" statutes have been adopted by states which model their corporation laws on Delaware.[19]

* * *

Problem 7-3[20]

In each of the following phases in a corporation's life, it has the balance sheet shown below. Determine the maximum permissible distribution in Delaware and an MBCA state.

(1) The stockholders buy 100 shares of $1 par common stock for $5 each.

Assets		Liabilities and Equity	
Cash	500	Common stock	100
		Additional paid-in capital	400
Total	500	Total	500

(2) During its first year, the corporation borrows money to buy land, and has net income of $100. At the end of the year, its position is as follows.

Assets		Liabilities and Equity	
Cash	200	Current liabilities	100
Accounts receivable	500	Long-term debt	1,000
Land	1,000		
		Common stock	100
		Additional paid-in capital	400
		Retained earnings	100
Total	1,700	Total	1,700

19. *See, e.g.*, Kan. Stat. Ann. 17-6420 (cited in Cox & Hazen, *supra* note 17, at 563 n.1); William Foster, *The (Limited) Allure of Delaware*, 2013 Ark. L. Notes 1476 at ¶ 18 (citing Kansas and Oklahoma). California amended its corporation laws in 2011 to conform largely to the MBCA provisions described above, but also retained a provision permitting distributions if less than retained earnings, and allowing the term to be defined without reference to GAAP. This was described in the legislative proposal as "conceptually similar" to the nimble dividend statute. Harold R. Marsh, Jr. et al., Marsh's California Corporation Law § 14.07 (2016).

20. Problems 7-3 and 7-4 are adapted from Manning & Hanks, *supra* note 3, at 115–21.

(3) The second year doesn't go so well; the corporation has a net loss of $500.

Assets		Liabilities and Equity	
Cash	100	Current liabilities	200
Accounts receivable	200	Long-term debt	1,000
Land	1,000		
		Common stock	100
		Additional paid-in capital	400
		Retained earnings (deficit)	(400)
Total	1,300	Total	1,300

* * *

Sometimes, the decision under these dividend statutes requires business evaluation and judgment by your client's directors. The following case and statutes provide guidelines for the directors' decisions.

Randall v. Bailey

Supreme Court of New York, Trial Term, New York County, 1940
23 N.Y.S.2d 173
aff'd, 43 N.E.2d 43 (N.Y. 1942)

WALTER, Justice.

A trustee of Bush Terminal Company, appointed in a proceeding under Section 77B of the Bankruptcy Act, 11 U.S.C. § 207, here sues former directors of that company to recover on its behalf the amount of dividends declared and paid between November 22, 1928, and May 2, 1932.... At the times of the declarations and payments, the company's books concededly showed a surplus.... The plaintiff claims, however, that in fact there was no surplus ... and that the directors consequently are personally liable to the corporation for the amount [of the dividends] under Section 58 of the Stock Corporation Law.[21] Defendants claim that there was no impairment of capital and that the surplus was actually greater than the amount which plaintiff concedes as the amount shown by the books.

The ... plaintiff [claims that it was] improper to "write-up" the land values above cost and thereby take unrealized appreciation into account.

....

---

21. [Ed.] The statute provided, in pertinent part, that "[n]o stock corporation shall declare or pay any dividend which shall impair its capital or capital stock, nor while its capital or capital stock is impaired." The court engaged in extended construction of other statutory language and ultimately decided to rely upon the language quoted as "controlling."

Until 1915 the company's land was carried upon its books at cost. In 1915 the land was written up to 80% of the amount at which it was then assessed for taxation, and in 1918 it was written up to the exact amount at which it was then so assessed. Those two write-ups totalled $7,211,791.72, and the result was that during the period here in question the land was carried on the books at $8,737,949.02, whereas its actual cost was $1,526,157.30. Plaintiff claims that the entire $7,211,791.72 should be eliminated because it represents merely unrealized appreciation, and dividends cannot be declared or paid on the basis of mere unrealized appreciation in fixed assets irrespective of how sound the estimate thereof may be. That obviously and concededly is another way of saying that for dividend purposes fixed assets must be computed at cost, not value, and plaintiff here plants himself upon that position, even to the point of contending that evidence of value is immaterial and not admissible. If that contention be sound, the company indisputably had a deficit at all the times here involved in an amount exceeding the dividends here in question....

It is to be emphasized at the outset that the question is not one of sound economics, or of what is sound business judgment or financial policy or of proper accounting practice, or even what the law ought to be. My views of the business acumen or financial sagacity of these directors, as well as my views as to what the legislature ought to permit or prohibit, are entirely immaterial. The question I have to decide is whether or not an existing statute has been violated. The problem is one of statutory construction.

The words of the statute, as it existed during the period here involved, are: "No stock corporation shall declare or pay any dividend which shall impair its capital or capital stock, nor while its capital or capital stock is impaired...." Stock Corporation Law, § 58, as enacted by Laws 1923, c. 787.

....

It ... appears that after using surplus and surplus profits terminology for practically a hundred years the legislature [in the above statute] completely abandoned it, and I think that is quite significant as indicating a conscious intent to get away from the idea of profits earned as a result of completed transactions as the sole source of dividends.

....

[T]he capital or capital stock referred to in these statutes is the sum of the liability to stockholders, and any value which the corporation's property has in addition to that sum is surplus. And I cannot doubt that [the authority of prior cases would] include an appreciation in the value of property purchased whether realized or unrealized.

....

In summary, I think that it cannot be said that there is a single case in this State which actually decides that unrealized appreciation cannot be taken into consideration, or, stated in different words, that cost and not value must be used in determining whether or not there exists a surplus out of which dividends can be paid. I think, further, that such a holding would run directly counter to the meaning of the terms capital and capital stock as fixed by decisions of the Court of Appeals construing the earlier statutes, and that such construction of those terms must be deemed to have been adopted by the legislature in enacting the statute here involved....

....

I see no cause for alarm over the fact that this view requires directors to make a determination of the value of the assets at each dividend declaration. On the contrary, I think that is exactly what the law always has contemplated that directors should do. That does not mean that the books themselves necessarily must be altered by write-ups or write-downs at each dividend period, or that formal appraisals must be obtained from professional appraisers or even made by the directors themselves. That is obviously impossible in the case of corporations of any considerable size. But it is not impossible nor unfeasible for directors to consider whether the cost of assets continues over a long period of years to reflect their fair value, and the law does require that directors should really direct in the very important matter of really determining at each dividend declaration whether or not the value of the assets is such as to justify a dividend, rather than do what one director here testified that he did, viz. "accept the company's figures." The directors are the ones who should determine the figures by carefully considering values, and it was for the very purpose of compelling them to perform that duty that the statute imposes upon them a personal responsibility for declaring and paying dividends when the value of the assets is not sufficient to justify them. What directors must do is to exercise an informed judgment of their own, and the amount of information which they should obtain, and the sources from which they should obtain it, will of course depend upon the circumstances of each particular case. If directors have blindly or complacently accepted either cost or any other arbitrary figures as indicative of value, they have not exercised either discretion or judgment and no court is required to act as if they had. When directors have in fact exercised an informed judgment with respect to the value of the company's assets, the courts obviously will be exceedingly slow to override that judgment, and clear and convincing evidence will be required to justify a finding that such judgment was not in accordance with the facts. In the last analysis, however, the issue, in any case in which it is claimed that dividends have been paid out of capital, is the value of the assets and the amount of the liabilities to creditors and stockholders at the times the dividends were declared and paid.

Upon the evidence in this case I find that the directors here did in fact exercise an informed judgment with respect to ... the value of the land of the company ... and that such land and improvements were worth several millions of dollars more than the amounts at which they were carried on the books. At least one of the directors was thoroughly versed in real estate values by reason of long and extensive experience in buying and selling and in recommending mortgage loans on real estate and was personally and thoroughly familiar with the properties and business of all the companies just named, and of the development thereof, from the time of the organization of the company, and no one could criticise any other director for relying upon his knowledge and judgment as to the value thereof, or for basing a judgment thereon. His knowledge and judgment probably were as safe and sound a guide as any formal appraisal that could have been obtained. At least one other of the directors likewise had a thorough familiarity with these properties and business from the inception of their developments.

....

In summary, therefore, after considering all the evidence, I find that at the times these dividends were declared and paid the value of the assets exceeded the total liabilities to creditors and stockholders by an amount in excess of the total dividends, and that there accordingly was no impairment of capital or capital stock.

....

Model Business Corporation Act

§ 6.40. Distributions to Shareholders

(d) The board of directors may base a determination that a distribution is not prohibited under subsection (c) either on financial statements prepared on the basis of accounting practices and principles that are reasonable in the circumstances or on a fair valuation or other method that is reasonable in the circumstances.

§ 8.32. Directors' Liability for Unlawful Distributions

(a) A director who votes for or assents to a distribution in excess of what may be authorized and made pursuant to section 6.40(a) ... is personally liable to the corporation for the amount of the distribution that exceeds what could have been distributed without violating section 6.40(a)....

Delaware General Corporation Law

§ 172. Liability of directors and committee members as to dividends or stock redemption

A member of the board of directors, or a member of any committee designated by the board of directors, shall be fully protected in relying in good faith upon the records of the corporation and upon such information, opinions, reports or statements presented to the corporation by any of its officers or employees, or committees of the board of directors, or by any other person as to matters the director reasonably believes are within such other person's professional or expert competence and who has been selected with reasonable care by or on behalf of the corporation, as to the value and amount of the assets, liabilities and/or net profits of the corporation or any other facts pertinent to the existence and amount of surplus or other funds from which dividends might properly be declared and paid, or with which the corporation's stock might properly be purchased or redeemed.

* * *

Problem 7-4

In part (3) of Problem 7-3, our company had finished a bad year with a retained deficit, as follows:

Assets		Liabilities and Equity	
Cash	100	Current liabilities	200
Accounts receivable	200	Long-term debt	1,000
Land	1,000		
		Common stock	100
		Additional paid-in capital	400
		Retained earnings (deficit)	(400)
Total	1,300	Total	1,300

Suppose instead that the land were actually worth $1,400, based on reliable appraisals. Could the directors revalue it as follows?

Assets		Liabilities and Equity	
Cash	100	Current liabilities	200
Accounts receivable	200	Long-term debt	1,000
Land (market value)	1,400		
		Common stock	100
		Additional paid-in capital	400
		Retained earnings (deficit)	0
Total	1,700	Total	1,700

If so, what would be the maximum distribution permitted in Delaware or an MBCA state? What are the risks to the corporation's directors?

* * *

There is yet another source of similar rules applicable to the corporate distribution: your state's "fraudulent transfer" or "fraudulent conveyance" or "voidable transactions" statute. There are three different names, because the statute has been retitled during its historical development.

Uniform Voidable Transactions Act

§ 4. Transfer or obligation voidable as to present or future creditor

(a) A transfer made or obligation incurred by a debtor is voidable as to a creditor, whether the creditor's claim arose before or after the transfer was made or the obligation was incurred, if the debtor made the transfer or incurred the obligation:

(1) with actual intent to hinder, delay, or defraud any creditor of the debtor; or

(2) without receiving a reasonably equivalent value in exchange for the transfer or obligation, and the debtor:

(i) was engaged or was about to engage in a business or a transaction for which the remaining assets of the debtor were unreasonably small in relation to the business or transaction; or

(ii) intended to incur, or believed or reasonably should have believed that the debtor would incur, debts beyond the debtor's ability to pay as they became due.

§ 5. Transfer or obligation voidable as to present creditor

(a) A transfer made or obligation incurred by a debtor is voidable as to a creditor whose claim arose before the transfer was made or the obligation was incurred if the debtor made the transfer or incurred the obligation without receiving a reasonably equivalent value in exchange for the transfer or obligation and the debtor was insolvent at that time or the debtor became insolvent as a result of the transfer or obligation....

§ 7. Remedies of creditor

(a) In an action for relief against a transfer or obligation under this [Act], a creditor, ... may obtain:

(1) avoidance of the transfer or obligation to the extent necessary to satisfy the creditor's claim;

(2) an attachment or other provisional remedy against the asset transferred or other property of the transferee if available under applicable law; and

(3) subject to applicable principles of equity and in accordance with applicable rules of civil procedure:

(i) an injunction against further disposition by the debtor or a transferee, or both, of the asset transferred or of other property;

(ii) appointment of a receiver to take charge of the asset transferred or of other property of the transferee; or

(iii) any other relief the circumstances may require.

(b) If a creditor has obtained a judgment on a claim against the debtor, the creditor, if the court so orders, may levy execution on the asset transferred or its proceeds.

This is the most recent version of these uniform state law provisions. The basic substantive rules are very similar in each version of the act, so this language or very similar language is very likely the law in your state.[22] Important take-aways:

- § 5 replicates the "balance sheet" test.
- § 4 replicates the "equity insolvency" test.[23]
- A distribution by a corporation would be a transfer subject to this statute as well as the laws we studied above. So, for example, even in "nimble dividends" states, we must also consider the "equity insolvency" test.
- The remedies in § 7 (subject to exceptions not discussed here) for such a transaction include recovery of the transfer (or its value) from the transferee. This statute, being a remedy for creditors, does not focus on liability of the transferor (corporation).

b. Distribution of the Corporation's Stock

Occasionally a corporation distributes its own stock to the stockholders, known as a stock dividend. This event seems innocent enough at first but is one of the more perplexing areas of corporate accounting and finance.

Practical effect. Consider whether a stock dividend should make any difference at all to shareholders. Suppose a corporation has 100,000 shares of common stock outstanding, and it declares and pays to each stockholder a 10% common stock dividend. After giving effect to the dividend, there are 110,000 shares of common stock outstanding. A shareholder who previously owned 100 shares (out of 100,000) now owns 110 shares (out of 110,000). Has each stockholder's relative stake in the enterprise changed? Does it make a difference if the price of the stock also drops by 10%, or if it remains unchanged?

State law. State corporation statutes deal with stock dividends differently than other dividends. Delaware law is typical of those states which recognize the par value concept.

> If the dividend is to be paid in shares of the corporation's ... capital stock the board of directors shall, by resolution, direct that there be designated as capital in respect of such shares an amount which is not less than the aggregate par value of par value being declared as a dividend and, in the case of shares without par value being declared as a dividend, such amount as shall be determined by the board of directors....[24]

The Model Business Corporation Act, upon which the laws of many states are based, does not require par value for shares, and thus has simpler rules for stock dividends.

---

22. As of 2020, only Alaska, Louisiana, South Carolina and Virginia do not have some version of these Acts on their books.

23. Put aside for our purposes the difference in §§ 4–5 between recovery by present or future creditors.

24. Del. Gen. Corp. Law § 173.

"Unless the articles of incorporation provide otherwise, shares may be issued pro rata and without consideration to the corporation's shareholders.... An issuance of shares under this subsection is a share dividend."[25] Consider how each of these laws might influence the accounting treatment for a stock dividend.

* * *

Problem 7-5

A corporation is organized by selling 100,000 shares of its $1 par value common stock for $15 per share. The corporation's charter authorized 150,000 shares. The capital accounts would appear on the balance sheet thusly:

Common stock $1 par value	
150,000 shares authorized, 100,000 shares outstanding	100,000
Contributed capital in excess of par	1,400,000

The corporation issues a stock dividend of 10,000 shares, or 10% to each shareholder.

After the stock dividend, we would increase the capital account to reflect the newly issued stock. This is what Delaware Gen. Corp. Law § 173 (reprinted above) requires. So we would journal

Cr Common stock $1 par value	10,000

But what would be the debit entry to balance this increase in the common stock account? Contributed capital? Is that also "capital" under Delaware law? What about retained earnings? How would you advise this corporation, if it were incorporated in Delaware, to complete its accounting in order to comply with state law? What would be required if it were incorporated in a Model Act state?

* * *

You may wonder why all these complications arise for a transaction which distributes no assets and leaves no claims unchanged. Notice that no adjustment to capital accounts is required by Model Business Corporation Act § 6.23(a), since no par value is required thereunder.

Accounting rules. So much for the law. What does GAAP require in the case of stock dividends? Amazingly, the Committee on Accounting Procedures (the early predecessor to the FASB) decided in 1953 that a stock dividend *does* have economic effect, because, when stock dividends are small relative to the number of outstanding shares, "they do not have any apparent effect upon the share market price."[26] Therefore, GAAP requires companies issuing stock dividends to transfer

> from retained earnings to the category of capital stock and additional paid-in capital an amount equal to the *fair value* of the additional shares issued. Unless this is done, the amount of earnings that the shareholder may believe

25. Model Bus. Corp. Act § 6.23(a).

26. Accounting Research Bulletin No. 43, Chapter 7B, ¶ 10. No empirical research was cited supporting this conclusion. See the current version at Accounting Standards Codification ¶ 505-20-05-2.

> to have been distributed to him or her will be left, except to the extent otherwise dictated by legal requirements, in retained earnings subject to possible further similar stock issuances or cash distributions.[27]

Does this have any basis in the requirements of state law?

> The accounting required ... will likely result in the capitalization of retained earnings in an amount in excess of that called for by the laws of the state of incorporation; such laws generally require the capitalization only of the par value of the shares issued.... However, these legal requirements are, in effect, minimum requirements and do not prevent the capitalization of a larger amount per share.[28]

So we would answer Problem 7-5 *according to GAAP* differently. If the stock distributed as a stock dividend had a fair value of $15 per share, we would journal the stock dividend of 10,000 shares as follows.

Dr Retained Earnings	150,000	
Cr Common Stock $1 Par		10,000
Cr Contributed Capital		140,000

This is GAAP's mandate to "capitalize retained earnings." Has GAAP in effect changed state law?

Stock dividend or stock split? But our journey into the quaint world of par value continues. Suppose, in our opening illustration, the corporation's stock dividend was not 10% but 50%. This is known as a stock "split."[29] Recall that our common stock account looked like this before the storm:

Common stock, $1 par value, 150,000 shares authorized, 100,000 shares outstanding	100,000

The only change would be to "split" the shares on the corporation's books.[30]

Common stock, 66⅔¢ par value, 150,000 shares authorized and outstanding	100,000

No compensating entry to any other accounts needs be found, as we puzzled with in the above problem. No further changes are required by GAAP.[31]

* * *

27. Accounting Standards Codification ¶ 505-20-30-3.

28. *Id.* ¶ 505-20-30-4.

29. A "stock split" is defined as one which has a material impact on share market value, and is expected to be at a minimum of 20 to 25% of the percent of the number of previously outstanding shares. Accounting Standards Codification ¶¶ 505-20-25-2 and -3.

30. The corporation's articles would likely need to be amended to reflect the change in par value. This will also reduce the trading price, probably by one-third in our example, and is a useful device to adjust the per-share trading price. See *supra* note 7.

31. "In the case of a stock split, there is no need to capitalize retained earnings, other than to the extent occasioned by legal requirements." Accounting Standards Codification ¶ 505-20-30-6.

Problem 7-6

X Corporation's Owners' Equity portion of the balance sheet appears as follows:

Common stock $1 par value, 1,000,000 shares authorized, 750,000 outstanding	750,000
Additional paid-in capital	5,250,000
Retained earnings	4,000,000
	10,000,000

How will this section appear if the following actions were to be taken? Consider each independently.

(a) The corporation issues a cash dividend of $1 per share

(b) The corporation issues a stock dividend of 250,000 shares (one share for each three outstanding). Assume the fair market value of the stock distributed is $8.

(c) The corporation splits its common stock two-for-one

* * *

3. Distributions to Owners in Other Capacities

A slightly more complicated way to get money out of a business is to be paid *not as the owner* but in a different capacity, such as an employee, although occasionally it is that of a creditor. Thus, the business owner could pay herself a salary. This amount would appear as an expense in the income statement and would reduce the owner's or owners' equity accordingly, but would have the same "bottom line" effect.

Illustration. Winston's Widgets has been in business for one year. Winston has generated tentative profits of $100, and a balance in his owner's equity account of $100, each before preparation of end-of-year financial statements. But Winston has not taken any money to spend for himself. That would not happen until he withdraws money from the business for his own use. He could do this in one of two ways. First, he could simply distribute an amount to himself as the owner. Second, he could pay himself a "salary" of a certain amount. Suppose Winston wanted to take $15 from Winston's Widgets.

If he chose to take this $15 as a distribution to himself as owner, he would have made the following journal entry.

	Dr	Cr
Dr Owner's equity—Winston	15	
Cr Cash		15
To record distribution to owner.		

Now Winston's Widgets would still show $100 of net income for the period, but his equity account would be reduced from $100 to $85. Suppose instead that Winston decided to pay himself a salary, like any other employee. He would have made the following this journal entry.

Dr Salary expense	15	
Cr Cash		15

To record payment of salary to Winston.

His net income would be reduced to $85. Note that in either case, Winston would still have pocketed his $15 and his equity in the business would be reduced by $15.

Thus, as an economic or an accounting matter, we could say that we would be indifferent between the ways in which owners receive distributions. There may be legal differences between the two methods, however. Payments to employees are different from distributions to owners in their treatment under substantive laws of employment, creditors' rights, income tax, and perhaps other areas. But the issue in any of those cases is to use *those* applicable rules and policies (tax, bankruptcy, social security, etc.) to properly characterize a transaction about which the accountants are relatively indifferent.

D. Redemptions

1. Non-Corporate Entities

When a partnership receives a contribution, the partner's equity account is credited with the value of the contributed property. Subsequent gain or loss is added to or subtracted from the partner's equity account according to the allocation provided by the partnership agreement or the default rules of state partnership law.

However, if a partner's interest is redeemed (repurchased) by the partnership, the amount paid for the interest will be determined by the market value of the interest and by the bargaining power of the parties. Only rarely will the price be determined by reference to the amount in the partners' equity accounts. Therefore, it will be unlikely that the amount paid by the partnership to redeem the partner's interest will equal the amount of that partner's equity account.

Ordinarily, if the amount paid is greater than the book value of the partner's account, the difference is a loss allocated among the remaining partners' accounts as they have agreed to share losses or as state law requires losses to be shared.

Illustration. Suppose that Able, Baker and Charlie formed a partnership, with each contributing $10,000 cash, and each agrees to share profits and losses equally. Over the years, the partnership has recognized income of $30,000. Therefore, the assets of the partnership (net of liabilities) would total $60,000, and each partner's equity account would have a balance of $20,000. If Able were to retire and the partnership agreed to pay him $30,000 for his partnership interest (based on the parties' bargain or a valuation of the interest in the partnership), the excess would be borne by Baker and Charlie equally as follows.

Dr Able — Equity	20,000	
Dr Baker — Equity	5,000	
Dr Charlie — Equity	5,000	
Cr Cash		30,000

To record redemption of Able's partnership interest for $30,000.

If the price paid were for some reason *less* than the value of Able's equity account, the resulting "gain" would be credited to Baker's and Charlie's equity accounts equally.

Ordinarily, the generic (non-tax) accounting for partnership redemptions is relatively unimportant. There will be separate and likely different rules governing the amount of tax gain or loss recognized by Able, Baker, Charlie and the partnership. The answers will depend on, among other things, the nature of each partner's contribution to the partnership, the amount of debt incurred by the partnership, and the decision by the partners to revalue the interests as permitted by federal tax law. The same would be true for a non-corporate entity other than a partnership, such as a limited liability company, which is treated as a partnership for tax purposes.

2. Corporations

Recall that when a corporation issues stock, it debits the asset received (usually cash), credits "Common Stock (par value)" for the par value amount, if there is one, and credits "Contributed capital in excess of par" for the remainder. When a corporation repurchases its stock, it simply reverses these entries. It will debit the common stock and contributed capital accounts, and credit the cash or other asset distributed in payment.

The only complication is that we don't keep careful inventory of shares, and there is likely no record of how much "contributed capital" was paid for a particular share when it was originally sold. Furthermore, those amounts might vary widely over time as shares of stock were sold for different amounts. Usually, the total amount of contributed capital is simply averaged over the number of outstanding shares. The remaining amount is debited to (subtracted from) retained earnings.

Illustration. Recall the example from Xerox Corp. on page 217. Based on the information on its balance sheet, each share of Xerox common stock has $1 in par value and, on average, $14.08 of contributed capital. And let's say that Xerox wants to purchase 100 shares of its stock, and that the market price is $28 per share. To do this the company would journal as follows.

Dr Common stock ($1 par value)	100	
Dr Contributed capital	1408	
Dr Retained earnings	1292	
Cr Cash		2800

To repurchase and retire 100 shares at market price

This example assumes that Xerox does not account for the purchased stock as "treasury stock" under state law, a concept as outmoded as par value.[32] If, for some reason, the price of Xerox stock has dropped to an amount below the capital accounts, say to $14 per share, the amount taken from the contributed capital account would be reduced as follows.

Dr Common stock ($1 par value)	100	
Dr Contributed capital	1300	
Cr Cash		1400

It would *not* be appropriate to reduce contributed capital for the full amount and to *credit* retained earnings for the difference. GAAP normally prohibits a company from increasing "earnings" by transactions in its own stock.[33]

State law normally treats a repurchase like a distribution. In Model Act jurisdictions, the two are treated identically, as a "distribution" is defined to include a repurchase.[34] Other states provide similar rules for repurchases.[35]

* * *

Problem 7-7

Franz, Gregor, and Orkin have been in their pest control business for several years. Prepare journal entries for a redemption by the business of Orkin's ownership interest in exchange for $15,000 cash under each of the following arrangements.

(a) The business is a partnership, and they have agreed to share profits and losses equally. Each partner's equity account has a balance of $9,000.

(b) The business is a corporation, in which Franz, Gregor, and Orkin each own 100 shares of $1 par value stock. The corporation's capital accounts appear as follows:

Common stock $1 par value	300
Contributed capital in excess of par	29,700
Retained earnings	30,000

32. Most modern statutes do not permit a corporation to carry repurchased stock as "treasury stock," but require it to be cancelled, and the accounting in those cases would be as discussed in the text. *See e.g.*, Model Bus. Corp. Act § 6.31(a): "A corporation may acquire its own shares, and shares so acquired constitute authorized but unissued shares." Xerox is a New York corporation, and New York law, like Delaware law, permits a corporation to retain reacquired shares as "treasury" shares, without reducing the stated capital accounts, if the shares are to be resold by the corporation later. N.Y. Bus. Corp. L. § 515(a) and (d); Del. Gen. Corp. L. § 160(a).

33. Accounting Standards Codification ¶ 505-30-25-8.

34. Model Bus. Corp. Act § 1.40 ("A distribution may be in the form of a payment of a dividend; a purchase, redemption, or other acquisition of shares; a distribution of indebtedness; or otherwise.").

35. *See, e.g.*, Del. Gen. Corp. L. § 160(a) ("[N]o corporation shall ... redeem its own shares ... when the capital of the corporation is impaired or redemption would cause any impairment...."). Impairment can be measured using current values of assets in some cases, as was done in *Randall v. Bailey* for a cash dividend. *See* Klang v. Smith's Food and Drug Centers, Inc., 702 A.2d 150 (Del. 1997).

Problem 7-8

X Corporation's Owners' Equity portion of the balance sheet appears as follows:

Common stock $1 par value, 1,000,000 shares authorized, 750,000 outstanding	750,000
Additional paid-in capital	5,250,000
Retained earnings	4,000,000
	10,000,000

How should the corporation account for the repurchase (and cancellation) of 100 shares for:

(a) $1,000 cash?

(b) $600 cash?

Chapter 8

Business Combinations

One of the fundamental assumptions of GAAP is what we have called the "economic entity" assumption. Financial statements are relevant only if they present the position of a distinct entity. How do we determine what is the proper entity?

The *legal* entity is often not the proper accounting entity. When investment by one entity in another constitutes control of the other, GAAP's "economic entity" assumption requires *combination* of two otherwise legally separate entities.[1]

This chapter discusses the two basic conceptual issues about combinations. In Part A, we discuss the rules for accounting for combinations of two businesses into one economic entity. In Part B, we discuss how to treat "uncombined" entities which are nonetheless still related to one another.

A. Principles of Consolidation

Consolidation is required when a business (the "acquirer") obtains control of another business (the "acquiree"). This is a "business combination." There are many terms in the preceding sentence which need further definition.

- ***Business.*** A "business" is defined under GAAP as "an integrated set of activities and assets" that can be managed for the purpose of making a profit for its owners.[2] If the acquisition is *not* of a "business," then is simply an acquisition of assets, for which we already know how to account.[3]
- ***Acquirer*** and ***Acquiree.*** This "business" is owned or controlled by the "acquiree" entity. The "acquirer" entity is the one seeking to obtain control or ownership.
- ***Control.*** The acquirer obtains control if it has the "ability to determine the direction of management and policies" of the acquiree.[4] The acquirer gets control

1. "There is a presumption that consolidated financial statements are more meaningful than separate financial statements and that they are usually necessary for a fair presentation when one of the entities in the consolidated group directly or indirectly has a controlling financial interest in the other entities." Accounting Standards Codification (ASC) ¶ 810-10-10-1.

2. ASC ¶ 805-10-20.

3. ASC ¶¶ 805-50-30-1 to -4. This might be a good time to review. The entity would debit the new asset at its fair value, and credit the asset(s) given or liability(ies) recognized in exchange. There would be no recognition of gain unless the assets surrendered were carried at less than fair value and the transaction was not with a related party.

4. ASC ¶ 805-10-20.

by buying assets and assuming liabilities of the acquiree, or by buying ownership interests in the acquiree.[5]

Once these prerequisites are met, GAAP requires the acquirer to present consolidated financial statements which combine the two entities. This is the subject of Part 1 below. In addition, a new asset, known as "goodwill," may be recognized in the consolidation. This is the subject of Part 2 below.

1. Combination of Assets and Liabilities

Consolidated financial statements are prepared by combining the financial statements of the two separate entities as if the parent acquired the assets (and liabilities) of the subsidiary.[6]

Illustration

Parent Corp. agrees to acquire control of Sub Corp. by purchasing all of its stock. Sub Corp.'s simplified balance sheet is as follows.

Sub Corp. Balance Sheet

Assets	500	Liabilities	150
		Comm. Stock	50
		Contributed capital	100
	___	Retained earnings	200
	500		500

Parent Corp. could acquire Sub Corp.'s stock either for cash or by issuing its own stock to Sub Corp. shareholders in exchange for their shares. Assume that Sub Corp.'s assets and liabilities are stated at "fair values" on its balance sheet and thus require no adjustments.[7] In this case, Parent Corp. would journal as follows to bring Sub Corp.'s net assets onto its own balance sheet.

In a cash transaction:

Dr Sub Corp. Assets	500	
Cr Sub Corp. Liabilities		150
Cr Cash		350

5. ASC ¶ 805-10-55-2.

6. ASC ¶ 805-20-25-1. You may wonder why a business would want to acquire another business' liabilities. Normally, that is the bargain struck. It could be agreed (for a higher price, of course) to purchase only the assets and leave some or all of the liabilities behind.

7. We will remove this simplifying assumption later.

In a stock transaction (assuming Parent's common stock has a par value of $1 and Parent issued 50 shares)

Dr Sub Corp. Assets	500	
Cr Sub Corp. Liabilities		150
Cr Common Stock		50
Cr Contributed capital		300

Variations: Purchase of less than 100% of control of Sub. In many instances, Parent Corp. doesn't acquire all of the Sub Corp. stock. Perhaps Parent Corp. only needs to buy 75% of the stock of Sub Corp. to get the control it desires. If Parent acquires control, the accounting remains the same; all of Sub Corp.'s assets and liabilities are brought on to Parent Corp. books. On the equity side, if Parent does not own 100% of the subsidiary, there will be a remaining "non-controlling" interest to be accounted for. The details are not important at this introductory stage, but you will see many real-world financial statements with a "noncontrolling interest in a consolidated subsidiary" reported with, but separate from, the parent company's equity.[8]

Variations: Purchase of assets. If Parent Corp. purchases Sub Corp. assets, the accounting will look identical to a business combination. The difference, of course, is that in a sale of assets, the consideration credited (cash or stock) is transferred to the seller of the *assets* (the corporation or other entity), rather than to the shareholders directly.

* * *

Problem 8-1

Parent Corp. has determined to purchase all the assets of Sub Corp., which consist of the following at fair market value:

Cash	10,000
Accounts receivable	20,000
Inventory	30,000
Property, plant and equipment	40,000
Total fair market value	100,000

Sub Corp.'s liabilities consist of $10,000 of accounts payable and $20,000 of long-term debt (both of which are fair market values). What would be the journal entry

8. ASC ¶ 810-10-45-16.

to reflect this acquisition if the consideration paid by Parent Corp. for all of Sub Corp.'s stock were:

(a) $70,000 cash?

(b) 7,000 shares of Parent Corp. common stock, with a $1 par value and a total fair market value of $70,000?

Problem 8-2

Suppose that in addition to the assets and liabilities listed in the previous problem, Sub Corp. had applied for and received a patent on its production process. Sub Corp. had spent $10,000 on obtaining the patent. Parent agreed to pay $20,000 for the patent, so that the total consideration was now $90,000 cash. What would the journal entry be to reflect the acquisition by Parent Corp.?

Problem 8-3

Two years ago, Bidder Corp. purchased 25% of the voting common stock of Target Corp. for $25,000.

Now, Target Corp. has the following assets and liabilities.

	Item	Book Value	Fair Value
Assets	Cash	10,000	10,000
	Accounts Receivable	20,000	20,000
	Inventory	30,000	30,000
	Property, Plant and Equipment	35,000	40,000
	Trademark	-0-	20,000
Liabilities	Accounts payable	10,000	10,000
	Long-term Debt	10,000	10,000

Make the required journal entries if Bidder now purchases:

(a) all of the remaining voting common stock for $75,000 cash. In order to make your journal entry balance, you will need to know what entry was made when Bidder purchased Target stock two years ago, and understand that Bidder is no longer treated as the owner of that stock (for accounting purposes).

(b) all of the remaining voting common stock for $75,000 cash, *but* Bidder's purchase two years ago of the initial 25% cost only $15,000. In order to make your journal entry balance, you will need to take account of the economic fact that an asset which cost bidder $15,000 is now being valued in this transaction at $25,000.

* * *

Accounting Challenges for the Acquisition Lawyer

The entities still exist separately. Despite the accounting consolidation, Parent Corp. and Sub Corp. continue their separate legal and practical existence. Either entity may need its own separate financial statements for internal or regulatory purposes. But these statements are rarely seen by others.[9]

The entities will probably engage in transactions with each other. GAAP requires, in preparing the consolidated income statement for Parent Corp. and its subsidiaries, that these intra-entity transactions be eliminated. Thus, a sale from Sub Corp. to Parent Corp. would not result in any income recognized for the consolidated entity; that would happen only if Parent Corp. sells the goods to an unrelated third party. This is one reason that entities in the Parent-Sub situation may wish to have Parent and Sub be considered "unrelated" for accounting purposes — so that sales from one to the other can be recognized. This is our subject in Part B of this Chapter.

The accounting is separate from and mostly indifferent to the legal form of the transaction. The consolidation of the entities for *accounting* purposes has paid no attention to the *legal* machinations involved. Therefore, the lawyer representing Parent and/or Sub in such a transaction will need to keep the accounting treatment in mind. Even if the legal transaction is a "merger" or a "stock purchase," the accounting will represent a purchase of assets and assumption of liabilities.

How does the acquired corporation account for the transaction?
Remember that Sub Corp. retains its own legal existence and financial statements. If the "fair value" paid to Sub shareholders by Parent exceeds Sub Corp.'s historical cost in its assets, Sub Corp.may choose to revalue its assets and recognize gain (and in most cases, public companies are required to do so) by using what is known as ***pushdown accounting***, as it "pushes" the new value paid by Parent "down" to Sub's financial statements too.

The challenge of valuation. The acquisition and consolidation require all assets of the acquired entity to be stated at "fair value." This can be an extremely complicated undertaking. We will study some of the basics of valuation in Chapter 11. The lawyer and accountant will likely closely advise management of the acquiring entity in its valuation analysis.

Prior to 2001, GAAP authorized another type of accounting for combinations. This was called "pooling of interests" accounting which, if certain requirements were met governing the *form* of the transaction, provided for an historical-cost combination of the two entities. Substantial criticism over the years of the "pooling of interests" method led the FASB to abolish it.

---

9. For example, if Sub Corp. were to pay a dividend to Parent Corp., it may need its own financial statements to determine the legality of the dividend under state law according to the rules discussed in Chapter 7.

2. Goodwill

The term "goodwill" can have a number of different meanings depending on the context. But the accountant has a singular and simple meaning for "goodwill."

> **Goodwill has only one meaning for accounting purposes**
>
> Goodwill is the *nonidentifiable intangible asset* which arises only upon acquisition of assets constituting a separate business, and is defined as "an asset representing future economic benefits arising from other assets acquired in a business combination ... that [is] not individually identified and separately recognized."
>
> Source: ASC ¶ 805-30-20

Goodwill is measured as the excess of consideration paid over net fair value of identifiable assets acquired.[10]

Why might a buyer pay ***more*** for a business than the fair value of seller's assets? This is a larger question — how to value a business — which is our subject in Chapter 11. Suffice it to say, for now, that a buyer decides how much to pay for something based on its value to the buyer. And in the case of the purchase of a business, that business is *something more* than the simple combination of the identifiable assets and liabilities. A buyer will pay an amount for the assets of a business which represents the value *to the buyer* of that business, that is, the profits it will produce. That is not necessarily measured by the value of seller's assets.

There are three key aspects of goodwill for the lawyer to understand.

- First, goodwill is ***not separately identifiable***. It is thus distinguished from *identifiable intangible assets*, which we discussed in Chapter 5(B)(2)(b). Those assets are identifiable because they have characteristics similar to tangible assets: they can be owned, conveyed, and others can be excluded from using them. Goodwill, on the other hand, is a nonidentifiable asset because it does not separately exist apart from — and cannot be bought or sold separately from — the combined assets of the business entity purchased.
- Second, accountants are concerned with goodwill only as it may result from a ***business combination***. Some goodwill might be "self-developed," that is, additional value might accrete to a business over time apart from the separate value of its identifiable assets. But GAAP's fundamental principle of "reliability" requires an actual transaction before goodwill can be measured.
- Third, goodwill arises ***only*** in a business combination.[11] This statement has two consequences.
    - ***If goodwill is recognized, then the transaction is, by definition, a business combination.*** If an acquisition is structured legally as a purchase and sale of

10. ASC ¶ 805-30-30-1.

11. See the general rule, and exceptions not important for our purposes, at ASC ¶ 350-20-15-2.

assets, and the consideration paid exceeds the fair values of all of the tangible and intangible assets, then a "business" has been acquired under GAAP, not just a few assets. Remember, the GAAP definition of a "business" is not based on legal form, but is "an integrated set of activities and assets" that can be managed for the purpose of making a profit for its owners.[12] The distinction is important, because in order to revalue goodwill in future periods, the entity will need to identify the group of assets which constitute the "business," even if it is not a separate legal entity.

- ***Not every business combination results in recognition of goodwill.*** Goodwill is recognized only when the consideration paid exceeds the fair market value of all identifiable assets. That will be true in many, perhaps most, business combinations. But not necessarily all of them.

Illustration

Once again, let's look at Sub Corp. with the following balance sheet.

Sub Corp. Balance Sheet

Assets	500	Liabilities	150
		Comm. Stock	50
		Contributed capital	100
	___	Retained earnings	200
	500		500

In our first illustration, we assumed that Parent Corp. would pay $350 for Sub Corp.'s voting common stock. Let's now assume that Parent Corp. pays ***$400*** for Sub Corp.'s voting common stock. We would begin to journal as before, but we would soon run into trouble.

Dr Sub Corp. Assets	500	
Cr Sub Corp. Liabilities		150
Cr Cash		**400**

How do we make the journal entry balance? We would first look at Sub Corp.'s assets individually, to determine if any should be revalued to a "fair value" in excess of book value. But if the answer to that is "no," or the answer is "yes," but our journal entry still doesn't balance, GAAP requires recognition of a separate asset known as "goodwill." Our completed journal entry is thus:

Dr Sub Corp. Assets	500	
Dr Goodwill (asset)	**50**	
Cr Sub Corp. Liabilities		150
Cr Cash		400

12. ASC ¶ 805-10-20.

Since the value paid for the seller's business is determined independent of the value of the seller's identifiable assets, it is also possible that the buyer might be able to pay *less* than the identifiable value of the assets. If this happens, the buyer recognizes gain on the "bargain purchase." In the above illustration, if Parent paid $300 for Sub's assets and liabilities (perhaps because Sub was in a distressed position requiring a forced sale), Parent would then journal as follows:

Dr Sub Corp. Assets	500	
Cr Sub Corp. Liabilities		150
Cr Cash		300
Cr Gain on purchase (revenue)		**50**

* * *

Problem 8-4

Buyer Corp. has determined to purchase all the assets of Seller Corp., which consist of the following at fair market value:

Cash	10,000
Accounts Receivable	20,000
Inventory	30,000
Property, Plant and equipment	40,000
Total fair market value	100,000

Seller Corp.'s liabilities consist of $10,000 of Accounts Payable and $20,000 of long-term debt (both of which are fair market values). The acquisition agreement provides that the assets are purchased subject to the liabilities, so that Seller Corp.'s liabilities are also "purchased" by Buyer Corp., which agrees to pay $90,000 cash for the deal.

(a) What would be the journal entry to reflect this acquisition?

(b) What would be the journal entry if Buyer Corp. instead purchases all the common stock of Seller Corp.?

* * *

Once goodwill is recognized, it is not amortized,[13] but is carried at its initial value and revalued each year, with any decrease in value recognized as an expense.

How is goodwill identified? Goodwill is identified at the "reporting unit" level, which is a component of the business for which discrete financial information is available and is regularly reviewed.[14]

What is "value"? As with identifiable intangible assets, the value to be measured is the "fair value" of the reporting unit, compared with its carrying (or "book") value. The fair value can be determined by market prices, if reliable market prices exist for the equity interest in the reporting unit. For example, the reporting unit may be a separately-incorporated subsidiary, where the outstanding minority com-

13. There is an exception for private companies which may choose to amortize goodwill. *See* ASC ¶ 350-20-35-63.

14. ASC ¶ 350-20-35-34.

mon stock is publicly-traded. Otherwise, more complex valuation methods may be needed for determining the value of the reporting unit, which we will study in Chapter 11.[15]

When is goodwill tested? Goodwill must be valued every year. However, since the above valuation process can be quite involved, GAAP does not require that it be repeated every year. It should be done when the reporting unit is first acquired, and need not be repeated unless an examination of facts and circumstances make it more likely than not that fair value is below carrying value. Examples of relevant factors include:

- Broad macroeconomic conditions or industry or market considerations which affect business generally or the industry in which the company operates;
- Entity-specific factors, such as changes in costs, performance of the economic unit, change in management, strategy, or customers, or a sustained decline in share price.[16]

Even with this annual review, goodwill must be tested for impairment anytime "an event occurs or circumstances change that would more likely than not reduce the fair value of a reporting unit below its carrying amount."[17] If that fair value of the goodwill as measured at the "reporting unit" level is less than the carrying value, the goodwill must be written down to its fair value with an expense recognized for that period.

* * *

Problem 8-5

In 20x1, Parent Corp. purchased all the common stock of Sub Corp. for $10 million in cash. The assets of Sub Corp. had a fair value of $9 million, so Parent Corp. recorded $1 million of goodwill on its balance sheet in accounting for the purchase.

(a) In 20x2, if no other combinations have occurred, and the business of Sub Corp. has not changed materially and continues to be profitable, must Parent Corp. test its goodwill for impairment?

(b) Regardless of your answer to (a), suppose that a fair value determination was made of Sub Corp. at the following amounts. What (if any) journal entries would be required?

(1) $11 million

(2) $9.5 million

(3) $8 million

(c) Regardless of your answer to (b), suppose that in 20x2 the goodwill was considered impaired and a charge of $1 million was taken. In 20x3, the fair value of Sub Corp. is determined to again be $10 million, as it was at the original acquisition. How would this change be reflected on Parent Corp.'s balance sheet?

---

15. ASC ¶¶ 350-20-35-22 to -24.
16. ASC ¶ 350-20-35-3C.
17. ASC ¶ 350-20-35-30.

Problem 8-6

Parent Corp. purchased 33% of the common stock of Sub Corp. for $3.3 million in cash. The net assets of Sub Corp. (assets minus liabilities) had a book value of $9 million. Would Parent Corp. record $300,000 of goodwill? How should the transaction be accounted for?

* * *

B. Related Party Transactions

Not all entities which have some common ownership are consolidated. There are many business entities which are related through common ownership or influence, but whose relationship falls short of "control" requiring consolidation.[18] There are two important consequences to this arrangement of "influence" short of "control."

- First, sales to this entity—over which you have "significant influence"—can be recognized, even though you might have an ability to name the price and thus create profits at any time and for any amount.
- Second, you can transfer to this other company assets which have unrecognized losses, and arrange for the transfer to be at prices which will not show a loss to your company, and leave the later losses (or even bankruptcy) in the unconsolidated entity.

Of course, if the two entities in these examples are consolidated, these transactions will all be for naught, because they will be erased in the consolidation accounting. It is obviously critical that GAAP be able to distinguish between companies which should be treated as unrelated parties who can conduct arm's-length transactions, and those companies which should be consolidated because one has control over the other.

Many entities were able to have the best of both worlds, and used unconsolidated subsidiaries over which they really *did* have control to manufacture profits at artificial prices and hide troubled assets. Whether they were able to do this because of failures of GAAP or because they were able to successfully bend the rules is the subject of much debate.[19]

1. The Old Abuses

Prior to 2003, entities seized upon an interpretation[20] which allowed an entity to avoid consolidation if at least three percent of the equity (ownership) interests were

18. Recall from Chapter 4(B)(1)(b) that if one entity has only "significant influence" over the other, it may use the "equity method" of accounting for the investment.

19. See Chapter 3(A)(3) on how to make a duck out of a dog.

20. EITF Issue No. 90-15. "EITF" refers to the *Emerging Issues Task Force* of the FASB. According to the FASB, the EITF

> was designed to promulgate implementation guidance within the framework of the Accounting Standards Codification to reduce diversity in practice on a timely basis.... Make-

provided by a third party and if those ownership interests had voting control. A company could, for example, create a limited partnership and provide 97% of the money in exchange for nonvoting limited partnership interests, and have an independent third party provide three percent of the money in exchange for all the voting interests. Even *that* investment could be provided indirectly by the company, as was the case with special-purpose entities created by Enron and by American International Group (AIG).

Edward J. Janger, *Brandeis, Business Ethics, and Enron*, in Enron: Corporate Fiascos and Their Implications 63, 65–66 (2004).

> The principal tool that Andrew Fastow, Enron's Chief Financial Officer, appears to have used in the creation of the celebrated LJM, Chewco, and Raptor partnerships is called "structured finance." The magic was accomplished through manipulation of legitimate structures and the malleable accounting rules for "off balance sheet" treatment of entities.
>
> Let's start with a legitimate use of structured finance, and then explore how Fastow manipulated that device. Let's assume that Enron entered into a deal to sell a piece of heavy equipment for $500,000, and the buyer promised to pay for it over the next ten years, at a steady rate of $50,000 plus interest. Let's further assume that Enron wanted the cash now, instead of the income stream. Enron would have two options: it could borrow $500,000 against the income stream..., or it could sell the income stream (or "financial asset") for $500,000. The loan transaction would alter both the left side and the right side of the balance sheet. Cash would increase by $500,000 on the left side, while the $500,000 would be booked as debt on the right side of the balance sheet. The sale transaction, by contrast, operates only on the left side of the balance sheet. One asset ... would become cash.... One important thing to note, however, is that neither the sale nor the loan transaction alters the book value of Enron. Shareholder equity remains constant.
>
> Neither of these transactions is controversial. Neither of them is deceptive. The advantage of the sale transaction, for Enron's purposes, is that after the sale, Enron would book the full $500,000 value of the receivable as income in the quarter in which the asset was sold. This is permissible under accounting rules if the sale is a "true sale" to a "separate entity." In other words, Enron must have truly transferred the benefits and risks of ownership to the purchaser....

> up of the Task Force is designed to include persons in a position to be aware of emerging issues before they become widespread and before divergent practices become entrenched. Therefore, if the group can reach a consensus on an issue, usually that is taken by the FASB as an indication that no Board action is needed.

www.fasb.org/jsp/FASB/Page/SectionPage&cid=1218220137512.

> Here's where the smoke and mirrors come in. What if the value of the income stream is $500,000, but Enron chose to book it as a $1 million deal? Well, that is a fraud, and that is basically what Enron did. How could Enron have done this without being detected? The sleight of hand was accomplished by manipulating and pressing the limits of the accounting rules for off-book transactions. Since nobody would pay $1 million for a $500,000 asset, Enron sold it to a partnership that it controlled, and Enron guaranteed to the purchasing partnership that the $500,000 asset would in fact yield $1 million. In the case of the LJM and Chewco partnership set up by Fastow, the enhancements took different forms for each partnership, but in both cases, Enron essentially guaranteed (in various ways too complicated to detail here) that, if [Enron] defaulted on its obligation to pay for the assets, Enron would make up the difference.... The problem is that Enron never disclosed this recourse. In this simplified example, Enron essentially borrowed $500,000 from the buyer and didn't list that debt on the balance sheet.
>
> Having explained what Enron did, recognize one other important fact: these numbers were made up. In the real Enron deals, the undisclosed recourse totaled $1.2 billion. When the magnitude of the undisclosed recourse was finally disclosed, the value of Enron's stock collapsed.

Bethany McLean and Peter Elkind, The Smartest Guys in the Room: The Amazing Rise and Scandalous Fall of Enron 151 (2003).

> Enron continued to fund its growth — to the tune of billions of dollars each year — through the miracle of structured finance. Structured finance enabled Enron to raise capital off its balance sheet to an extent no one imagined possible. According to an Enron board presentation, Fastow's Global Finance group was raising around $20 billion worth of capital a *year*, mostly through structured finance deals. As Fastow himself once told the board, his job was to "feed the beast."
>
> In business terms, it was as if the company had discovered a way to defy the laws of gravity. Using off-balance-sheet vehicles and other complex transactions, Enron seemed to be able to make money magically appear without either adding debt or issuing stock. And that's precisely how many Enron executives felt, especially those who worked directly for Fastow: they thought they *were* magicians, reinventing corporate finance, rewriting the rules of the game, thumbing their nose at the way business had always been done.
>
> One wonders now whether Fastow recognized that he was creating an illusion, especially as the pressure increased, and the sums became larger, and the chicanery required to pull it all off grew more brazen. For the most part, Fastow seemed to exhibit great pride in the work he was doing — he even bragged about some of Enron's more clever structures. But every once in a while, he would show that he could glimpse a more terrifying reality. Once,

a banker asked him what would happen to Enron if the deal flow ever stopped.

"It implodes," Fastow responded.

Mark Cheffers and Michael Pakaluk, Accounting Ethics and the Near Collapse of the Entire Financial System of the World 48–49, 60–61 (2011).

> Coral Re[insurance Co.] may be viewed as the "Mother" of all Special Purpose Entities (SPEs) and Off Balance Sheet (OBS) irregularities. It was created long before Enron perfected that accounting manipulation.... AIG [American International Group]'s subsidiaries survived the deterioration of business in the [insurance] market through having AIG create an OBS entity, shift all of those potential ... losses to this putative third-party entity, and only record a loss internally when the amount was paid—because one does not need to book the loss. (When the time came for paying the loss, AIG would tell Coral Re, and at that time there would be a round trip of cash between AIG and Coral Re.
>
> A key aspect of Coral Re's existence was that it had to be perceived as independent of AIG, since otherwise consolidation principles would eliminate any of the loss deferral benefits. Hence, despite the fact that AIG originated, managed and controlled every aspect of Coral Re's business, AIG was successful in hiding this entity from every auditor or regulator ... for more than seven years.
>
> ....
>
> The next improper transaction of AIG which came to light, involving PNC Financial Services, was also similar to Coral Re, insofar as it involved creating an entity which appeared to be independent and was not consolidated, but which actually was not independent and should have been consolidated.
>
> In the scheme which AIG sold to PNC, AIG created a Special Purpose Entity (SPE) which would be putatively independent of PNC, because the entity would be in part initially funded by AIG. PNC then transferred badly performing investments to this SPE, thereby removing them from its balance sheet.
>
> ....
>
> The transactions were irregular because the SPEs did not meet the minimal GAAP standards for non-consolidation; moreover, AIG did not have a true ownership stake in the entity.... The ... SPEs nominally met the GAAP third-party investment requirement for non-consolidation, because AIG agreed to contribute cash to the SPE equivalent to 3% given the value of the investments contributed by PNC. However, in substance, AIG's investment fell below that mark. Through [origination fees and payments on a note by PNC to AIG] ... AIG's interest in the SPE would fall below minimum GAAP requirements.

2. The New Rules

GAAP has been substantially revised to take account of the abuses of the early part of the new century. The underlying question is the same as always—should an entity be consolidated with one of its owners?

We begin with the general rule that consolidation is normally appropriate where an entity owns a majority of the voting control of another entity. But this does not answer all our questions. Could it be that in some cases the owner of a majority of the voting control does not actually exercise control, so that consolidation with that owner is not appropriate? And similarly, could it be the case that an owner of some other kinds of interests would be able to exercise control even though it owns far less than a majority of the voting control? Given the abuses of the previous several years, the answer to these questions was obviously "yes." Accounting standards needed to take account of all this diversity. Thus was born accounting for the "special purpose entity" or SPE, which was rechristened a ***"variable interest entity" or VIE*** in modern GAAP.

The general rule: control requires consolidation. Recall GAAP's general requirement that "control" of one entity by another requires consolidation of the two as if the controlling entity acquired the controlled entity.[21] "Control" means "the ability to determine the direction of management and policies."[22] Normally control exists with ownership of a majority of the outstanding voting shares or interests. But control may be exercised with lesser voting power, "for example, by contract, lease agreement with other stockholders, or by court decree."[23] We apply the general rule unless the exception for a VIE applies.[24]

HOW TO APPLY THE EXCEPTIONS FOR VARIABLE INTEREST ENTITIES

We apply these rules whenever the question to be answered is: ***does this entity potentially need to be consolidated with another?*** To answer the question, follow these three steps.

1. **Does the entity have variable interests?** A variable interest is an ownership or other pecuniary interest that "change[s] with the changes in the fair value of the VIE's net assets.... Equity interests are [normally] considered variable interests" (ASC ¶ 810-10-20).

21. ASC ¶ 810-10-10-1.

22. ASC ¶ 805-20-10.

23. ASC ¶ 810-10-15-8.

24. There are other exceptions such as partnerships, research and development arrangements or contractual control by one entity of another. See ASC ¶ 810-10-15-10 for the list of exceptions. These are minor compared to the VIE rules for our initial inquiry and we focus here only on the VIE rules.

2. **If "yes," is the entity a variable interest entity?** This might seem obvious, but the term VIE has a special meaning. It is essentially a business enterprise which is not going to be successful without some additional arrangements for funding.

   (If "no," we follow the general rules for consolidation.)

3. **If "yes," does the VIE need to be consolidated with a variable interest holder?** Here we apply special rules to determine whether a variable interest holder "controls" the VIE.

   (If "no," we follow the general rules for consolidation.)

A detailed flowchart appears at ASC ¶ 810-10-05-6.

Let's examine each of these steps in turn.

1. Does the entity have variable interests? This should be fairly obvious. Any right or ownership interest in the entity is variable if it "change[s] with the changes in the fair value of the VIE's net assets...."[25] Any equity interest can be a variable interest,[26] but not all variable interests are equity interests. The terms of each right or interest must be carefully examined according to the contracts or organizational documents of the entity.

Illustration

Common stock is a "variable interest" because its value changes with the value of the corporation's assets. If A owns 30% of the common stock of B Corp., A holds variable interests in B Corp. Although the answer to the first VIE question is "yes," we still need to determine if B Corp. is a VIE. *Only then* do we consider whether to follow the special VIE rules with respect to A's ownership of B Corp. common stock.

2. Is the entity a VIE? An entity is a VIE if it is designed in ***either*** of these ways:

- First: the total equity investment is insufficient to finance its activities without additional financial support, that is, additional commitments to provide assets or to absorb losses.

25. ASC ¶ 810 10 20.
26. *Id.*

- Second, the equity investors, taken as a whole, lack ***any one*** of these characteristics:
  - The power to direct the entity's main economic activity. This characteristic is lacking if the voting rights of investors are not proportionate to their obligations to absorb losses, or if substantially all of the entity's activities are directed by investors with few voting rights.
  - The obligation to absorb expected losses
  - The right to receive expected residual returns.[27]

3. Does the VIE need to be consolidated with the variable interest holder? A variable interest holder has a controlling financial interest, and thus consolidation of the VIE with that holder is appropriate, if those variable interests have ***both*** these characteristics:

- The power to direct the VIE's main economic activity; and
- The obligation to absorb losses or to receive benefits that could be potentially significant to the VIE.

Obviously, more than one VIE holder could satisfy the second condition, but it is expected that only one VIE holder could satisfy the first condition.[28]

Significant judgment must be exercised. Obviously, these can be complicated inquiries. The answer often can be found only after careful legal and economic analysis and testing of the entity.

> In determining the purpose for which the legal entity was created and the variability the legal entity was designed to create and pass along to its interest holders..., all relevant facts and circumstances shall be considered, including, but not limited to, the following factors:
>
> a. The activities of the legal entity
>
> b. The terms of the contracts the legal entity has entered into
>
> c. The nature of the legal entity's interests issued
>
> d. How the legal entity's interests were negotiated with or marketed to potential investors
>
> e. Which parties participated significantly in the design or redesign of the legal entity.[29]

---

27. ASC ¶ 810-10-15-14.
28. *Id.* ¶ 810-10-25-38A.
29. *Id.* ¶ 810-10-25-25.

Examples

Most companies use variable interest entities (VIEs) to take assets they own and sell interests in them in smaller pieces. Verizon Communications, Inc., for example, has put their cell-phone payment plan receivables into a separate entity, and then sold interests in that entity for cash. This allows them to receive cash earlier than simply waiting for you to pay your cell phone bill. The "separate entity" is a VIE, according to the notes to Verizon's 2018 financial statements, because

> The ... Entities meet the definition of a VIE for which we have determined that we are the primary beneficiary as we have both the power to direct the activities of the entity that most significantly impact the entity's performance and the obligation to absorb losses or the right to receive benefits of the entity. Therefore, the assets, liabilities and activities of the ABS Entities are consolidated in our financial results and are included in amounts presented on the face of our consolidated balance sheets.

Notice how Verizon almost quotes the GAAP standards in its disclosure. Ford Motor Co. has a similar program; it loans money to buyers of its vehicles. Here is how Ford describes its VIE in notes to its 2018 financial statements.

> Securitization Entities. Through Ford Credit, we securitize, transfer, and service financial assets associated with consumer finance receivables, operating leases, and wholesale loans. Our securitization transactions typically involve the legal transfer of financial assets to bankruptcy remote [entities]. We generally retain economic interests in the asset-backed securitization transactions, which are retained in the form of senior or subordinated interests, cash reserve accounts, residual interests, and servicing rights.... In most cases, the bankruptcy remote [entities] meet the definition of VIEs for which we have determined we have both the power to direct the activities of the entity that most significantly impact the entity's performance and the obligation to absorb losses or the right to receive benefits of the entity that could be significant....

There is a wider variety of VIEs in financial firms. Bank of America Corporation discloses several lines of VIEs in these excerpts from notes to its 2018 financial statements.

> **Variable Interest Entities**
>
> The Corporation consolidates a VIE if it has both the power to direct the activities of the VIE that most significantly impact the VIE's economic performance and an obligation to absorb losses or the right to receive benefits that could potentially be significant to the VIE. On a quarterly basis, the Corporation reassesses its involvement with the VIE and evaluates the impact of changes in governing documents and its financial interests in the VIE. The consolidation status of the VIEs with which the Corporation is involved may change as a result of such reassessments.

The Corporation primarily uses VIEs for its securitization activities, in which the Corporation transfers whole loans or debt securities into a trust or other vehicle. When the Corporation is the servicer of whole loans held in a securitization trust, including non-agency residential mortgages, home equity loans, credit cards, and other loans, the Corporation has the power to direct the most significant activities of the trust. The Corporation generally does not have the power to direct the most significant activities of a residential mortgage agency trust except in certain circumstances in which the Corporation holds substantially all of the issued securities and has the unilateral right to liquidate the trust. The power to direct the most significant activities of a commercial mortgage securitization trust is typically held by the special servicer or by the party holding specific subordinate securities which embody certain controlling rights.

The Corporation utilizes VIEs in the ordinary course of business to support its own and its customers' financing and investing needs. The Corporation routinely securitizes loans and debt securities using VIEs as a source of funding for the Corporation and as a means of transferring the economic risk of the loans or debt securities to third parties. The assets are transferred into a trust or other securitization vehicle such that the assets are legally isolated from the creditors of the Corporation and are not available to satisfy its obligations. These assets can only be used to settle obligations of the trust or other securitization vehicle. The Corporation also administers, structures or invests in other VIEs.

First-lien Mortgage Securitizations

As part of its mortgage banking activities, the Corporation securitizes a portion of the first-lien residential mortgage loans it originates or purchases from third parties, generally in the form of [residential-mortgage-backed securities] guaranteed by government-sponsored enterprises.

Value of first-mortgage securitization VIEs, Dec. 31, 2018 ($ billions)

Unconsolidated:	$187.5
Consolidated:	13.3

Collateralized Debt Obligation VIEs

The Corporation receives fees for structuring VIEs which hold diversified pools of fixed-income securities, typically corporate debt or [asset-backed securities], which the VIEs fund by issuing multiple tranches of debt and equity securities. The VIEs are generally managed by third-party portfolio managers.The Corporation typically transfers assets to these entities, holds securities issued by them and may be a derivative counterparty.

Investment VIEs

The Corporation sponsors, invests in or provides financing, which may be in connection with the sale of assets, to a variety of investment VIEs that hold loans, real estate, debt securities or other financial instruments and are designed to provide the desired investment profile to investors or the Corporation.

Leveraged Lease Trusts

The trusts hold long-lived equipment such as rail cars, power generation and distribution equipment, and commercial aircraft. The Corporation structures the trusts and holds a significant residual interest. Debt issued by the leveraged lease trusts is non-recourse to the Corporation.

Tax Credit VIEs

The Corporation holds investments in unconsolidated limited partnerships and similar entities that construct, own and operate affordable housing, wind and solar projects. An unrelated third party is typically the general partner or managing member and has control over the significant activities of the VIE. The Corporation earns a return primarily through the receipt of tax credits allocated to the projects.

Value of all other VIEs, Dec. 31, 2018 ($ billions)

Unconsolidated:	$94.7
Consolidated:	4.3.

* * *

Problem 8-7

NorthWestern Retail Co. (NWC) owns a chain of department stores and has a significant online retail business. NWC plans to sell $1.1 million of its customer accounts receivable. It will form a corporation called Invesco Inc. NWC will transfer the accounts receivable to Invesco in exchange for $1 million cash, which Invesco will borrow from National Bank, assigning the accounts as security for the loan. The Bank insists on more "cushion" for its investment, so Invesco will sell $100,000 of common stock to unrelated investors. Invesco has a traditional corporate structure: the shareholders elect directors, and the directors hire managers. Invesco management will select the accounts to be purchased by Invesco, oversee the collections, and Invesco is responsible for the loan payments to the Bank.

(a) Is there a business purpose for this arrangement? Why doesn't NWC simply borrow the money from National Bank and pledge the receivables itself?

(b) Should Invesco be consolidated with NWC?

(c) Regardless of your answer in (b), how would you change the arrangement to obtain the opposite result?

(d) Suppose NWC and Invesco management both knew that the accounts receivable had a fair market value well below $1.1 million. How is this deal still possible?

Problem 8-8[30]

Mortgage Investors Group was created as follows. MIG sold three levels of debt instruments, Level I, Level II and Level III bonds, for a total of $940,000. MIG's equity is owned by Midwest Brokerage Services, Inc. (MBSI), a regional investment banker, which invested $60,000. MIG took the $1 million and purchased BB-rated fixed-rate commercial mortgage loans with seven-year maturities from First National Bank (which is not affiliated with MBSI). Each month, payments received from the pool of mortgage loans are paid over first to the Level I bondholders, then the Level II bondholders, then the Level III bondholders. If there is a shortfall in the mortgage payments, the equity tranche will absorb the losses, then the Level III bonds, and so on up to the Level I bonds. The mortgage loans will continue to be serviced by First National Bank, which collects payments and takes care of the escrow accounts (for taxes and insurance). However, if there is a default on any mortgage, First National will transfer servicing to MBSI, which agrees to take over the servicing. MBSI then takes all responsibility for managing the foreclosed property. MBSI retains the right to monitor the mortgage loans prior to any delinquency to assure itself that it can act quickly to preserve collateral value in the case of any default. MBSI earns a fixed fee plus a percentage of the unpaid principal balance on the underlying loans. Neither First National nor MBSI may be removed from their positions as primary or secondary servicer of the underlying mortgages.

Identify the holders of variable interests in MIG and the nature of those interests. With whom, if anyone, should MIG be consolidated?

Problem 8-9[31]

The following is from the 2010 Annual Report of Papa John's International, Inc.

Through December 2010, we had a purchasing agreement with BIBP, a special-purpose entity formed at the direction of our Franchise Advisory Council, for the sole purpose of reducing cheese price volatility to domestic system-wide restaurants. BIBP is an independent, franchisee-owned corporation. BIBP purchases cheese at the market price and sells it to our distribution subsidiary, PJ Food Service, Inc. ("PJFS"), at a fixed price. PJFS in turn sells cheese to Papa John's restaurants (both Company-owned and franchised) at a set price. PJFS purchased $153.0 million, $142.4 million and $165.4 million of cheese from BIBP during 2010, 2009 and 2008, respectively.

Should BIBP be consolidated with Papa John's International, Inc.?

---

30. See ASC ¶¶ 810-10-55-96 to -109.

31. Adapted from Lawrence Revsine, *et al.*, Financial Reporting and Analysis 1003 (5th ed. 2012).

Problem 8-10[32]

Royal Co. is a beverage manufacturer, and Crown Co. is a distributer and retailer of beverages. The two companies have formed Cola Corp. to manufacture, distribute, and sell a new cola product. The entity is funded with $1 million of stock purchased in equal portions by Royal and Crown, and $99 million in 20-year fixed-rate bonds sold to widely-dispersed unrelated investors. All decisions about manufacture, distribution and sale of the Cola Corp. products must be made jointly by the two shareholders. Each company elects three of Cola's six directors. The stockholders have agreed to submit unresolved disputes to binding arbitration.

Should Cola Corp. be consolidated with any other entity?

32. See ASC ¶¶ 810-10-55-183 to -192.

Part Three

Legal Issues Involving Accounting Concepts

Part Two covered the basic accounting issues which you will likely encounter as a practicing lawyer—the areas where accounting questions will create legal problems for a client. This part discusses the reverse arrangement—primarily legal problems which will intimately involve the accounting issues you have already mastered. In short, it is time to put your accounting knowledge to work in a law practice.

Chapter 9

Internal Controls

Internal controls are the systems, policies, plans, approvals, and security devices, among other things, which allow an entity to operate in the way its management intends. They are the key to understanding management of any entity, and the legal standards relating to internal controls have assumed great significance in recent years, especially as courts require directors to exercise close and careful oversight of corporations, and as policy makers require internal control systems to bear much of the weight of detection and prevention of financial fraud.

We will study internal controls as they have developed historically. First, we turn to the law of internal *accounting* controls. They are, of course, more closely related to the financial statements and decisions we have studied so far. Second, we will discuss the law of business organizations which requires managers of those organizations to exercise effective oversight of the business generally, not just the accounting systems, often known as "Enterprise Risk Management."

A. The Modern Development of Internal Accounting Controls

1. The Foreign Corrupt Practices Act

The law of internal accounting controls began in modern times with the passage of the Foreign Corrupt Practices Act of 1977 (FCPA).[1] The portion of the Act which is our focus here does not deal directly with foreign corrupt practices. Rather, it imposes upon companies the obligation to have controls and systems in place.

In addition to the statutory provisions of the FCPA, the Securities and Exchange Commission has adopted two important rules in furtherance of this statute, and brought the first and still one of the most important FCPA cases. Each is excerpted below.

1. For a summary of internal controls developments prior to 1977, see Parveen P. Gupta *et al.*, *Sarbanes-Oxley and Public Reporting on Internal Control: Hasty Reaction or Delayed Action?*, 27 Accounting Horizons 371 (2013).

Securities and Exchange Act of 1934

Section 13(b)(2)

Every issuer which has a class of securities registered pursuant to section [12] of this title and every issuer which is required to file reports pursuant to section [15(d)] of this title shall—

(A) make and keep books, records, and accounts, which, in reasonable detail, accurately and fairly reflect the transactions and dispositions of the assets of the issuer;

(B) devise and maintain a system of internal accounting controls sufficient to provide reasonable assurances that—

> **Who is covered?** An issuer is subject to these rules (under sections 12 or 15(d) of the Act) if (1) its shares are traded on a stock exchange; (2) it has more than $10 million in assets or 500 shareholders of record (2000 if at least 1500 of them are "accredited" investors, that is, wealthy individuals and certain institutions); or (3) it has recently made a registered public offering of securities. This is usually what people refer to when they speak of "public" companies.

(i) transactions are executed in accordance with management's general or specific authorization;

(ii) transactions are recorded as necessary

(I) to permit preparation of financial statements in conformity with generally accepted accounting principles or any other criteria applicable to such statements, and

(II) to maintain accountability for assets;

(iii) access to assets is permitted only in accordance with management's general or specific authorization; and

(iv) the recorded accountability for assets is compared with the existing assets at reasonable intervals and appropriate action is taken with respect to any differences.

Rules and Regulations under the Securities and Exchange Act of 1934

Rule 13b2-1. **Falsification of accounting records.**

No person shall, directly or indirectly, falsify or cause to be falsified, any book, record or account subject to Section 13(b)(2)(A) of the Securities Exchange Act.

Rule 13b2-2. **Representations and conduct in connection with the preparation of required reports and documents.**

(a) No director or officer of an issuer shall, directly or indirectly:

(1) Make or cause to be made a materially false or misleading statement to an accountant in connection with; or

(2) Omit to state, or cause another person to omit to state, any material fact necessary in order to make statements made, in light of the circumstances under which such statements were made, not misleading, to an accountant in connection with:

(i) Any audit, review or examination of the financial statements of the issuer required to be made pursuant to this subpart; or

(ii) The preparation or filing of any document or report required to be filed with the Commission pursuant to this subpart or otherwise.

....

Securities And Exchange Commission v. World-Wide Coin Investments, Ltd.

United States District Court, Northern District of Georgia, 1983
567 F. Supp. 724

VINING, District Judge.

This is a securities fraud action in which the Securities and Exchange Commission (SEC) seeks a permanent injunction against World-Wide Coin Investments, Ltd. (World-Wide) and the individual defendants as well as an order for a full accounting and disclosure of wrongfully received benefits....

Factual Background

World-Wide Coin Investments, Ltd., is a Delaware corporation with its principal offices in Atlanta, Georgia, and is engaged primarily in the wholesale and retail sale of rare coins, precious metals, gold and silver coins, bullion, and, until 1979, in the retail sale of camera equipment.... Its inventory of rare coins comes from its purchases of collections from estates and private individuals, purchases from dealers, purchases on domestic commodities exchanges, and purchases at coin shows. Sales are transacted at the Atlanta office and at many major coin shows held in the United States. For some time it published a trade journal, *The Coin Wholesaler*, which carried both news and feature stories of special interest to coin collectors and investors, who comprised the majority of subscribers....

World-Wide's common stock is registered with the SEC pursuant to the Securities Exchange Act of 1934, and until late 1981 was listed on the Boston Stock Exchange. Prior to July 1979, the company's assets totaled over $2,000,000, and it had over 40 employees. In August 1981, the time of the filing of this lawsuit, the company's assets amounted to less than $500,000, and it had only three employees.

Defendant Joseph H. Hale took over the management and control of World-Wide on July 24, 1979, as the controlling shareholder, chairman of the board, chief executive officer, and president....

....

III. EVENTS FOLLOWING HALE'S TAKEOVER

... It is the deterioration of World-Wide's internal controls and accounting procedures that constitutes the primary thrust of the SEC's complaint. The SEC contends that the combination of late filings, lack of internal controls, transactions unsupported by adequate documentation, and a total disregard for proper accounting procedures resulted in the precarious position of the company at the time the lawsuit was filed. This court will attempt to examine each of the various problems of the company from 1979 through 1981.

C. Problems with Internal Controls and Accounting Procedures

... The problems that occurred at the company with respect to internal controls and accounting procedures can be divided into [two] areas: (1) inventory problems, [and] (2) problems with separation of duties and the lack of documentation of transactions....

(1) *Inventory Problems*

The safeguarding of World-Wide's physical inventory was one of its most severe problems; there was considerable testimony at trial to the effect that the company's vault, where most of the rare coins were kept, was unguarded and left open all day to all employees. Furthermore, no one employee was responsible for the issuance of coins from the vault....

Hale also failed to initiate an adequate system of itemizing World-Wide's physical inventory. Rather than maintaining a perpetual inventory system, the company relied on a manual quarterly system, which, in light of the company's inadequate securities measures, was not effective in safeguarding the assets or in keeping an accurate account of the inventory. World-Wide's system made it relatively simple for an employee to improperly value and/or misappropriate large items of inventory undetected. Furthermore, employees were allowed to take large amounts of inventory off the premises of World-Wide for purposes of effecting a sale without giving a receipt.

....

(2) *Separation of Duties*

... World-Wide maintains no separation of duties in the area of purchase and sales transactions, and valuation procedures for ending inventory. For instance, a single salesperson can do all the following tasks without supervision or review by another employer or officer: appraise a particular coin offered for purchase by a customer, purchase that coin with a check that the salesperson alone has drawn, count that same coin into inventory, value the coin for inventory purposes, and sell the coin to another purchaser.

Employees, none of whom was bonded, were also allowed to take large amounts of inventory off the company's premises for purposes of effecting a sale without giving a receipt, as well as being given cash to purchase the precious metals and coins at various locations, also without giving a receipt....

Additionally, there were no procedures enforced with respect to writing checks; for instance, no system has been implemented to ensure that the purpose for which a check is written can be ascertained. Since employees have been allowed to write checks without noting the purpose of the transaction on the instrument or on any other document, source documents for most checks do not exist....

Evidence introduced at trial further revealed that approximately $1.7 million worth of checks were written to Hale, his affiliates, or to cash, all without supporting documentation or any indication of the purpose of the checks....

APPLICATION OF LAW

The Foreign Corrupt Practices Act ... ("FCPA") was enacted by Congress as an amendment to the 1934 Securities Exchange Act and was the legislative response to numerous questionable and illegal foreign payments by United States corporations in the 1970's. Although one of the major substantive provisions of the FCPA is to require corporate disclosure of assets as a deterrent to foreign bribes, the more significant addition of the FCPA is the accounting controls or "books and records" provision, which gives the SEC authority over the entire financial management and reporting requirements of publicly held United States corporations.

The FCPA was enacted on the principle that accurate recordkeeping is an essential ingredient in promoting management responsibility and is an affirmative requirement for publicly held American corporations to strengthen the accuracy of corporate books and records, which are "the bedrock elements of our system of corporate disclosure and accountability." A motivating factor in the enactment of the FCPA was a desire to protect the investor, as was the purpose behind the enactment of the Securities Acts. It is apparent that investors are entitled to rely on the implicit representations that corporations will account for their funds properly and will not channel funds out of the corporation or omit to include such funds in the accounting system so that there are no checks possible on how much of the corporation's funds are being expended in the manner management later claims.

....

Section 13(b)(2) contains two separate requirements for issuers in complying with the FCPA's accounting provisions: (1) a company must keep accurate books and records reflecting the transactions and dispositions of the assets of the issuer, and (2) a company must maintain a reliable and adequate system of internal accounting controls. In applying these two separate requirements to the instant case, the court will examine the requirements of each provision and the problems inherent in their interpretation.

The "books and records" provision, contained in section 13(b)(2)(A) of the FCPA has three basic objectives: (1) books and records should reflect transactions in conformity with accepted methods of reporting economic events, (2) misrepresentation, concealment, falsification, circumvention, and other deliberate acts resulting in inaccurate financial books and records are unlawful, and (3) transactions should be properly reflected on books and records in such a manner as to permit the preparation of financial statements in conformity with GAAP and other criteria applicable to such statements.

....

The only express congressional requirement for accuracy is the phrase "in reasonable detail." Although section 13(b)(2) expects management to see that the corporation's recordkeeping system is adequate and effectively implemented, how the issuer goes about this task is up to management; the FCPA provides no guidance, and this court cannot issue any kind of advisory opinion.

Just as the degree of error is not relevant to an issuer's responsibility for any inaccuracies, the motivations of those who erred are not relevant. There are no words in section 13(b)(2)(A) indicating that Congress intended to impose a scienter requirement, although there is some support among officials at the Securities and Exchange Commission for the addition of a scienter requirement and a form of a materiality standard to the FCPA....

The second branch of the accounting provisions — the requirement that issuers maintain a system of internal accounting controls — appears in section 13(b)(2)(B). Like the recordkeeping provisions of the Act, the internal controls provision is not limited to material transactions or to those above a specific dollar amount. While this requirement is supportive of accuracy and reliability in the auditor's review and financial disclosure process, this provision should not be analyzed solely from that point of view. The internal controls requirement is primarily designed to give statutory content to an aspect of management stewardship responsibility, that of providing shareholders with reasonable assurances that the business is adequately controlled.

Internal accounting control is, generally speaking, only one aspect of a company's total control system; in order to maintain accountability for the disposition of its assets, a business must attempt to make it difficult for its assets to be misappropriated. The internal accounting controls element of a company's control system is that which is specifically designed to provide reasonable, cost-effective safeguards against the unauthorized use or disposition of company assets and reasonable assurances that financial records and accounts are sufficiently reliable for purposes of external reporting. "Internal accounting controls" must be distinguished from the accounting system typically found in a company. Accounting systems process transactions and recognize, calculate, classify, post, summarize, and report transactions. Internal controls safeguard assets and assure the reliability of financial records, one of their main jobs being to prevent and detect errors and irregularities that arise in the accounting systems of the company. Internal accounting controls are basic indicators of the reliability of the financial statements and the accounting system and records from which financial statements are prepared.

....

Although not specifically delineated in the Act itself, the following directives can be inferred from the internal controls provisions: (1) Every company should have reliable personnel, which may require that some be bonded, and all should be supervised. (2) Account functions should be segregated and procedures designed to prevent errors or irregularities. The major functions of recordkeeping, custodianship, authorization, and operation should be performed by different people to avoid the temptation for abuse of these incompatible functions. (3) Reasonable assurances should be maintained that transactions are executed as authorized. (4) Transactions should be properly recorded in the firm's accounting records to facilitate control, which would also require standardized procedures for making accounting entries. Exceptional entries should be investigated regularly. (5) Access to assets of the company should be limited to authorized personnel. (6) At reasonable intervals, there should be a comparison of the accounting records with the actual inventory of assets, which would usually involve the physical taking of inventory, the counting of cash, and the reconciliation of accounting records with the actual physical assets. Frequency of these comparisons will usually depend on the cost of the process and upon the materiality of the assets involved.

The main problem with the internal accounting controls provision of the FCPA is that there are no specific standards by which to evaluate the sufficiency of controls; any evaluation is inevitably a highly subjective process in which knowledgeable individuals can arrive at totally different conclusions. Any ruling by a court with respect to the applicability of both the accounting provisions and the internal accounting control provisions should be strictly limited to the facts of each case.

....

The definition of accounting controls does comprehend reasonable, but not absolute, assurances that the objectives expressed in it will be accomplished by the system. The concept of "reasonable assurances" contained in section 13(b)(2)(B) recognizes that the costs of internal controls should not exceed the benefits expected to be derived....

... It is true that a cost/benefit analysis is particularly relevant here, but it remains undisputed that it was the lack of any control over the inventory and inadequate accounting procedures that primarily contributed to World-Wide's demise. No organization, no matter how small, should ignore the provisions of the FCPA completely, as World-Wide did. Furthermore, common sense dictates the need for such internal controls and procedures in a business with an inventory as liquid as coins, medals, and bullion.

....

Individually, the acts of these defendants do not appear so egregious as to warrant the full panoply of relief requested by the SEC nor to impose complete liability under the FCPA. However, the court cannot ignore the all-pervasive effect of the combined failure to act, failure to keep accurate records, failure to maintain any type of inventory control, material omissions and misrepresentations, and other activities which caused World-Wide to decrease from a company of 40 employees and assets over $2,000,000 to a company of only three employees and assets of less than $500,000. It is evident that World-Wide [and] Hale ... violated all provisions contained in section 13(b)(2)(A) and (B) and the SEC's rules promulgated thereunder.

....

Notes and Questions

1. Concern continued about the level of detail required for records and controls under the FCPA. Section 13(b)(7), added in 1988, provides that:

> For purposes of paragraph (2) of this subsection, the terms "reasonable assurance" and "reasonable detail" mean such level of detail and degree of assurance as would satisfy prudent officials in the conduct of their own affairs.

2. The accounting and record keeping provisions of the FCPA apply only to "public" companies (see definition in the box accompanying Section 13(b)(2) above). Would you find that these rules are good guides for a client of yours of more modest size? What portions of what Judge Vining said about controls needed at World Wide Coin might not be appropriate for a much smaller operation?

---

2. The COSO Standards

In the mid-1980s, public attention focused on the auditing profession in light of financial frauds uncovered in numerous SEC and private lawsuits, some of the more notorious cases being the *Mattel* and *Cenco* cases. In addition, accounting and auditing rules were coming under scrutiny in the then-incipient savings and loan crisis.

One notable result was the creation and funding by several industry groups of the National Commission on Fraudulent Financial Reporting (NCFFR), also known as the "Treadway Commission" after its chair, former SEC Commissioner James C. Treadway, Jr. The NCFFR identified as one of its three objectives to "[i]dentify attributes of corporate structure that may contribute to acts of fraudulent financial reporting or to the failure to detect such acts promptly."[2] Although the Commission discussed the structure of the internal audit staff and the audit committee of the board of directors, its main emphasis was on management.

> The tone set by top management — the corporate environment or culture within which financial reporting occurs — is the most important factor contributing to the integrity of the financial reporting process. Notwithstanding an impressive set of written rules and procedures, if the tone set by management is lax, fraudulent financial reporting is more likely to occur.[3]

The organizations which sponsored the NCFFR continued work after the report was issued, concentrating mostly on the issue of internal controls. This group was known as "The Committee of Sponsoring Organizations of the Treadway Commission," or

---

2. Report of the National Commission on Fraudulent Financial Reporting 2 (1987).

3. *Id.* at 32.

COSO for short.[4] COSO completed a follow-up study providing an "integrated framework" for internal controls. It defined internal controls as:

> a process, effected by an entity's board of directors, management, and other personnel, designed to provide reasonable assurance regarding the achievement of objectives in the following categories:
>
> - Effectiveness and efficiency of operations.
> - Reliability of reporting.
> - Compliance with applicable laws and regulations.

An internal control system, according to COSO, has five integrated components, and within them seventeen principles, reprinted below.[5]

> **Control Environment**
>
> The control environment is the set of standards, processes, and structures that provide the basis for carrying out internal control across the organization. The board of directors and senior management establish the tone at the top regarding the importance of internal control and expected standards of conduct.
>
> There are five principles relating to Control Environment:
>
> 1. The organization demonstrates a commitment to integrity and ethical values.
> 2. The board of directors demonstrates independence from management and exercises oversight of the development and performance of internal control.
> 3. Management establishes, with board oversight, structures, reporting lines, and appropriate authorities and responsibilities in the pursuit of objectives.
> 4. The organization demonstrates a commitment to attract, develop, and retain competent individuals in alignment with objectives.
> 5. The organization holds individuals accountable for their internal control responsibilities in the pursuit of objectives.
>
> **Risk Assessment**
>
> Risk assessment involves a dynamic and iterative process for identifying and analyzing risks to achieving the entity's objectives, forming a basis for determining how risks should be managed. Management considers possible changes in the external environment and within its own business model that may impede its ability to achieve its objectives.

---

4. Those organizations are: the AICPA, The American Accounting Association, The Institute of Internal Auditors, The Institute of Management Accountants, and The Financial Executives Institute. See www.coso.org/aboutus.htm.

5. COSO, Internal Control—Integrated Framework (May 2013); see the Executive Summary at https://www.coso.org/Documents/990025P-Executive-Summary-final-may20.pdf. Internal Control—Integrated Framework Executive Summary © 2013 Committee of Sponsoring Organizations of the Treadway Commission (COSO). All rights reserved. Used with permission.

There are four principles relating to Risk Assessment:

6. The organization specifies objectives with sufficient clarity to enable the identification and assessment of risks relating to objectives.
7. The organization identifies risks to the achievement of its objectives across the entity and analyzes risks as a basis for determining how the risks should be managed.
8. The organization considers the potential for fraud in assessing risks to the achievement of objectives.
9. The organization identifies and assesses changes that could significantly impact the system of internal control.

Control Activities

Control activities are the actions established by policies and procedures to help ensure that management directives to mitigate risks to the achievement of objectives are carried out. Control activities are performed at all levels of the entity and at various stages within business processes, and over the technology environment.

There are three principles relating to Control Activities:

10. The organization selects and develops control activities that contribute to the mitigation of risks to the achievement of objectives to acceptable levels.
11. The organization selects and develops general control activities over technology to support the achievement of objectives.
12. The organization deploys control activities through policies that establish what is expected and procedures that put policies into action.

Information and Communication

Information is necessary for the entity to carry out internal control responsibilities in support of achievement of its objectives. Communication occurs both internally and externally and provides the organization with the information needed to carry out day-to-day controls. Communication enables personnel to understand internal control responsibilities and their importance to the achievement of objectives.

There are three principles relating to Information and Communication:

13. The organization obtains or generates and uses relevant, quality information to support the functioning of internal control.
14. The organization internally communicates information, including objectives and responsibilities for internal control, necessary to support the functioning of internal control.
15. The organization communicates with external parties regarding matters affecting the functioning of internal control.

Monitoring Activities

Ongoing evaluations, separate evaluations, or some combination of the two is used to ascertain whether each of the five components of internal control, including controls to effect the principles within each component, is present and functioning. Findings are evaluated and deficiencies are communicated in a timely manner, with serious matters reported to senior management and to the board.

There are two principles relating to Monitoring Activities:

16. The organization selects, develops, and performs ongoing and/or separate evaluations to ascertain whether the components of internal control are present and functioning.
17. The organization evaluates and communicates internal control deficiencies in a timely manner to those parties responsible for taking corrective action, including senior management and the board of directors, as appropriate.

The above three objectives (operations, reporting and compliance) and the five components (control environment, risk assessment, control activities, information and communication, and monitoring activities) create a 3x5 matrix of internal control design and implementation. And there is a "third dimension," because each of these is considered at each operating level of the entity (overall, by division, by operating segment, and so on).[6]

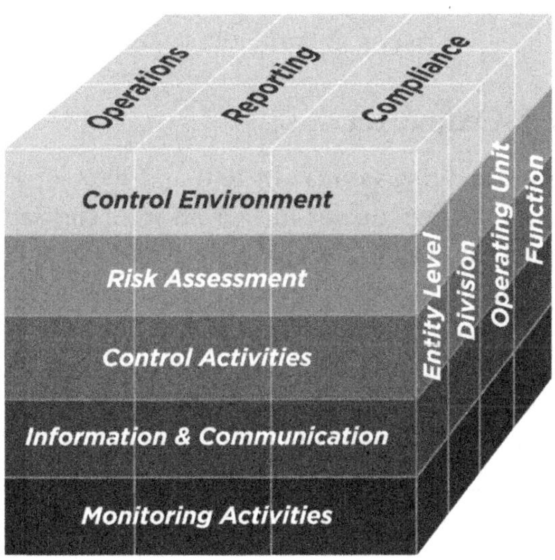

6. *See id.* at 6.

As indicated below, the COSO framework has become the *de facto* standard for internal control systems in the United States, with its endorsement by the SEC pursuant to federal legislation known as the Sarbanes-Oxley Act.

Consider the following textbook's check-list for preventing financial statement fraud. How does it relate to the seventeen COSO principles?

> Strategic reasoning refers to the ability to anticipate a fraud perpetrator's likely method of concealing a fraud.... When engaged in strategic reasoning, an auditor will consider several questions, including the following:
>
> 1. What types of *fraud schemes* is management likely to use to commit financial statement fraud? For example, is management likely to improperly record sales before goods have been shipped to customers?
>
> 2. What *typical tests* are used to detect these schemes? For example, auditors often examine shipping documents to validate shipments to customers.
>
> 3. How could management *conceal the scheme* of interest from the typical test? For example, management may ship goods to an off-site warehouse so as to be able to provide evidence of shipment to an auditor.
>
> 4. How could the *typical test be modified* so as to detect the concealed scheme? For example, the auditor may gather information about the shipping location to ensure that it is owned or leased by the customer or interview shipping personnel to determine if sold goods are always shipped to the customer.[7]

3. The Sarbanes-Oxley Act

The accounting and auditing scandals of 2001 and 2002—particularly Enron and WorldCom—created the impetus for further reform. The Sarbanes-Oxley Act of 2002 (commonly referred to as "SOX") required the SEC to adopt rules requiring a report by management of "public" companies on the company's internal controls, and a report on the management report by the company's auditors under standards to be developed by the PCAOB.[8] These two reports are known colloquially as the "Section 404 reports" or "SOX 404 reports." They have been much criticized as creating significant costs for, and competitive disadvantages to, U.S. public companies. The audit report requirement was subsequently limited by Congress in 2010 to much larger public companies.[9]

---

7. W. Steve Albrecht *et al.*, Fraud Examination 368–69 (4th ed. 2009).

8. SOX § 404(b), Pub. L. 107-204, 116 Stat. 745, 789, *codified at* 15 U.S.C. § 7262(b)(2002).

9. Dodd-Frank Act § 989(G)(a), Pub. L. 111-203, 124 Stat. 1376, 1948, *codified at* 15 U.S.C. § 7262(c) (2010). For a good history of the development of reporting on internal accounting controls, see Gupta *et al.*, *supra* note 1.

Rules and Regulations under the Securities Exchange Act of 1934

Rule 13a-15 — Issuer's Disclosure Controls and Procedures Related to Preparation of Required Reports

c. The management of each such issuer ... must evaluate, with the participation of the issuer's principal executive and principal financial officers, or persons performing similar functions, the effectiveness, as of the end of each fiscal year, of the issuer's internal control over financial reporting. The framework on which management's evaluation of the issuer's internal control over financial reporting is based must be a suitable, recognized control framework that is established by a body or group that has followed due-process procedures, including the broad distribution of the framework for public comment.

Where Rule 13a-15(c) refers to a "framework" to be used by management upon which to base its evaluation, the SEC specifically endorsed the COSO framework. The SEC stated that other suitable frameworks *may* be developed for domestic issuers (it didn't list any examples) and that other frameworks exist for issuers outside the United States (it *did* list examples of these).[10] In particular, the SEC noted that the COSO framework was relevant only insofar as it addresses internal controls related to *financial statements.* The other parts of the COSO internal control framework, addressing operations and compliance with laws and regulations, were not considered part of Congress' requirements.[11]

Pursuant to this directive in the Sarbanes-Oxley Act, the Public Company Accounting Oversight Board (PCAOB)[12] prepared internal control auditing standards, which have been updated to indicate that the audit of internal controls is integrated with the audit of the financial statements themselves.[13] The auditor should use the same "control framework" as did the company whose effectiveness is being audited, so that in practice means that the COSO framework will form the basis for the auditor's internal control opinion as well.[14]

The internal control auditing standards use a "top-down approach," meaning that the initial focus is on the financial statements themselves. From there, the auditor considers entity-level controls and the control environment as those relate to the company's period-end financial reports.[15] The auditor then identifies the significant financial statement accounts and, within each, the likely sources of misstatement.

---

10. Securities Act Rel. No. 8238, Management's Report on Internal Control Over Financial Reporting and Certification of Disclosure in Exchange Act Periodic Reports, 68 Fed. Reg. 36,636, 36,442 (2003).

11. *Id.* at 36,640. We will expand our inquiry beyond financial statements in part B below.

12. For background on the PCAOB, see Ch.3(B).

13. PCAOB Auditing Standards AS 2201.07.

14. *Id.*, AS 2201.05.

15. Note these terms ("entity-level controls" and "control environment") from the COSO description, p. 272, and summarized in the "COSO cube" on p. 273.

With that background the auditor tests both the design and operation of selected internal accounting controls. The testing of the controls' design and operation considers many of the same issues of collection of appropriate evidence for the financial statement audit which we discussed in Chapter 3(B)(3). The results are analyzed, deficiencies evaluated, and an opinion stated on the controls.

Example

In its 2019 annual report, Facebook, Inc.'s management reports on its internal controls.

> **Management's Report on Internal Control over Financial Reporting**
>
> Our management is responsible for establishing and maintaining adequate internal control over financial reporting.... Management conducted an assessment of the effectiveness of our internal control over financial reporting based on the criteria set forth in Internal Control—Integrated Framework issued by the Committee of Sponsoring Organizations of the Treadway Commission (2013 framework). Based on the assessment, management has concluded that its internal control over financial reporting was effective as of December 31, 2019, to provide reasonable assurance regarding the reliability of financial reporting and the preparation of financial statements in accordance with U.S. GAAP. Our independent registered public accounting firm, Ernst & Young LLP, has issued an audit report with respect to our internal control over financial reporting ...

Ernst & Young's report, in turn, provides the following assessment.

> **Opinion on Internal Control over Financial Reporting**
>
> We have audited Facebook, Inc.'s internal control over financial reporting as of December 31, 2019, based on criteria established in Internal Control—Integrated Framework issued by the Committee of Sponsoring Organizations of the Treadway Commission (2013 framework) (the COSO criteria). In our opinion, Facebook, Inc. (the Company) maintained, in all material respects, effective internal control over financial reporting as of December 31, 2019, based on the COSO criteria.
>
> ....
>
> **Definition and Limitations of Internal Control Over Financial Reporting**
>
> A company's internal control over financial reporting is a process designed to provide reasonable assurance regarding the reliability of financial reporting and the preparation of financial statements for external

> purposes in accordance with generally accepted accounting principles. A company's internal control over financial reporting includes those policies and procedures that (1) pertain to the maintenance of records that, in reasonable detail, accurately and fairly reflect the transactions and dispositions of the assets of the company; (2) provide reasonable assurance that transactions are recorded as necessary to permit preparation of financial statements in accordance with generally accepted accounting principles, and that receipts and expenditures of the company are being made only in accordance with authorizations of management and directors of the company; and (3) provide reasonable assurance regarding prevention or timely detection of unauthorized acquisition, use, or disposition of the company's assets that could have a material effect on the financial statements.
>
> Because of its inherent limitations, internal control over financial reporting may not prevent or detect misstatements. Also, projections of any evaluation of effectiveness to future periods are subject to conditions, or that the degree of compliance with the policies or procedures may deteriorate.

* * *

Problem 9-1

On pp. 268–69, Judge Vining lists six different "directives" which he believes can be "inferred" from the language of the FCPA. How would you classify those directives under the five-part COSO framework?

Problem 9-2

You are General Counsel to Gas-n-Go, Inc., which owns and operates 650 self-service gas stations and convenience stores in the region. Because of your accounting expertise, management has asked for your thoughts on a "fraud control" handbook to be given to local store and station managers.

Each Gas-n-Go location is run by two to seven workers as cashiers and stockers. The manager hires and supervises all employees. The manager prepares daily sales reports, detailing total sales broken down by cash/credit and time of day. The manager prepares weekly inventory reports of products on the store shelves and purchases made during the week. Gas-n-Go does not use laser-scanning point-of-sale terminals to keep continuous track of sales of each product, because management believes these systems are too expensive in the company's low-margin line of business.

What are the risks for fraud (on even a small scale) in operation of the Gas-n-Go franchises? How would you address them using the COSO framework?

B. Business Oversight and Enterprise Risk Management

We have seen the importance of internal controls, particularly the requirements in the law that an entity have a functioning system of internal *accounting* controls. Note that the specific focus on accounting and financial reporting comes from Congress, not from COSO (or other standards organizations).

Internal control standards can be applied everywhere in a business, not just with financial records. Understanding internal controls is key to understanding legal concepts about how those in charge of a business oversee that business.

> In the real world, the language of corporate governance is accounting. Boards of directors are concerned with whether they were adequately informed before making a decision. But they express this concern in such terms as, "Do we have adequate internal controls?" "Was that process sufficiently audited?" To teach corporate law ... while generally ignoring the significance of auditing and internal controls to business decision making, runs the risk of systematically misunderstanding [it].[16]

Internal controls are operative once we have identified the business risk involved. But businesses need a broader focus, one that identifies which risks should be borne at all. This additional inquiry is part of a framework known as *enterprise risk management* or ERM.

> The most recent innovations revolve around the notion that the firm should avoid "risk silos" and instead seek to quantify and coordinate risk across the business enterprise. Naturally, this effort must be coordinated at the highest managerial levels of the firm as only senior management holds the authority and the firm-wide perspective to survey all sources of risk throughout the business. This integrated, continuous, and comprehensive approach to risk management and coordination at the highest managerial levels of the firm emerged in the 1990s as enterprise-wide risk management, or ERM.[17]

Not surprisingly, the COSO team which developed internal controls also has a framework for enterprise risk management, called *Enterprise Risk Management—Integrating with Strategy and Performance.*[18] The COSO ERM framework consists of five components incorporating 20 principles.[19]

---

16. Joel Seligman, *Accounting and the New Corporate Law*, 50 Wash. & Lee L. Rev. 943, 945 (1993).

17. Kristin N. Johnson & Steven A. Ramirez, *New Guiding Principles: Macroprudential Solutions to Risk Management Oversight and Systemic Risk Concerns*, 11 U. St. Thomas L.J. 386, 396 (2014).

18. COSO, Enterprise Risk Management—Integrating with Strategy and Performance (June 2017). This is a revised version of the first ERM framework published in 2004.

19. This graphic is from the Executive Summary at https://www.coso.org/Documents/2017-COSO-ERM-Integrating-with-Strategy-and-Performance-Executive-Summary.pdf. © 2017 Committee of Sponsoring Organizations of the Treadway Commission (COSO). All rights reserved. Used with permission.

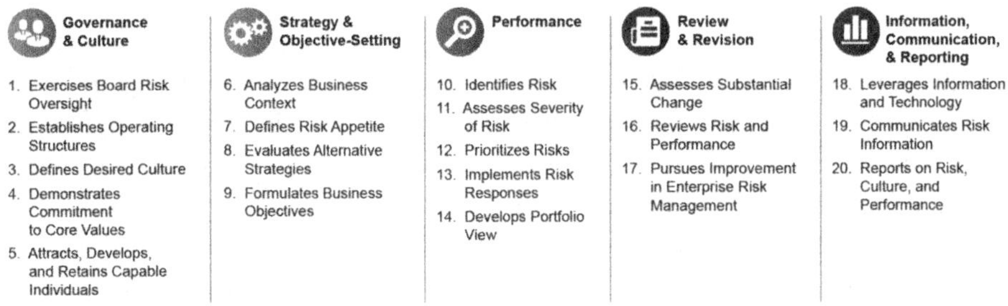

The ERM framework is different in that it is a wider ranging inquiry. The second component in the above framework, and the detail in the first component, are parts which were not included in the internal control framework.

> Enterprise risk management incorporates some concepts of internal control. "Internal control" is the process put into effect by an entity to provide reasonable assurance that objectives will be achieved. Internal control helps the organization to identify and analyze the risks to achieving those objectives and now to manage risks. It allows management to stay focused on the entity's operations and the pursuit of its performance targets while complying with relevant laws and regulations.[20]

But what does this have to do with you as a lawyer? Your clients will be subject to legal standards in the oversight of their businesses. Let's see how the law has developed, and then we can see how it relates to ERM.

The relevant law has developed around the standards governing the conduct of a corporation's directors. This is because most large businesses are corporations, and therefore most of the business failures or oversights significant enough to result in reported litigation involve corporations. Most of the law in this area not statutory, but common-law. The excerpt below is from the text of and comments to the Model Business Corporation Act, which is the basis of the corporation law in many states.

Model Business Corporation Act § 8.30

Standards of Conduct for Directors

(b) The members of the board of directors ... when ... devoting attention to their oversight function, shall discharge their duties with the care that a person in a like position would reasonably believe appropriate under similar circumstances.

20. COSO ERM, *supra* note 18, at 6. "Perhaps the largest open question is the integration of internal control and enterprise risk management.... COSO states that internal control is a subset of a broader enterprise risk management process, which is itself encompassed within the even broader concept of governance." Kyleen Prewett & Andy Terry, *COSO's Updated Enterprise Risk Management Framework—A Quest for Depth and* Clarity, Journal of Corporate Accounting & Finance, (July 2018) 16, at 21–22.

OFFICIAL COMMENT

The phrase "devoting attention," in the context of the oversight function, refers to concern with the corporation's information and reporting systems and not to proactive inquiry searching out system inadequacies or noncompliance. While directors typically give attention to future plans and trends as well as current activities, they should not be expected to anticipate the problems which the corporation may face except in those circumstances where something has occurred to make it obvious to the board that the corporation should be addressing a particular problem. The standard of care associated with the oversight function involves gaining assurances from management and advisers that systems believed appropriate have been established, coupled with ongoing monitoring of the systems in place, such as those concerned with legal compliance or internal controls (followed up with a proactive response when alerted to the need for inquiry ...).

According to the MBCA commentary quoted above, directors fulfill their duty of oversight by:

- establishing a system sufficient in scope and detail in relation to the corporation's business (relying on management's assurance of sufficiency)
- monitoring the system's reports and information, and
- responding when the reports indicate a need for further inquiry or corrective action.

This should sound similar to the five components of the COSO ERM framework: governance/culture, strategy/objective setting, performance, review/revision, and information/communication. An important addition in the ERM process, reflected in step 2 in the five-step chart above, is assessing the company's willingness to bear some part of identified risks, its so-called "risk appetite."

State corporate law deals with risk management with two potentially conflicting rules. On the one hand, it is clear that directors may be held liable for ignoring evidence that the company's controls are not working. But on the other hand, directors are expected to take risks, indeed, they are rewarded for taking business and entrepreneurial risks, and the law traditionally does not hold them liable for bad business judgments. How to reconcile these two doctrines has been the subject of much litigation, most of it in the leading corporate law state of Delaware. The following recent opinion provides a good history of Delaware jurisprudence — particularly the famous cases of *Graham v. Allis Chalmers* and *Caremark* — and applies them to a case arising from the sub-prime mortgage crisis.

In re Citigroup Inc. Shareholder Derivative Litigation

Delaware Court of Chancery, 2009
964 A.2d 106

CHANDLER, Chancellor.

This is a shareholder derivative action brought on behalf of Citigroup Inc. ("Citigroup" or the "Company"), seeking to recover for the Company its losses arising from exposure to the subprime lending market. Plaintiffs, shareholders of Citigroup, brought this action against current and former directors and officers of Citigroup, alleging, in essence, that the defendants breached their fiduciary duties by failing to properly monitor and manage the risks the Company faced from problems in the subprime lending market and for failing to properly disclose Citigroup's exposure to subprime assets. Plaintiffs allege that there were extensive "red flags" that should have given defendants notice of the problems that were brewing in the real estate and credit markets and that defendants ignored these warnings in the pursuit of short term profits and at the expense of the Company's long term viability.

....

Pending before the Court is defendants' motion ... to dismiss the complaint for failure to state a claim under Court of Chancery Rule 12(b)(6) and for failure to properly plead demand futility under Court of Chancery Rule 23.1. For the reasons set forth below, the ... claims are dismissed for failure to adequately plead demand futility pursuant to Rule 23.1.

I. BACKGROUND

....

B. Citigroup's Exposure to the Subprime Crisis

Plaintiffs allege that since as early as 2006, defendants have caused and allowed Citigroup to engage in subprime lending[21] that ultimately left the Company exposed to massive losses by late 2007. Beginning in late 2005, house prices, which many believe were artificially inflated by speculation and easily available credit, began to plateau, and then deflate. Adjustable rate mortgages issued earlier in the decade began to reset, leaving many homeowners with significantly increased monthly payments. Defaults and foreclosures increased, and assets backed by income from residential mortgages began to decrease in value. By February 2007, subprime mortgage lenders began filing for bankruptcy and subprime mortgages packaged into securities began experiencing increasing levels of delinquency. In mid-2007, rating agencies downgraded bonds backed by subprime mortgages.

Much of Citigroup's exposure to the subprime lending market arose from its involvement with collateralized debt obligations ("CDOs")—repackaged pools of lower rated securities that Citigroup created by acquiring asset-backed securities, including

21. "Subprime" generally refers to borrowers who do not qualify for prime interest rates, typically due to weak credit histories, low credit scores, high debt-burden ratios, or high loan-to-value ratios.

residential mortgage backed securities ("RMBSs"),[22] and then selling rights to the cash flows from the securities in classes, or tranches, with different levels of risk and return. Included with at least some of the CDOs created by Citigroup was a "liquidity put"—an option that allowed the purchasers of the CDOs to sell them back to Citigroup at original value.

According to plaintiffs, Citigroup's alleged $55 billion subprime exposure was in two areas of the Company's Securities & Banking Unit. The first portion totaled $11.7 billion and included securities tied to subprime loans that were being held until they could be added to debt pools for investors. The second portion included $43 billion of super-senior securities, which are portions of CDOs backed in part by RMBS collateral.[23]

By late 2007, it was apparent that Citigroup faced significant losses on its subprime-related assets, including the following as alleged by plaintiffs:

- *October 1, 2007:* Citigroup announced it would write-down approximately $1.4 billion on funded and unfunded highly leveraged finance commitments.
- *October 15, 2007:* Citigroup issued a press release reporting a net income of $2.38 billion, a 57% decline from the Company's prior year results.
- *November 4, 2007:* Citigroup announced significant declines on the fair value of the approximately $55 billion in the Company's U.S. subprime-related direct exposures, and estimated that further write downs would be between $8 and $11 billion.
- *November 6, 2007:* Citigroup disclosed that it provided $7.6 billion of emergency financing to the seven SIVs[24] the Company operated after they were unable to repay maturing debt. The SIVs drew on the $10 billion of so-called committed liquidity provided by Citigroup. On December 13, 2007 Citigroup bailed out seven of its affiliated SIVs by bringing $49 billion in assets onto its balance sheet and taking full responsibility for the SIVs' $49 billion worth of assets.
- *January 15, 2008:* Citigroup announced it would take an additional $18.1 billion write-down for the fourth quarter 2007 and a quarterly loss of $9.83 billion. Citigroup also announced that the Company lowered its dividend to $0.32 per share, a 40% decline from the Company's previous dividend disbursement.
- By March 2008, Citigroup shares traded below book value and the Company announced that it would lay off an additional 2,000 employees, bringing Citigroup's total layoff since the beginning of the subprime market crisis to more than 6,000.
- July 18, 2008: Citigroup announced it lost $2.5 billion in the second quarter, largely caused by $7.2 billion of write-downs of Citigroup's investments in mortgages and other loans and by weakness in the consumer market.

---

22. RMBSs are securities whose cash flows come from residential debt such as mortgages.

23. Rights to cash flows from CDOs are divided into tranches rated by credit risk, whereby the senior tranches are paid before the junior tranches.

24. [Ed.] Structured Investment Vehicles.

Plaintiffs also allege that Citigroup was exposed to the subprime mortgage market through its use of SIVs. Banks can create SIVs by borrowing cash (by selling commercial paper) and using the proceeds to purchase loans; in other words, the SIVs sell short term debt and buy longer-term, higher yielding assets. According to plaintiffs, Citigroup's SIVs invested in riskier assets, such as home equity loans, rather than the low-risk assets traditionally used by SIVs.

The problems in the subprime market left Citigroup's SIVs unable to pay their investors. The SIVs held subprime mortgages that had decreased in value, and the normally liquid commercial paper market became illiquid. Because the SIVs could no longer meet their cash needs by attracting new investors, they had to sell assets at allegedly "fire sale" prices. In November 2007, Citigroup disclosed that it provided $7.6 billion of emergency financing to the seven SIVs the Company operated after they were unable to repay maturing debt. Ultimately, Citigroup was forced to bail out seven of its affiliated SIVs by bringing $49 billion in assets onto its balance sheet, notwithstanding that Citigroup previously represented that it would manage the SIVs on an arms-length basis.

C. Plaintiffs' Claims

Plaintiffs allege that defendants are liable to the Company for breach of fiduciary duty for failing to adequately oversee and manage Citigroup's exposure to the problems in the subprime mortgage market, even in the face of alleged "red flags".... By way of example only, plaintiffs' "red flags" include the following:

- *May 27, 2005:* Economist Paul Krugman of the *New York Times* said he saw "signs that America's housing market, like the stock market at the end of the last decade, is approaching the final, feverish stages of a speculative bubble."
- *May 2006:* Ameriquest Mortgage, one of the United States' leading wholesale subprime lenders, announced the closing of each of its 229 retail offices and reduction of 3,800 employees.
- *February 12, 2007:* ResMae Mortgage, a subprime lender, filed for bankruptcy. According to *Bloomberg,* in its Chapter 11 filing, ResMae stated that "[t]he subprime mortgage market has recently been crippled and a number of companies stopped originating loans and United States housing sales have slowed and defaults by borrowers have risen."
- *April 18, 2007:* Freddie Mac announced plans to refinance up to $20 billion of loans held by subprime borrowers who would be unable to afford their adjustable-rate mortgages at the reset rate.
- *July 10, 2007:* Standard and Poor's and Moody's downgraded bonds backed by subprime mortgages.
- *August 1, 2007:* Two hedge funds managed by Bear Stearns that invested heavily in subprime mortgages declared bankruptcy.
- *August 9, 2007:* American International Group, one of the largest United States mortgage lenders, warned that mortgage defaults were spreading beyond the

subprime sector, with delinquencies becoming more common among borrowers in the category just above subprime.

- *October 18, 2007:* Standard & Poor's cut the credit ratings on $23.35 billion of securities backed by pools of home loans that were offered to borrowers during the first half of the year. The downgrades even hit securities rated AAA, which was the highest of the ten investment-grade ratings and the rating of government debt.

....

III. THE MOTION TO DISMISS UNDER RULE 23.1

The decision whether to initiate or pursue a lawsuit on behalf of the corporation is generally within the power and responsibility of the board of directors.... Accordingly, in order to cause the corporation to pursue litigation, a shareholder must either (1) make a pre-suit demand by presenting the allegations to the corporation's directors, requesting that they bring suit, and showing that they wrongfully refused to do so, or (2) plead facts showing that demand upon the board would have been futile.

....

Demand is not excused solely because the directors would be deciding to sue themselves. Rather, demand will be excused based on a possibility of personal director liability only in the rare case when a plaintiff is able to show director conduct that is "so egregious on its face that board approval cannot meet the test of business judgment, and a substantial likelihood of director liability therefore exists."[25]

.... Plaintiffs' argument is based on a theory of director liability famously articulated by former-Chancellor Allen in *In re Caremark.*[26] Before *Caremark,* in *Graham v. Allis-Chalmers Manufacturing Company,*[27] the Delaware Supreme Court, in response to a theory that the Allis-Chalmers directors were liable because they should have known about employee violations of federal anti-trust laws, held that "absent cause for suspicion there is no duty upon the directors to install and operate a corporate system of espionage to ferret out wrongdoing which they have no reason to suspect exists."[28] Over thirty years later, in the context of approval of a settlement of a class action, former-Chancellor Allen took the opportunity to revisit the duty to monitor under Delaware law. In *Caremark,* the plaintiffs alleged that the directors were liable because they should have known that certain officers and employees were violating the federal Anti-Referral Payments Law. In analyzing these claims, the Court began, appropriately, by reviewing the duty of care and the protections of the business judgment rule.

With regard to director liability standards, the Court distinguished between (1) "*a board decision* that results in a loss because that decision was ill advised or 'neg-

25. *Aronson v. Lewis,* 473 A.2d 805, 815 (Del. 1984).
26. *In re Caremark Int'l Inc. Derivative Litigation,* 698 A.2d 959 (Del.Ch.1996).
27. 188 A.2d 125 (Del.1963).
28. *Id.* at 130.

ligent'" and (2) "an *unconsidered failure of the board to act* in circumstances in which due attention would, arguably, have prevented the loss." ...

In the latter class of cases, where directors are alleged to be liable for a failure to monitor liability creating activities, the *Caremark* Court, in a reassessment of the holding in *Graham*, stated that while directors could be liable for a failure to monitor, "only a sustained or systematic failure of the board to exercise oversight — such as an utter failure to attempt to assure a reasonable information and reporting system exists — will establish the lack of good faith that is a necessary condition to liability."[29]

In *Stone v. Ritter*,[30] the Delaware Supreme Court approved the *Caremark* standard for director oversight liability.... As the *Stone* Court explained:

> *Caremark* articulates the necessary conditions predicate for director oversight liability: (a) the directors utterly failed to implement any reporting or information system or controls; *or* (b) having implemented such a system or controls, consciously failed to monitor or oversee its operations thus disabling themselves from being informed of risks or problems requiring their attention. In either case, imposition of liability requires a showing that the directors knew that they were not discharging their fiduciary obligations. Where directors fail to act in the face of a known duty to act, thereby demonstrating a conscious disregard for their responsibilities, they breach their duty of loyalty by failing to discharge that fiduciary obligation in good faith.[31]

Thus, to establish oversight liability a plaintiff must show that the directors *knew* they were not discharging their fiduciary obligations or that the directors demonstrated a *conscious* disregard for their responsibilities such as by failing to act in the face of a known duty to act. The test is rooted in concepts of bad faith; indeed, a showing of bad faith is a *necessary condition* to director oversight liability.

....

The Delaware Supreme Court has stated that bad faith conduct may be found where a director "intentionally acts with a purpose other than that of advancing the best interests of the corporation, ... acts with the intent to violate applicable positive law, or ... intentionally fails to act in the face of a known duty to act, demonstrating a conscious disregard for his duties."[32] More recently, the Delaware Supreme Court held that when a plaintiff seeks to show that demand is excused because directors face a substantial likelihood of liability where "directors are exculpated from liability except for claims based on 'fraudulent,' 'illegal' or 'bad faith' conduct, a plaintiff must also plead particularized facts that demonstrate that the directors acted with scienter, *i.e.*, that they had 'actual or constructive knowledge' that their conduct was legally improper."[33] A plaintiff can thus plead bad faith by alleging with particularity that a

29. *Caremark*, 698 A.2d at 971.

30. [Ed.] 911 A.2d 362 (Del. 2006).

31. *Id.* [at 370] (footnotes omitted).

32. *In re Walt Disney Co. Derivative Litigation*, 906 A.2d 27, 67 (Del.2006).

33. *Wood v. Baum*, 953 A.2d 136, 141 (Del. 2008).

director *knowingly* violated a fiduciary duty or failed to act in violation of a *known* duty to act, demonstrating a *conscious* disregard for her duties.

....

In this case, plaintiffs allege that the defendants are liable for failing to properly monitor the risk that Citigroup faced from subprime securities. While it may be possible for a plaintiff to meet the burden under some set of facts, plaintiffs in this case have failed to state a *Caremark* claim sufficient to excuse demand based on a theory that the directors did not fulfill their oversight obligations by failing to monitor the business risk of the company.

The allegations in the Complaint amount essentially to a claim that Citigroup suffered large losses and that there were certain warning signs that could or should have put defendants on notice of the business risks related to Citigroup's investments in subprime assets. Plaintiffs then conclude that because defendants failed to prevent the Company's losses associated with certain business risks, they must have consciously ignored these warning signs or knowingly failed to monitor the Company's risk in accordance with their fiduciary duties. Such conclusory allegations, however, are not sufficient to state a claim for failure of oversight that would give rise to a substantial likelihood of personal liability, which would require particularized factual allegations demonstrating bad faith by the director defendants.

Plaintiffs do not contest that Citigroup had procedures and controls in place that were designed to monitor risk. Plaintiffs admit that Citigroup established the ARM[34] Committee and in 2004 amended the ARM Committee charter to include the fact that one of the purposes of the ARM Committee was to assist the board in fulfilling its oversight responsibility relating to policy standards and guidelines for risk assessment and risk management. The ARM Committee was also charged with, among other things, (1) discussing with management and independent auditors the annual audited financial statements, (2) reviewing with management an evaluation of Citigroup's internal control structure, and (3) discussing with management Citigroup's major credit, market, liquidity, and operational risk exposures and the steps taken by management to monitor and control such exposures, including Citigroup's risk assessment and risk management policies. According to plaintiffs' own allegations, the ARM Committee met eleven times in 2006 and twelve times in 2007.

Plaintiffs nevertheless argue that the director defendants breached their duty of oversight either because the oversight mechanisms were not adequate or because the director defendants did not make a good faith effort to comply with the established oversight procedures. To support this claim, the Complaint alleges numerous facts that plaintiffs argue should have put the director defendants on notice of the impending problems in the subprime mortgage market and Citigroup's exposure thereto. Plaintiffs summarized some of these "red flags" in their answering brief as follows:

---

34. [Ed.] Audit and Risk Management.

- the steady decline of the housing market and the impact the collapsing bubble would have on mortgages and subprime backed securities since as early as 2005;
- December 2005 guidance from the FASB staff—"The FASB staff is aware of loan products whose contractual features may increase the exposure of the originator, holder, investor, guarantor, or servicer to risk of nonpayment or realization.";
- the drastic rise in foreclosure rates starting in 2006;
- several large subprime lenders reporting substantial losses and filing for bankruptcy starting in 2006;
- billions of dollars in losses reported by Citigroup's peers, such as Bear Stearns and Merrill Lynch.

....

The warning signs alleged by plaintiffs are not evidence that the directors consciously disregarded their duties or otherwise acted in bad faith; at most they evidence that the directors made bad business decisions.... That the director defendants knew of signs of a deterioration in the subprime mortgage market, or even signs suggesting that conditions could decline further, is not sufficient to show that the directors were or should have been aware of any wrongdoing at the Company or were consciously disregarding a duty somehow to prevent Citigroup from suffering losses.

To recognize such claims under a theory of director oversight liability would undermine the long established protections of the business judgment rule. It is well established that the mere fact that a company takes on business risk and suffers losses—even catastrophic losses—does not evidence misconduct, and without more, is not a basis for personal director liability.[35] ...

This Court's recent decision in *American International Group, Inc. Consolidated Derivative Litigation*[36] demonstrates the stark contrast between the allegations here and allegations that are sufficient to survive a motion to dismiss. In *AIG*, the Court faced a motion to dismiss a complaint that included "well-pled allegations of pervasive, diverse, and substantial financial fraud involving managers at the highest levels of AIG." In concluding that the complaint stated a claim for relief under Rule 12(b)(6), the Court held that the factual allegations in the complaint were sufficient to support an inference that AIG executives running those divisions knew of and approved much of the wrongdoing. The Court reasoned that huge fraudulent schemes were unlikely to be perpetrated without the knowledge of the executive in charge of that division of the company. Unlike the allegations in this case, the defendants in *AIG* allegedly failed to exercise reasonable oversight over pervasive *fraudulent* and *criminal*

35. *See Gagliardi v. TriFoods Int'l, Inc.*, 683 A.2d 1049, 1051 (Del.Ch.1996) ("The business outcome of an investment project that is unaffected by director self-interest or bad faith, cannot itself be an occasion for director liability.") (footnote omitted).

36. 965 A.2d 763 (Del.Ch.2009).

conduct. Indeed, the Court in *AIG* even stated that the complaint there supported the assertion that top AIG officials were leading a "criminal organization" and that "[t]he diversity, pervasiveness, and materiality of the alleged financial wrongdoing at AIG is extraordinary."

Contrast the *AIG* claims with the claims in this case. Here, plaintiffs argue that the Complaint supports the reasonable conclusion that the director defendants acted in bad faith by failing to see the warning signs of a deterioration in the subprime mortgage market and failing to cause Citigroup to change its investment policy to limit its exposure to the subprime market. Director oversight duties are designed to ensure reasonable reporting and information systems exist that would allow directors to know about and prevent wrongdoing that could cause losses for the Company. There are significant differences between failing to oversee employee fraudulent or criminal conduct and failing to recognize the extent of a Company's business risk. Directors should, indeed must under Delaware law, ensure that reasonable information and reporting systems exist that would put them on notice of fraudulent or criminal conduct within the company. Such oversight programs allow directors to intervene and prevent frauds or other wrongdoing that could expose the company to risk of loss as a result of such conduct. While it may be tempting to say that directors have the same duties to monitor and oversee business risk, imposing *Caremark*-type duties on directors to monitor business risk is fundamentally different. Citigroup was in the business of taking on and managing investment and other business risks. To impose oversight liability on directors for failure to monitor "excessive" risk would involve courts in conducting hindsight evaluations of decisions at the heart of the business judgment of directors. Oversight duties under Delaware law are not designed to subject directors, even expert directors, to *personal liability* for failure to predict the future and to properly evaluate business risk.

....

Notes and Questions

1. *In re American International Group, Inc., Consolidated Derivative Litigation*, 965 A.2d 763 (Del. Ch. 2009), was referred to by the court in *Citigroup* as a case where adequate bad faith was alleged. Here is a flavor of the conduct involved.

> Most of the wrongdoing alleged ... involved action by AIG insiders to misstate AIG's financial performance in order to deceive investors into believing that AIG was more prosperous and secure than it really was. The single largest act of deception alleged involved a fraudulent $500 million reinsurance transaction in which various AIG insiders staged an elaborate artificial transaction with defendant Gen Re Corporation. Although AIG portrayed the transaction as providing Gen Re with reinsurance, in reality the transaction had no substance and was simply staged to make AIG's balance sheet look better. In other instances, AIG insiders allegedly used secret offshore subsidiaries to mask AIG losses, blatantly misstated accounts with no basis for their adjust-

> ments, failed to correct well-documented accounting problems in an AIG subsidiary, and hid AIG's involvement in controversial insurance policies that involved betting on when elderly people would die.
>
> But, the complaint alleges, [AIG Chairman Hank] Greenberg and his Inner Circle were not content with merely hiding AIG's financial performance. Various insiders ... allegedly involved AIG in conspiracies with other companies to rig markets. In both the municipal derivative and general insurance markets, AIG supposedly conspired with competitors and others to subvert supposedly competitive auctions by secretly pre-selecting the winners.
>
> Finally, the [p]laintiffs allege that Greenberg and other defendants exploited their own familiarity with improper financial machinations by causing AIG to sell its "expertise" in balance sheet manipulation. AIG sold insurance policies that did not involve the actual transfer of insurable risk to other companies with the improper purpose of helping those companies report better financial results. AIG also created special purpose entities for other companies without observing the required accounting rules for the similarly improper purpose of helping those companies hide impaired assets that they did not want on their balance sheets.
>
> Eventually, all of these schemes were uncovered. As a result, AIG suffered serious harm. The corporation was forced to restate years of financial statements, eventually reducing stockholder equity by $3.5 billion. And, AIG still faces litigation and regulatory proceedings on a number of fronts, an ongoing process that has already required the corporation to pay over $1.6 billion in fines and other costs necessary to resolve proceedings against it.

965 A.2d at 774–75. A recent analysis puts the combined cost of the AIG meltdown, including both lost share value and the cost of the ultimate government "bailout," at roughly $400 billion, more than double the size of the WorldCom bankruptcy (discussed in Chapter 5) and eight times the size of the Enron bankruptcy (discussed in Chapter 3).[37]

2. Has Delaware developed a coherent theory of what constitutes an adequate internal control system? There is no Delaware statutory counterpart to MBCA § 8.30(b), but nonetheless, how do you think Delaware's rules compare with the MBCA?

3. How well do your summaries of either the Delaware or MBCA rules compare with the COSO ERM framework summarized on p. 279? Where in the COSO framework did the Citicorp directors face the biggest challenges? What about the AIG directors?

* * *

37. Mark Cheffers & Michael Pakaluk, Accounting Ethics and the Near Collapse of the Entire Financial System of the World 30 (2011).

Problem 9-3

Mid States Healthcare Corporation (MSHC) operates seven hospitals and five different health insurance plans in a three-state area.

(a) As counsel to the board of directors of MSHC, what would you suggest be done by the directors to assure the company's compliance with:

(1) state and local hospital licensing and inspection laws;

(2) certification of physicians, nurses, and other health care professionals employed in that capacity by MSHC;

(3) compliance with Medicare, Medicaid, and other government programs which provide payments to hospitals for insured individuals' care;

(4) state insurance laws governing the marketing of health insurance plans and policies; or

(5) state insurance laws governing the required types of custodianship and investment of insurance premiums?

Assume that under each law, MSHC's directors could face personal liability of the company were found to have violated any of these laws or regulations.

(b) Suppose MSHC had been fined by federal and state officials for overcharging the Medicare program and for allowing certain medical procedures to be performed by unlicensed or unqualified individuals. Does this mean that the procedures you suggested in part **(a)** have failed? How, if at all, should they then be modified?

Problem 9-4

Frosty Freeze, Inc. (FF) is a regional producer of ice cream. FF's three production facilities are under constant inspection by federal and state officials. Over the past few years, these officials have reported violations such as condensation dripping into processing vats (3 different instances), ceiling in disrepair, and general sanitation concerns including some reports of contamination. FF's board of directors has not discussed the food safety aspects of its operations, though. In recent years there has been one mention in board meetings of the subject—the president's report that FF had passed its "food safety audit" done by a third-party company.

Conditions at FF's plants led to a widespread outbreak of a *listeria* contamination in FF Ice Cream. Virtually all of the product had to be recalled and the company closed one of its facilities, and barely escaped bankruptcy. Irate shareholders have sued FF's directors alleging breach of the duty of oversight. Is it sufficient for the board to rely on federal and state food safety inspectors and the "food safety audit"?

Chapter 10

Accounting Terms in Agreements and Litigation

Good lawyers understand three important aspects of financial information in the bargaining process. First, they understand the specific meanings and limitations of financial statement terms, whatever the transactional context. This is the subject of Part A of this chapter. Second, they apply their knowledge of financial statement generation in advising their clients when the financial statements themselves are the subject of an agreement. This is the subject of Part B. Finally, they understand how accounting terminology works to *influence* the terms and future of the bargain reached by the client. This is discussed in the following chapter using the specific context of valuation of a business. Because business valuation is significant both in and out of court, it is covered separately.

A. Definition of Accounting Terms

A lawyer should be careful with terminology in drafting any agreement. The very purpose of a contract is to reduce uncertainty. By now, you've seen that accounting terms have specially defined meanings, many of them contrary to your intuitive sense before you began Chapter 1.

This part focuses on definitions in three different areas common for lawyers. First is the meaning of "income" in the context of compensation. Second is the evaluation of the balance sheet accounts of a business when that business is being purchased. Finally, there are many covenants in debt agreements which involve financial statement accounts.

1. Income

Of all accounting terms used in a business, "income" or "profit" may be paramount. It is pursuit of this profit that drives the parties to the bargaining table. They expect to make profits, but they have probably spent very little time considering what "profit" is. This makes the descent to litigation over unclear terms much more likely. And there is no guarantee that the results will be right or certain. We will look at some exemplary cases and then try our hand at writing an agreement about income.

Powel v. Burke

Supreme Court of Connecticut, 1979
178 Conn. 384, 423 A.2d 97

PETERS, Associate Justice.

This case concerns the sale of an accounting business. This suit by the plaintiff seller sought recovery from the defendants, the purchasers of the business, of amounts allegedly due under the contract of sale. After a trial before a state referee, the court found all disputed issues for the plaintiff and rendered judgment in his favor for $23,254. The defendants have appealed, assigning error to several aspects of the court's interpretation of the contract for sale....

All parties to this action are certified public accountants. The plaintiff, John Powel, prior to June 1963, owned and operated an accounting business in Bridgeport; the defendants, Thomas G. Burke, Alfred Hollis and B. James Burke, doing business as Thomas G. Burke & Company, conducted an accounting business in New York City with an office in Westport. In June, 1963, the plaintiff took a job in New York and offered to sell his accounting practice to the defendants. The defendants agreed and the parties entered into an informal oral agreement for the sale whereby the defendants took over the operation of the plaintiff's practice on July 1, 1963. Approximately one year later, the parties attempted to reduce their agreement to writing. The basic terms of the agreement were contained in a proposal written on the back of a check. Thereafter, following further discussion and modification, the parties executed a two-page, handwritten agreement dated July 7, 1964.

The agreement is in two parts. Part one provides for certain lump sum payments for furniture and good will and is undisputed in this appeal. Part two, entitled "Sale of Practice," calls for payments to the plaintiff, based on financial results, over a five-year "buy-out" period from June 30, 1963, to June 30, 1968. The plaintiff was to be paid either (1) 15 percent of gross collections during the five-year contract period, or (2) 50 percent of the profit on accounts collected, whichever was less. It is undisputed that, in fact, the second alternative formula, under any interpretation, would yield the lower figure. Thus, the dispute between the parties centers on the calculation of "50 percent of profit on accounts collected" under the second formula.

The contract defined "profit" as gross collections, less staff payroll cost, less $10 per hour for partners' time, less 30 percent of staff payroll cost as a charge for overhead. If actual overhead cost was less than 30 percent of staff payroll cost, the actual figure was to be used. Despite substantial agreement about the underlying raw data, the parties differ about the method of computation required as a matter of interpretation of several of the provisions of the contract.

At the outset, the defendants contend that the court's interpretation of the contract as a whole is unreasonable because it produces paper profits when in fact the business lost money. According to the defendants, the parties intended that the plaintiff would be paid only if the business proved profitable, and the formula set out in the contract for determining "profit" was intended merely to simplify computations, not to distort reality. The defendants have gone to elaborate lengths to attempt to prove that the plaintiff's business, under so-called "generally accepted accounting principles," experienced a net loss during the five-year buy-out period. Such calculations are, however, wholly irrelevant to the interpretation of the parties' agreement in this case.

It is the general rule that a contract is to be interpreted according to the intent expressed therein, and not by an intent the court may believe existed in the minds of the parties.... Had the parties wished to define profit according to generally accepted accounting principles, they could easily have done so. They chose instead a definition of profit as gross collections less certain stipulated deductions for partners' time, staff payroll, and overhead. Whether or not application of this definition produces a profit that would not have resulted under another definition, it is still the parties' agreement, rather than some alternate "real world" figure, that must control. The defendants "cannot now be heard to claim, for (their) own benefit, that the actual undertaking of the parties was other than that which appears in their written agreement." *Osborne v. Locke Steel Chain Co.*, 153 Conn. 527, 531, 218 A.2d 526, 529 (1966).

The defendants next claim that the court erred in computing staff payroll cost for employees who worked more than 1800 hours in a year. The contract provides for an employee's hourly rate to be computed by dividing his or her annual base salary by 1800 hours. The court, however, by accepting the plaintiff's calculations on all disputed issues, read an implied exception into this contract language for employees who actually worked more than 1800 hours. For those employees, the payroll cost chargeable to the plaintiff was limited to their actual salary, because if their actual hours worked had been multiplied by the hourly rate called for by the agreement, the plaintiff would have been charged for more payroll cost than was actually incurred. This approach, although logical, finds no support in the contract language. The contract provides a clear and unambiguous formula for the calculation of staff payroll cost; an implied exception cannot be read into the contract by the interpretation of the court....

....

The defendants lastly claim error concerning the interpretation of the contract provision that, after the fifth year, at the end of the buy-out period, the plaintiff was to receive 15 percent of the June 1968 receivables collected after that date, and that no costs were to be applied to these receivables. The receivables thus collected totalled $20,210, an amount not now disputed. Of this amount, the court awarded the plaintiff 50 percent, rather than 15 percent, in apparent reliance on the 50 percent formula applied in the calculation of the plaintiff's compensation for moneys received during the five-year buy-out period. The defendants urge that the 50 percent figure is an inappropriate measure for the entirely separate entitlement to collections subsequent to Junc, 1968, and we agree. The 50 percent figure applies to a different time frame, and by its terms is inapplicable to subsequently collected receivables, whereas the 15 percent figure is consistent with the exclusion of all costs.

....

There is error in part; the judgment is to be modified in accordance with this opinion by reducing the plaintiff's recovery by the amount of $8936.

In this opinion the other Judges concurred.

What if, instead of defining "profits," you agree to have a third party determine the profits? What principles should guide the third party?

Smith v. Peninsula House, Inc.

Superior Court of New Jersey, Appellate Division, 1961
65 N.J. Super. 341, 167 A.2d 807

The opinion of the court was delivered by GOLDMANN, S.J.A.D.

[Plaintiff] sought an accounting with respect to his share of defendant's net profits under the employment agreement.... [T]he [trial] court determined that defendant's net profits for 1958 amounted to $7,460.54, and therefore entered judgment for plaintiff in half this amount, as provided by the agreement....

[Plaintiff appealed the trial court's adverse judgment on another issue.] ... Defendant has taken a cross-appeal from so much of the judgment as awarded plaintiff $3,730.27, half of the total net profits, contending that under the employment agreement the firm of auditors therein mentioned found there was no net profit for the purposes of the profit-sharing provision of the agreement.

....

In March 1958 the parties entered into an employment agreement whereby defendant agreed to employ plaintiff as manager of its Peninsula House, Sea Bright, N.J., a hotel with restaurant, bar and bathing facilities....

....

The provision of the March 1958 employment agreement under which plaintiff claims one-half of the net profits reads:

> "2. As full compensation for your services, you are to receive one-half of any net profit (before income taxes) earned by the corporation during each calendar year of your employment, as determined by the corporation's independent auditors (presently Harris, Kerr, Forster & Co.), whose determination of net profit shall be conclusive."

The auditing firm's statement of profit and loss for the year 1958 showed that the hotel operation had resulted in a net loss of $6,120.22; there had been an $11,591.91 profit realized from the sale of the so-called Elliott property owned by the defendant, and the net profit for the year was therefore $5,471.69. The trial judge used this last figure ... half of which he gave plaintiff as his share of the net profits for 1958.

The meaning of the term "net profit" is not fixed and invariable, but depends upon the setting in which it is used. The trial court obviously believed that Harris, Kerr,

Forster & Co., the auditors, were not authorized by the employment agreement to determine "net profit" for the purpose of compensating plaintiff, but were merely authorized to determine "net profit" for the corporation in general. But this cannot have been the intent of the parties.

The "net profit" of a corporation cannot be determined in a vacuum. Its precise meaning must be garnered from the context in which it is used. Thus, net profit for federal income tax purposes might be quite different from net profit for the purposes of a corporate financial statement. The agreement here in question itself indicates the context of the subject matter with which the parties were dealing, and may be resorted to in aid of ascertaining their intent with respect to "net profit."

The agreement took the form of a letter from the brother of defendant's president, apparently acting as attorney and agent for the company. It begins:

> "In connection with our plans to operate the Peninsula House as a beach club and motel, this will confirm our understanding of the arrangements between us:
>
> "(1) You will enter into the employ of Peninsula House, Inc., as manager of the operation for the current calendar year and from year to year thereafter, subject to termination by either party as of December 31 in any year * * *."

Then follows paragraph 2, quoted above. The third paragraph states that plaintiff would not incur any obligations on behalf of the corporation for capital improvements, nor obligations for unpaid operating expenses aggregating more than $5,000 at any one time, without prior written consent of a director of the corporation. Paragraph 4 provides that all monies received by him on behalf of the corporation were to be deposited promptly at the local bank, where the corporation would maintain a special account with a maximum balance of $5,000 upon which he could draw for corporate expenses....

The agreement clearly relates to the hotel operation, and to nothing else. Plaintiff's right to share in any profit made from the sale of corporate property is pinpointed and limited to the hotel premises, described as a "beach club and motel." To conclude, as did the trial judge, that he was entitled to share in an entirely separate asset of the corporation, the Elliott property, is to read something into the employment agreement which is not there and thus write a new contract for the parties.

It seems entirely clear that the parties had three purposes in mind: (1) to provide an incentive to plaintiff as manager of the hotel business to build up an operating profit by permitting him to share in the fruits of his efforts in that direction; (2) to permit him to share in any profit resulting from the sale of the Peninsula House for a sum exceeding $190,000; and (3) to give him first refusal if the company received an offer to purchase the property for a lower sum. The very fact that the agreement provided for what should be done in the event that the hotel property was sold is the strongest kind of indication that the profit-sharing arrangement otherwise contemplated only an operating profit.

We find no ambiguity in the term "net profit" considered in the context of the agreement. But were there any ambiguity, the parties expressly stipulated that the company's independent auditors were to determine the net profit during each calendar year, and that such determination "shall be conclusive."

We must conclude that if the stipulation of the parties is to be given any reasonable meaning, they intended that the auditors determine the net profit for the purposes of the employment agreement, and this determination was to be binding. This does not mean that the determination of the auditors is conclusive in the sense that it is not subject to judicial review. It merely means that their decision will be upheld in the absence of bad faith or an unreasonable departure from approved accounting practices.

....

When Francis J. English, a certified public accountant in the employ of Harris, Kerr, Forster & Co., attempted to explain how the determination of net profit was arrived at, the trial judge prevented it. His refusal to admit into evidence the formal determination of the auditors as to corporate net profit for the purposes of the employment agreement, and their reasons therefor, was reversible error. This offer of proof by defendant was relevant and proper. It is clear from the record that the auditors concluded there was no net corporate profit for the purposes of the agreement, defendant having suffered a net loss of $6,120.22 in the operation of Peninsula House.

True, some profit-sharing contracts contain clauses expressly excluding non-operating income from gross revenues. However, this does not necessarily mean that in every instance where such income is not expressly excluded, the parties did not intend to exclude it....

Accordingly, in the context of the profit-sharing arrangement here in question, the purpose of which was to create a direct relationship between plaintiff's performance as hotel manager and his compensation, thereby providing him with maximum incentive to produce a favorable operating result, we hold that a reasonable interpretation of "net profit" requires that it be limited to those profits related to plaintiff's specific function in managing the beach club and motel. It cannot include capital gains wholly unrelated to that aspect of the business with which plaintiff was concerned. The auditors therefore properly excluded the capital gain on the sale of the Elliott property from their determination of net profit under the employment agreement.

....

... We reverse the judgment entered in plaintiff's favor in the sum of $3,730.27 plus interest and costs. We therefore direct that judgment be entered in favor of defendant, and remand the case for that purpose.

Siteman v. Marine Petroleum Co.

Missouri Court of Appeals, 1974
511 S.W.2d 436

CLEMENS, Acting Presiding Judge.

Plaintiff Sid Siteman, formerly president and general manager of defendant Marine Petroleum Company, sued ... for a stipulated salary of ten per cent of defendant's net profits....

....

Marine's first board of directors met in October, 1947 and adopted this resolution: 'It was regularly moved and seconded that Mr. Sid Siteman be the General Manager of the Company; ... and that, for his services as General Manager of this Company, he be paid as salary an amount equal to ten per cent (10%) of the net profits of the Company before taxes, said salary to be paid at the end of each fiscal year and as soon as the net profits are determined....

At the beginnings of the second to seventeenth fiscal years the directors adopted similar resolutions....

Defendant Marine's Appeal

Marine appeal[s] from plaintiff's judgment on Count IV for his fiscal 1965–1966 salary. The issue ... [is] whether the term "net profits" was limited to Marine's operating profits or also included a large gain Marine made on the sale of its original terminal.

....

"Profit' is an elastic and ambiguous word." 34 Words and Phrases, page 405. In *Sidney Smith, Inc. v. Steinberg*, 316 S.W.2d 243(3) (Mo.App.1958), the court adopted Webster's definitions of "profit" as "the excess of returns over expenditure in a given transaction or a series of transactions; as: a. The excess of the price received over the price paid for goods sold. b. The excess of the price received over the cost of purchasing and handling, or of producing and marketing, particular goods * * *" or, "the advantage remaining after all costs, charges and expenses have been deducted from income." By these definitions, Marine did make a "net profit" on the sale of its original terminal. While there is an obvious distinction between "gross profits" and "net profits," the word "profit" is equivalent to "net profit." (See "Profit" at page 1376 of Black's Law Dictionary, Fourth Edition (1950)). We interpret the meaning of "net profits" in accord with the contracting parties' intention so as to reach an interpretation that is fair and reasonable considering "the relationship of the parties, the subject matter of the contract, the usages of the business, the surrounding facts and circumstances attending the execution of the contract and its interpretation by the parties." *Gabel-Lockhart Co. v. Gabel*, 360 Mo. 518, 229 S.W.2d 539 (1950). Here it is conceded Marine sold its original terminal in 1965 for $850,000 and thereby realized a gain of $720,190 over its costs of buying the terminal. Marine argues this was a "capital gain," and that term is "the creature of the internal revenue code and not a part of 'net profit,'" as that term is "used in our society." This is a straw-man issue. Shorn of this hollow argument, the sale of Marine's terminal did beyond doubt produce a net profit of $720,190.

Of more substance, but no more merit, is Marine's contention its "net profit" is limited to operating profit. Nowhere in the record is the phrase "net profit" either expressly or impliedly so limited. We hold the term "net profit" means the difference between Marine's income and its expenses, and that, prima facie, includes the gain on the sale of its terminal.

On the meaning of "net profits" used in an employment contract both plaintiff and Marine cite *Harvey v. Missouri Valley Electric Co.*, 268 S.W.2d 820, 821 (Mo.1954), holding "the meaning of 'net profits' and what is included therein varies according to the context in which, and the circumstances under which, the words are used...."

On this issue Marine also cites *Sidney Smith, supra*. That case was decided on its own facts (as are all cases in this field of law), and the court pointed out that Steinberg had a contract for a fixed salary, plus one-third of the "net profits." But with reference to the elements constituting net profits, the contract said: "It is expressly understood that party of the second part (employee Steinberg) has no interest vested or contingent in the merchandise, equipment, trade name or good will of said business, either during the term of this contract or after its termination." With that provision in the contract, the court necessarily held the gain from the sale of a customer's list was not intended to be included in the computation of net profits. Here there were no such limitations on plaintiff's share of Marine's profits. Unlike Sidney Smith plaintiff was an incorporator, officer and shareholder and participated in the corporate business leading up to the profitable sale. The opinion there does not help Marine.

....

Several contrasting factors in our case persuade us to find the parties evidenced no intention to limit "net profits" to operating profits. Purchase of the original terminal, its sale, the purchase of a site for a new one and the attendant financing, were integral parts of Marine's wholesale fuel business. Over the years plaintiff participated in these transactions even to the extent of personally guaranteeing loans. Marine used income from the sale of the original terminal in part to buy tow boats, purchase securities, finance the new terminal and to pay increased dividends to stockholders. All this contrasts sharply with *Smith [v. Peninsula House]*, *supra*, where the plaintiff-employee came into the defendant corporation, already established, to manage one hotel and the questioned profits arose from the sale of an unrelated property.

We find still another indication of the parties' lack of intent to limit plaintiff's income to a share of operating profits. In previous years the depreciation of Marine's physical assets was treated as a corporate expense in computing net profits. By so charging plaintiff's share of Marine's profits with the depreciation of physical assets a logical corollary would be that the parties intended plaintiff's income would be increased by appreciation when realized. This is a persuasive factor against Marine's contention plaintiff's compensation was to be limited to operating profits.

....

Ennis v. Warm Mineral Springs, Inc.

Florida Court of Appeal, 1967
203 So. 2d 514

PIERCE, Judge.

This is an appeal by Thomas H. Ennis, plaintiff below, from a Final Decree entered by the Sarasota County Circuit Court in a suit wherein Ennis sought a declaratory decree, together with an accounting and a money judgment, with reference to an employment contract entered into by him and Warm Mineral Springs, Inc., hereinafter referred to as the corporation.

The contract, of which Ennis sought a judicial interpretation, was in the form of a resolution of the corporation, and, in its essential part, was as follows:

> "(5) that the Vice-President, Thomas H. Ennis, be paid twenty-five (25%) per cent of the gross profits before Federal Income Taxes, and * * * the corporation reserves the right to terminate the services of Thomas H. Ennis any time at the discretion of the Directors."

....

Plaintiff Ennis and one Frederick Matthew Daley had been acquaintances, then friends, over a period of some thirty years. Daley was aware that Ennis had either promoted or been associated with some highly successful Florida real estate developments.... An arrangement was then worked out whereby Ennis would investigate various real property holdings being offered for sale in Florida and made recommendations to Daley as to suitability for development purposes. As his contribution to the joint venture, Ennis was to locate a suitable investment and after acquisition was to furnish the "know-how" and devote full time to the development and promotion of the project. Daley was to provide the necessary funds. Ennis and Daley were to split the profits 50-50, but later Ennis agreed to take 25%.

[Suitable property was then identified and purchased, and Warm Mineral Springs, Inc. was created to subdivide, develop, and sell lots.]

Things rocked along for a few years, the corporation enjoying a notable degree of success, with Ennis providing the necessary impetus and know-how. An annual accounting was made and Ennis was paid a share of the profits, admittedly not amounting to "25% of gross profits." In April, 1958, Ennis was fired (later permitted to submit his resignation)....

On September 15, 1958, Ennis filed his instant complaint, alleging the corporate resolution and his employment thereunder, and seeking a declaratory decree as to his rights and status, directed mainly at an interpretation of the term, "gross profits" as used in the contract, and particularly whether "accounts receivable" should be included in "gross profits"; also whether sums used for capital improvements, i.e., in developing more lots for future sale, were properly deductible by the corporation before computation of the 25% Share for Ennis.

....

... Upon a rather painstaking review of the entire record, we are impelled to hold with Ennis on both items, although we must leave to the Court below the final determination of the accounting.

Ennis contends that, in construing the employment contract, the term "gross profits" should be held to include accounts receivable, i.e., the unpaid deferred balances upon the purchase price of parcels of the Warm Mineral Springs property sold to purchasers and evidenced and secured by notes and mortgages or by executory contracts of sale. He also contends that revenue derived by the corporation from the sale of lots which was "ploughed back" into the developing and improvement of other lots for future sale by the corporation, thereby increasing its capital worth at the expense of what would otherwise be presently enhanced profits, should likewise be included in "gross profits".

The corporation disputes these assertions, and, while admitting the employment contract, contends that under the contract Ennis was to share only in Cash received from current sales less operating expenses and costs of land improvements for future sales....

Ennis denies any such "understanding" on his part and asserts his understanding to be that "gross profits" meant whatever was received by the corporation, either presently or in evidenced anticipation, over and above only the current expenses and liabilities.

....

The corporation argues that if Ennis were allowed to participate in accounts receivable, it could result in his "getting rich" in a year in which the corporation suffered loss. This position is untenable for the reason that Ennis would not have to be paid in cash upon what the corporation earned in a year in both cash and deferred payments. But it would not necessarily follow that his right to be paid his requisite share would "go down the drain" merely because the corporation was willing to take a part, even most, of the purchase price in deferred payments rather than cash. He would simply receive his additional compensation if and when the future payments were made.

Furthermore, carried to its logical extreme, the corporation could require as little as 1% Down on the installment sales of lots, which conceivably could result in Ennis owing money to the corporation during years in which he had actually generated thousands of dollars in business for the benefit of the corporation. Such a result would be unconscionable, and ... the employment contract cannot be so interpreted.

Perhaps the real "philosophy" influencing the corporation in its contentions may be gleaned from the uncontroverted testimony of Ennis, who stated that when he was fired, Daley told him "you are not entitled to participate in the accounts receivable". When asked why, Daley said, "Because they have not accrued; and when they do accrue you won't be here".

Another circumstance of significance in this connection occurred after Ennis left the corporation. An audit of the corporation books was made by the Federal Internal Revenue, resulting in an adjustment totalling $165,458.54 as additional taxable income for the years in which Ennis was employed. The discrepancy was apparently not a wilful attempt at evasion of taxes but resulted from an improper accounting method, i.e., the corporation was reporting only *cash* received on the installment sales, whereas it should have reported the full amount of sale.

The corporation conceded that, predicated on the Federal computation of additional taxable income, the amount payable to Ennis would be increased by $21,002.80. Ennis contended additional sums due to him should have placed the figure in the neighborhood of $40,000.00, but this is something the lower Court must examine after remand.

....

We reverse on the merits and hold that Ennis was entitled to have a decree entered declaring his rights in the employment contract, that he is entitled to an accounting of the "gross profits" during the time he was employed, according to the meaning of such term as herein held, and to have a money judgment entered up for 25% of the amount so found and not heretofore paid, and such other relief as is necessary or incidental thereto. Such accounting shall be under the supervision of the Chancellor upon remand, to be followed accordingly by entry of a new final decree.

Reversed and remanded, with directions aforesaid.

SHANNON, Acting C.J., concurs.

ADAMS, GEORGE E., Associate Judge (dissenting).

I respectfully dissent. The majority opinion in this case merely weighs the testimony which was adduced before the trial court. This Court can only determine whether there was substantial competent evidence to support the judgment of the lower court. There are substantial conflicts in the testimony produced before the trial court on nearly every critical fact recited in the majority opinion.

It appears to this writer that since the contract of employment as contained in the minutes of the corporation was ambiguous, that testimony and evidence adduced before the trial court must be resorted to in order to determine what the contract meant. There was substantial competent evidence before the trial judge from which he could have found that the contract of employment was a contract for 25% of the gross profits received in cash by the corporation, the term gross profits meaning actually profits after all expenses were paid, except payment of federal income taxes. This, in fact, appears to be the construction placed upon the contract by the Plaintiff....

....

The majority in this case further holds that the Plaintiff is entitled to a declaration of his rights. At the time of the action herein, whatever rights the Plaintiff had had accrued to him and whatever sums were due were then determinable. I can think of no more effective way to declare such a Plaintiff's rights than to deny him any relief.

For the reasons above stated, I would affirm the judgment of the lower court.

Notes and Questions

1. The difference of opinion here is important. Is the "ambiguous contract" interpreted as a matter of fact (discretion given to the lower court's judgment) or as a matter of law? Should it matter that the trial court's interpretation would have been "unconscionable"?

2. Daley is quoted as saying the accounts receivable "have not accrued." How can that be? If there had been no accrual, there would be no account receivable. Does he mean that no sale has been recognized? If so, Ennis is not entitled to payment, right?

3. *Should* the accounts receivable be considered part of "gross profits"? What about money reinvested in capital improvements?

4. A and B form a partnership to own and operate apartment buildings. A invests 75% of the required amount, B the remaining 25%. Specifically, they agree to "embark upon a joint venture for the purpose of acquiring, developing, operating, holding and selling the property." They agree that "net profits or net losses from the property" shall be divided 15% to A and 85% to B. They agree that net profits "shall be determined through the use of generally accepted accounting practices consistently applied on a cash basis." When the apartment buildings are sold, does B receive 85% of the profit (if covered by the agreement) or 25% of the profit (presumably his default share if there is no other arrangement)? *See Eriksson v. Eriksson*, 203 Ga. App. 611, 417 S.E.2d 165 (1992).

5. What if the agreement specified that B were to receive 85% of the "operating income"? *See Jones & Scully, Inc. v. O'Connell*, 604 So. 2d 867 (Fla. App. 1992).

6. The following advice applies to the sale of a business but is relevant when considering the dynamics of the negotiations in defining "profits" of a business.

> Sellers will have no control after the deal closes over [how the accounting will be done], and so will prefer an agreement drafted with an orientation toward the top line (sales), to minimize the role the buyer's judgment can play in the process. Buyers, in control, will prefer a focus at or near the bottom line, enabling them to exercise judgment concerning a variety of matters over which GAAP gives discretion.[1]

* * *

---

1. Lawrence A. Cunningham, *Sharing Accounting's Burden: Business Lawyers in Enron's Dark Shadows*, 57 Bus. Law. 1421, 1433 (2002).

Problem 10-1

Your client, John Megabyte, has been contacted by MyComputer Corp. (MCC) which franchises personal computer repair and training in major cities nationwide. MCC wants John to set up a new office in Metropolis, population 350,000. MCC would provide initial planning and operations advice. John would be responsible for obtaining office space, as well as hiring and supervising the sales and training staff. MCC would handle advertising, billing and collections from its national office. The company's normal procedure is to record services for training and repairs from the local offices daily, and to send out bills immediately to occasional customers, and every three months to institutional customers. Local offices are not responsible for collections and are to forward any payments they do receive directly to the national office.

(1) MCC proposes to pay John a small salary plus a negotiated percentage of the sales from the Metropolis office. How would you define "sales" in John's employment agreement with MCC? Would you propose a different definition if you were counsel for MCC?

(2) Suppose instead John's incentive pay is to be based on the "profits" of the Metropolis store. How would you define this term? Again, how would it differ if you were counsel for MCC?

* * *

Definitions of "income" and related accountings terms are at issue not only in small companies, as in our cases, but in large public companies. Most executive compensation systems use incentive or bonus payments which are tied to achievement of certain target amounts or ratios based on the company's accounting information. The lawyer's role here would include being alert for perverse incentives for management to "manage" these numbers for self-interest.

> [C]onsider an executive who [would receive a bonus if earnings per share (EPS) exceeds $3.00 for the year. The executive] believes current business conditions will allow the company to earn only $2.80 EPS for the year. The executive can still achieve the $3.00 minimum EPS required for a bonus by curtailing needed expenditures, say, simply by cutting back on critical research and development. Research expenses go down, reported earnings go up, and bonuses are paid! This short-term strategy can prove costly in the long term if a competitor introduces a new product based on the technology the company had been researching.[2]

2. Lawrence Revsine, *et al.*, Financial Reporting and Analysis 394 (5th ed. 2012).

2. Balance Sheet Accounts

A business may buy or sell assets (or even liabilities) and therefore agree on the description and value of those assets. Alternatively, an agreement may require a business to retain a certain type or value of assets. As a lawyer familiar with financial statement generation, you should be able to write and review contract language about those items.

* * *

Problem 10-2

Your client is selling $250,000 (book value) of her company's accounts receivable to a "factor," who will be paying $225,000 cash. What representations or warranties should you be prepared to make about the accounts? Recall what you know about the process of how these accounts receivable were created in the first place.

Problem 10-3

You are on the legal staff of Commonwealth Bank. One of the bank's loan officers specializes in relatively high-risk loans to start-up businesses. She has come to you with the following proposal: the bank will lend $500,000 to an individual who intends to open a bookstore in one of the city's new shopping malls. The loan would be secured by the store's inventory and accounts receivable. The bank intends to charge 8% annually on the unpaid loan balance plus 10% of the store's net income. The borrower would covenant to keep at all times inventory, accounts receivable and cash totaling at least 80% of the outstanding unpaid balance. Prepare provisions of the loan contract specifying what are "cash," "inventory," and "accounts receivable," and how they are to be valued.

Problem 10-4

This is a covenant relating to balance sheet items from a commercial loan taken by Acme United Corporation, presented as an exhibit to its 2011 annual report.

> **Tangible Net Worth.** Borrower on a consolidated basis shall, at all times, maintain a Tangible Net Worth of not less than $18,000,000.00. "Total Liabilities" shall mean all liabilities of Borrower, including capitalized leases and all reserves for deferred taxes and other deferred sums appearing on the liabilities side of a balance sheet of Borrower, in accordance with GAAP applied on a consistent basis. "Tangible Net Worth" shall mean the total assets minus Total Liabilities. For purposes of this computation, the aggregate amount of any intangible assets of Borrower including, without limitation, goodwill, franchises, licenses, patents, trademarks, trade names, copyrights, service marks, prepaid pension costs and brand names, shall be subtracted from total assets. This covenant shall be tested quarterly.

(a) This covenant defines "net worth" essentially as assets-liabilities. Could the covenant instead state that "net worth" means the total of the owners' equity accounts?

(b) "Total Liabilities" is defined in accordance with GAAP. Why does it specifically mention "capitalized leases" and "reserves for deferred taxes"? Aren't those already liabilities under GAAP? Why do they need specific mention?

(c) Why isn't "total assets" a defined term? [You can tell it is not defined because, according to custom in these agreements, defined terms have Initial Capitals.] And why subtract intangible assets? Is there something less certain about the value of these assets?

* * *

3. Financial Ratios and Performance Measures

When a business seeks funding from lenders, typically those lenders seek assurance that they will be repaid. A lender may, among other things, insist on covenants governing the business' condition and operation. Just as you are not being trained to be an accountant, neither are you to be a banker. But competence is required in any event.

> Lawyers won't be asked to develop financial covenants and don't need to analyze the bankers' spreadsheets.... But with just a basic understanding of financial statements, and the company's financial statements before you, you should be able to make sense of the financial covenants you are asked to draft. This is important. The lawyers will be held responsible for the document. If there are mistakes, the fact that the lawyers did not understand what they were writing is not a particularly strong defense.[3]

Covenants are generally of two different types. *Coverage* covenants are those which measure the debtor's ability to pay or "cover" the debt. *Balance sheet* covenants are less precisely directed, more about the company's general financial structure, including transactions with owners.[4] "In general, financial covenant adjustments to generally accepted accounting principles are toward cash and away from accrual accounting, and toward realizable value, instead of book value."[5]

---

3. Carolyn E.C. Paris, Drafting for Corporate Finance 207–08 (2d ed. 2014).
4. *Id.* at 209.
5. *Id.* at 208.

Example

This is a simplified covenant to maintain debt service coverage in a 2010 loan agreement by Campus Crest Communities for its student housing construction projects, included as an exhibit to the company's 2010 annual report. Also included are the necessary definitions from the beginning of the agreement.

Covenant

The Project shall satisfy an Aggregate Debt Service Coverage Ratio of no less than 1.10 to 1.0. In order to evidence the satisfaction of such Aggregate Debt Service Coverage Ratio, Borrower shall deliver to Administrative Agent within thirty (30) days after the end of each calendar quarter, an executed Debt Service Coverage Test for each Project on the form attached hereto as Exhibit A and certified by the Borrower as true, correct and complete and as fairly and accurately presenting the information contained therein.

Definitions

Aggregate Debt Service Coverage Ratio shall mean the ratio, as determined by Administrative Agent, of the aggregate amount of each Projects Net Operating Income to the aggregate amount of each Project's Debt Service.

Net Operating Income shall mean a Projects Gross Revenues minus a Projects Operating Expenses.

Gross Revenues shall mean the pro forma gross rental income for the applicable Calculation Period from all executed Leases (approved by Lender in accordance with the terms set forth in this Agreement) with tenants in occupancy for that academic year for a Property.

Operating Expenses shall mean the pro forma expenditures of all kinds for the applicable Calculation Period, calculated on an annualized basis, made with respect to the operation of a Property in the normal course of business including, but not limited to, expenditures for taxes (assuming the full assessment of each Property), insurance, repairs, replacements, maintenance, management fees, salaries, advertising expenses, professional fees, wages and utility costs, and reasonable additions to, or creations of, reserves for repairs and replacements and for capital expenditures.

Debt Service shall mean the sum of the actual principal and interest payable under the Notes which is attributable to the applicable Project.

Calculation Period shall mean the twelve (12) month period immediately following any Determination Date.

EXHIBIT A

Debt Service Coverage Test

Borrower:		Project Name:
Determination date (end of quarter):		
Debt service for following year:		Debt amount:
Gross Revenues		
Tenant		Rental
Total Gross Revenues:		
Operating Expenses		
Real estate taxes		
Insurance		
Maintenance		
Management fee		
Reserves		
Other		
Total Operating Expenses:		
Net Operating Income (Gross Revenues less Operating Expenses):		
Debt Service (from above):		
Debt Service Coverage Ratio (Net Operating Income / Debt Service):		
Borrower signature:		Date:

Questions

1. Do the formulas for revenues and expenses move "toward cash and away from accrual accounting" as the text quoted above suggests?

2. Would one- or two-month variations in revenues or expenses affect the calculation of this ratio? Suppose the company prepaid an expense? Suppose a student's lease payments were several months behind?

B. Agreements about Financial Statements

Apart from using accounting terms in substantive provisions of a transaction, the parties may agree about financial statements themselves.

1. One-Time Transactions

If financial statements are an important part of the economic bargaining between the parties, for reasons discussed in this Chapter, the parties should understand how those statements were prepared, and warrant that they conform to that understanding. In an offering of securities subject to the Securities Act, the agreements about financial statements are much more complex. Those issues are discussed in detail in courses in securities regulation. The following discussion highlights the main questions to be considered in a small transaction.

Independent review. Should the financial statements be audited? Answering this question depends upon the client's evaluation (with the attorney) of the likelihood of significant variations between what those statements purport to represent and what either party believes that those statements represent. If it is likely that the two parties are speaking different languages, and the differences could be significant in terms of economic gain or loss or future litigation to sort things out, some independent review should be considered.

Audits, of course, add significantly to the cost of the transaction, especially so if an air of distrust exists from the beginning. Maybe there are even two accountants already at battle along with the parties and counsel. However, one text puts it bluntly: "The smaller the company, the greater the need for an audit."[6] Financial statements can be reviewed by an independent accountant by standards less demanding than GAAS.[7] Such review may be appropriate where an audit, despite its advantages, is impossible because of cost or because of the condition of the company's financial records.

* * *

Problem 10-5

Commonwealth Bank is considering a $500,000 loan to a local used book seller to expand the business. The Bank's loan officer has reviewed the borrower's most recent financial statements, shown below.

---

6. 2 Irving Kellogg & Loren B. Kellogg, Fraud, Window Dressing and Negligence in Financial Statements at 29-12 (1994).

7. See, for example, a "review" engagement, where both the extent of procedures and level of accuracy are different than in an audit. Don M. Pallais, Audits and Other Accountants' Services: A Handbook for Lawyers 135 (2010).

Ex Libris Bookstore
Balance Sheet 12/31/xx

Cash	$100,000	Accounts Payable	$100,000
Accounts Receivable, net	250,000	Current amount of loan	50,000
Inventory	400,000	Long-term debt	450,000
		Owner's equity	150,000
	$750,000		**$750,000**

Ex Libris Bookstore
Income Statement for year ended 12/31/xx

Sales		4,000,000
Cost of sales	3,000,000	
Store clerks: salary and benefits	500,000	
Uncollectible accounts	50,000	
Lease expense	250,000	
Interest, taxes, insurance	100,000	3,900,000
Net income		100,000

At this level of business, an audit is too expensive. What covenants do you recommend be included in the loan agreement about the financial statements presented to the Bank?

* * *

2. Continuing Disclosure Obligations

The financial disclosure obligations of a business with publicly-traded securities are set primarily in the Exchange Act and its rules, along with the rules of the marketplace where those securities are traded. The small business, however, does not have a corresponding set of obligations. The nature and extent of obligations relating to financial disclosure varies with the type of organization.

A corporation is ordinarily required to keep financial records, but there is little detail provided by the statutes.[8] The statutes governing more informally-organized

8. Model Business Corporation Act § 16.01(c) provides that "[a] corporation shall maintain accounting records in a form that permits preparation of its financial statements." Comment 3 provides some detail.

The accounting records to be maintained under section 16.01(c) depend upon the form of the corporation's financial statements. For example, annual tax returns filed with the relevant taxing au-

associations such as partnerships[9] and limited liability companies[10] are even less demanding.

But in general, more attention is paid in state statutes and in the case law to when and whether partners, members or shareholders may have *access* to the records kept than to the types of records which must be kept. And when relationships deteriorate, the accounting becomes critical to the determination of the rights of each business person.

Couri v. Couri

Supreme Court of Illinois, 1983
95 Ill. 2d 91, 447 N.E.2d 334

UNDERWOOD, Justice:

This litigation began in 1974, approximately 6½ months after the dissolution of a partnership that had existed for some 20 years between the plaintiff, Joseph Couri, and his brother, Anthony Couri, the defendant. Pursuant to plaintiff's complaint, the circuit court of Peoria County ordered defendant to render a formal accounting to plaintiff, and on June 30, 1980, a court-appointed receiver wound up the partnership affairs. A final judgment was entered, in February 1981, for plaintiff in the amount of $122,690 and costs. Defendant appealed, plaintiff cross-appealed, and the appellate court reversed. We allowed plaintiff's petition for leave to appeal.

In 1941, plaintiff, defendant, and their brother Peter Couri orally agreed to operate as equal partners the "Couri Brothers Supermarket," a business which their father began in 1928. The brothers agreed that they would have equal control of the partnership, share equally in profits and losses and have equal rights in the partnership property. The agreement was of indefinite duration.

Plaintiff began working full time in his father's store in 1935 and continued to do so until 1941, when he entered the United States Army. Defendant began working in the store in the early '30s and in 1941, following his father's death, assumed responsibility for the books and records of the newly formed partnership. Defendant

thorities may be the only annual financial statements prepared by small businesses operating on a cash basis and, in those instances, the requisite accounting records to be maintained might consist of only a check register, vouchers and receipts.

9. The Uniform Partnership Act does not require any records. The official comment to § 408 states:

> A general partnership is often a very informal organization. Accordingly, this subsection states a default-required location for any books and records a partnership may have but does not require that books and records be kept. Other law may so require, however — particularly tax law. This subsection applies to any books and records kept to satisfy other law.

10. The Uniform Limited Liability Company Act similarly does not require any records. The official comment to § 410, dealing with production of information, notes that "[t]his section generally concerns providing existing information, not creating it."

continued to work full time at the store until 1946, when plaintiff returned from the Army and resumed his full-time position. Thereafter defendant apparently worked part time for several years until he formed another unrelated partnership, a tavern called the "Western Tap." From approximately 1949 until 1956, defendant devoted most of his time to that business while plaintiff continued to work full time in the supermarket. It was apparently during that time that Peter Couri entered medical school, and in 1954 plaintiff and defendant purchased his interest in the partnership. Their oral agreement was of indefinite duration, and provided that they would, in all respects, be equal partners.

Defendant sold the Western Tap in 1956, and for the next 10 years devoted a good deal of his time to real estate ventures on behalf of the supermarket partnership. During this period, plaintiff gave his full time to the store, working as a clerk as well as a butcher in the meat department.

The brothers continued to operate the partnership, with both now apparently working full time, until September 29, 1973, at which time they had an irreconcilable disagreement, resulting in plaintiff's leaving the store permanently. The circumstances under which the disagreement and dissolution of the partnership occurred were sharply disputed: Plaintiff claimed that he was precluded by defendant from full participation in the management and operation of the partnership, while defendant claimed that plaintiff abandoned the business and thereafter refused to participate. Although neither party acquiesced in the other's characterization of the circumstances surrounding plaintiff's departure, the trial court determined that the partnership was rightfully dissolved, a finding which has not been challenged on appeal.

In November 1973, plaintiff visited defendant at his home and requested and received some of the partnership records for the prior two years. The parties, however, were unable to resolve their differences, and plaintiff consequently demanded that defendant wind up the partnership affairs. Instead, in July 1974, defendant changed the locks on the store, closed out the partnership checking account, opened a new account which was in his exclusive control, changed the name of the grocery store from "Couri Brothers Supermarket" to "Couri's Supermarket," and continued to operate the store until the court-appointed receiver wound up the partnership affairs and disposed of its assets.

The books and records of the partnership as well as the tax returns were prepared and maintained by defendant throughout the partnership's existence. There were daily reports, and monthly and yearly summaries. The tax returns were prepared from the latter two. The daily reports were theoretically restated in the monthly and yearly summaries; however, at least for the years 1971 through 1974, income was admittedly substantially understated so that the summaries and tax returns for those periods did not accurately reflect actual income. The parties agreed at trial and in the appellate court that income could be reliably verified from the daily reports, a concession which the appellate court found difficult to accept because of its belief that those records could not have accurately reflected the partnership's net profit. It seems clear, however, that those records, if adequately explained, represented the most accurate description of the financial operation of the partnership. Unfortunately, the vast majority of the daily reports, which were in defendant's possession and under his control, were destroyed approximately two years after this litigation began. Despite a court order prohibiting defendant from destroying, altering or otherwise modifying any of the partnership's books and records, defendant's son cleaned his parents' attic, while the latter two were vacationing, resulting in the disposal of several boxes containing daily reports. According to the boy's testimony, he was instructed to clean the garage and attic by his mother, who testified she acted without consulting defendant.

The parties stipulated at trial that there would be no accounting of the partnership's financial affairs prior to 1957. Thus, the trial court's judgment was based upon the partnership's financial status from 1957 through June 1980. In response to the court's order requiring defendant to account for this period, defendant produced books, records, bank statements, and tax returns which may, at best, be described as contradictory and incomplete. Such daily reports as were available were mainly copies which plaintiff had fortuitously made of reports which he had received prior to trial but which were returned by him and were among those destroyed. To exacerbate matters further, defendant's bookkeeping practices were not in accord with generally accepted accounting principles.

Although neither party could provide precise calculations, both submitted memoranda and affidavits based upon the available evidence indicating the manner in which the income should be computed. Defendant's total figures varied from approximately $433,600 to $487,000, whereas plaintiff asserted that defendant's figures should be increased by approximately $527,000, resulting in a total in excess of $1 million. The estimated reported income (tax returns for four or five years were not produced and were no longer available from the Internal Revenue Service) was approximately $424,000. The trial judge ... determined that the accounting filed by defendant for the years 1957 through June 30, 1980, did not accurately reflect the net income of the partnership. Rather, the court found that the actual net income was $750,000....

... The appellate court, accepting one of defendant's arguments, reversed and dismissed plaintiff's petition for an accounting. It held that, notwithstanding defendant's duty to account, based upon the available incomplete evidence as well as the unreliability of the tax returns, plaintiff had failed to demonstrate an amount to which he was entitled. Although doubting the reliability of the daily reports, the court stated that once those documents were "innocuously swept away," an accounting became not only impractical but unattainable, and it was thus impossible to compute how much was due either party.

In our judgment the basic flaw in the appellate court's reasoning is its mischaracterization of the consequences of the breaches of defendant's fiduciary duties and the destruction of the daily records which the court had ordered him to preserve. Those records were in defendant's sole possession and control, and while the defendant's proof indicates he did not know they were being destroyed, it is clear that he had not informed his family of their importance and the necessity of their preservation.

Plaintiff's inability to be more specific in his proof is the direct result of the breach of defendant's obligations under the court order as well as his failure to adequately discharge his fiduciary duties.

The basic partnership principles involved here are well settled. A fiduciary relationship existed between the partners and embraced all matters relating to the partnership business; each was bound to exercise the utmost good faith and honesty in all dealings and transactions relating to the partnership. As the managing partner who was admittedly responsible for virtually all of the financial aspects of the partnership, defendant had a duty, as trustee, to maintain regular and accurate records and to account for partnership transactions. All doubts and obscurities created by his own negligent failure to keep adequate records were properly resolved against him by the trial court.

Despite the imprecise nature of some of plaintiff's proof, there was sufficient evidence from which the trial court could fashion an equitable decree, and we do not believe, as the appellate court apparently did, that in these circumstances the trial court was required to detail the nature or method of its calculations. Thus, ... the evidence here, although voluminous, is not in such a state of uncertainty that it is impossible to determine whether any amount is due....

Defendant's argument here that "right or wrong" the only concrete evidence available shows that net income was approximately $546,143 ignores the record and the applicable fiduciary principles. Based upon the available books and records, the testimony and reports of two accountants, the testimony of the parties, and the reasonable inferences from the evidence, the trial court could have reasonably concluded that income was substantially greater than defendant contended. Indeed it was evident that the tax returns were not accurate, as the appellate court (whose statement of facts has been adopted by defendant in this court) conceded. The trial court had evidence from which it could determine the approximate amount of the understatement for the years 1971–74. Further, the court could well have rejected much of defendant's evidence and testimony concerning the period from 1974–80, given the absence of any daily reports (which he no longer prepared) or other supporting documents to verify actual income, and the obvious disparity between the profits defendant claimed and the known profits for the period in which he admitted the understatements. Too, the probative value of defendant's explanation concerning his change of accounting methods and his testimony concerning the accrual method upon which he had previously operated was not great. Even assuming that he had attempted to follow that method in previous years — which an accountant commissioned by the court was unable to verify from records which seemed to indicate the contrary — his methods were inconsistent with accepted accounting principles. Thus, had the court, based upon this evidence, determined that defendant continued to understate income during the years 1974–80, albeit in a somewhat lesser amount, it could have reasonably concluded that the net income of the partnership over the period in question was $750,000. While we express no opinion on defendant's testimony concerning his blamelessness in the destruction of the daily reports, we do point out that had defendant preserved those records as he was ordered to do, he might have been able to overcome or rebut some of the presumptions which were resolved against him. His inability to do so is the result of his own handling of the partnership's affairs.

....

For the reasons stated, the appellate court's judgment is reversed. Since this case has been in litigation for nearly nine years, in lieu of a remand, we affirm the circuit court's judgment ... and we enter judgment here for plaintiff for an additional amount of $32,500 and costs.

Appellate court reversed; circuit court affirmed; additional judgment entered here.

Notes and Questions

1. If you take $487,000, the highest figure calculated by the defendant for the cumulative net income, and add one-half of $527,000, the plaintiff's proposed increases, you come up with $750,500, which, rounded off, would be $750,000, the amount of net income "found" by the trial court and affirmed here. The case seemed to turn more on the fiduciary duty of one party keeping the records, no?

2. To what actions does this fiduciary duty extend? The principal case suggests the duty extends at least to the *keeping of records*. But we saw above that modern entity law does not have firm record-keeping requirements. Therefore, the fiduciary duty extends more often to the *duty to disclose*. See the Comment to § 409 of ULLCA:

> [S]ome cases characterize owners' information rights as reflecting a fiduciary duty of those with management power. *E.g., Bakerman v. Sidney Frank Importing Co., Inc.*, No. Civ.A. 1844-N, 2006 WL 3927242 at *14 (Del. Ch. Oct. 16, 2006) (holding that an LLC manager owed "certain duties to members of the LLC" and stating that "[w]hen fiduciaries communicate with their beneficiaries in the context of asking the beneficiary to make a discretionary decision—such as whether to consent to a sale of substantially all the assets of an LLC—the fiduciary has a duty to disclose all material facts bearing on the decision at issue") (citing *Loudon v. Archer-Daniels-Midland Co.*, 700 A.2d 135, 137 (Del.1997)).

Accord, Comment to RUPA 409(a) ("many cases characterize a manager's duty to disclose as a fiduciary duty.").

3. Cases discussing partnership records invariably arise against the backdrop of dissolution. Often the court's decision is made easier by the fact that the party alleging the inadequacy of the records provided is the one with few equities on his or her side to begin with. *See, e.g., Holcomb v. Davis*, 431 S.W.2d 881 (Ky. 1968), *Hansen v. Hansen*, 297 P.2d 879 (Mont. 1956), and the particularly compelling case of *Duncan v. Bartle*, 216 P.2d 1005 (Or. 1950), vindicating the efforts of a woman who, despite a heart attack and broken arm, continued to operate a restaurant herself 18 hours a

day *and* keep accounting records. However, where the opposite is true, courts will leave the burden of proof where it first lodged. *See Mayeux v. Winder*, 131 P.3d 85, 91 (N.M. 2005) ("Plaintiffs' awareness of and involvement in the financial affairs of the company further support our conclusion that it was fair for Plaintiffs to bear the burden of showing that Defendant's facially legitimate expenditures were improper.").

* * *

Problem 10-6

You are a new associate in a large law firm. Having heard that you have completed a course in Legal Accounting, a partner asks you to review and suggest changes to the firm's limited liability company operating agreement form, which reads, in relevant part, as follows:

> **Article 4. Books, records and reports**
>
> **§ 4.1.** ***Record keeping.*** Proper, complete and accurate books and records shall be kept in accordance with standard accounting practices.
>
> **§ 4.2.** ***Reports.*** The Treasurer will prepare and send to each member monthly a profit and loss statement. At the end of the year, each member will receive a balance sheet, as well as a statement of each member's profit or loss share for the year for that member's tax returns and records.
>
> **§ 4.3.** ***Estimates for tax purposes.*** Each year, no later than two months before the end of the company's fiscal year, each member shall receive an estimate of the member's share of the company's profit or loss for the year, so that the member may estimate his or her income tax obligations for the year.
>
> **§ 4.4.** ***Distributions.*** There shall be distributed annually to each member, from the company's excess cash flow as determined by the Treasurer, the member's share of such cash flow.

Chapter 11

Business Valuation

Valuation of a business is an issue which pervades the practice of law. In this chapter we focus on the lawyer's use of financial information in tackling that task. The task is complicated for many reasons.

- ***This is not individual asset valuation.*** The valuation techniques herein are for valuing a group of assets in a business. In some cases, only a portion of an entity must be valued for a specific purpose. In Chapter 5, for example, we learned that assets are tested for impairment under GAAP based on their "fair value," taking the value of the assets as a productive group. The principles in this chapter will apply broadly to most of GAAP's "fair value" requirements. This is a fast-growing area of GAAP.
- ***We are concerned with valuation of a closely-held business.*** We are not discussing how to value a publicly-traded company or any of its stocks or bonds. Rather, the concern is valuation of a business with only a few owners and, therefore, without a current market for the interests we seek to value.
- ***We are concerned with valuation of a business as a "going concern."*** This means that we are assuming the business will be continued in operation, not broken up or liquidated.
- ***We are concerned with the value of the business in a specific context.*** This is especially important, because the reason we are asking the question provides much of the basis for the decision. "'Value' is a judicial chameleon of sorts; its attendant meanings change with the factual contexts in which it arises."[1]
- ***Our financial statements will not determine value.*** Although we have spent most of this textbook creating and using the numbers financial statements, they will be of limited use in determining the value of the business. This is primarily because they focus on past transactions (historical income, historical cost) and they omit important types of assets from the calculation of value. Nonetheless, the financial statements will provide a starting point for business valuation. Analysts use that information to begin their search for value.

1. W. Terrance Schreier & O. Maurice Joy, *Judicial Valuation of "Close" Corporation Stock:* Alice in Wonderland *Revisited*, 31 Okl. L. Rev. 853, 853 (1978).

What you will learn. This chapter proceeds in five parts.

- First, we will survey the situations in which business valuation becomes a legal issue.
- Second, we will learn the basics of valuation theory.
- Third, we will study the valuation methods based on the income of the business entity.
- Fourth, we will study the valuation methods based on the market value of the entity or comparable entities.
- Finally, we consider the situations in which these values should be discounted or increased based on the type of interest we are valuing.

A. The Legal Contexts

There are perhaps dozens of ways in which the value of a business could become a legal issue. There are a handful of contexts, however, which account for most reported cases, and we are left to use those to determine their applicability in other contexts.

1. State Business Entity Law

Many valuation cases arise from provisions common to most state's corporation and limited liability company (LLC) laws. These involve three related areas in which those dissatisfied with an action by the business are entitled to a valuation of their interests.

a. Dissenter's Appraisal Rights

State corporation law allows a shareholder whose shares have been converted into a specified amount of cash or other property pursuant to certain corporate actions the right to have the "fair value" of those shares determined in a court proceeding, and to receive that value in cash instead of the amount of cash or other consideration specified.[2] Suppose, for example, that A Corp. and B Corp. agree to merge, and the merger agreement is that A Corp. will be the surviving entity and that each share of B Corp. common stock will be converted into one share of A Corp. common stock. State law normally provides that the holders of B Corp. common stock must approve the merger for it to be effective, usually by majority vote. If the agreement is approved, a B Corp. shareholder who voted "no" will nonetheless see his share converted into one share of A Corp. common stock when the merger becomes effective. But if that shareholder so desires, he or she may bring suit against B Corp. to be paid, in cash,

2. *See, e.g.*, Model Business Corporation Act Ch. 13.

the "fair value" of his or her shares.[3] These rights are typically referred to as "dissenter's" appraisal rights, because only those who did not approve the underlying corporate action are entitled to maintain the lawsuit.[4] The rule in LLCs ordinarily depends on the contractual agreement governing the company; the law does not typically provide an absolute appraisal right.[5]

b. Buyout in a Dissolution Proceeding

Strife and discord are a fact of life in any business. In a corporation, a shareholder who is dissatisfied with the conduct of business might simply sell his or her shares. However, if the corporation's stock is closely-held, there may be no buyers for those shares. In many instances, the shareholders resort to a lawsuit seeking liquidation of the corporation due to misconduct on the part of those in control of the corporation. Typical is § 14.30(2) of the Model Business Corporation Act, which provides that a court may dissolve a corporation in a proceeding by a shareholder

> if it is established that:
>
> ....
>
> (ii) the directors or those in control of the corporation have acted, are acting, or will act in a manner that is illegal, oppressive, or fraudulent.
>
> ....
>
> (iv) the corporate assets are being misapplied or wasted.

In applying these statutory rules, courts came to recognize that dissolution of the corporation was a drastic remedy for what was essentially a problem of shareholder liquidity. In many cases, therefore, courts began to allow the majority shareholders (the defendants) to "buy out" the minority shareholder (the plaintiff) instead of ordering dissolution. They were willing to do this without explicit statutory authority.[6]

Many state legislatures then legitimized this "buy out" option in their statutes. As an example, Model Business Corporation Act § 14.34 states that if judicial dissolution is sought by a shareholder under § 14.30 (reprinted above), the corporation or the other shareholders may elect to purchase the plaintiff's shares. If the two sides cannot work out a price, then the court shall "determine the fair value of the petitioner's shares."[7]

---

3. The cases we read all involve mergers, but these rights are available in other situations, such as sale of substantially all the assets of the corporation or amendment of the articles in a way which fundamentally changes the rights of a class of stock. *See generally* Model Business Corporation Act § 13.02(a). In addition, there are many exceptions and legal issues involved in these statutory proceedings which are beyond the scope of our study here.

4. Under the Model Act, all that is required is that the shares "not vote ... in favor of the proposed action." *Id.* § 13.21(a)(2).

5. *See* Uniform Limited Liability Company Act § 1006, Del. Lim. Liab. Co. Act, 6 Del. Code § 18-210.

6. *See, e.g.*, Davis v. Sheerin, 754 S.W.2d 375 (Tex. App. 1st Dist.1988).

7. Model Business Corporation Act § 14.34(d).

Similar rules may apply in the LLC situation. The Uniform Limited Liability Company Act provides for judicial dissolution

> on the grounds that:
>
> ... (C) the managers or those members in control of the company:
>
> (i) have acted, are acting, or will act in a manner that is illegal or fraudulent; or
>
> (ii) have acted or are acting in a manner that is oppressive and was, is, or will be directly harmful to the applicant....[8]

The Act also permits a buyout rather than dissolution.[9]

c. *"Fairness" Determination Required*

In other circumstances, state corporation law requires that the directors' conduct meet certain legal standards. If it does not, the directors may face liability for their actions unless it is shown that the conduct in question was fair to the corporation. One aspect of fairness is the value or price involved,[10] and therefore valuation of a business or a segment of a business may be at issue when the fairness of the directors' conduct is litigated.

2. Federal Income, Estate, and Gift Taxes

All the property of a decedent is subject to the federal estate tax according to its value at the time of death.[11] Similarly, gifts of property are subject to the federal gift tax based on their value.[12] When the estate or gift includes an interest in a business, the same valuation issues arise. In addition, a gift which qualifies as a charitable contribution is deductible from income by a taxpayer in determining federal income tax, again according to the value of the property given.[13] In each instance, the Treasury Department has given the following definition as a starting point. Value is "fair market value" and

> fair market value is the price at which the property would change hands between a willing buyer and a willing seller, neither being under any compulsion to buy or sell and both having reasonable knowledge of relevant facts.[14]

---

8. ULLCA §701(a)(4).

9. *Id.* §701(b).

10. *See* Weinberger v. UOP, Inc., 457 A.2d 701 (Del. 1983); Delaware Open MRI Radiology Associates v. Kessler, *infra* p. 338.

11. I.R.C. §§2001(a) (tax), 2031(a) (value).

12. *Id.* §§2501(a)(1) (tax), 2512(a) (value).

13. *Id.* §170(a). For valuation rules regarding charitable contributions of interests in closely-held businesses, see Treas. Reg. §1.170A-13(c). In general, an appraisal is required if the claimed deduction exceeds $5,000. *See id.* §1.170A-13(c)(2).

14. Treas. Reg. §§1.170A-1(c)(2) (charitable contribution deduction), 20.2031-3 (estate tax), 25.2512-1 (gift tax).

The income tax context of business valuation is especially relevant because the specific guidance given by the Treasury Department in this area,[15] which is often relied on by courts in other contexts.

3. Division of Property on Divorce

Dissolution of a marriage involves, apart from all the other enormous issues, the division of a formerly single economic unit. In many instances, one spouse is the sole proprietor of a small business — upon divorce, the value of that business must be determined. The valuation process is significantly impacted by the proscriptions of applicable state laws.

4. Agreements

A business needs to be valued if it is closely-held and the owners have planned exit strategies which are reflected in a repurchase or "buy-sell" agreement. Typically, a value is agreed upon for the amount to be paid for an owner's interest, which in turn reflects the parties' estimations about the value of the business. We learned in Chapter 10 how to use accounting terminology in agreements. That knowledge can be combined with valuation theories to provide a contractual solution to the valuation issue.

5. Other Contexts

Many other varieties of legal situations exist requiring business valuation.[16] Damages might be assessed to the unsuccessful defendant in a contract, tort or antitrust case, based in part on the decrease in value of the business.[17] Forfeiture or condemnation proceedings can involve small business property,[18] or the property may be subject to property tax based on its value. Bankruptcy or insolvency proceedings and the related negotiations with creditors constantly involve questions of the business' value under various scenarios.[19] Various regulatory statutes may require valuation.[20]

---

15. *See* Rev. Ruls. 59-60 and 68-609, *infra* pp. 323 and 345.

16. For examples other than those in this paragraph, see Gary R. Trugman, Understanding Business Valuation: A Practical Guide to Valuing Small to Medium Sized Businesses 2–7 (3d ed. 2008).

17. *See, e.g.*, Zokoych v. Spalding, *infra* p. 354.

18. *See, e.g.*, New Haven Unified School District v. Taco Bell Corp., 24 Cal. App. 4th 1473, 30 Cal. Rptr. 2d 469 (1st Dist. 1994) (valuation of goodwill in condemnation of restaurant by school district).

19. *See* Harry J. Haynsworth IV, *Valuation of Business Interests*, 33 Mercer L. Rev. 457, 457–58 (1982).

20. *See, e.g.*, I.R.C. § 401(a)(28)(C) (valuation of employer securities held in trust under an employee stock ownership plan (ESOP), where those employer securities are not publicly traded).

B. Basic Valuation Theory

Before we consider methods of valuation, let's briefly consider theories of valuation. That will help organize our study. In general, things have value because they can be exchanged for future benefits.[21] If we agree that the most sensible way to evaluate future benefits is a cash equivalent, then we can calculate value in cash terms.[22]

The difficulty arises when we apply this theory. These cash values can be measured in two different ways.

- First, we could directly look at future benefits in terms of **cash payments**, but receipt of those amounts is subject to risk. We need a way to convert or translate those estimated future benefits into present cash terms. This describes the "income" methods of valuation discussed in Part C below.
- Second, we could look for a **market price**. This will be difficult because, by definition, we are valuing a small or closely-held business which does not have a current market for its ownership interests. We might, however, find a comparable item for sale at an established market price, and that might approximate the value of what we have. This describes the "market" method of valuation discussed in Part D below.

Theories of valuation and the application of those theories is an expert's subject. A list of reference works for further study is at the end of this chapter. We begin here with brief overview, provided by a Treasury Department revenue ruling. This may seem like an odd place to begin. Revenue Ruling 59-60 is an early interpretation of the elusive term "fair market value" in the context of estate and gift taxes. Although it is now over 60 years of age, it remains an authoritative statement of business valuation procedures in many contexts. Everyone who deals with business valuation will be familiar with it. One professional business valuation analyst sums up the impact of this publication.

> Revenue Ruling 59-60 is said to be one of the greatest business valuation treatises ever written.... [It] is quoted more often than any other source in the valuation field.... Because of its wide acceptance, many other authorities have looked to this ruling for guidance in [valuation] ... for many reasons other than taxes.... Regardless of the set of standards followed in performing a business valuation, they all send the same message: Consider the factors set forth in Revenue Ruling 59-60.[23]

---

21. Shannon P. Pratt & Alina V. Niculita, Valuing A Business: The Analysis and Appraisal of Closely Held Companies 56 (5th ed. 2008). *See also* Gary R. Trugman, Understanding Business Valuation: A Practical Guide to Valuing Small to Medium Sized Businesses 105–12 (5th ed. 2017).

22. The valuation analyst's assignment is to determine the equivalent of cash that would be paid for the item being valued as of the valuation date.... No one will buy property if there will be no future benefits, whether in the form of income or the appreciation to be realized upon subsequence resale.

Trugman, *supra* note 21, at 106.

23. Trugman, *supra* note 21, at 693 & 704.

Revenue Ruling 59-60

1959-1 C.B. 237

....

SECTION 1. PURPOSE.

The purpose of this Revenue Ruling is to outline and review in general the approach, methods and factors to be considered in valuing shares of the capital stock of closely held corporations for estate tax and gift tax purposes. The methods discussed herein will apply likewise to the valuation of corporate stocks on which market quotations are either unavailable or are of such scarcity that they do not reflect the fair market value.

....

SECTION 3. APPROACH TO VALUATION.

.01 A determination of fair market value, being a question of fact, will depend upon the circumstances in each case. No formula can be devised that will be generally applicable to the multitude of different valuation issues arising in estate and gift tax cases. Often, an appraiser will find wide differences of opinion as to the fair market value of a particular stock. In resolving such differences, he should maintain a reasonable attitude in recognition of the fact that valuation is not an exact science. A sound valuation will be based upon all the relevant facts, but the elements of common sense, informed judgment and reasonableness must enter into the process of weighing those facts and determining their aggregate significance.

.02 The fair market value of specific shares of stock will vary as general economic conditions change from "normal" to "boom" or "depression," that is, according to the degree of optimism or pessimism with which the investing public regards the future at the required date of appraisal. Uncertainty as to the stability or continuity of the future income from a property decreases its value by increasing the risk of loss of earnings and value in the future. The value of shares of stock of a company with very uncertain future prospects is highly speculative. The appraiser must exercise his judgment as to the degree of risk attaching to the business of the corporation which issued the stock, but that judgment must be related to all of the other factors affecting value.

.03 Valuation of securities is, in essence, a prophesy as to the future and must be based on facts available at the required date of appraisal. As a generalization, the prices of stocks which are traded in volume in a free and active market by informed persons best reflect the consensus of the investing public as to what the future holds for the corporations and industries represented. When a stock is closely held, is traded infrequently, or is traded in an erratic market, some other measure of value must be used. In many instances, the next best measure may be found in the prices at which the stocks of companies engaged in the same or a similar line of business are selling in a free and open market.

SECTION 4. FACTORS TO CONSIDER.

.01 It is advisable to emphasize that in the valuation of the stock of closely held corporations or the stock of corporations where market quotations are either lacking or too scarce to be recognized, all available financial data, as well as all relevant factors affecting the fair market value, should be considered. The following factors, although not all-inclusive are fundamental and require careful analysis in each case:

a) The nature of the business and the history of the enterprise from its inception.
b) The economic outlook in general and the condition and outlook of the specific industry in particular.
c) The book value of the stock and the financial condition of the business.
d) The earning capacity of the company.
e) The dividend-paying capacity.
f) Whether or not the enterprise has goodwill or other intangible value.
g) Sales of the stock and the size of the block of stock to be valued.
h) The market price of stocks of corporations engaged in the same or a similar line of business having their stocks actively traded in a free and open market, either on an exchange or over-the-counter.

.02 The following is a brief discussion of each of the foregoing factors:

(a) The history of a corporate enterprise will show its past stability or instability, its growth or lack of growth, the diversity or lack of diversity of its operations, and other facts needed to form an opinion of the degree of risk involved in the business.... The history to be studied should include, but need not be limited to, the nature of the business, its products or services, its operating and investment assets, capital structure, plant facilities, sales records and management, all of which should be considered as of the date of the appraisal, with due regard for recent significant changes. Events of the past that are unlikely to recur in the future should be discounted, since value has a close relation to future expectancy.

(b) A sound appraisal of a closely held stock must consider current and prospective economic conditions as of the date of appraisal, both in the national economy and in the industry or industries with which the corporation is allied. It is important to know that the company is more or less successful than its competitors in the same industry, or that it is maintaining a stable position with respect to competitors. Equal or even greater significance may attach to the ability of the industry with which the company is allied to compete with other industries.... The loss of the manager of a so-called "one-man" business may have a depressing effect upon the value of the stock of such business, particularly if there is a lack of trained personnel capable of succeeding to the management of the enterprise....

(c) Balance sheets should be obtained, preferably in the form of comparative annual statements for two or more years immediately preceding the date of appraisal, together with a balance sheet at the end of the month preceding that date, if corporate accounting will permit. Any balance sheet descriptions that are not self-explanatory, and balance sheet items comprehending diverse assets or liabilities, should be clarified in essential detail by supporting supplemental schedules. These statements usually will disclose to the appraiser (1) liquid position (ratio of current assets to current liabilities); (2) gross and net book value of principal classes of fixed assets; (3) working capital; (4) long-term indebtedness; (5) capital structure; and (6) net worth. Consideration also should be given to any assets not essential to the operation of the business, such as investments in securities, real estate, etc. In general, such nonoperating assets will command a lower rate of return than do the operating assets, although in exceptional cases the reverse may be true. In computing the book value per share of stock, assets of the investment type should be revalued on the basis of their market price and the book value adjusted accordingly....

(d) Detailed profit-and-loss statements should be obtained and considered for a representative period immediately prior to the required date of appraisal, preferably five or more years. Such statements should show (1) gross income by principal items; (2) principal deductions from gross income including major prior items of operating expenses, interest and other expense on each item of long-term debt, depreciation and depletion if such deductions are made, officers' salaries, in total if they appear to be reasonable or in detail if they seem to be excessive, contributions (whether or not deductible for tax purposes) that the nature of its business and its community position require the corporation to make, and taxes by principal items, including income and excess profits taxes; (3) net income available for dividends; (4) rates and amounts of dividends paid on each class of stock; (5) remaining amount carried to surplus; and (6) adjustments to, and reconciliation with, surplus as stated on the balance sheet. With profit and loss statements of this character available, the appraiser should be able to separate recurrent from nonrecurrent items of income and expense, to distinguish between operating income and investment income, and to ascertain whether or not any line of business in which the company is engaged is operated consistently at a loss and might be abandoned with benefit to the company. The percentage of earnings retained for business expansion should be noted when dividend-paying capacity is considered. Potential future income is a major factor in many valuations of closely-held stocks, and all information concerning past income which will be helpful in predicting the future should be secured. Prior earnings records usually are the most reliable guide as to the future expectancy, but resort to arbitrary five-or-ten-year averages without regard to current trends or future prospects will not produce a realistic valuation. If, for instance, a record of progressively increasing or decreasing net income is found, then greater weight may be accorded the most recent years' profits in estimating earning power....

(e) Primary consideration should be given to the dividend-paying capacity of the company rather than to dividends actually paid in the past.... Where an actual or effective controlling interest in a corporation is to be valued, the div-

> We discussed in Ch. 7 the different ways owners can extract cash payments from their businesses. See pp. 234–35.

idend factor is not a material element, since the payment of such dividends is discretionary with the controlling stockholders. The individual or group in control can substitute salaries and bonuses for dividends, thus reducing net income and understating the dividend-paying capacity of the company. It follows, therefore, that dividends are less reliable criteria of fair market value than other applicable factors.

(f) [Valuation of] goodwill is based upon earning capacity. The presence of goodwill and its value, therefore, rests upon the excess of net earnings over and above a fair return on the net tangible assets. While the element of goodwill may be based primarily on earnings, such factors as the prestige and renown of the business, the ownership of a trade or brand name, and a record of successful operation over a prolonged period in a particular locality, also may furnish support for the inclusion of intangible value. In some instances it may not be possible to make a separate appraisal of the tangible and intangible assets of the business. The enterprise has a value as an entity....

(g) Sales of stock of a closely held corporation should be carefully investigated to determine whether they represent transactions at arm's length. Forced or distress sales do not ordinarily reflect fair market value nor do isolated sales in small amounts necessarily control as the measure of value. This is especially true in the valuation of a controlling interest in a corporation. Since, in the case of closely held stocks, no prevailing market prices are available, there is no basis for making an adjustment for blockage. It follows, therefore, that such stocks should be valued upon a consideration of all the evidence affecting the fair market value. The size of the block of stock itself is a relevant factor to be considered. Although it is true that a minority interest in an unlisted corporation's stock is more difficult to sell than a similar block of listed stock, it is equally true that control of a corporation, either actual or in effect, representing as it does an added element of value, may justify a higher value for a specific block of stock.

> Later in this Chapter, we will see courts evaluate the market which is trading the security whose value we seek. If the market is robust, this may be the best evidence of value. See *Dell, Inc. v. Magnetar Global Event Driven Master Fund Ltd.*, infra p. 360.

(h) [I]n valuing unlisted securities the value of stock or securities of corporations engaged in the same or a similar line of business which are listed on an exchange should be taken into consideration along with all other factors. However, if sufficient comparable companies whose stocks are listed on an exchange cannot be found, other comparable companies which have stocks actively traded in on the over-the-counter market also may be used. The essential factor is that whether the stocks are sold on an exchange or over-the-counter there is evidence of an active, free public market for the stock as of the valuation date. In selecting corporations for comparative purposes, care should be taken to use only comparable companies. Although the only restrictive requirement as to comparable corporations specified in the statute is that their lines of business be the same or similar, yet it is obvious that consideration must be given to other relevant factors in order that the most valid comparison possible

> If the security we are trying to value is not traded in a market, we will try to find "comparable" securities that are traded in a market. See *Zokoych v. Spalding, infra* p. 354.

will be obtained. For illustration, a corporation having one or more issues of preferred stock, bonds or debentures in addition to its common stock should not be considered to be directly comparable to one having only common stock outstanding. In like manner, a company with a declining business and decreasing markets is not comparable to one with a record of current progress and market expansion.

....

SECTION 5. WEIGHT TO BE ACCORDED VARIOUS FACTORS.

The valuation of closely held corporate stock entails the consideration of all relevant factors as stated in section 4. Depending upon the circumstances in each case, certain factors may carry more weight than others because of the nature of the company's business. To illustrate:

(a) Earnings may be the most important criterion of value in some cases whereas asset value will receive primary consideration in others. In general, the appraiser will accord primary consideration to earnings when valuing stocks of companies which sell products or services to the public; conversely, in the investment or holding type of company, the appraiser may accord the greatest weight to the assets underlying the security to be valued.

SECTION 6. CAPITALIZATION RATES.

In the application of certain fundamental valuation factors, such as earnings and dividends, it is necessary to capitalize the average or current results at some appropriate rate. A determination of the proper capitalization rate presents one of the most difficult problems in valuation.... Wide variations will be found even for companies in the same industry. Moreover, the ratio will fluctuate from year to year depending upon economic conditions. Thus, no standard tables of capitalization rates applicable to closely held corporations can be formulated. Among the more important factors to be taken into consideration in deciding upon a capitalization rate in a particular case are: (1) the nature of the business; (2) the risk involved; and (3) the stability or irregularity of earnings.

> The capitalization rate or discount rate is the factor used to convert future cash flows into an equivalent present value. Whether it is a *discount* or *capitalization* rate depends on the mathematics of your situation. The distinction is explained *infra* p. 332–33.

SECTION 7. AVERAGE OF FACTORS.

Because valuations cannot be made on the basis of a prescribed formula, there is no means whereby the various applicable factors in a particular case can be assigned mathematical weights in deriving the fair market value. For this reason, no useful purpose is served by taking an average of several factors (for example, book value, capitalized earnings and capitalized dividends) and basing the valuation on the result. Such a process excludes active

> Despite this exhortation, analysts average their results from different valuation methods *all the time*. One expert suggests that it is within the spirit of this paragraph to "thoughtfully consider" all the Revenue Ruling's factors in assigning weights to each value. Pratt & Niculita, *supra* note 21, at 481.

consideration of other pertinent factors, and the end result cannot be supported by a realistic application of the significant facts in the case except by mere chance.

....

C. Cash Flow Methods

Several factors mentioned in Revenue Ruling 59-60 focus on cash flow. The Ruling recommends that you obtain income statements for the entity, and to consider:

- What are the major deductions (expenses)?
- What is the firm's dividend-paying capacity?
- What items of income and expense can be expected to recur?
- How can we determine the future amounts of recurring items?

This indicates that one measure of value of a business is its future cash flows.

Turning these future cash flows into a present value is done by estimating those amounts and then converting them into a number representing the value of those amounts today. We present below the standard method for so doing (part 1) and a specialized method to use in situations where intellectual property or other intangible assets are a material part of the business (part 2).

1. Discounted Cash Flow

A valuation analyst can estimate the present value of a business by translating estimated future cash flows into present-day amounts. This translation is done with the help of a *discount* or *capitalization* rate, a percentage amount which converts future dollars into their current dollar equivalents. This theory of valuation is called, not surprisingly, the ***discounted cash flow or DCF*** method of valuation, and is the most widely accepted method used in valuation.[24]

Discounted Cash Flow Formula

$$PV = \frac{CF_1}{1+r} + \frac{CF_2}{(1+r)^2} + \ldots$$

PV = Present value of the future cash flows
CF_i = Estimated cash flow for period i
r = discount rate (expressed as a decimal: 8% = 0.08)

24. See, *e.g.*, Pratt & Niculita, *supra* note 21, at 174 ("the very heart of valuation"); McKinsey & Co., Valuation: Measuring and Managing the Value of Companies 331 (6th ed. 2015) ("the most accurate and flexible method for valuing companies").

We will examine each component of this formula in turn.

a. The Discount Rate

The discount rate is based upon two basic principles of finance.[25]

Basic Principles of Finance
1. A dollar today is worth more than a dollar tomorrow.
2. A safe dollar is worth more than a risky one.

The discount rate has two components, corresponding to these two basic principles: a "risk free" rate and a "risk premium."[26]

The "risk free" rate is intended to capture only the time-value of the investment. There is, of course, no investment which is entirely riskless. However, most valuation analysts will assume that the closest approximation is U.S. government securities, because the default risk is low. Ordinarily, analysts will use a long-term U.S. treasury bond, because the investment being evaluated is also long-term.

The "risk premium" typically consists of at least three additional parts:

- The additional rate required because of risks in this business or industry ***generally*** ("equity risk premium").
- The additional rate required because smaller companies are generally more risky than larger companies ("size premium")
- The additional rate (or reduction in rate) due to the ***specific*** characteristics of the company or investment being evaluated.

A discount rate calculation such as this is known as the "build-up" method. This discount rate would be used to discount to present value the future amounts which will accrue to the owners or equity holders.

25. Richard A. Brealey, Stewart C. Myers, and Franklin Allen, Principles of Corporate Finance 20, 25 (13th ed. 2020).

26. It could not be more confusing to refer to this rate as either a "discount" or "capitalization" rate and then, to add the idea of a "premium." These are terms which analysts and courts typically employ, however. Be sure you understand the arithmetic, regardless of the term. What is being added to what, and how does that affect the result?

Illustration: A Discount Rate for X Co.

The current interest rate on 20-year U.S. bonds is about 2%. The average return on all equity securities (from published data) is about 10%, and our analyst has determined that X Co. is more risky than average, so this additional business risk component is 5%. X Co. is a small company, so the analyst may include another 5% addition for the small size of the company. Finally, X Co. depends for its business acumen on the founder, and its revenues come from sales to primarily two customers, so the analyst may include a 5% addition for X Co.'s specific risk. The discount rate for returns to X Co. stock would be the sum of these five rates, 2 +10 + 5 + 5 + 5 = 27%.

b. Future Cash Flows

Determining the appropriate discount rate is only half the job. The future cash flows must still be estimated. This is where our knowledge of accounting is most valuable, because we will use the business' past financial information to help determine future income or cash flows. In general, the valuation analyst looks at the balance sheet and income statement to determine cash flows which are:

- recurring;
- resulting from the core business; and
- reliable current numbers, not historical values.

If the business is small, the analyst might directly calculate future cash flows from the business' records. But usually, the analyst begins with the income statement and adjusts it to

- remove non-cash items (as we studied in Chapter 2)
- remove non-recurring items
- include cash expenditures which are not expenses, that is, capital investments and principal debt repayments
- include (as cash outflows) additional amounts of working capital needed in the business.

The analyst will then forecast the growth of these items, beginning with sales and assuming an appropriate profit margin. The forecasting will include company-specific items as well as assumptions about the industry and the economy.

Sensitivity Analysis:
The Relationship between Future Cash Flows and Discount Rates

Discounting has an awesome power to make the far-off future irrelevant. When you consider that discount rates typically applied to small businesses range between 20 and 40 percent, anything received more than ten years from now becomes inconsequential. The present value of $1 received in ten years at a 30% discount rate is a mere 7.25¢! Because even the lowest discount rate will have a profound effect on later years, you can change the present value the most by altering the *amount of future flows* rather than the discount rate. Thus, you know where to spend your time evaluating the work of the business valuation analyst, whether your client's analyst or the other side's analyst.

Illustration. Assume Wanda's Widgets will produce a net cash flow of $10,000 per year for the next five years, and then be worth nothing. Assume also that the appropriate discount rate for the cash flows from Wanda's Widgets, considering both the time value of money and the risk inherent in the widget business, is ten percent (10% or 0.10).

With these assumptions, we would calculate the present value of Wanda's Widgets to be about $37,910.

$$37{,}910 = \frac{10{,}000}{1.1} + \frac{10{,}000}{(1.1)^2} + \frac{10{,}000}{(1.1)^3} + \frac{10{,}000}{(1.1)^4} + \frac{10{,}000}{(1.1)^5}$$

It is important to note that each of these numbers is an ***estimate***. We should be aware, as attorneys, that changes in the estimates will produce changes in the results. We can engage in a rudimentary form of ***sensitivity analysis*** in determining how a change in inputs will change outputs. Your client's valuation and financial experts can provide detail here, but let's look at a couple of introductory examples.

Cash flows. A change in the flows will translate directly. If we double the anticipated flows from $10,000 to $20,000, the present value will be about double, that is, $75,820.

Discount rate. The impact of a change in the discount rate is less straightforward. If we were to reduce the discount rate from 10% to 5%, the present value will be about $43,290, not nearly as impressive an increase.

c. Terminal Value and Capitalization of Cash Flows

Recall the DCF formula,

$$PV = \frac{CF_1}{1 + r} + \frac{CF_2}{(1 + r)^2} + \ldots$$

which suggests that we should continue this estimating and discounting process into perpetuity. That is obviously impossible. Thus, some assumptions must be made about the long-term or "steady state" cash flows.

The analyst usually assumes that, once the business reaches a stable condition, that it will continue indefinitely. There may be some growth, perhaps due to the business model which will permit expansion. The revenues may also grow at least from general price increases. So after the useful discrete prediction period, which in the formula below is *t* years, the analyst calculates a "terminal value" for the business:

$$PV = \frac{CF_1}{1 + r} + \frac{CF_2}{(1 + r)^2} + \ldots + \frac{CF_t}{(1 + r)^t} + \frac{TV}{(1 + r)^t}$$

where *TV* refers to the terminal value. In the final projection year *t*, the formula provides the cash flow for that year, and the hypothetical terminal value for the business, also received at that same time.[27]

In order to calculate the terminal value, the analyst needs to know how to value a cash flow stream which will continue infinitely. Fortunately, there is an elegant answer. If I am to receive $\$X$ each year in perpetuity, and the appropriate discount rate is *r*, then

$$PV = X / r.$$

So, for example, the present value of $1,000 in perpetuity at a discount rate of 5% is $20,000:

$$20{,}000 = 1{,}000 / 0.05.$$

This makes intuitive sense. If you were to create a fund which would pay $1,000 annually forever, and the appropriate interest rate were 5%, you would need to have $20,000 as the "endowment" which would generate $1,000 each year.

This perpetuity formula will allow the analyst to create a terminal value. The analyst forecasts a "steady state" cash flow after the projection period of *t* years, CF_{t+1}. The present value of that perpetual flow is

$$TV = CF_{t+1} / r.$$

There is one more modification to the formula. Normally a growth rate is assumed to exist even in this "steady state" period. The business may add sales, customers, or locations, or the rate may simply reflect the increase in population (new customers) or the general rise in prices assumed to continue over time. If the analyst can forecast a growth rate, that is factored into the perpetuity formula. If CF_{t+1} is the perpetual payment, and *g* is the growth rate, then

$$TV = CF_{t+1} / r\text{-}g.$$

So the entire discounted cash flow formula becomes:

27. It would be a mistake to have the terminal value be received in year *t+1*, but this is commonly done. The terminal value is assumed to be received immediately at the beginning of the terminal year. Jeffrey M. Risius, Business Valuation: A Primer for the Legal Professional 77 (2007).

$$PV = \frac{CF_1}{1 + r} + \frac{CF_2}{(1 + r)^2} + \ldots + \frac{CF_t}{(1 + r)^t} + \frac{\frac{CF_{t+1}}{r - g}}{(1 + r)^t}$$

where CF_{t+1} is the "steady state" cash flow and g is the growth rate. This is the standard DCF valuation model.

d. How to Handle Debt

Our DCF model has not dealt with others who may have claims on the business' value—its creditors. Fortunately, our model can be easily adjusted to deal with a business which has debt.

First, we can dismiss most of the short-term debt. It is routinely assumed by a business valuation analyst that the accounts payable and accounts receivable will balance out over the long term, so ordinary short-term credit is not something which needs to be separately considered.[28]

Second, we will need to adjust the discount rate. If some of the business' capital consists of debt, it has a lower risk. Debt is normally less risky than equity because, among other things, it has priority in payment, and it is often collateralized. This is reflected in a lower discount rate, using the "weighted average cost of capital" (WACC) method. This calculates the discount rate as a combination of:

- the rate calculated for return on equity (see part 1(a) above) multiplied by the percentage of invested capital which is equity, and
- a rate for the debt securities which is normally the interest rate on the debt instruments, reduced to account for the fact that interest payments to debt-holders are tax-deductible, and multiplied by the percentage of invested capital which is debt.

The weighted average cost of capital is the average of these two rates, weighted by the relative percentage of debt and equity in the business:

$$r = \left(r_E x \frac{E}{D + E} \right) + \left(r_D x \frac{D}{D + E} \right)$$

r = the weighted average cost of capital
r_E = discount rate for equity (see part 1(a) above)
r_D = discount rate for debt (calculated as indicated just above)
D = value of the business' debt
E = current market value of the business' equity.

Finally, the valuation analyst must remember that the value calculated by this method, PV, is the *total value* of the business. It must be divided between the stakeholders.

28. *See* Brealey, Myers, and Allen, *supra* note 25, at 518. Obviously, this assumption should be checked with the reality of the subject business, however. If either payables or receivable are growing in a sustained fashion, the company should be asked why this is so.

If the analyst needs to know only the value of the equity (normally what is desired) the value of debt must be subtracted.

A Simple Example

Simple Co. needs to be valued, and we are using the DCF method. Our analyst has made the following calculations and assumptions:

Risk-free rate of return: 1%
Equity risk premium: 10%

Estimates of future business: the analyst has projected income and cash flows for the next three years. After that, the analyst estimates that the business will grow at 2% per year.

	First year	Second year	Third year	Terminal value	Total
Income	100,000	105,000	120,000	125,000	
+ depreciation	10,000	10,000	10,000	12,500	
- additional cash needs	5,000	5,000	5,000	7,500	
= cash flow	105,000	110,000	125,000	130,000	
Present value	95,455	90,909	93,914	1,085,232	1,365,510

Math notes. Here is how these present values were derived. Begin with our formula from p. 11-18:

$$PV = \frac{CF_1}{1+r} + \frac{CF_2}{(1+r)^2} + \ldots + \frac{CF_t}{(1+r)^t} + \frac{\frac{CF_{t+1}}{r-g}}{(1+r)^t}$$

From the facts above, we have the following values for the variables:

r = 1% + 10% (no other adjustments for Simple Co.) = 11% or 0.11
g = 2% or 0.02
t = 3
CF_1 = 105,000 CF_2 = 110,000 CF_3 = 125,000 CF_4 = 130,000

So the formula with these numbers works like this:

$$PV = \frac{105{,}000}{1.1} + \frac{110{,}000}{1.21} + \frac{125{,}000}{1.331} + \frac{\frac{130{,}00}{0.09}}{1.331}$$

$$PV = 95{,}455 + 90{,}909 + 93{,}914 + \frac{1{,}444{,}444}{1.331}$$

$$PV = 95{,}455 + 90{,}909 + 93{,}914 + 1{,}085{,}232 = 1{,}365{,}510$$

Note how much of the value (79.4%) is represented by the terminal value. This is not unusual in DCF valuation, especially with a relatively short time horizon and relatively low risk premium.

A Simple Example with Debt

Simple Co. needs to be valued, and we are using the DCF method. Our analyst has made the same calculations as in the previous example.

Simple Co. has long-term debt of $100,000, which bears interest at 5%. Our analyst assumes that this debt level will continue indefinitely. Our analyst also estimates the current value of Simple Co.'s equity at $400,000.

We need to modify our previous example in two respects. *First*, the interest expense ($5,000/yr) must be subtracted from net income, and affects all cash flows accordingly. *Second*, we must calculate *r* according to the WACC formula:

$$r = \left(r_E x \frac{E}{D+E} \right) + \left(r_D x \frac{D}{D+E} \right)$$

r_E = discount rate for equity = 11% or 0.11
r_D = discount rate for debt = 5% or 0.05
D = $100,000
E = $400,000

Therefore r = (0.11 x 0.8) + (0.05 x 0.2) = 0.098. The other numbers are the same, so our present value table is recalculated as follows:

	First year	Second year	Third year	Terminal value	Total
Income	95,000	100,000	115,000	120,000	
+ depreciation	10,000	10,000	10,000	12,500	
- additional cash needs	5,000	5,000	5,000	7,500	
= cash flow	100,000	105,000	120,000	125,000	
Present value	91,075	87,093	90,651	1,210,621	1,479,440

Important note. The present value we have calculated here is the value of *all* invested capital. In order to calculate the value of the equity alone, we now subtract the face value of the debt:

Value of equity = $1,479,440 – $100,000 = $1,379,440.

It is no accident that the two formulas produced almost the same number. The numbers would be exactly the same if our growth assumptions were smooth throughout. For more robust examples, see Pratt & Niculita, *supra* note 21, 221–25, and Brealey, Myers & Allen, *supra* note 25, at 512–16.

Case Illustration

DFC Global Corp. was a publicly-traded consumer financial services firm. It was purchased by a private equity firm in 2014. Dissenting shareholders sought appraisal in court under Del. Gen. Corp. L. § 262. Experts on both sides used DCF to value DFC (sorry about that), and the court engaged in its own independent review and calculations.

Cash flow. The court began with DFC's projected net income, and then adjusted those projections to estimate cash flow by (1) adding the depreciation and amortization expense, (2) subtracting estimated capital expenditures and (3) subtracting estimated additional needs for working capital. This resulted in the "free cash flow" for each of the next four years.

Discount rate. The court calculated the equity discount rate using a risk-free rate of 3.14%, a risk premium of 6.18%, and a size premium of 3.52%, making the equity rate 12.84%. The debt discount rate was estimated by looking at the company's existing senior notes, and the rate was estimated at 10%. The court then calculated a weighted average cost of capital (WACC) of 10.72% based on the company's relative debt and equity amounts. So the 2015 "free cash flow" of \$33.2 million has a present value of \$33.2/1.1072 = \$30,0 million. The 2016 "free cash flow" of \$61.4 million has a present value of $\$61.4/(1.1072)^2$ = \$50.1 million, and so on with the other two years.

Terminal value. The court used the cash flow projection for the final year (\$130.1 million) and used the perpetuity formula to compute the terminal value. The court used a 3.1% growth rate for the terminal period valuation, based primarily on long-term inflation rates. Using the terminal value = CF_{t+1} / (r-g) formula, the 2018 free cash flow of \$130.1 million becomes \$130.1/(0.1072 – 0.031) = \$1687.4 million, which is discounted to $\$1687.4/(1.1072)^4$ = \$1122.8 million

These calculations combined as follows (\$ millions):

	2015	2016	2017	2018	Terminal*	Total
Net income	72.7	112.1	156.0	200.8		
Plus depreciation	45.1	46.4	46.6	46.6		
Less capital expenditures	35.8	42.6	44.1	45.7		
Less additional working capital	48.8	54.5	69.8	71.6		
Free cash flow	33.2	61.4	88.7	130.1	1687.4	
Present value	30.0	50.1	65.3	86.6	1122.8	1354.8

* Terminal value = CF_{t+1} / (r-g) as we determined in the text.

> Note that the terminal value is about 83% of the final number. This is not unusual in DCF analysis, as with the Simple Co. example above. The court's calculation came out to $13.07 per share, versus the petitioner's expert's number of $17.90 and the respondent's expert at $7.81. Unfortunately, this is also not unusual in DCF analysis.
>
> Source: *In re Appraisal of DFC Global Corp.*, 2016 WL 3753123 (Del. Ch. Jul. 8, 2016). On appeal, the Delaware Supreme Court reversed in part, taking little issue with these calculations, but concerned about the overall weight the Chancellor gave to the DCF method versus other methods discussed later in this chapter. *DFC Global Corp. v. Muirfield Value Partners, L.P.*, 172 A.3d 346 (2017).

You should be facile enough with DCF calculations to understand and reproduce the above simple examples. You are *not* a valuation analyst, but this analyst's work is going to be used by you in competent representation of your client. Some examples of items a lawyer should attend to:[29]

- Because the terminal value is such a high percentage of the total value, other valuation methods should also be consulted as a "check on the reasonableness of the terminal value."
- The WACC calculation assumes that the business' capital structure will remain constant over time.
- Any change in each of the inputs will change the result dramatically. Your expert should test his/her valuation and any other valuation to see how it responds to changes in some of the assumed values.[30]
- There are also many common errors made by valuation analysts in their assumptions and calculations.

This means there is work for the lawyer to do in evaluating how the analyst's work will be treated in court, should it come to that, or in further negotiations regarding the business' value. See how the parties did in the following valuation case.

Delaware Open MRI Radiology Associates, P.A. v. Kessler

Court of Chancery of Delaware, 2006
898 A.2d 290

STRINE, Vice Chancellor.

... In this case, the key question is whether the minority stockholders of Delaware Open MRI Radiology Associates, P.A. ("Delaware Radiology") received fair value in a squeeze-out merger with an acquisition vehicle of the majority stockholders,

29. Summarized from Pratt & Niculita, *supra* note 21, at 229–31.
30. *See* "Sensitivity Analysis" box p. 331.

Delaware Open Acquisition, P.A. ("Delaware Acquisition"). The majority and minority stockholders were all radiologists who formed Delaware Radiology to capture additional revenues by owning the centers at which patients would be scanned by MRI machines (the "MRI Centers"). The squeeze-out merger at Delaware Radiology occurred after the radiologists' underlying radiology practice split up, turning the eight Delaware Radiology stockholders into two discrete blocks. The majority group, the "Broder Group," was comprised of five of the stockholders and controlled 62.5% of the Delaware Radiology shares. The minority group, the "Kessler Group," was comprised of three of the stockholders and owned the remaining 37.5% of the Delaware Radiology shares.

....

II. *Factual Background*

A. *The Radiology Practice Of The Kessler And Broder Groups*

This case has its origins in the common radiology practice in which the Kessler and Broder Groups had interests....

The formation of the entity whose value is at issue in this litigation—Delaware Radiology—resulted from the desire of the partners ... to take advantage of the more favorable insurance reimbursement and medical malpractice rates then available in Delaware. To enter the Delaware market, the partners had to form a Delaware entity and obtain licenses to practice medicine in Delaware.

For business reasons, the partners also wanted to join up with a respected Delaware physician who could help secure patients for the MRI Centers they would open in Delaware. To that end, the partners enlisted a locally-renowned doctor, Steven Edell, as a joint venturer.... The division of responsibility was relatively clear. Delaware Radiology would put up capital to form the MRI Centers and would ensure that high-quality MRI reading services were provided to the patients coming through the Centers. Meanwhile, Edell would provide input into possible locations for MRI Centers and use his plentiful contacts in the Delaware medical community to ensure that the MRI Centers would benefit from patient referrals.

....

The stability of this arrangement was short-lived. In June 1999, ... the Kessler Group left ... to form their own radiology practice....

....

On December 15 [2002], the Broder Group first formally notified the Kessler Group of a merger whereby the Kessler Group would be squeezed out of Delaware Radiology....

... On January 9 [2003], the individual members of the Kessler Group submitted written demands for appraisal of their shares pursuant to 8 Del. C. § 262.... As contemplated, the Broder Group met and approved the merger.... The final per share merger consideration, after adjustments, was $16,228.55, which would have provided each minority stockholder with $811,427.50.

Soon after the merger, the Broder Group capitalized on the substantial planning already underway for [three] new MRI Centers....

III. *Framework For Analysis*

The resolution of this case is complicated by the presence of both an equitable entire fairness claim and a statutory appraisal claim. The key issues relevant to each type of claim are common, and the differing rubrics have relatively little influence on the bottom line outcome of the case, which turns on whether the merger was financially fair.

....

... Here, there is no question that the merger implicates the entire fairness doctrine, as the Broder Group comprised all the members of the Delaware Radiology board and the acquiring company's board, and used its majority control to vote through the merger....

Therefore, the Broder Group bears the burden to prove that the merger was entirely fair. That burden has been said to require that the proponents of a conflicted merger demonstrate that they proceeded in a manner that was both procedurally and substantively fair.[31] ... In a non-fraudulent transaction, therefore, "price may be the preponderant consideration outweighing other features of the merger."[32]

....

V. *The Fairness Of The Merger Price*

....

At trial, the Broder Group relied on the same expert it used to set the merger price in the first instance, Timothy Reed of Diversified Medical Management. Reed premised his opinion of value on a discounted cash flow analysis that attributed no value to [the centers opened after the merger, and] that accepted the reading and management fees as proper expenses of the MRI Centers.... After doing all this, and using high discount rates ... Reed came to a value of $6,815,400, or $17,038.67 per share, which translated to $2,555,800 overall to the Kessler Group. This was slightly higher than the value offered to the Kessler Group in the merger, which was a value set in reliance on Reed's earlier work.

For its part, the Kessler Group employed John Mitchell of Gocial Gerstein, LLC as its valuation and damages expert. Like Reed, Mitchell relied on a DCF analysis. But Mitchell: (1) included in his valuation an estimate of the value of [two of the centers opened after the merger]; (2) treated the majority of Reading Fees entirely as profit to Delaware Radiology rather than as proper expenses to the MRI Centers; (3) reduced the management fee to Tri-State, as well as the fees to Edell, as being ex-

31. *See Weinberger v. UOP, Inc.*, 457 A.2d 701, 711 (Del.1983).

32. *Id. See also Onti* [*Inc. v. Integra Bank*, 751 A.2d 904] at 930 n. 108 [Del. Ch. 1999] ("[W]here the claims of unfair dealing do not rise to the level of fraud ... the Court should primarily focus on whether the price was unfair.").

cessive; and (4) did not tax affect Delaware Radiology's future earnings at all. Mitchell also used a lower discount rate. Using these inputs, Mitchell arrived at a value for Delaware Radiology on the merger date of $26,429,722, which translates into $66,074 per share or $9,911,100 to the Kessler Group for its 37.5% share.

In determining which side is closer to the mark, I will proceed as follows. For the sake of clarity, I begin by determining how the expansion plans affected Delaware Radiology's value on the merger date.... Finally, I endeavor to put all the pieces together and come to a bottom-line determination of the value of Delaware Radiology as of the merger date, for the purposes of making a determination of fairness and shaping the Kessler Group's award.

Delaware law is clear that "elements of future value, including the nature of the enterprise, which are known or susceptible of proof as of the date of the merger and not the product of speculation, may be considered." Obviously, when a business has opened a couple of facilities and has plans to replicate those facilities as of the merger date, the value of its expansion plans must be considered in the determining fair value. To hold otherwise would be to subject our appraisal jurisprudence to just ridicule. The dangers for the minority arguably are most present when the controller knows that the firm is on the verge of break-through growth, having gotten the hang of running the first few facilities, and now being well-positioned to replicate its success at additional locations—think McDonald's or Starbucks. Here, the business plan of Delaware Radiology involved the strategy of opening additional MRI Centers in Delaware with Edell. This strategy was part of what the Supreme Court would call the "operative reality" of Delaware Radiology on the merger date and must be considered in determining fair value.[33]

On this record, it is easy to conclude that the value of the expansion plans ... must be considered in valuing Delaware Radiology as of the merger date....

VI. *The Appraisal Valuation And Fair Value Determination*

....

Both of the experts in the case used a discounted cash flow analysis as the foundation for their valuations of Delaware Radiology. The basic elements of a DCF analysis are

33. In essence, when the court determines that the company's business plan as of the merger included specific expansion plans or changes in strategy, those are corporate opportunities that must be considered part of the firm's value. *See [Cede & Co. v.] Technicolor,* [684 A.2d 289,] at 298–99 (Del. 1996) (discussing that the company's value should take into account the new strategy implemented by a majority shareholder before the minority was cashed-out). *See also Montgomery Cellular Holding Co., Inc. v. Dobler,* 880 A.2d 206, 222 (Del.2005). As a thoughtful academic paper notes, there is an obvious relation between the need to evaluate what the business plans of the company being valued in appraisal were as of the merger date, and the equitable corporate opportunity doctrine.... The Chancellor's decision in *Onti v. Integra* illustrates well the interaction of these concerns. In that case, the Chancellor took into account a corporation's similar plans to expand in shaping his remedy in a combined appraisal/entire fairness proceeding. *Onti,* 751 A.2d at 925–26.

not novel and need not be repeated here.[34] In computing my own DCF value for Delaware Radiology on the merger date, I will focus on the major remaining differences between the testimonial experts, then use the resolution of those differences along with the inputs formerly determined to reach a final determination of fair value.

Before I complete that work, a few factors that influence my approach are worth noting. Delaware Radiology is a small, privately owned entity. As shall be seen, using even an income-based approach such as a DCF model to value such an entity has its challenges, principally in the area of calculating a proper cost of capital. In this situation, the absence of both market information about the subject company and good public comparables force the court to rely even more than is customary on the testimonial experts. That reality is inescapable.

That has led me to consider carefully which of the two experts, the Broder Group's expert Reed or the Kessler Group's expert Mitchell, was the more reliable. Although I have done my own independent analysis and reach a conclusion materially different than either expert, when there is doubt and there is not a more reliable basis to decide a question, I will use the approach advocated by the expert whose testimony I found more credible and well-grounded in finance and fact. As a general matter, I easily conclude that Mitchell's testimony was far closer to the mark in all respects. Mitchell approached his task in a conservative and restrained manner that, although still reflecting a desire to advance his clients' objectives, reasonably took into account factors limiting the value of Delaware Radiology.

By contrast, Reed's testimony seemed more aggressively driven by his goal of reducing what the Broder Group would be ordered to pay. Moreover, Reed was given marching orders in his work before and after the merger that led him to undervalue Delaware Radiology. Indeed, those orders were such that Reed did not even know he was valuing Delaware Radiology itself before he finished his valuation in October 2003....

Even when he realized that the value of [centers opened after the merger] might be considered in this case, Reed took the position that it was impossible to value businesses that were soon to, but not yet, open using a DCF analysis. That position would come as a revelation to finance professors, owners of franchisable retail establishments, and businesspersons of all kinds. Put simply, this did not instill confidence in me and seemed to be a posture designed simply to advance the Broder Group's interest in not according the Kessler Group any share of [that] value.... Likewise, Reed's knowledge of the relevant facts regarding Delaware Radiology seemed unduly constrained by his clients, and his blinkered view of the business impaired his ability to reach a reasoned determination of value. For these reasons, I give more weight to Mitchell's testimony and lean on his analysis when there is no better method to break an impasse.

34. For the standard classroom description, *see* Richard A. Brealey & Stewart C. Myers, Principles of Corporate Finance 75–80 (7th Ed.2003); Bradford Cornell, Corporate Valuation: Tools for Effective Appraisal and Decision Making 100–41(1993). For a good judicial summary, *see Onti,* 751 A.2d at 917.

A. *Calculating Net Cash Flows*

The most important input necessary for performing a proper DCF is a projection of the subject company's cash flows. Without a reliable estimate of cash flows, a DCF analysis is simply a guess. Fortunately, Delaware Radiology was not engaged in a complex business and [its] operations ... provided a foundation for making some reasonable estimates of future performance. Of even greater utility, [Michael] Carr of Tri-State [an entity formed for the non-medical management of Delaware Radiology] made detailed projections of the performance of [three of the centers] for non-litigation use....

... Traditionally, this court has given great weight to projections of this kind because they usually reflect the best judgment of management, unbiased by litigation incentives. That is especially so when management provides estimates to a financing source and is expected by that source (and sometimes by positive law) to provide a reasonable best estimate of future results. Therefore, we have regarded with rightful suspicion attempts by parties who produced such projections to later disclaim their reliability, when that denial serves their litigation objective.

Here, the Broder Group has done that in material ways....

For his part, Mitchell used the extant projections as the beginning for his analysis and built off of them in a manner that I find to be reasonable and conservative....

....

Overall, I find Mitchell's estimated growth realistic and appropriate when compared to the historic scan volume of the MRI Centers and the management projections for new MRI Centers....

I also find that Mitchell made reasonable assumptions regarding the revenues that Delaware Radiology would receive for doing scans.... Reed, by contrast, assumed reductions in reimbursement rates of 9% ... in year two, or 2005, and then increased them at 3%, the rate of inflation, annually. Essentially, the basis for Reed's reduction was speculation by Carr, and Reed's own opinion that Delaware reimbursement rates were high relative to neighboring states and that they were likely to fall. But the record is devoid of information from more objective sources to substantiate that viewpoint, which, like other elements of Reed's and Carr's testimony, fits with the self-interest of the Broder Group.

[The court then calculates five-year projections of revenues and costs, assumes a 29.4% tax rate (since Delaware Radiology was an S-Corporation), and then adds back non-cash expense to approximate five-year cash flows, and subtracts estimated capital expenditures required for those five years.]

B. *Calculating Terminal Value*

Both experts use a form of the capitalization method to calculate a terminal value for the MRI Centers. Mitchell assumed a constant perpetuity growth rate of 4%. Reed assumed a perpetuity growth rate of 3%. As between the two, I find Mitchell's rate more realistic. Reed essentially assumes no real growth in the value of Delaware Radiology after the projection period, which I believe is unduly pessimistic. Mitchell captures a modest increment of growth for the MRI Centers above the growth in the entire economy that is realistically achievable, and I adopt his perpetuity assumption.

I depart from Mitchell in one material respect in calculating Delaware Radiology's terminal value. Mitchell assumed no capital expenditures during the terminal period in an alleged attempt to capture value from his assumption that the MRI equipment would last well beyond the end of its period of financing, which would allow the MRI Centers to have a period where they would be making no payments on their equipment. Essentially, I find credible the trial testimony that the useful life of the MRI equipment does exceed the period of financing, but I also find that, at some point, replacement will become necessary....

C. Calculating The Weighted Average Cost Of Capital ("WACC")

The experts also haggle over the correct discount rate to calculate the value of the future expected cash flows of Delaware Radiology on the merger date. Testimonial feuds about discount rates often have the quality of a debate about the relative merits of competing alchemists. Once the experts' techniques for coming up with their discount rates are closely analyzed, the court finds itself in an intellectual position more religious than empirical in nature, insofar as the court's decision to prefer one position over the other is more a matter of faith than reason.

This unfortunate reality flows from the status of principles of corporate finance. Even as to public companies, there is much dispute about how to calculate the discount rate to use in valuing their future cash flows, even when one tries to stick as closely as possible to the principles undergirding the capital asset pricing model [CAPM] and the semi-strong form of the efficient capital markets hypothesis. Witness the serious academic debate about whether the so-called size premium received by investors in smaller public companies is a durable indicia of their greater risk, or whether there are attributes of stocks with a low book-to-market ratio that require the consideration of that factor in estimating a discount rate....

Situations like this one inspire even less confidence, when experts are required to calculate a cost of capital for a very small, non-public company, for which neither of the experts has identified reliable public comparables. In this context, the ability of the experts or the court to hew literally to the teaching of the high church of academic corporate finance is essentially non-existent....

The experts in this case have used the proxy that has found the most favor among professional appraisers: the so-called "build-up model." The build-up model begins with the core factors considered by CAPM: a risk-free rate and an equity premium rate. From there, however, the build-up model begins to diverge from CAPM. A size premium ... is de rigueur under the build-up model. Much more heretical to CAPM, however, the build-up method typically incorporates heavy dollops of what is called "company-specific risk," the very sort of unsystematic risk that the CAPM believes is not rewarded by the capital markets and should not be considered in calculating a cost of capital. The calculation of a company specific risk is highly subjective and often is justified as a way of taking into account competitive and other factors that endanger the subject company's ability to achieve its projected cash flows. In other words, it is often a back-door method of reducing estimated cash flows rather than adjusting them directly. To judges, the company specific risk premium often seems like the device experts employ to bring their final results into line with their clients' objectives, when other valuation inputs fail to do the trick.

....

In view of the unavoidable imprecision of the exercise, I adopt Mitchell's approach for use in my remedy award. I do so in large part because of my determination that his analysis is, on balance, the more reliable. I also do so because his approach to calculating the discount rate comes the closest to putting into practice the thinking behind the CAPM in circumstances when [it] cannot be applied in its pure form. Mitchell's inclusion of a small stock premium is consistent with a good deal of academic and practitioner thinking.[35]

F. *The Total Value Of Delaware Radiology*

From the total enterprise value, I deduct each MRI Center's debt as of December 31, 2003. In addition, as Delaware Radiology was not the 100% owner of any MRI Center, each entity value is multiplied by Delaware Radiology's ownership percentage....

[M]y analysis results in a value of Delaware Radiology of $13,292,903.22, which results in a per share value of $33,232.26. The Kessler Group's 37.5% ownership of Delaware Radiology has a total value, then, of $4,984,838.71.

....

2. Capitalized Excess Earnings: The "Treasury Formula"

In the introduction to this chapter, we read Revenue Ruling 59-60, an early fundamental statement of valuation concepts. The Treasury Department has opined on valuation theories and methods many other times, however. Another notable effort, Revenue Ruling 68-609, was promulgated to guide valuation when intellectual property or intangible assets are a material part of the entity's value. It modifies somewhat the general discounted cash flow analysis.

Although the I.R.S. disclaims the authoritative value of this procedure in the very same announcement in which it is promulgated, Rev. Rul. 68-609 is, like Rev. Rul. 59-60, the theoretical basis for much valuation, including nontax cases.

---

35. *E.g.*, Rolf W. Banz, *The Relationship between Return and Market Value of Common Stocks*, 9 J. Fin. Econ. 3 (1981); Eugene F. Fama & Kenneth R. French, *The Cross-Section of Expected Stock Returns*, 47 J. Fin. 427 (1992); Shannon P. Pratt, et al., Valuing a Business: The Analysis and Appraisal of Closely Held Companies 170 (4th ed.2000).

Revenue Ruling 68-609

1968-2 C.B. 327

....

The question presented is whether the "formula" approach, the capitalization of earnings in excess of a fair rate of return on net tangible assets, may be used to determine the fair market value of the intangible assets of a business

The "formula" approach may be stated as follows:

A percentage return on the average annual value of the tangible assets used in a business is determined, using a period of years (preferably not less than five) immediately prior to the valuation date. The amount of the percentage return on tangible assets, thus determined, is deducted from the average earnings of the business for such period and the remainder, if any, is considered to be the amount of the average annual earnings from the intangible assets of the business for the period. This amount (considered as the average annual earnings from intangibles), capitalized at a percentage of, say, 15 to 20 percent, is the value of the intangible assets of the business determined under the "formula" approach.

The percentage of return on the average annual value of the tangible assets used should be the percentage prevailing in the industry involved at the date of valuation, or (when the industry percentage is not available) a percentage of 8 to 10 percent may be used.

The 8 percent rate of return and the 15 percent rate of capitalization are applied to tangibles and intangibles, respectively, of businesses with a small risk factor and stable and regular earnings; the 10 percent rate of return and 20 percent rate of capitalization are applied to businesses in which the hazards of business are relatively high.

The above rates are used as examples and are not appropriate in all cases. In applying the "formula" approach, the average earnings period and the capitalization rates are dependent upon the facts pertinent thereto in each case.

The past earnings to which the formula is applied should fairly reflect the probable future earnings. Ordinarily, the period should not be less than five years, and abnormal years, whether above or below the average, should be eliminated. If the business is a sole proprietorship or partnership, there should be deducted from the earnings of the business a reasonable amount for services performed by the owner or partners engaged in the business. Further, only the tangible assets entering into net worth, including accounts and bills receivable in excess of accounts and bills payable, are used for determining earnings on the tangible assets. Factors that influence the capitalization rate include (1) the nature of the business, (2) the risk involved, and (3) the stability or irregularity of earnings.

The "formula" approach should not be used if there is better evidence available from which the value of intangibles can be determined. If the assets of a going business are sold upon the basis of a rate of capitalization that can be substantiated as being realistic, though it is not within the range of figures indicated here as the ones ordinarily to be adopted, the same rate of capitalization should be used in determining the value of intangibles.

Accordingly, the "formula" approach may be used for determining the fair market value of intangible assets of a business only if there is no better basis therefor available.

....

Example

The "Treasury formula" approach is illustrated below, with assumed values. Our business has tangible assets of $100,000. Its average of earnings for the previous five years is $15,000. We have calculated (from industry data) that a comparable return on tangible assets is 10%. Therefore:

Return on tangible assets is $100,000 x 10% [0.10] = $10,000.

The difference of the actual earnings from the return on tangible assets ($15,000 – $10,000 = $5,000) is the return on *intangible* assets. We have calculated (from industry data) that a comparable return on intangible assets is 20%. We can capitalize the annual return (see p. 332) as follows:

Value of intangible assets = $5,000 / 20% [0.20] = $25,000.

The total value of the business is the sum of the values of the tangible and intangible assets:

$100,000 + $25,000 = $125,000.

Case Illustration

Philip Morris, Inc. (PMI) purchased Seven-Up Co. in 1978, by purchasing all the Seven-Up stock. It then liquidated the company, that is, Seven-Up's assets were distributed to its shareholder (a PMI subsidiary). The then-applicable federal income tax regulations required that PMI's cost of purchasing the Seven-Up stock should be allocated to the Seven-Up assets received in liquidation "in proportion to the net fair market values of such assets on the date received." Because many of Seven-Up's assets were intangible assets which had never been bought or sold (formulas, trademarks, distribution contracts with bottlers), they needed to be valued for this purpose.

The valuation expert chose to apply the "Treasury" method as no other valuation method was deemed appropriate under the circumstances. The expert began by finding average earnings; but instead of using an average of past earnings, the expert used average discounted future earnings (as with the DCF method). The expert used 10% as an appropriate rate of return on Seven-Up's tangible assets. The difference between the average future earnings and 10% of the tangible assets would be the return on Seven-Up's intangible assets; that amount was $16 million. The expert then selected 20% as the appropriate rate for capitalizing the return on intangible assets and determined the value of those intangible assets to be $16 million / 20% (0.20) or $80 million. This added to the value of Seven-Up's tangible assets of $180 million yielded a total fair market value of the company of $260 million.

Source: *Philip Morris, Inc. v. Comm'r*, 96 T.C. 606, 632–39 (1991), *aff'd. mem.* 970 F.2d 897 (2d Cir. 1992).

Blake v. Blake Agency, Inc.

New York Supreme Court, Appellate Division, 1985
107 A.D.2d 139, 486 N.Y.S.2d 341

Before MOLLEN, P.J., and TITONE, THOMPSON and WEINSTEIN, JJ.

THOMPSON, Justice.

These appeals concern the valuation of a minority interest in the shares of a closely held corporation, where the minority shareholder has commenced a special proceeding pursuant to Business Corporation Law § 1104-a to dissolve the corporation, and the corporation has elected to buy out the minority shareholder pursuant to Business Corporation Law § 1118. Specifically, we are called upon in this case to determine whether Special Term correctly valued petitioner Lawrence R. Blake's 25% interest in the common stock of Blake Agency, Inc.…

THE FACTS

Blake Agency, Inc. is a storefront insurance brokerage firm, located in Queens County, which specializes in property and casualty insurance. The agency was incorporated in 1954 by William Blake, Sr. Upon his death in 1968, four of his sons each received a 25% share of the stock in the corporation. In 1971 William Blake, one of the sons of William Blake, Sr., bought his brother Richard Blake's 25% share of the corporation, thereby acquiring effective control of the company. The corporation has never declared or paid any dividends.

Petitioner Lawrence R. Blake apparently had various disagreements with his brother William Blake with regard to corporate operations. Petitioner believed he had been "frozen out" of the corporation's affairs, as evidenced by the fact that he was never consulted before corporate decisions were made and the fact that he was never paid any dividends. On August 4, 1981, he filed a petition pursuant to Business Corporation Law § 1104-a for the judicial dissolution of Blake Agency, Inc. On October 30, 1981, the corporation elected to purchase Lawrence R. Blake's shares in the corporation for their "fair value", pursuant to Business Corporation Law § 1118(a). By order dated November 19, 1981 (Graci, J.), the dissolution proceeding was stayed pursuant to Business Corporation Law § 1118(b), pending negotiations undertaken by the parties in an attempt to agree on the "fair value" of the minority shares. On April 5, 1982, the parties stipulated that they were unable to agree on the value of petitioner's shares. Special Term (Graci, J.), on or about April 8, 1982, appointed Samuel S. Tripp, Esq., as a referee to help determine the question of the "fair value" of petitioner's shares in the corporation. The "fair value" of the shares had to be determined as of August 3, 1981, the day immediately preceding the filing of the petition and order to show cause (Business Corporation Law § 1118[b]).

After hearing the testimony of various witnesses, including four experts, the referee determined the "fair value" of petitioner's shares to be $64,834. The referee's calculations commenced by multiplying adjusted gross revenue from insurance commissions by a factor of one (a capitalization rate of 100%), in order to determine the value of the corporation's goodwill. Gross commission revenue was determined to be $254,210. This amount was then reduced by subtracting "Subproducer Revenues" of $32,744 and "Contingent Income" of $9,872, leaving a balance of $211,594.* The referee divided the $211,594 by four to determine petitioner's 25% share of the goodwill of the corporation, resulting in a figure of $52,898. He then applied a discount of 40% to this figure because petitioner's shares represented a minority interest in the corporation and because they were not readily marketable. After application of this discount, petitioner's share of the intangible value of the corporation (goodwill) was determined to have a fair value of $31,739. The referee also found that petitioner's share of the corporation's net tangible value was $33,095, representing 25% of the corporation's assets ($321,443.03) less its current liabilities ($189,060.25). He did not apply a discount to net tangible value. Combining the intangible value and the net tangible value, the referee concluded that the fair value of petitioner's shares in the corporation as of August 3, 1981 was $64,834. He found that the investment value should be considered in the determination of fair value in this case, and that neither "net asset value" nor "market value" should be considered. Additionally, the referee found that William Blake's annual compensation of approximately $84,000 was not excessive.

The referee's valuation of petitioner's 25% interest in Blake Agency, Inc. can be summarized as follows:

Intangible Value	
Gross Commission Revenue for the period ended June 30, 1981	$254,210
Less: "Subproducer Revenues"	(32,744)
Less: "Contingent Income"	(9,872)
Adjusted Gross Commission Revenue	$211,594
Petitioner's 25% share	$52,898
Less: 40% combined minority interest and lack of marketability discount	(21,159)
Petitioner's share of goodwill	$31,739

* "Subproducer Revenue" constitutes commissions earned from business referred to the corporation from other insurance agents who apparently had an oral agreement with the agency. "Contingent Income" represents funds received from insurance companies if the loss ratios on the policies handled by the agency fall below a certain average.

Net Tangible Value	
Assets	$321,443
Less: Current Liabilities	(189,060)
Net Tangible Value	$132,383
Petitioner's 25% share	$33,095
Intangible Value	$31,739
Net Tangible Value	$33,095
Fair Value	$64,834.

By judgment dated May 11, 1983, Special Term adjudged the "fair value" of petitioner's shares in Blake Agency, Inc. to be $64,834 as of August 3, 1981....

THE STATUTORY FRAMEWORK

Business Corporation Law § 1104-a and § 1118 were enacted in 1979 for the specific purpose of enabling minority shareholders of closely held corporations to obtain relief, when they found themselves in a situation of being denied participation in or being "frozen out" of corporate management and being refused employment by the corporation and/or participation in dividends. The statutes were enacted to afford a minority shareholder the right to bring a proceeding to dissolve the corporation and to distribute its assets among the shareholders. Section 1118 counterbalances section 1104-a by affording the corporation the option of electing to purchase the minority's shares, thereby avoiding dissolution. [The court quotes N.Y. Business Corporation Law §§ 1104-a and 1118.]

DETERMINING "FAIR VALUE"

A court's obligation to determine the "fair value" of the petitioner's shares in a closely held corporation presents a difficult problem. The statute does not define the term "fair value", and it fails to provide any criteria for determining "fair value". In making the necessary determination, courts should generally look for guidance to the criteria set forth by the cases interpreting Business Corporation Law § 623, the appraisal rights statute. The factors to be considered are, inter alia, market value, investment value, and net asset value. The weight to be accorded each factor depends upon the circumstances of the particular case. The value of the corporation should be determined on the basis of what a willing purchaser, in an arm's length transaction, would offer for the corporation as an operating business, rather than as a business in the process of liquidation.

Within the context of a closely held corporation, market value is usually of little or no significance because the shares of stock are not traded on any public market. Moreover, other than certain bona fide offers to purchase all of the outstanding stock of a corporation (i.e., through a merger or acquisition), a sale of the stock of a closely held corporation usually does not qualify as an arm's length transaction because the sale usually involves corporate officers, employees or family members. Net asset value is generally the standard applicable in evaluating manufacturing corporations or real estate and investment holding companies. With a corporation like the one in issue herein, investment value will usually be the primary criterion upon which "fair value" is based.

In addition, the Internal Revenue Service has developed the following factors to be considered in determining the fair market value of closely held corporate stock for estate and gift tax purposes (see Rev.Rul. 59-60, 1959-1 CB 237, pp. 238–239):

> "(a) The nature of the business and the history of the enterprise from its inception.
>
> "(b) The economic outlook in general and the condition of the specific industry in particular.
>
> "(c) The book value of the stock and the financial condition of the business.
>
> "(d) The earning capacity of the company.
>
> "(e) The dividend paying capacity.
>
> "(f) Whether or not the enterprise has goodwill or other intangible assets.
>
> "(g) Sales of the stock and the size of the block of stock to be valued.
>
> "(h) The market price of stocks of corporations engaged in the same or a similar line of business having their stocks actively traded in a free and open market, either on an exchange or over-the-counter."

Investment value is usually a function of the earning power of the corporation. Thus, acceptable methods of determining investment value include (1) a "discounted income approach", by which either average earnings of the corporation measured over a number of years, or a weighted average of corporate earnings (giving greater weight to corporate earnings of the most recent years) is capitalized at a predetermined percentage, and using the capitalization rate, a multiplier is developed and that multiplier is then applied to earnings; (2) capitalization of dividends, if the corporation has a history of payment of dividends; or (3) a "comparative appraisal" approach, which utilizes a comparison with the price-to-earnings ratios of publicly traded stocks in similar industries and financial situations of the closely held corporation (*see generally* Haynsworth, Valuation of Business Interests, 33 Mercer L.Rev. 457; Schreier & Joy, Judicial Valuation of "Close" Corporation Stock: *Alice in Wonderland* Revisited, 31 Okla.L.Rev. 853 ...).

This list of methods of valuation is not all-inclusive. In various cases, courts may need to examine the compensation paid to a principal shareholder, the corporation's cash flow, or some other measure of corporate earnings. Furthermore, if goodwill is an element in evaluating the corporation, the court will necessarily have to make a determination regarding its value. One generally accepted method of determining the value of goodwill is by capitalizing the corporation's net earnings after making a deduction for earnings attributable to net tangible assets (see Rev.Rul. 68-609, 1968-2 CB 327 ...).

THE "FAIR VALUE" OF PETITIONER'S SHARES AND THE NATURE OF HIS AWARD

A

Contrary to petitioner's contention, we find that the referee was justified in applying a multiplier of only one to gross commission revenue in determining the value of the corporation's goodwill. The referee credited the testimony of the corporation's expert, Kenneth Pollock, that the insurance industry was "soft" due to direct billing of premiums by insurance companies, and that the value of the goodwill of an insurance agency should thus be measured by applying a multiplier of one to gross commission revenue. The insurance industry, according to the testimony, had become "soft" because agencies had to remit premiums to the insurance companies on an "account rendered basis" (within 45 days of receipt). This situation, coupled with the insurance companies' policy of directly billing policyholders for premiums in order to take advantage of higher interest rates, greatly reduced the insurance agencies' ability to invest premiums in high-interest certificates of deposit. We decline to disturb the referee's finding because he properly considered the characteristics of the industry as a whole in making his determination.

Petitioner's reliance on *Donehoo v. United States* (21 AFTR2d 1700) is misplaced. Although the court in that case applied a multiplier of 1.5 to the gross commission revenue of an insurance agency, that case involved the valuation of a Pittsburgh, Pennsylvania insurance agency in 1962. Furthermore, the multiplier of 1.5 was expressly agreed to by the parties.

The referee was also justified in deducting "Contingent Income" from gross commission revenue. The uncontroverted evidence is that such income is dependent on the agency's policies generating less than average loss ratios. In any particular year there may be no "Contingent Income" whatsoever. Thus, the referee's deduction of this item was proper.

Petitioner, however, is entitled to a percentage of the "Subproducer Revenue" earned by the corporation. Although the record shows that the subproducing insurance agents associated with Blake Agency, Inc. had no contractual or family relationship with the agency and were free to terminate their association with the agency at will, the subproducers did generate 20% of the agency's gross commission revenue, and all of the corporation's five subproducers have been associated with the corporation for at least three years. Therefore, in calculating "fair value" we have added 50% of "Subproducer Revenue", to wit, $16,372, to gross commission revenue.

B

With regard to the discount applied by the referee and approved by Special Term, we believe that that discount should be reduced from 40% to 25%. Said discount should only reflect the lack of marketability of petitioner's shares in the closely held corporation. No discount should be applied simply because the interest to be valued represents a minority interest in the corporation.

Business Corporation Law § 1104-a was enacted for the protection of minority shareholders, and the corporation should therefore not receive a windfall in the form of a discount because it elected to purchase the minority interest pursuant to Business Corporation Law § 1118. Thus, a minority interest in closely held corporate stock should not be discounted solely because it is a minority interest.

However, a discount recognizing the lack of marketability of the shares of Blake Agency, Inc. is appropriate, and, under the circumstances of this case, the amount of the discount should be 25%. A discount for lack of marketability is properly factored into the equation because the shares of a closely held corporation cannot be readily sold on a public market. Such a discount bears no relation to the fact that the petitioner's shares in the corporation represent a minority interest.

Applying the 25% discount of petitioner's shares and adding back 50% of subproducer revenue increases, the "fair value" of petitioner's shares is as follows:

Adjusted Gross Commission Revenue	$211,594.00
Add: 50% of "Subproducer Revenues"	16,372.00
Total	$227,966.00
Petitioner's Share of Goodwill	$56,911.50
Less: 25% Discount	(14,247.88)
Discounted Share of Goodwill	42,743.62
Petitioner's Share, Net Tangible Value	33,095.00
Fair Value	$75,838.62.

C

The referee was fully justified in finding that William Blake's compensation was not excessive in light of his abilities and duties. Petitioner's expert opined that an executive who generated $850,000 per year in business should be paid a base salary of $25,000 plus a 30% bonus for additional new business. The corporation's expert testified that the Blake Agency did over $1,800,000 in business per year, and that this would usually require two executives earning a total of $82,000 in salaries and bonuses, not including pension contributions and perquisites. Thus, the referee was fully justified in finding that William Blake's compensation and benefits of $84,000 were not excessive.

....

E

Turning to the issues raised in the corporation's cross appeal, the referee was justified in not discounting petitioner's share of net tangible assets, despite the argument that this approach fails to account for the working capital needs of the corporation. Under the circumstances of this particular case it was unnecessary to apply a discount to net tangible value because the corporation admittedly has never paid any dividends, and because the corporation's June 30, 1981 balance sheet shows that it has more than $70,000 cash in savings accounts and over $48,000 in marketable securities. These assets will leave the corporation with sufficient working capital, even after it has paid petitioner the fair value of his shares. Finally, contrary to the corporation's contention, the referee's determination that its goodwill amounted to $211,594 was not unwarranted in light of the corporate assets of more than $320,000 and the combined net earnings to the corporation (approximately $8,000) and compensation to William Blake ($84,000) of $92,000.

CONCLUSION

The judgment should be modified, on the law and the facts, by ... increasing the amount ordered and adjudged to be the "fair value" of the 50 shares of capital stock owned by petitioner Lawrence R. Blake from $64,834 to $75,838.62....

Question

The starting point for the referee's calculation of "goodwill" was not cash or earnings, but "Gross Commission Revenue." We learn only at the very end of the opinion that the net earnings were only $8,000. Does it make sense that the "fair value" of 25% of Blake Agency, Inc. should be measured by gross revenues?

D. Market Value Methods

The use of any valuation technique assumes that there is no properly functioning "market" which will provide a fair value of the business interest in question. If there is such a market, there is no need for any other valuation. For example, Delaware law denies dissenters' appraisal rights if the dissenters' shares are traded on a securities exchange or held of record by more than 2,000 persons.[36]

However, there are two situations where market values can be useful in valuation.

- The analyst can find "comparable" companies which have market values, and can therefore estimate a value for the business being valued.
- There is evidence of relevant market value of the business being valued because it was the subject of a full and fair negotiation by buyer and seller.

We discuss each of these situations below.

1. Comparable Companies or "Multiplier" Method

This method of business valuation is applied in the following manner. First, the earnings of the business in question are calculated. Probably some normalizing assumptions will be made. Then, the evaluator searches for comparable publicly-traded companies. Finding some (we hope), the evaluator determines the price-earnings ratios of those companies. This can be done because, unlike the business in question, the shares of the comparable company have market prices. Finally, the evaluator takes the price-earnings ratio (a multiplier), and multiplies it by the subject company earnings. The result is the price of the subject company.

$$\frac{Price_{market}}{Earnings_{market}} \times Earnings_{subject} = Price_{subject}$$

market = observed values for comparable company or companies
$Earnings_{subject}$ = computed value for subject company

An evaluator can use the same method as above applied to any financial statistic which can be calculated both for the company in question and publicly-traded companies.

36. Del. Gen. Corp. L. § 262(b)(1). There are some exceptions as further stated in that subsection, which are not important to our example here.

Other measures used include EBIT (earnings before interest and taxes), EBITDA (same, before depreciation and amortization), and MVIC (market value of invested capital). The choice of the comparable item, whether earnings or some more complicated measure, is normally within the professional judgment of the evaluator.

Case Illustration

A shareholder in a mailing list brokerage firm sued to dissolve the corporation under state law, and the corporation elected to buy out the shareholder for the "fair value" of the shares as provided by law. *See* N.Y. Bus. Corp. L. § 1118(a). All experts agreed to use the "multiplier" method to value the shares, using earnings as the measure to be multiplied, similar to the formula in the text above.

First, the company's reported earnings were adjusted by reducing the salary expenses paid to some of the officer-shareholders to an amount reflecting salaries paid to similar officers who were *not* shareholders. This earnings figure, so adjusted, was $80,425.32.

Second, an appropriate price/earnings multiplier (or ratio) was selected. The valuation experts looked at publicly-traded companies "with similar specialties and growth characteristics, and a comparison with the range of multipliers that prevailing wisdom considers acceptable for companies with high, middle, or low growth and future promise." This multiplier, based on the comparable companies' price/earnings ratios was ten.

The value of the company was therefore $80,425.32 x 10 or $804,253.20.

Source: *Raskin v. Walter Karl, Inc.*, 514 N.Y.S.2d 120 (N.Y. App. Div. 1987).

Zokoych v. Spalding

Appellate Court of Illinois, 1984
123 Ill. App. 3d 921, 463 N.E.2d 943

WILSON, Justice:

This appeal arises from the third trial between plaintiff and defendants where evidence was presented on the question of the value of Ample Tool and Manufacturing, Inc. ("Ample"), a closely held company in which Stephen Zokoych and Bruce Spalding ("Spalding") were the principal shareholders. Ample ceased doing business in 1970.

In the first appeal, we affirmed the trial court's award to plaintiff of compensatory damages [including the value of the plaintiff's one-half share of Ample which was appropriated by the defendant].... The court's decision that the evidence did not establish a value for Ample was reversed, however, and the case was remanded with directions to determine the value of Ample and to award plaintiff additional damages for one-half that amount.

... The trial court found that Ample's value was $420,000 and entered judgment for plaintiff.... Defendants now appeal. The allegation[] presented for review [is] whether the trial court improperly relied on testimony given by plaintiff's expert, John Langum, as to the value of Ample....

....

OPINION

The principal question for our determination concerns the trial court's finding as to the value of Ample, a closely held corporation which ceased doing business in 1970. We note at the outset, however, that upon review the trial court's finding (which, in this case was the basis upon which plaintiff's damages were determined), will not be reversed unless it is palpably or manifestly contrary to the weight of the evidence.

I.

Challenging the evidence presented, particularly that of plaintiff's expert, Langum, defendants initially contend that Langum's method of valuation was based on a superficial, one factor analysis which relied on the price earnings ratios of 32 publicly traded companies whose only potential similarity to Ample was product line or business activity.[37] Because these companies were incorrectly chosen, defendants posit, the trial court's acceptance of Langum's analysis and conclusions was in error. We disagree.

Contrary to defendants' postulation, we believe that there was sufficient evidence upon which the court could reasonably conclude that a meaningful comparison could be made because the comparative companies were properly selected.... [Langum] "selected and studied particularly thoroughly" the price earning ratios for 32 companies according to their standard industrial classification code and the description of their business according to Standard and Poor's. These companies all used iron and steel and were engaged in metal work.

Langum then stated that he further "made several studies of these companies from different standpoints to consider their proper use as a guide." These "different standpoints" included the companies' earnings and dividend ranges to ensure that their stocks were not highly priced, the "behavior of sales [from] year to year," the "company as a whole," and "certain aspects of their net income." Langum made a chart showing the price earnings ratio for each company and decided to use the lowest ratio of the

37. We note that in valuing the stock of a closely held corporation, the use of the listed stock prices of comparable, publicly traded corporations has received both judicial and legislative sanction. See, *Central Trust Co. v. United States* (1962), 158 Ct.Cl. 504, 305 F.2d 393; I.R.C. § 2031(b) (1983).

companies that were engaged in metal work. As a result of this analysis, the ratio figure selected was the number seven.

Langum further testified that in his opinion, the 32 selected companies were the most closely comparable to Ample. He explained that "that certainly doesn't mean identical. * * * There never will be [an identical company]. But comparable to means affording a reasonable and meaningful comparison. * * * [T]hese are larger companies, but they are engaged in the similar line of business, and hence, comparable * * *."

The question of whether publicly held corporations are truly comparable remains a question of fact for the trial court....

In *Estate of Victor P. Clarke v. Commissioner*, 35 T.C.M. (CCH) 1482, 1501 (1976), the court determined that comparable does not mean "essentially identical" because that interpretation would be "* * * unduly restrictive, as it strips the inquiry into the valuation of a closely-held stock of the flexibility needed to make an informed judgment. Rare indeed would be the corporation identical to that being valued * * *." The court stated further that a meaningful comparison involved an interplay of a myriad of complex factors and features, including the companies' products, management, earnings, dividend paying capacity, book value and their position in the industry.

Also, *Righter v. United States* (1971), 194 Ct.Cl. 400, 439 F.2d 1204, the court held that the comparative appraisals used were entitled to "little if any weight." In that case, a small closely held company manufactured two principal products, "Scrabble," a popular crossword puzzle game, and "Parcheesi," a backgammon game. In determining the value of the company's stock for estate tax purposes, however, the defendant selected several publicly held companies that manufactured either toys or toys *and* games. Defendant's comparison was thus rejected because, the court ruled, the products of the comparative companies "appeal to and are used by different age groups." 439 F.2d 1204, 1217.

In the case at bar, defendants further point out that "the great preponderance" of the 32 companies was dissimilar to Ample because they manufactured railroad cars, automobile parts, heating and ventilating equipment, bottle caps, and other items. The record also shows that defendants offered the testimony of their expert, Bissell, who stated that unlike Ample, several of the companies were "large enterprises" and all showed a positive net worth.

As the preceding cases suggest, however, there is no fixed rule for determining comparability. Rather, our focus is on the fact that each of the comparative companies had the same standard industrial classification as Ample, each supplied parts, machinery or equipment to other companies engaged in basic manufacturing, all were engaged in metal work and, as Bissell acknowledged, all were affected by the same economic factors. Equally important, *Langum testified that he considered other factors* in determining comparability. These factors were: (1) the products of the respective companies; (2) the markets served by the companies; (3) the dividend history of the comparables; (4) book value; (5) each company's position in the industry; and (6) management performance. Langum also testified that he considered the companies' sales behavior each year, whether the companies were listed on the stock exchanges (Langum stated that 11 were not) and the companies' net income. In our view, these additional refinements to Langum's initial selection of companies based on their industrial classification renders his analysis highly credible and effectively distinguishes this case from those cited by defendant where the court rejected the comparative companies used.

....

We thus conclude that the weight of the evidence in the case at bar supports the trial court's decision that Langum's testimony was credible.

II.

Further challenging the sufficiency of the evidence presented, defendants next contend that even if the 32 companies selected by Langum were comparable in terms of product line or business undertaking, they were dissimilar in several other respects. Defendants point to Langum's testimony under cross-examination where he stated that he did not conduct a comparison between Ample and the 32 companies with regard to the following features:

1. number of employees;
2. number of plant facilities;
3. dividend history;
4. debt structure;
5. management performance;
6. whether any of the companies had a negative working capital or negative net worth as shown on their balance sheet;
7. The ability of the companies to service their debts;
8. The nature of the comparative companies' debt to their net worth as compared to Ample's.

By way of comparison, however, the cases defendants cite on this issue set forth the following "fundamental" factors which, along with other relevant considerations depending on the facts of each case, should "ordinarily" be considered in determining the comparability between a closely held corporation and those to which it is compared:

1. products;
2. market;
3. management;
4. earnings;
5. dividend paying capacity;
6. book value;

7. position in the industry of each company;
8. capital structure;
9. credit status;
10. personnel experience;
11. maturity of the business.

Our review of the record reveals that of the 11 factors cited in the cases above, Langum testified either under direct or cross-examination that he had considered at least seven of these items....

....

The foregoing testimony convinces us that the weight of the evidence supports the trial court's finding that Langum properly considered relevant factors in determining the value of Ample and the comparability of the 32 companies. For this reason, defendants' argument on this issue will be rejected.

III.

Further challenging Langum's analysis, defendants contend that his valuation was improperly based on a price earnings ratio of only 10 months and that he failed to make any adjustments for the sale of machinery, the failure to pay Spalding a regular salary upon his return or for the lack of marketability of Ample's stock. We cannot agree.

First, when asked as to why he used the 10 month period from July 1, 1969 to April 30, 1970 to compute Ample's net income, Langum stated that he did so because (1) after reading the first trial testimony of Jack Schwartz, who began to keep the books of the company in July 1969, Langum said that he felt he could "rely on his [Schwartz] statements and accounts as a basis for determining [Ample's] income"; (2) Spalding came back into the business at that time; (3) McCauley had testified in the first trial that Spalding and plaintiff "were a good combination * * * and a very good team * * * with good customers"; (4) the recession in the tool and die industry had "run its course" by that time and had begun a period of recovery; and (5) the company experienced a "breakup" by May 1970 since plaintiff had left shortly before then, tools and equipment were physically transferred and sales were diverted because Ample's customers were informed of a change in the business.

Additionally, the record reveals that McCauley again testified in this trial that in his opinion, Ample experienced a dramatic change for the better in sales and an appreciable decline in the amount of money expended for outside labor services during this 10 month period. Plaintiff also testified as to the favorable changes in the company after Spalding's return. We additionally note that defendant's expert, Bissell, agreed that Ample's sales volume was impressive after Spalding came back and that in analyzing Ample, Bissell "would put more emphasis on the recent period, but I would * * * also consider historical results as well."

In view of all of the foregoing testimony, along with the fact that Langum and McCauley were knowledgeable as to the history, growth and subsequent demise of

Ample, that they so testified and reasonably chose to place greater emphasis on the 10 month period in question, we believe that the evidence supports the trial court's decision to adopt Langum's use of the 10 month period to determine the value of Ample. Moreover, the cases defendants cite on this issue are unpersuasive since based on the unique facts involved, the court in those instances decided that the valuation should not be based on less than a year's sales earnings. Unlike Ample, however, none of the closely held corporations in those cases had experienced a dramatic change in earnings and management performance which precipitated a cessation of business.

As far as Langum's adjustments for the sale of machinery are concerned, the record shows that in setting the value of Ample's machinery and equipment, Langum deducted $16,325 for the sale of equipment during the fiscal year ending February 1970 and that he added $22,931 in machinery and equipment purchases. Adjustments for the depreciation of equipment (a deduction of $79,683) and the acquisition of small tools (an addition of $25,500) were also made. We further believe that Langum's failure to make an adjustment for Ample's failure to pay Spalding a regular salary did not render his evaluation implausible since defendants have failed to bring to our attention any authority which mandates this consideration.

IV.

We next consider defendants' contention that Langum failed to make an adjustment for the unmarketable nature of Ample's stock. While it is true that Langum did not make a "dollar amount" deduction to compensate for this factor, he specifically stated under direct examination that he was well aware of the fact that there were no market prices for the stock of a privately held corporation.[38] Moreover, we distinguish *In re Marriage of Rossi* (1983), 113 Ill.App.3d 55, 68 Ill.Dec. 801, 446 N.E.2d 1198, cited by defendants on this issue, where the court rejected the evaluation of a closely held corporation. Unlike the expert witness in that case, Langum did not place a premium on plaintiff's share of ownership which would inflate its value. 113 Ill.App.3d 55, 61, 68 Ill.Dec. 801, 446 N.E.2d 1198.

For these reasons, we conclude that the trial court's judgment as to the value of Ample was not manifestly or palpably contrary to the weight of the evidence and therefore will not be disturbed.

....

Questions

The figure given as the value for Ample, $420,000, together with the multiple of seven times earnings, means that plaintiff's expert had decided Ample's annual earnings,

38. We acknowledge the fact that in evaluating a closely held corporation, an expert witness may take a deduction for its unmarketability, however, our review of the cited cases on this issue convinces us that this is not a mandatory requirement, as long as other relevant factors are properly considered.

based on that ten-month period, were $60,000. Do you think it is significant that no deduction was made for failure to pay the defendant a salary? Can that decision be squared with the conclusion reached by the court in *Blake*, the preceding case?

2. Valuation from Market Prices

The valuation exercise is necessary because we do not have direct market evidence of the price of the business to be valued. But sometimes, we do! In business transactions, the so-called "deal price" may be good evidence of market value, sometimes, the best evidence.

One commentator suggests that some sort of market value will be available in most valuation cases, and that it should be the "go to" standard for courts to use before resort is had to expensive and unproductive expert valuation.[39] Furthermore, another analysis opines that, although the "deal price" may be flawed, this does not necessarily mean that the valuation process will be better. "Even when the process through which a deal price is determined was flawed, the deal price may still provide the best information about the value of a company's shares, because the alternative valuation methodologies are even more flawed."[40] Consider how these alternatives are balanced by the Delaware Supreme Court in the following case.

Dell, Inc. v. Magnetar Global Event Driven Master Fund Ltd.

Supreme Court of Delaware, 2017
177 A.3d 1

VALIHURA, Justice:

The petitioners left standing in this long-running appraisal saga are former stockholders of Dell Inc. ("Dell" or the "Company") who validly exercised their appraisal rights instead of voting for a buyout led by the Company's founder and CEO, Michael Dell, and affiliates of a private equity firm, Silver Lake Partners ("Silver Lake"). In perfecting their appraisal rights, petitioners acted on their belief that Dell's shares were worth more than the deal price of $13.75 per share—which was already a 37% premium to the Company's ninety-day-average unaffected stock price.

Our appraisal statute, 8 Del. C. § 262, allows stockholders who perfect their appraisal rights to receive "fair value" for their shares as of the merger date instead of the merger consideration. The appraisal statute requires the Court of Chancery to assess the "fair value" of such shares and, in doing so, "take into account all relevant factors." The trial court complied: it took into account all the relevant factors presented by

39. Michael W. Schwartz & David C. Bryan, *Campbell, Iridium, and the Future of Valuation Litigation*, 67 Business Lawyer 939 (Aug. 2012).

40. Jonathan Macey & Joshua Mitts, *Asking the Right Question: The Statutory Right of Appraisal and Efficient* Markets, 74 Business Lawyer 1015, 1018 (2019).

the parties in advocating for their view of fair value—including Dell's stock price and deal price—and then arrived at its own determination of fair value.

....

Here, the trial court gave no weight to Dell's stock price because it found its market to be inefficient. But the evidence suggests that the market for Dell's shares was actually efficient and, therefore, likely a possible proxy for fair value. Further, the trial court concluded that several features of management-led buyout ("MBO") transactions render the deal prices resulting from such transactions unreliable. But the trial court's own findings suggest that, even though this was an MBO transaction, these features were largely absent here. Moreover, even if it were not possible to determine the precise amount of that market data's imperfection, as the Court of Chancery concluded, the trial court's decision to rely "exclusively" on its own DCF analysis is based on several assumptions that are not grounded in relevant, accepted financial principles.

We REVERSE, in part, and AFFIRM, in part, and REMAND for these reasons and those that follow....

I.

A. Dell

In June 2012, when the idea of an MBO first arose, Dell was a mature company on the brink of crisis: its stock price had dropped from $18 per share to around $12 per share in just the first half of the year.... Yet despite ... [founder Michael] Dell's attempts to persuade Wall Street to buy into the Company's future, the market still "didn't get" Dell, as Mr. Dell lamented. It still viewed the Company as a PC business, and its stock hovered in the mid-teens.

....

B. The Sale Process

... [A]fter Silver Lake's Egon Durban also proposed the idea of an MBO [in August, 2012], Mr. Dell enlisted the advice of friend and private equity executive George Roberts of Kohlberg Kravis Roberts & Co. L.P. ("KKR").... [H]e received positive feedback, including an indication that KKR might be interested in participating should the Company go that route. Mr. Dell then brought the idea to Dell's Board [of Directors] ... on Friday, August 14, 2012.

The following Monday, the Board met and created an independent special committee composed of four independent directors (the "Committee") to evaluate possible transactions to acquire the Company proposed by Mr. Dell and/or any other party, as well as to explore possible strategic alternatives. The Board empowered the Committee to hire its own legal and financial advisors, and the Committee selected Debevoise & Plimpton LLP as legal counsel and JP Morgan Chase & Co. as financial advisor. (The Committee eventually hired Evercore Partners as a second financial advisor in January 2013.) ...

....

On February 3, [2013,] Silver Lake presented the Committee two options ... : either (i) $13.60 per share if it allowed the Company to continue its regular quarterly dividend payment through closing, or (ii) $13.75 all-cash with no additional dividends. After the Committee told Silver Lake that $13.60 would not suffice under the first alternative, Silver Lake boosted the cash component to $13.65 per share on February 4, its "best and final offer."

The Committee met with its financial advisors on the afternoon of February 4: both Evercore and JPMorgan indicated that they considered $13.65 per share fair to the unaffiliated stockholders from a financial point of view. The Committee recommended that the Board accept Silver Lake's offer, and, aside from Mr. Dell, who was not present, the Board unanimously adopted resolutions approving the transaction. The next morning, February 5, 2013, the Company and three entities affiliated with Silver Lake and Mr. Dell (collectively the "Buyout Group") entered into the merger agreement dated February 5, 2013 (collectively with amendments, the "Merger Agreement"), and they publicly announced the planned transaction.

....

The Merger Agreement ... provided for a forty-five-day go-shop period ending March 23, 2013; ... and termination fees of $180 million if the Company agreed to a Superior Proposal as defined in the Merger Agreement that materialized during the go-shop period, or $450 million if the Company agreed to a non-Superior Proposal or to bids produced after the go-shop period.

[The "go-shop" period resulted in other indications of interest sufficient to require the Buyout Group to raise the proposed consideration for the merger to $13.75 per share.] [T]he Board approved the revised transaction (hereinafter, the "Merger") and amended the Merger Agreement to reflect the changed deal terms. A vote was scheduled for September 12, 2013.

At the special meeting held September 12, 2013, 57% of all Dell shares approved the Merger (70% of the shares present at the meeting). The Merger closed October 29, 2013, and the shares of non-dissenting Dell stockholders were converted into $13.75 per share in cash.... [H]olders of 38,765,130 shares of Dell common stock demanded appraisal.

D. The Appraisal Trial

The four-day appraisal trial in October 2015 featured 1,200 exhibits, seventeen depositions, live testimony from seven fact witnesses and five expert witnesses, a 542-paragraph-long pre-trial order, and 369 pages of pre- and post-trial briefing. Petitioners argued that, as demonstrated through their expert's DCF analysis, the fair value of the Company's common stock at the effective time of the Merger was actually $28.61 per share — more than double the deal price of $13.75.... In contrast, Dell maintained that its DCF analysis yielding a $12.68 per share valuation was a more appropriate approximation of fair value, but that, in light of the uncertainties facing the PC industry, fair value could be as high as the deal price (but not greater).

E. *The Court of Chancery's Determination of Fair Value*

The Court of Chancery acknowledged that "[t]he consideration that the buyer agrees to provide in the deal and that the seller agrees to accept is one form of market price data, which Delaware courts have long considered in appraisal proceedings." However, the court believed that flaws in Dell's sale process meant that the deal price of $13.75 should not be afforded any weight here since it was "not the best evidence of [the Company's] fair value." Accordingly, the trial court disregarded both Dell's pre-transactional stock price and the deal price entirely.

....

But, given that the trial court deemed it "illogical" to believe that another bidder would not have topped the Buyout Group's offer if the Company were actually worth the $28.61 per share advocated by the petitioners, the Court of Chancery rejected petitioners' DCF and arrived at its "fair value" determination of $17.62 per share through its own DCF analysis, using a mix of the inputs proposed by the petitioners' and the Company's experts and adjustments of its own.

F. *This Appeal*

The Company ... claims that the trial court erred by disregarding Section 262(h)'s requirement that it "take into account all relevant factors" in determining fair value.

....

In response, the petitioners argue that the Court of Chancery *did* consider "all relevant factors"—including the deal price—in determining fair value as the Court of Chancery outlined a litany of reasons why the sale process distorted the deal price's worth as a proxy for fair value....

II. *Analysis*

We agree with petitioners that the trial court *did consider* all relevant factors presented, including Dell's stock price and deal price. But we reverse because the reasoning behind the trial court's decision to give no weight to any market-based measure of fair value runs counter to its own factual findings. After reviewing our appraisal statute and accompanying jurisprudence, we explore why the facts fail to support the Court of Chancery's reasoning for disregarding, in particular, the deal price. To the extent the trial court can justify giving any weight to its DCF analysis on remand, we conclude that, for the most part, the trial court did not abuse its discretion as to the asserted errors.

A. *The Relevant Legal Framework*

....

Appraisals are odd. Unlike other cases, where one side loses if the other side fails to persuade the court that the evidence tilts its way, appraisals require the court to determine a number representing the fair value of the shares after considering the trial presentations and submissions of parties who have starkly different objectives: petitioners contend fair value far exceeds the deal price, and the company argues that fair value is the deal price or lower. In reality, the burden "falls on the [trial] judge to determine fair value, using 'all relevant factors.'"[41]

....

Given the human element in the appraisal inquiry—where the factfinder is asked to choose between two competing, seemingly plausible valuation perspectives, forge its own, or apportion weight among a variety of methodologies—it is possible that a factfinder, even the same factfinder, could reach different valuation conclusions on the same set of facts if presented differently at trial. There may be no perfect methodology for arriving at fair value for a given set of facts, and the Court of Chancery's conclusions will be upheld if they follow logically from those facts and are grounded in relevant, accepted financial principles. "To be sure, "fair value" does not equal "best value."[42]

B. The Court of Chancery's Reasons for Disregarding Deal Price Do Not Follow from the Record

....

The three central premises that the Court of Chancery relied upon to assign no weight to the deal price were flawed. First, the court believed that a "valuation gap" existed between Dell's stock price and the Company's intrinsic value, and this conclusion—contrary to the efficient market hypothesis—led it to hypothesize that the bidding over Dell as a company was anchored at an artificially low price that depressed the ultimate deal price below fair value. Second, the court suggested that the lack of strategic buyers in the sale process—and, accordingly, the involvement of only private equity bidders—also pushed the deal price below fair value. Third, the court concluded that several factors endemic to MBO go-shops further undercut the deal price's credibility. We consider each of these premises in turn and find them untenable in view of the Court of Chancery's own findings of fact as considered in light of established principles of corporate finance. Without these premises, the trial court's support for disregarding the deal price collapses. Accordingly, the trial court's reliance on them as a basis for granting no weight to the market-based indicators of value constituted an abuse of discretion meriting reversal.

---

41. *See* Eric L. Talley, *Finance in the Courtroom: Appraising Its Growing Pains*, Del. Lawyer, Summer 2017, at 16–17 ("[U]nlike highly trained (and highly remunerated) investment bankers—whose job requires generating a 'football field' *range* of discounted cash flow (DCF) valuations—a judge presiding over an appraisal proceeding must conjure up a *single number* at the end of the process.").

42. *See DFC Global Corp. v. Muirfield Value Partners, L.P.*, 172 A.3d 346, 369–71 (Del. 2017). Rather, as framed in another context, a fair price "means a price that is one that a reasonable seller, under all of the circumstances, would regard as within a range of fair value; one that such a seller could reasonably accept." *Id.* (quoting *Cinerama, Inc. v. Technicolor, Inc.*, 663 A.2d 1134, 1143 (Del. Ch. 1994), *aff'd*, 663 A.2d 1156 (Del. 1995)). And "[t]he fact that a transaction price was forged in the crucible of objective market reality (as distinguished from the unavoidably subjective thought process of a valuation expert) is viewed as strong evidence that the price is fair." *Van de Walle v. Unimation, Inc.*, 1991 WL 29303, at *17 (Del. Ch. Mar. 7, 1991). *See also Applebaum v. Avaya, Inc.*, 812 A.2d 880, 889–90 (Del. 2002) (stating that "in many circumstances a property interest is best valued by the amount a buyer will pay for it" and "a well-informed, liquid trading market will provide a measure of fair value superior to any estimate the court could impose.").

i. The Trial Court Lacked a Valid Basis for Finding a "Valuation Gap" Between Dell's Market and Fundamental Values

The Court of Chancery presumed "investor myopia" ... produced a "valuation gap" between Dell's fundamental and market prices. That presumption contributed to the trial court's decision to assign no weight to Dell's stock price or deal price. The trial court believed that short-sighted analysts and traders impounded an inadequate—and lowball—assessment of all publicly available information into Dell's stock price, diminishing its worth as a valuation tool. But the record shows just the opposite: analysts scrutinized Dell's long-range outlook when evaluating the Company and setting price targets.... Further, the Court of Chancery's analysis ignored the efficient market hypothesis long endorsed by this Court. It teaches that the price produced by an efficient market is generally a more reliable assessment of fair value than the view of a single analyst, especially an expert witness who caters her valuation to the litigation imperatives of a well-heeled client.

....

The record before us provides no rational, factual basis for such a "valuation gap." Indeed, the trial court did not indicate that Dell lacked a vast and diffuse base of public stockholders, that information about the Company was sparse or restricted, that there was not an active trading market for Dell's shares, or that Dell had a controlling stockholder—or that the market for its stock lacked any of the hallmarks of an efficient market....

....

ii. The Lack of Strategic Bidders Is Not a Credible Reason for Disregarding the Deal Price

....

The Court of Chancery stressed its view that the lack of competition from a strategic buyer lowered the relevance of the deal price. But its assessment that more bidders—both strategic and financial—should have been involved assumes there was some party interested in proceeding. Nothing in the record indicates that was the case. Fair value entails at minimum a price some buyer is willing to pay—not a price at which no class of buyers in the market would pay. The Court of Chancery ignored an important reality: if a company is one that no strategic buyer is interested in buying, it does not suggest a higher value, but a lower one. "[O]ne should have little confidence she can be the special one able to outwit the larger universe of equally avid capitalists with an incentive to reap rewards by buying the asset if it is too cheaply priced."

....

iii. Features of MBOs Which Could Theoretically Undermine the Probative Value of the Deal Price Are Not Present Here.

The Court of Chancery focused on three problems supposedly present in all MBOs to show that the deal price here is not evidence of fair value: (a) structural issues; (b) the "winner's curse"; and (c) management's perceptive value to the company. Yet none of these theoretical characteristics detracts from the reliability of the deal price on the facts presented here. As a result, the trial court's reliance on these themes to disregard the deal price in its fair value analysis was error.

Though it is true that "[t]he structure of the go-shop is an obvious factor that affects a participant's pathway to success," even the petitioners' expert characterized the structure here as "rais[ing] fewer structural barriers than the norm" and found no disqualifying fault with the design of Dell's go-shop....

The "winner's curse" describes a theory that, in outbidding incumbent management to "win" a deal, a buyer likely overpays for the company because management would presumably have paid more if the company were really worth it. Recognizing this phenomenon, prospective bidders supposedly resist outbidding incumbent management for fear they might later discover the information that prevented management from bidding even higher in the first place. But the likelihood of a winner's curse can be mitigated through a due diligence process where buyers have access to all necessary information. And, here, Dell allowed [bidders] to undertake "extensive due diligence," diminishing the "information asymmetry" that might otherwise facilitate a winner's curse.

....

The Court of Chancery also presumed that "Mr. Dell's value to the Company" imposed another impediment to the likelihood of rival bidders succeeding and thus dissuaded them from even trying. But, again, the Court of Chancery's own fact findings contradict and do not rationally support this conclusion.

....

[E]ven if one could accept the trial court's view that Mr. Dell's service as CEO added per-share value to the Company's stock, the record does not suggest that he would have stopped serving the Company if ... another reputable buyer had prevailed. He was contractually obligated to explore "any such potential counterparty or financing source if requested by the Committee," though he had "discretion" as to whether to continue after such exploration....

C. Market Data Conclusion

The actual facts concerning Dell's market values — the particularities of its stock market and the sale process — demonstrate that the Court of Chancery's reasons for assigning no weight to the market values are flawed....

In so holding, we are not saying that the market is always the best indicator of value, or that it should always be granted some weight. We only note that, when the evidence of market efficiency, fair play, low barriers to entry, outreach to all logical buyers, and the chance for any topping bidder to have the support of Mr. Dell's own votes is so compelling, then failure to give the resulting price heavy weight because the trial judge believes there was mispricing missed by all the Dell stockholders, analysts, and potential buyers abuses even the wide discretion afforded the Court of Chancery in these difficult cases....

D. The Discounted Cash Flow Analyses

... When ... an appraisal is brought in cases like this where a robust sale process of that kind in fact occurred, the Court of Chancery should be chary about imposing the hazards that always come when a law-trained judge is forced to make a point estimate of fair value based on widely divergent partisan expert testimony.

As is common in appraisal proceedings,[43] each party — petitioners and the Company — enlisted highly paid, well-credentialed experts to produce DCF valuations. But their valuations landed galaxies apart — diverging by approximately $28 billion, or 126%. Petitioners' expert arrived at a per-share valuation of $28.61 as of the merger date, and the Company's expert produced a valuation of $12.68 per share. The Court of Chancery recognized that "[t]his is a recurring problem," and even believed the "market data is sufficient to exclude the possibility, advocated by the petitioners' expert, that the Merger undervalued the Company by $23 billion." Thus, the trial court found petitioners' valuation lacks credibility on its face. We agree. Yet, the trial court believed it could reconcile these enormous valuation chasms caused by the over 1,100 variable inputs in the competing DCFs and construct a DCF that more appropriately reflected the fair value of Dell's stock than the market data. And, reconciling the various agreements and divergences among the experts, the trial court determined fair value to be $17.62.

... [T]he Court of Chancery's DCF value was the antithesis of any economist's definition of fair market value. The Court of Chancery conceded that its DCF value did not reflect a value deemed attractive to the buyers of Dell's 1,765,369,276 publicly traded shares. Further, it did not reflect the value that private equity buyers ... put on it, as it was too high for any of them to pay....

....

In addition to the relatively sound economic reasons, there are also important policy reasons supporting this result. If the reward for adopting many mechanisms designed to minimize conflict and ensure stockholders obtain the highest possible value is to risk the court adding a premium to the deal price based on a DCF analysis, then the incentives to adopt best practices will be greatly reduced. Although widely considered the best tool for valuing companies when there is no credible market information and no market check, DCF valuations involve many inputs — all subject to disagreement by well-compensated and highly credentialed experts — and even slight differences in these inputs can produce large valuation gaps....

III. Fair Value Conclusion

Despite the sound economic and policy reasons supporting the use of the deal price as the fair value award on remand, we will not give in to the temptation to dictate that result. That said, we give the Vice Chancellor the discretion on remand

43. *See, e.g.*, *DFC*, 172 A.3d at 388 (describing "briefs and expert reports written by highly-skilled litigators in concert with men and women of valuation science that often come to ridiculously varying positions").

to enter judgment at the deal price if he so chooses, with no further proceedings.... If he chooses to weigh a variety of factors in arriving at fair value, he must explain that weighting based on reasoning that is consistent with the record and with relevant, accepted financial principles.

E. Discounts and Premiums

Once the evaluator has come up with a value, using the methods we previously studied, it may be adjusted for one or more reasons. These can be categorized based on where the adjustments occur in the valuation process. Once the evaluation process has concluded that the company's value is $X, if our investor owns 3% of the company, the investor's share may be 3% of $X. If adjustments are made to the $X value, such an adjustment is at the "company level." If adjustments are made to the 3% of $X value, such an adjustment is at the "investor level."

1. Investor-Level Adjustments

There are three common adjustments made to the value of an individual interest, based on the realities of the marketplace in which such interest are or might be sold.

- ***Marketability discount.*** The value of the shares or interests may be reduced because they may be difficult to sell. There are very few people interested in buying shares of a business with just a few owners.
- ***Minority-interest discount.*** An amount of the total shares or interests which does not control the business will be worth less than its *pro rata* share, reflecting this inability to make basic business decisions.
- ***Control premium.*** The opposite of the minority-interest discount, recognizing that an ownership interest becomes more valuable to the extent that it allows the holder to change how the business operates.

In most valuations required in dissenter's appraisal or oppression valuation (see description *supra*, pp. 318–20), the governing legal standard is that the owner is to receive the "fair value" of his or her interest. Most courts have held in this context that marketability and minority-interest discounts are **not** appropriate. The owner is entitled to his or her proportionate share of the value of the company, regardless of the fact this his interest may be difficult or impossible to sell otherwise. This is true in leading court opinions[44] as well as the most recent (1999) revision of the Model Business Corporation Act, which defines the entitlement of the owners to be

> "Fair value" [which] means the value of the corporation's shares determined:
>
> (i) immediately before the effectiveness of the corporate action to which the shareholder objects;

---

44. One of the leading cases is *Cavalier Oil Corp. v. Harnett*, 564 A.2d 1137, 1144 (Del. 1989). The issue was also discussed in *Blake v. Blake Agency, supra*, pp. 351–52.

(ii) using customary and current valuation concepts and techniques generally employed for similar businesses in the context of the transaction requiring appraisal; and

(iii) without discounting for lack of marketability or minority status....[45]

However, there are exceptions. California's statute refers to "fair *market* value" as the entitlement, which suggests that discounts are appropriate.[46] Many states do not have statutory law which addresses discounts, and regardless of statutory language, courts are often given discretion to apply such discounts.[47]

A control premium may be justified if the proportion of ownership entitled the holder to direct important parts of the business operations or finance. There is no "bright line" test here, because the control exercised by any owner depends on the specific arrangements made in the company's governance documents and the relative percentage ownership(s) of the other owners. It would be rare to see any control premium discussed in dissenters' appraisal or dissolution cases, of course, because those proceedings almost inherently involve owners with little or no control over the business to begin with. However, in other situations, mostly in valuation for income or estate tax purposes, a control premium is more common. The theories and calculations of these premiums are a matter for your expert evaluator and beyond our scope here.

2. Company-Level Adjustments

The evaluator usually calculates a value for the entire enterprise before dividing it by the share which is involved in the case. In the valuation for the entire firm, as you may recall, we have used (in most cases) forecasted cash flows or market multiples to arrive at estimates of value. In each instance, these estimates and the discount or interest rates involved took into account the uncertainties of the business, the broader industry, and even the economy (when considering inflation, for example).

Many evaluators take an additional step of making "specific company" adjustments at this level, recognizing the fact that this business may pose unique risks. Usually, such risks are not considered by financial theories, because unique risks faced by one business are normally avoidable if an investor holds a diversified port folio of assets.[48] These adjustments may include, for example, reducing the value of the company because it depends on a key employee or manager, or its business

45. Model Bus. Corp. Act § 13.01 (1999). Although this is the most recent incarnation of the model act, most states follow earlier and less clear versions. For a good history of the Delaware and Model rules in this area, see Robert B. Thompson, *The Case for Iterative Statutory Reform: Appraisal and the Model Business Corporation Act*, 74 Law and Contemporary Problems 253 (Winter 2011).

46. Cal. Corp. Code § 1300(a)(1).

47. Shannon Pratt & Alina Niculita, The Lawyer's Business Valuation Handbook 298–99 (2d ed. 2010).

48. For this reason, the *Kessler* court decried the use of "company-specific risk" as "unsystematic" and "heretical" to modern portfolio theory. *See* Pt. VI(C) of the opinion, p. 11-26.

relies on a key customer, or it is a small business with greater variability in cash flows or profits.

A recent example is the decision of the Kentucky Supreme Court rejecting shareholder-level discounts and allowing entity-level discounts due to the company's small size and due to its specific business

> but with the strong caveat, that any entity-level discount must be based on particular facts and authority germane to the specific company being valued, *i.e.*, there can be no automatic 15–25% discount of the whole entity's value simply because it is closely held and not publicly traded. [R]ecognized entity-level discounts that may be appropriate in a given case include, but are not limited to, a key manager discount, a limited customer or supplier base discount, a "trapped-in" capital gains discount, an environmental liability discount, a pending litigation discount, a "portfolio" discount, a small-size discount or a privately-held company discount.[49]

Such discounts are recognized in the appraisal literature.[50] It is important for the reviewing attorney to consider whether the adjustment should take the form of a wholesale percentage reduction in the calculated value of the company, or if the analyst should instead revise estimates of cash flows or risk measures to take into account the specific items at hand. This suspicion was clearly stated by then Vice-Chancellor Strine in the *Kessler* case:

> it is often a back-door method of reducing estimated cash flows rather than adjusting them directly. To judges, the company specific risk premium often seems like the device experts employ to bring their final results into line with their clients' objectives, when other valuation inputs fail to do the trick.[51]

And so, armed with an appropriate degree of skepticism, note that here, as with the investor-level adjustments, the theories and calculations are a matter for your expert evaluator and beyond our scope here.

Comprehensive Problem

Bill and Ted have become big-time entrepreneurs. They incorporated their business five years ago, becoming Collegetown Coffee Company (CCC). Bill owns 75 shares and Ted owns 25 shares of CCC's common stock, no par value. To do so, each contributed his partnership interests, which were valued (at the time of contribution) at $150,000 for Bill and $50,000 for Ted. Bill is the President of CCC, but Ted refused to sell out to the lame mainstream lifestyle. He has picked up new members for the Wyld Stallyns rock band and is constantly on the road, with no management role in CCC.

---

49. Shawnee Telecom Resources Inc. v. Brown, 354 S.W.3d 542, 562 (Ky. 2011).

50. See generally, Pratt & Niculita, *supra* note 21, at 460–65.

51. Delaware Open MRI Radiology Associates, P.A. v. Kessler, 898 A.2d. 290, 339 (Del. Ch. 2006), reprinted in this chapter at p. 344.

CCC owns six coffee houses in the area, with 50 employees in all. Its brand and hipster attitude have resulted in a great reputation and most resplendent profits. When Bill and Ted incorporated, they hired a local CPA firm as their auditors. Its most recent balance sheet and income statement are presented below, along with some basic financial statistics from the past five years.

Collegetown Coffee Company Balance Sheet as of Dec. 31, 20x5 (most recent year)			
Assets		**Liabilities and Equity**	
Cash	100,000	Accounts payable	50,000
Accounts receivable	200,000	Current portion of long-term debt	100,000
Inventory	300,000	Loan—Collegetown Nat'l Bank	1,000,000
Equipment	500,000		
Furnishings	600,000	Contributed capital (200 shares outstanding, no par value)	400,000
	1,700,000	Retained earnings	150,000
			1,700,000

Collegetown Coffee Company Income Statement for year ended Dec. 31, 20x5		
Revenues		
Cash sales	2,000,000	
Credit sales	13,000,000	15,000,000
Expenses		
Cost of sales	14,000,000	
Advertising	500,000	
Administrative expenses	250,000	
Interest	50,000	
Taxes	30,000	14,830,000
Net Income		**170,000**

Five-year financial history. CCC added one store in 20x4 and two stores in 20x2. A brief spike in coffee prices in 20x5 reduced profits in that year, but the coffee markets have now returned to normal.

	20x5	20x4	20x3	20x2	20x1
Total assets	1,700,000	1,750,000	1,250,000	1,100,000	850,000
Long-term debt	1,100,000	1,000,000	600,000	600,000	500,000
Gross receipts	15,000,000	12,000,000	10,000,000	900,000	750,000
Net income	170,000	200,000	110,000	100,000	65,000
ROA	0.147	0.16	0.12	0.127	0.111
ROE	0.309	0.381	0.244	0.235	0.163

Ted seeks more return from the company to support his rock star lifestyle. Bill finds Ted's constant carping for more dividends less charming than decaf, and the two have been at odds for months. Now, Ted has gotten a lawyer and sued to have CCC dissolved, alleging that Bill is "freezing out" Ted from a sustainable return on his investment. Bill has opted, as permitted by relevant state law, to have Ted's shares purchased by CCC for their "fair value" instead of facing dissolution.

Bill's expert values CCC as follows: She uses discounted-cash-flow analysis. She forecasts that CCC will add one store each year, with each store adding about $50,000 to net income. The discount for each year is set at 40%, which is the industry average for similar companies with publicly-traded stock (coffee and fast-food restaurants) of 35% plus 5% premium to take into account CCC's small size compared to the public companies. She then makes a steady-state assumption (no further growth) after five years. Total value of equity: $704,000, so Ted's one-eighth share would be $88,000.

	20x6	20x7	20x8	20x9	Terminal	**Total**
Estimates	220,000	270,000	320,000	370,000	1,050,000	
Discounted	157,000	138,000	116,000	96,000	197,000	704,000

She also notes that there have been recent sales of CCC shares among the other shareholders at prices of about $4000/share, which would make Ted's 25 shares worth $100,000. She therefore opines that the value of Ted's interest is the average of these numbers, or $94,000.

Ted's expert values CCC as follows: Price-earnings ratios of the companies in the coffee and fast-food business average about 15. CCC's earnings, using 20x4's earnings of $200,000 as a representative year (before the coffee-cost problems) yields a total value for CCC of $3 million, so Ted's one-eighth share would be $375,000.

Advise the court as to the outcome of the case. Under relevant state law, the court is to exercise its own informed judgment and not just pick one expert valuation over the other.

Useful References

Valuation analysis is an expert's field. We have reviewed this material at an introductory level. If you are looking for further study, read on. All the information summarized in this chapter is found in these books.

References for attorneys. There are three shorter reference books written specifically for attorneys' use in understanding valuation:

- Robert B. Dickie & Peter R. Russo, Financial Statement Analysis and Business Valuation for the Practical Lawyer (Am. Bar Ass'n, Section of Business Law, 3d ed. 2020).
- Shannon P. Pratt & Alina V. Niculita, The Lawyer's Business Valuation Handbook (Am. Bar Ass'n, Section of Family Law, 2d ed. 2010).
- Jeffrey M. Risius, Business Valuation: A Primer for the Legal Professional (Am. Bar Ass'n, Section of Business Law, 2007).

Standard Reference works. The following works are the standards in the field. These are the texts with which your valuation analysts are likely familiar.

- Shannon P. Pratt & Alina V. Niculita, Valuing a Business: The Analysis and Appraisal of Closely Held Companies (McGraw Hill, 5th ed. 2008).
- Gary R. Trugman, Understanding Business Valuation: A Practical Guide to Valuing Small to Medium Sized Businesses (AICPA, 5th ed. 2017).
- McKinsey & Company, Valuation: Measuring and Managing the Value of Companies (Wiley, 6th ed. 2015).
- Robert W. Holthausen & Mark E. Zmijewski, Corporate Valuation: Theory, Evidence & Practice (Cambridge, 2d ed. 2020) (course textbook).
- Krishna G. Palepu & Paul M. Healy, Business Analysis & Valuation: Using Financial Statements (South-Western Cengage, 5th ed. 2013) (course textbook).

Chapter 12

Accounting Changes, Mistakes, and Liability

Mistakes happen in accounting and auditing just as they do everywhere else. Whether a mistake or correction leads to liability on the part of the accountant or auditor depends on the nature of the change and the legal context.

What you will learn. In this chapter we discuss first the accounting standards for making corrections. Some corrections are necessary because of changes in the rules, some because of mistakes. Second, we consider whether mistakes will lead to liability under either state or federal law, as each has its own rules.

A. Standards for Reporting Accounting Changes

1. Types of Changes

Under GAAP, changes to financial statements can be the result of any one of four causes.

(1) A change in accounting principle. This could be the result of new GAAP standards. Alternatively, an entity may make a different selection from among the GAAP "menu." If the latter is the reason for the change, however, the new method must be ***preferable.***[1] This requirement is in keeping with GAAP's overall requirement of consistency in presentation.[2] If the financial statements are audited, the auditor's opinion must separately report on the accounting change and whether the requirements (including the requirement of preferability) are met.[3]

(2) A change in an estimate. If an entity has new information, such as new data on collection of accounts receivable, useful lives of fixed assets, or inventory obsolescence, it should adjust the allowances and expenses accordingly. A change in es-

1. ASC § 250-10-45-2(b). See the following part for a discussion of preferability.

2. ASC § 250-10-45-1 and -11.

3. Public Company Accounting Oversight Board, Auditing Standards AU 2820.08 and 3101.17A-E.

timate, because it is based on ***new*** information, does not render prior period statements incorrect.[4]

(3) A change in the reporting entity. The entity may be combined with or separated from another entity (recall the rules for combinations in Chapter 8).

(4) An error. This could be either unintentional or deliberate. It could be an error in calculation, display, or application of GAAP.[5] This is normally where actionable accounting violations are found.

2. What Makes a Change "Preferable"?

There are two questions to be addressed here. First, what is "preferable?" Second, who makes that decision? However, these two questions are intertwined. Management makes the decision of course, but it is reviewed by the company's accountants and auditors. Management's standards are likely to be business standards, of course. But the proper level of scrutiny by the accountant or auditor is uncertain.

Where do we see the most changes? SEC regulations require a change in accounting principle by an SEC-registered company to be accompanied by a preferability letter from the company's auditor. One reviewer tallying up these letters[6] noted the most frequent letters concern the date for measuring the impairment of goodwill.[7] The subject coming in second was inventory changes, given the modern trend away from LIFO to FIFO or average cost.[8]

A recent analysis by Ernst & Young indicated that firm's suggestion that preferability considerations revolve around the following three criteria:

- The method should have specific support in the GAAP standards or accounting literature;
- Management's justification should be rational "in terms of presenting financial position and results of operations (as distinguished from other considerations, such as reducing taxes)"; and
- The method should be widely-recognized or prevalent in the industry.[9]

---

4. ASC §250-10-45-17. The following paragraph recognizes that distinguishing between a change in estimate *alone* and a change in estimate *required by a change in accounting principle* "is sometimes difficult."

5. ASC §250-10-05-1.

6. Derrick Coleman, "Preferability Letters: A 15-Year Review," *Audit Analytics* (posted Jan. 2, 2015) at http://www.auditanalytics.com/blog/preferability-letters-a-15-year-review/.

7. See Chapter 8, p. 247, "When is goodwill tested?"

8. On the use of inventory flow assumptions, see p. 153.

9. Ernst & Young, *Financial Reporting Developments: Accounting Changes and Error Corrections* (Rev. May 2015) at 16–17, available at http://www.ey.com/UL/en/AccountingLink/Publications-library-Financial-Reporting-Developments.

Securities and Exchange Commission Codification of Staff Accounting Bulletins

Topic 6: Interpretations of Accounting Series and Financial Reporting Releases

www.sec.gov/interps/account/sabcodet6.htm#P125_19708

G. Interim Financial Reporting

2. Amendments to Form 10-Q

b. Reporting requirements for accounting changes

1. Preferability

....

Question 2: Management may offer, as justification for a change in accounting principle, circumstances such as: their expectation as to the effect of general economic trends on their business (*e.g.*, the impact of inflation), their expectation regarding expanding consumer demand for the company's products, or plans for change in marketing methods. Are these circumstances which enter into the determination of preferability?

Interpretive Response: Yes. Those circumstances are examples of business judgment and planning and should be evaluated in determining preferability. In the case of changes for which objective criteria for determining preferability have not been established by authoritative bodies, business judgment and business planning often are major considerations in determining that the change is to a preferable method because the change results in improved financial reporting.

Question 3: What responsibility does the independent accountant have for evaluating the business judgment and business planning of the registrant?

Interpretive Response: Business judgment and business planning are within the province of the registrant. Thus, the independent accountant may accept the registrant's business judgment and business planning and express reliance thereon in his letter. However, if either the plans or judgment appear to be unreasonable to the independent accountant, he should not accept them as justification. For example, an independent accountant should not accept a registrant's plans for a major expansion if he believes the registrant does not have the means of obtaining the funds necessary for the expansion program.

Are changes in accounting principles worth the costs? There are not only the risks of perception by outsiders, but the actual costs of reworking prior years' financial statements. Consider these predictions made in 2007, when these preferabilty rules were first adopted, about whether changes in accounting principles were "worth it."

> In assessing the cost-benefit trade-off of future [accounting] principle changes, the controller and chief accounting officer of one *Fortune* 500 company said any improvements from a change in principle probably would not be worth the effort. He questioned the practicality of the [accounting standards] and

> believes there will be fewer voluntary changes as a result of [these standards]. However, an audit partner at a national CPA firm disagrees and says if a change would enable a company to better communicate the results of its business to its stakeholders, the company should make the change even if costs are higher, especially if it is motivated by a need for capital.[10]

Note, interestingly, that the business manager takes an accountant's view, while the CPA takes more of a manager's view. Do you think that "need for capital" is a sufficient business motivation to make a change in accounting principle "preferable"?

Change in Accounting Estimate Boosts Microsoft's Q1 2021 Gross Margin

Nicole Hallas, *Audit Analytics Blog*, Oct. 28, 2020.

Tech giant Microsoft announced its first quarter 2021.... Growth in Microsoft's gross margin and operating income was driven by a change in accounting estimate for the useful lives of server and network equipment....

Microsoft's gross margin increased in Q1 2021 to $26.15 billion — up 15% from Q1 2020 — and operating income increased to $15.9 billion — an increase of 25% — driven by growth in all their segments, and, notably, a reduction in depreciation expenses due to the change in estimated useful lives of equipment.

... The estimated useful life of server equipment increased from three years to four, while the estimated useful life of network equipment increased from two years to four.

The seemingly slight change in accounting estimate to extend the depreciable life for these assets does not impact historical depreciation expenses, total depreciation expenses over the life of the asset, or cash flows; however, the change does impact the timing of depreciation expense in the future, as can be seen in Microsoft's Q1 2021 results.

For full fiscal year 2021, Microsoft anticipates that their operating income will be positively impacted by the change by approximately $2.7 billion, or $0.09 per share.... Microsoft expected all of its EPS growth in Q1 2021 to come from this change in estimate.

https://blog.auditanalytics.com/change-in-accounting-estimate-boosts-microsofts-q1-2021-gross-margin/.

* * *

10. Jack O. Hall & C. Richard Aldridge, *Changes in Accounting for Changes*, 203 Journal of Accountancy (Feb. 2007), 47–48 available at http://www.journalofaccountancy.com/issues/2007/feb/changesinaccountingforchanges.html.

Problem 12-1

Recall Dime Store Supply Corp.'s inventory reclassification proposal in Problem 5-5, p. 155. Is the change preferable?

* * *

3. Treatment of Changes

All changes other than changes in estimates should be reported ***retrospectively***, that is, by issuing ***restated financial statements***, going back to prior periods as far as necessary to account for the change.[11] The restated financials must provide disclosure in each case of the voluntary or mandatory change in accounting principle, accounting entity, or the nature of the error and the effects of the correction.[12]

* * *

Problem 12-2

How would each of the following changes be accounted for?

(a) X Corp. had previously depreciated its plant and equipment (with a total depreciable cost of $1 million) over a useful life of 25 years. This had been done for the previous ten years. Now, in the eleventh year, X Corp. determines that the useful life must be reduced to a total of 20 years, that is, 10 more years remaining. What should be the proper depreciation expense for this year? Should prior years' expenses be restated?

(b) Y, LLC is a small used-book retailer. In year 2, Y employees discovered that the roof in one of their warehouses is leaking and has substantially damaged inventory. Most of the books have, in fact, been destroyed since sometime in year 1.

(c) Z Co. would like to change its accounting for one of its main inventory groups from LIFO to FIFO. They believe this will better track inventory flow and allow for closer management of inventory and lower costs. The company has inventory purchase and sales records going back ten years.

* * *

B. Liability of Auditors

The auditor's report (see p. 104) is an opinion that the client's financial statements are fairly presented. This can be styled as a representation or assertion. Thus, it makes sense that when the opinion is potentially incorrect, the legal wrong is in the nature of a ***misrepresentation***. This began as an intentional tort (deceit) but can be either

11. ASC § 250-10-45-5, unless it is impracticable to do so, see *id.* and § 250-10-45-9.

12. *See* ASC part 250-10-50.

intentional or negligent, depending on the defendant's conduct when making the misrepresentation.

> Courts list anywhere from four to nine elements of the common law ... misrepresentation claim, but whatever the number, they agree in substance that the plaintiff must prove (1) ... misrepresentation (2) of fact or opinion (as distinct from a promise) (3) that is material and (4) intended to induce and (5) does induce reasonable reliance by the plaintiff, (6) proximately causing pecuniary harm to the plaintiff.[13]

Misrepresentation actionable ***standing alone*** as a cause of ***pecuniary injury*** (as opposed to physical injury) is a separate species of tort liability. To add to it the confusing label of "fraud" will not ordinarily advance the inquiry further.[14]

Once the misrepresentation has come to light, the business may have few assets from which recovery can be had. The same is often true with the individuals who controlled the reporting entity, although they too might have "made" the misrepresentation. However, one entity left standing, usually with lots of assets, is the accounting firm which prepared and/or audited the financial statements. Upon what theory could the accountant be held liable? We discuss two distinct but overlapping doctrines, the first based in state common law and the second based in federal securities law.

1. Misrepresentation at Common Law

The issue with a misrepresentation made by an auditor in an audit opinion is that its intended audience is usually much wider than just the audit client. The extent to which liability should run beyond the privity of contract is a subject which has developed over many years.

- On the one hand, should the auditor's potential liability run to everyone who reads the opinion? Is there any limit to such liability?
- On the other hand, should the auditor's potential liability run only to the client—limited by privity of contract? Surely the auditor is aware that others will use and rely on this information.

The following recent opinion summarizes the developments and current state of the law, striving to reach a compromise between these two extremes.

---

13. Dan B. Dobbs, The Law of Torts 1345 (2000).

14. "There has been a good deal of overlapping of theories, and no little confusion, which has been increased by the indiscriminate use of the word 'fraud,' a term so vague that it requires definition in nearly every case." W. Page Keeton et al., Prosser and Keeton on The Law of Torts 727 (5th ed. 1984).

NYCAL Corporation v. KPMG Peat Marwick LLP

Supreme Judicial Court of Massachusetts, 1998
426 Mass. 491, 688 N.E.2d 1368

GREANEY, Justice.

On May 24, 1991, the plaintiff, allegedly in reliance on an auditors' report of the 1990 financial statements of Gulf Resources & Chemical Corporation (Gulf) prepared by the defendant, entered into a stock purchase agreement with the controlling shareholders of Gulf and, on July 12, 1991, the sale was completed. Gulf filed for bankruptcy protection in October, 1993, rendering the plaintiff's investment worthless. The plaintiff filed a civil complaint against the defendant seeking damages and costs incurred as a result of its alleged reliance on the auditors' report. The plaintiff claimed that the report materially misrepresented the financial condition of Gulf,[15] and should have included a "going concern" qualification. After applying the liability standard embodied in § 552 of the Restatement (Second) of Torts (1977), a judge in the Superior Court granted summary judgment for the defendant. We granted the parties' applications for direct appellate review of the final judgment. We conclude that the defendant did not breach any legal duty owed to the plaintiff and, accordingly, we affirm the judgment.

1. The following material facts are undisputed. Gulf retained the defendant to audit its 1990 financial statements. At that time, Gulf was listed on the New York Stock Exchange, and was controlled by several of its officers and directors who held their Gulf shares through two other entities (Inoco P.L.C. and Downshire N.V.). The financial statements were prepared by, and were the responsibility of, Gulf's management.

In February, 1990, D.S. Kennedy & Co. (Kennedy) reported to the Securities and Exchange Commission (SEC) that it had acquired 2,033,600 shares of Gulf common stock, and that it intended to acquire a controlling interest in Gulf. The defendant was aware of Kennedy's SEC filing. Gulf's controlling shareholders responded to the filing by increasing Inoco P.L.C.'s holdings in Gulf through purchasing and exercising warrants. Gulf management discussed with the defendant the potential for purchasing Kennedy's shares. Thus, the defendant was aware of Kennedy's interest in acquiring a controlling interest in Gulf and that Gulf intended to treat Kennedy as a hostile takeover threat.

The minutes of a September 14, 1990, meeting of Gulf's board of directors (board) reflect that the board discussed a possible sale to Aviva Petroleum, Inc. (Aviva). The minutes of an October 4, 1990 meeting indicate that the board discussed acquiring a 17% interest in Aviva, and adoption of a "poison pill" to defend against a hostile takeover by Aviva. Gulf ultimately purchased Aviva stock. The defendant reviewed

15. The plaintiff asserted that the report failed to take into account recurring substantial losses from operations, the extent of liability for environmental clean-up costs, inadequate accruals of pension and retirement obligations, and restrictions on transfers in certain bank accounts.

the minutes from the board's meetings in preparing the audit report, and was aware of Gulf's purchase of Aviva stock.

The defendant's completed auditors' report was included in Gulf's 1990 annual report, which became publicly available on February 22, 1991. In March, 1991, the plaintiff entered into discussions with Gulf concerning the possible purchase of a large block of Gulf shares, and during the course of those discussions, Gulf provided the plaintiff with a copy of its 1990 annual report. Thereafter, the plaintiff purchased 3,626,775 shares of Gulf (approximately 35% of the outstanding shares) in exchange for $16,000,000 in cash and $18,000,000 in the plaintiff's stock. The acquisition gave the plaintiff operating control of Gulf.

The defendant first learned of the transaction between the plaintiff and Gulf a few days prior to the July 12, 1991, closing. Until that time, the defendant did not know that any transaction between the plaintiff and Gulf had been contemplated.

2. We have not addressed the scope of liability of an accountant to persons with whom the accountant is not in privity. Three tests have generally been applied in other jurisdictions, either by common law or by statute, to determine the duty of care owed by accountants to nonclients. These include the foreseeability test, the near-privity test, and the test contained in § 552 of the Restatement.

The plaintiff urges our adoption of the broad standard of liability encompassed in the foreseeability test. Pursuant to this test, which is derived from traditional tort law concepts as first enunciated in *Palsgraf v. Long Island R.R.*, 248 N.Y. 339, 344, 162 N.E. 99 (1928), an accountant may be held liable to any person whom the accountant could reasonably have foreseen would obtain and rely on the accountant's opinion, including known and unknown investors. See, e.g., *H. Rosenblum, Inc. v. Adler*, 93 N.J. 324, 461 A.2d 138 (1983).[16] This test is generally disfavored, having been adopted by courts in only two jurisdictions. See *Touche Ross & Co. v. Commercial Union Ins. Co.*, 514 So.2d 315 (Miss.1987); *Citizens State Bank v. Timm, Schmidt & Co.*, 113 Wis.2d 376, 335 N.W.2d 361 (1983).

Our cases draw a distinction between the duty owed by a professional to a third party for personal injuries and that owed to a third party for pecuniary loss due to a professional's negligence. While we apply traditional tort law principles in cases involving the former, we have not done so in cases concerning the latter. Such principles are particularly unsuitable for application to accountants where, "regardless of the efforts of the auditor, the client retains effective primary control of the financial reporting process." *Bily v. Arthur Young & Co.*, 3 Cal.4th 370, 400, 11 Cal.Rptr.2d 51, 834 P.2d 745 (1992). The auditor prepares its report from statements and information supplied by the client, and once the report is completed and provided to the client, the client controls its dissemination. If we were to apply a foreseeability standard in these circumstances, "a thoughtless slip or blunder, the failure to detect a theft or forgery beneath the cover of deceptive entries, may expose accountants to a liability

16. This decision has been overruled by statute. See N.J. Stat. Ann. § 2A:53A-25 (West Supp.1997) (setting forth a near-privity standard).

in an indeterminate amount for an indeterminate time to an indeterminate class." *Ultramares Corp. v. Touche,* 255 N.Y. 170, 179, 174 N.E. 441 (1931). We refuse to hold accountants susceptible to such expansive liability, and conclude that Massachusetts law does not protect every reasonably foreseeable user of an inaccurate audit report.

The near-privity test, which originated in Chief Judge Cardozo's decision in *Ultramares Corp. v. Touche, supra,* and was modified by *Credit Alliance Corp. v. Arthur Andersen & Co.,* 65 N.Y.2d 536, 553, 493 N.Y.S.2d 435, 483 N.E.2d 110 (1985), limits an accountant's liability exposure to those with whom the accountant is in privity or in a relationship "sufficiently approaching privity." Under this test, an accountant may be held liable to noncontractual third parties who rely to their detriment on an inaccurate financial report if the accountant was aware that the report was to be used for a particular purpose, in the furtherance of which a known party (or parties) was intended to rely, and if there was some conduct on the part of the accountant creating a link to that party, which evinces the accountant's understanding of the party's reliance. *Id.* at 551, 493 N.Y.S.2d 435, 483 N.E.2d 110.

The defendant professes that the near-privity test is consistent with the standard we have previously applied to other professionals in the absence of privity. We disagree. A review of the relevant cases demonstrates that the first two elements of the near-privity test—reliance by the third party and knowledge that the party intended to rely—have analogs in our case law, but the third element—conduct by the accountant providing a direct linkage to the third party—does not.

....

We believe that the third test, taken from § 552 of the Restatement (Second) of Torts (1977), comports most closely with the liability standard we have applied in other professional contexts. Section 552 describes the tort of negligent misrepresentation committed in the process of supplying information for the guidance of others as follows:

> "(1) One who, in the course of his business, profession or employment, or in any other transaction in which he has a pecuniary interest, supplies false information for the guidance of others in their business transactions, is subject to liability for pecuniary loss caused to them by their justifiable reliance upon the information, if he fails to exercise reasonable care or competence in obtaining or communicating the information."

That liability is limited to

> "loss suffered (a) by the person or one of a limited group of persons for whose benefit and guidance he intends to supply the information or knows that the recipient intends to supply it; and (b) through reliance upon it in a transaction that he intends the information to influence or knows that the recipient so intends or in a substantially similar transaction."

Id.

The attendant comments explain the policy behind § 552 as follows:

> "[T]he duty of care to be observed in supplying information for use in commercial transactions implies an undertaking to observe a relative standard, which may be defined only in terms of the use to which the information will be put, weighed against the magnitude and probability of loss that might attend that use if the information proves to be incorrect. A user of commercial information cannot reasonably expect its maker to have undertaken to satisfy this obligation unless the terms of the obligation were known to him. Rather, one who relies upon information in connection with a commercial transaction may reasonably expect to hold the maker to a duty of care only in circumstances in which the maker was manifestly aware of the use to which the information was to be put and intended to supply it for that purpose."

Id. comment a, at 128.

The comments explain with regard to the requirement that the plaintiff be a member of a "limited group of persons for whose benefit and guidance" the information is supplied as follows:

> "[I]t is not required that the person who is to become the plaintiff be identified or known to the defendant as an individual when the information is supplied. It is enough that the maker of the representation intends it to reach and influence either a particular person or persons, known to him, or a group or class of persons, distinct from the much larger class who might reasonably be expected sooner or later to have access to the information and foreseeably to take some action in reliance upon it.... It is sufficient, in other words, insofar as the plaintiff's identity is concerned, that the maker supplies the information for repetition to a certain group or class of persons and that the plaintiff proves to be one of them, even though the maker never had heard of him by name when the information was given. It is not enough that the maker merely knows of the ever-present possibility of repetition to anyone, and the possibility of action in reliance upon it, on the part of anyone to whom it may be repeated."

Id. comment h, at 132–133.

We concur with the California Supreme Court's conclusion in *Bily v. Arthur Young & Co.*, 3 Cal.4th 370, 394, 11 Cal.Rptr.2d 51, 834 P.2d 745 (1992), that the Restatement test properly balances the indeterminate liability of the foreseeability test and the restrictiveness of the near-privity rule. Section 552 "recognizes commercial realities by avoiding both unlimited and uncertain liability for economic losses in cases of professional mistake and exoneration of the auditor in situations where it clearly intended to undertake the responsibility of influencing particular business transactions involving third persons." *Id.* at 408, 11 Cal.Rptr.2d 51, 834 P.2d 745.

Although the Restatement standard has been widely adopted by other jurisdictions, courts differ in their interpretations of the standard. The better reasoned decisions interpret § 552 as limiting the potential liability of an accountant to noncontractual third parties who can demonstrate "actual knowledge on the part of accountants of the limited—though unnamed—group of potential [third parties] that will rely upon the [report], as well as actual knowledge of the particular financial transaction that such information is designed to influence." *First Nat'l Bank of Commerce v. Monco Agency Inc.*, 911 F.2d 1053, 1062 (5th Cir.1990). See *Industrial Indem. Co. v. Touche Ross & Co.*, 13 Cal.App.4th 1086, 1095, 17 Cal.Rptr.2d 29 (1993). The accountant's knowledge is to be measured "at the moment the audit [report] is published, not by the foreseeable path of harm envisioned by [litigants] years following an unfortunate business decision." *First Nat'l Bank of Commerce v. Monco Agency Inc., supra* at 1059. See *Bethlehem Steel Corp. v. Ernst & Whinney*, 822 S.W.2d 592, 594 (Tenn.1991).[17]

The plaintiff argues that, by limiting § 552 to allow recovery only by those persons, or limited group of persons, that an accountant actually knows will receive and rely on an audit report, we will be rewarding an accountant's efforts to "remain blissfully unaware" of the report's proposed distribution and uses. We are unpersuaded by this argument. The axiom we have applied in other contexts applies to accountants as well: the Restatement standard will not excuse an accountant's "willful ignorance" of information of which the accountant would have been aware had the accountant not consciously disregarded that information.

2. The judge correctly concluded under § 552, that the undisputed facts failed to show that the defendant knew (or intended) that the plaintiff, or any limited group of which the plaintiff was a member, would rely on the audit report in connection with an investment in Gulf. To the contrary, the record suggests that the defendant did not prepare the audit report for the plaintiff's benefit and that the plaintiff was not a member of any "limited group of persons" for whose benefit the report was prepared. At the time the audit was being prepared, the plaintiff was an unknown, unidentified potential future investor in Gulf. The defendant was not aware of the existence of the transaction between the plaintiff and Gulf until after the stock purchase agreement had been signed and only a few days before the sale was completed.

The summary judgment record further indicates that the defendant neither intended to influence the transaction entered into by the plaintiff and Gulf nor knew that Gulf intended to influence the transaction by use of the audit report. While the

---

17. We reject the plaintiff's argument that § 552 encompasses the foreseeability doctrine of traditional tort law, and we decline to adopt the broad construction some courts have given to § 552 as the plaintiff requests. See, e.g., *Simpson v. Specialty Retail Concepts, Inc.*, 908 F.Supp. 323 (M.D.N.C.1995); *Blue Bell, Inc. v. Peat, Marwick, Mitchell & Co.*, 715 S.W.2d 408 (Tex.Ct.App.-Dallas, 1986). These cases apply such an expansive interpretation to § 552 that they effectively eliminate all of the restrictions that the Restatement sought to impose. The plaintiff also relies on *Fullmer v. Wohlfeiler & Beck*, 905 F.2d 1394 (10th Cir.1990) (applying Utah law), and *Merit Ins. Co. v. Colao*, 603 F.2d 654 (7th Cir.1979), cert. denied, 445 U.S. 929, 100 S.Ct. 1318, 63 L.Ed.2d 763 (1980) (applying Illinois law), in support of its broad interpretation of § 552. Neither case discusses § 552, nor analyzes the limitations on an accountant's liability under that standard. Furthermore, both cases have been overruled by legislative adoption of the near-privity rule. See Utah Code Ann. § 58-26-12 (1996); Ill.Ann.Stat. c. 225, § 450/30.1 (Smith-Hurd 1993).

defendant was aware of the circumstances surrounding the Kennedy and Aviva transactions, which had occurred prior to the completion of the audit report, the plaintiff's purchase of Gulf stock did not resemble either of those transactions, and it occurred subsequent to the issuance of the defendant's report. Furthermore, contrary to the plaintiff's contention, the Kennedy and Aviva transactions did not indicate to the defendant that Gulf's controlling shareholders intended to use the audit report to locate a purchaser for their stock. In fact, the record reveals that at the time the report was being prepared, Gulf's controlling shareholders were responding to expressions of interest in acquiring their stock by aggressively rejecting those advances and taking actions to defend against a hostile takeover.

Moreover, the record suggests that the defendant's audit report was prepared for inclusion in Gulf's annual report and not for the purpose of assisting Gulf's controlling shareholders in any particular transaction. The record does not exhibit that the defendant knew of any particular use that would be made of its audit report. Cf. *Guenther v. Cooper Life Sciences, Inc.*,759 F.Supp. 1437, 1443 (N.D.Cal.1990) (accountants knew that audit report would be placed in prospectus for public offering and had expressly consented to its inclusion). "Under the Restatement rule, an auditor retained to conduct an annual audit and to furnish an opinion for no particular purpose generally undertakes no duty to third parties." *Bily v. Arthur Young & Co., supra* at 393, 11 Cal.Rptr.2d 51, 834 P.2d 745.[18]

The rule we adopt today will preclude accountants from having to ensure the commercial decisions of non-clients where, as here, the accountants did not know that their work product would be relied on by the plaintiff in making its investment decision.

Judgment affirmed.

Negligence versus negligent misrepresentation. Courts often consider two related theories in auditor liability cases.

- ***Negligence.*** The auditor may be negligent in performance of his or her duties as measured by Generally Accepted Auditing Standards. Liability to the auditor's client can be established using traditional negligence analysis, but liability to *third parties* is less clear. It depends largely on whether the defendant owes a duty to the person not in privity.
- ***Negligent misrepresentation.*** The audit opinion is a representation which is clearly made to persons other than the audit client. This theory does not depend on creation of a duty. The problem is how to limit the liability to a somewhat smaller group than the world at large, or as Judge Cardozo so quotably charac-

18. We also note that the plaintiff had had the opportunity to conduct more detailed due diligence prior to its purchase of the Gulf shares, although it apparently did not do so. In addition, although the plaintiff asserts reliance on the defendant's report as the basis for making its investment in Gulf, such decisions typically involve other factors. See *Bily v. Arthur Young & Co.*, 3 Cal.4th 370, 401, 11 Cal.Rptr.2d 51, 834 P.2d 745 (1992).

terized the liability, "in an indeterminate amount for an indeterminate time to an indeterminate class." Liability usually depends not on duty, but rather the foreseeability of the plaintiff to the auditor.

It is easy to see that these two theories are closely related. It is less easy to see whether there should be much distinction between them. One is "duty" based, the other is "foreseeability" based, but sometimes even that distinction is less than clear, as a quick rereading of the *Palsgraf* case from your Torts class will make evident. Nonetheless, the Restatement 2d § 552 test is widely interpreted as endorsing the "negligent misrepresentation" theory of liability.[19]

Problem 12-3

LoanStar Corporation is a loan company. It borrows money and lends it to homeowners. In early 2019, LoanStar was short on funds, and borrowed $5 million from First National Bank. LoanStar prepared disclosure documents discussing its five-year results of operations and its five-year future business plan, and a complete set of income statements and balance sheets covering the most recently-completed fiscal years (2017 and 2018). The financial statements were audited by Shure & Serton, a local firm of certified public accountants. Shure & Serton gave an unqualified opinion on LoanStar's financial statements.

Later in 2019, a local newspaper's investigations discovered that LoanStar made loans based on inadequate documentation, continued to accrue interest income on loans in default, and the interest rates on its loans were in excess of state and federal limits. These revelations led to legal actions which reduced the price of LoanStar stock and caused LoanStar to default on its loan to First National Bank.

The Bank has sued Shure & Serton, claiming that its audit work should have uncovered and disclosed these problems at LoanStar. Assume that the question under state law is one of first impression in your jurisdiction. Advise Shure & Serton as to the likelihood of liability in the lawsuit.

* * *

Auditors may also be liable to their clients, of course, but such liability is not remarkably different from other areas of professional negligence. But suppose the client has also contributed to the misrepresentations. Who is more culpable?

---

19. For a good summary of the varied approaches, see Jay M. Feinman, *Liability of Lawyers and Accountants to Non-Clients: Negligence and Negligent Misrepresentation*, 67 Rutgers Univ. L. Rev. 127 (2015). The rule of Restatement (Second) of Torts § 552 has been carried over substantially intact to the Restatement (Third) of Torts: Liability for Economic Harm § 5, which received final approval in 2018.

Cenco Incorporated v. Seidman & Seidman

United States Court of Appeals, Seventh Circuit, 1982
686 F.2d 449

POSNER, Circuit Judge.

> You may recall that we have heard this story before. The same facts were the basis of an action by the SEC against Seidman & Seidman, which we looked at in the context of the types of evidence are required in an audit. See p. 100.

We consider in this case the standards under the common law of Illinois governing the liability of independent auditors for failing to detect fraud by the management of the company audited, and—*sua sponte*, as we are obliged to do—questions of federal subject-matter jurisdiction.

Between 1970 and 1975, managerial employees of Cenco Incorporated engaged in a massive fraud. The fraud began in Cenco's Medical/Health Division but eventually spread to the top management of Cenco, and by the time it was unmasked the chairman and president of Cenco plus a number of vice-presidents and other top managers were deeply involved. Not all the managers of Cenco were corrupt, however. Seven of the nine members of the board of directors were not in on the fraud, although there is evidence that they were negligent in allowing it to flourish undetected beneath their noses. The fraud was eventually discovered by a newly hired financial officer at Cenco who reported his suspicions to the Securities and Exchange Commission. Cenco's independent auditor throughout the period of the fraud, the accounting partnership of Seidman & Seidman, either never discovered the fraud or if it did failed to report it.

The fraud primarily involved the inflating of inventories in the Medical/Health Division far above their actual value. This increased the apparent worth of Cenco and greatly increased the market price of its stock (when the fraud was unmasked, the market price plummeted by more than 75 percent). The inflated stock was used to buy up other companies on the cheap. Cenco further benefited from the fraud by being able to borrow money at lower rates than if its inventories had been honestly stated and by getting its insurers to pay inflated claims for inventory lost or destroyed, since Cenco's insurance claims were based on inflated rather than actual inventory values. Thus, those involved in the fraud were not stealing from the company, as in the usual corporate fraud case, but were instead aggrandizing the company (and themselves) at the expense of outsiders, such as the owners of the companies that Cenco bought with its inflated stock, the banks that loaned Cenco money, and the insurance companies that insured its inventories.

The unmasking of the fraud led to the filing of a class action in federal district court against Cenco, its corrupt managers, and Seidman & Seidman. The class was composed of purchasers of Cenco stock during the period of the fraud, when the stock price was inflated. The suit charged the defendants with having violated various federal securities laws and SEC rules, notably Rule 10b-5, and common law strictures against fraud and related misconduct. Cenco—now under clean management—filed a cross-claim under Rule 13(g) of the Federal Rules of Civil Procedure against its co-defendant Seidman & Seidman, alleging that Seidman was liable to Cenco under both federal and state common law for having failed to prevent the fraud by Cenco's managers.

The case went to the jury on the three counts in Cenco's cross-claim alleging respectively breach of contract, professional malpractice (negligence), and fraud. Cenco's evidence tended to show that in the early stages of the fraud Seidman had been careless in checking Cenco's inventory figures and its carelessness had prevented the fraud from being nipped in the bud; that as the fraud expanded, Seidman's auditors became suspicious, but, perhaps to protect the very high fees that Seidman was getting from Cenco (about $1 million a year, which was 70 percent of Seidman's total billings), concealed their suspicions and kept giving Cenco a clean bill of health at their audit reports; that one partner in Seidman, asked by Cenco's general counsel (who was not in on the fraud) whether Seidman suspected anything, answered: "No one suspects fraud. Dismiss that." Seidman's evidence tended to show, to the contrary, that Seidman had diligently attempted to follow up all signs of fraud but had been thwarted by the efforts of the large group of managers at all levels at Cenco who were in on the fraud to prevent Seidman from learning about it.

The jury found for Seidman on all three counts. Cenco appeals both from the dismissal of its aiding and abetting and conspiracy counts and from the judgment entered against it on the jury's verdict, which it contends was based on erroneous instructions.

We can easily dispose of the charge that Seidman aided and abetted the fraud by Cenco's managers. There is no tort of aiding and abetting under Illinois law or, so far as we know, the law of any other state; all the cases that Cenco has cited with regard to this count are criminal cases. This is not a gap in tort law. Anyone who would be guilty in a criminal proceeding of aiding and abetting a fraud would be liable under tort law as a participant in the fraud, since aider-abettor liability requires participation in the criminal venture. The only utility of a separate tort of aiding and abetting in the commission of a tort would be to give plaintiffs' lawyers one more charge to fling at the jury in the hope that if enough charges are made the jury may accept at least one. In any event, creating a new Illinois tort is something for the Illinois courts or legislature to do rather than the federal courts.

We have much the same reaction to the conspiracy count, though the fact that Seidman does not argue that there is no tort of conspiracy makes us diffident about disposing of it on this ground. Tort law, unlike criminal law, does not punish "inchoate," which is to say purely preparatory, conduct; for wrongdoing to be actionable as a tort there must be an injury, as Cenco itself argues in defending the dismissal of Seidman's cross-claim. So while some torts, such as boycotts in restraint of trade, by their nature involve concerted activity, there is no basis in common law thinking for a tort of conspiracy to commit a tort. If there is a conspiracy and it fails, there is no injury and hence no tort liability; if it succeeds, the damages are fully recoverable in an action on the underlying tort.

In any event, Cenco could not have been prejudiced by the judge's dismissal of the conspiracy count. The judge allowed Cenco's fraud count to go to the jury, and Cenco has pointed us to no evidence that pertained only to Seidman's alleged participation in the conspiracy and not to its alleged participation in the fraud as well. In fact the fraud was a conspiracy, a conspiracy among numerous managers at Cenco; and by allowing the jury to consider whether Seidman had participated in the fraud the judge necessarily allowed the jury to consider whether Seidman had participated in a conspiracy to defraud. If it was error to withdraw the conspiracy count from the jury, which we doubt, it was harmless error.

This brings us to the main issue in the case — whether the district judge gave erroneous instructions to the jury. The challenged instructions relate to the question whether Seidman was entitled to use the wrongdoing of Cenco's managers as a defense against the charges of breach of contract, professional malpractice, and fraud. Despite the plurality of charges it is one question because breach of contract, negligence, and fraud, when committed by auditors, are a single form of wrongdoing under different names. The contract in question here (really a series of contracts) consists of the letters between Seidman and Cenco outlining the terms of Seidman's annual retention to audit Cenco's books. The material part of the letters is the incorporation by reference of general accounting standards which, so far as pertinent to this case, require the auditor to use his professional skill to follow up any signs of fraud that he discovers in the audit. The tort of negligence in the context of auditing is likewise a failure to use professional care and skill in carrying out an audit. And if such care and skill are not used, then the audit reports to the client will contain misrepresentations, either negligent or, if the auditor knows that the representations in the reports are untruthful or is indifferent to whether or not they are truthful, fraudulent.

Because these theories of auditors' misconduct are so alike, the defenses based on misconduct of the audited firm or its employees are also alike, though verbalized differently. A breach of contract is excused if the promisee's hindrance or failure to cooperate prevented the promisor from performing the contract. The corresponding defense in the case of negligence is, of course, contributory negligence.

Negligence is not a defense to an intentional tort such as fraud. But a participant in a fraud cannot also be a victim entitled to recover damages, for he cannot have relied on the truth of the fraudulent representations, and such reliance is an essential element in a case of fraud. If the misrepresentation is negligent rather than intentional, contributory negligence plays the same role it would play in an ordinary negligence case.

The jury instructions in this case stated these defenses accurately, but Cenco contends that the instructions should not have been given, because they related not to Cenco's conduct but to that of its managers. The judge was aware of the distinction but instructed the jury that the acts of a corporation's employees are the acts of the corporation itself if the employees were acting on the corporation's behalf. If this instruction was correct, then the instructions which allowed the jury to consider Cenco's misconduct as a defense to Seidman's alleged wrongdoing were proper.

To determine the correctness of the instruction requires us to decide in what circumstances, if any, fraud by corporate employees is a defense in a suit by the corporation against its auditors for failure to prevent the fraud. Illinois precedent allows us to reject one extreme position on this question, which is that the employee's fraud is always attributed to the corporation by the principle of respondeat superior. This position, which would exonerate auditors from all liability for failing to detect and prevent frauds by employees of the audited company, was rejected in *Cereal Byproducts Co. v. Hall*, 8 Ill.App.2d 331, 132 N.E.2d 27 (1956), where a company's independent auditors were held liable for negligently failing to detect embezzlement by the company's bookkeeper. Auditors are not detectives hired to ferret out fraud, but if they chance on signs of fraud they may not avert their eyes — they must investigate. The references to keeping an eye out for fraud that appear in the accounting standards incorporated (by reference) in the retention letters between Cenco and Seidman would have little point if not interpreted to impose a duty on auditors to follow up any signs of fraud that come to their attention.

But this does not tell us what the result should be if the fraud permeates the top management of the company and if, moreover, the managers are not stealing from the company — that is, from its current stockholders — but instead are turning the company into an engine of theft against outsiders — creditors, prospective stockholders, insurers, etc. On this question the Illinois cases on auditors' liability provide no guidance. In fact, to our knowledge the question has never been the subject of a reported case. Leeds Estate, Bldg. & Inv. Co. v. Shepherd, 36 (L.R.) Ch.D. 787, 802, 809 (1887), described by Cenco in its main brief as "the one squarely applicable common law decision on accountants' liability," is nothing of the sort. The auditor in that case had failed to discover that the company's manager, by misrepresenting the profits of the company, had caused the company to pay out dividends, directors' fees, and bonuses for himself — all in violation of the charter — as a result of which the company went broke. This was stealing from, not for, the company.

In predicting how the Illinois courts might decide the present case, we assume they would be guided by the underlying objectives of tort liability. Those objectives are to compensate the victims of wrongdoing and to deter future wrongdoing. With regard to the first, we must refine our earlier statement that the "victim" of Seidman's alleged laxity was Cenco Incorporated. A corporation is a legal fiction. The people who will receive the benefits of any judgment rendered in favor of Cenco on its cross-claim against Seidman are Cenco's stockholders, comprising people who bought stock in Cenco before the fraud began, people who bought during the fraud period and either sold afterwards when the stock price fell or continue to hold the stock at a loss, and people who bought after the fraud was unmasked. A judgment in favor of Cenco on its claim against Seidman would not differentiate among these classes, but would benefit every stockholder as of the date of the judgment (or the date when a judgment was anticipated with some precision) in proportion to the number of shares he owned.

Once the real beneficiaries of any judgment in favor of Cenco are identified, it is apparent that such a judgment would be perverse from the standpoint of compensating the victims of wrongdoing. Among the people who bought stock in Cenco before the fraud began are the corrupt officers themselves. To the extent they are still stockholders in the company, they would benefit pro rata from a judgment in favor of Cenco. The other stockholders in this class are innocent in a sense, but of course it is they who elected the board of directors that managed Cenco during the fraud. The people who bought during the fraud period and either sold at a loss or continue to hold at a loss are the plaintiffs in the recently settled class action in which both Cenco and Seidman were defendants. Seidman has already paid $3.5 million to them. Those who continue to own stock in Cenco (as distinct from those who sold at a loss) would receive additional compensation if Cenco prevailed in this action against Seidman. This is not to say they would be overcompensated; but it seems odd that the same shareholders should be able to recover damages from Seidman twice for the same wrong—once directly and once, in this suit, indirectly. Finally, the shareholders who bought after the fraud was unmasked lost nothing. The unmasking of the fraud caused the price of Cenco's stock to be bid down to reflect not only the true value of its inventories but also any anticipated injury to the company as a result of the fraud.

Because of shareholder turnover, there is always a potential mismatch between the recovery of damages by a corporation and the compensation of the shareholders actually injured by the wrong for which the damages were awarded. It is simply a more dramatic mismatch in this case than usual.

From the standpoint of deterrence, the question is whether the type of fraud that engulfed Cenco between 1970 and 1975 will be deterred more effectively if Cenco can shift the entire cost of the fraud from itself (which is to say, from its stockholders' pockets) to the independent auditor who failed to prevent the fraud. We think not. Cenco's owners—the stockholders—hired managers (directly, in the case of the president and chairman, who were both members of the board of directors, indirectly in the case of the others) who turned out to be thoroughly corrupt and to corrupt the corporation so thoroughly that it caused widespread harm to outsiders. If Seidman had been a more diligent auditor, conceivably if it had been a more honest auditor, the fraud might have been nipped in the bud; and liability to Cenco would make Seidman, and firms like it, more diligent and honest in the future. But if the owners of the corrupt enterprise are allowed to shift the costs of its wrongdoing entirely to the auditor, their incentives to hire honest managers and monitor their behavior will be reduced. While it is true that in a publicly held corporation such as Cenco most shareholders do not have a large enough stake to want to play an active role in hiring and supervising managers, the shareholders delegate this role to a board of directors, which in this case failed in its responsibility. And not all of Cenco's shareholders were "little people." During the period of the fraud Curtiss-Wright Corporation owned between 5 and 16 percent of Cenco's common stock and had its own accounting firm conduct a study of Cenco's operations—without discovering the fraud.

Thus, not only were some of Cenco's owners dishonest (and, to repeat, to the extent they still own stock in Cenco they would benefit from any judgment in Cenco's favor against Seidman), but the honest owners, and their delegates—a board of directors on which dishonesty and carelessness were well represented—were slipshod in their oversight and so share responsibility for the fraud that Seidman also failed to detect. In addition, the scale of the fraud—the number and high rank of the managers involved—both complicated the task of discovery for Seidman and makes the failure of oversight by Cenco's shareholders and board of directors harder to condone.

Cenco tries to draw a sharp contrast between an innocent Cenco and a Seidman that was (or so the jury could have found) an intentional tortfeasor. But if Cenco may be divorced from its corrupt managers, so may Seidman from the members and employees of the firm who suspected the fraud. If Seidman failed to police its people, Cenco failed as or more dramatically to police its own.

Furthermore, we must assume that Cenco's corrupt managers were acting for the benefit of the company, not against it as in the Cereal Byproducts case. The jury was instructed that it could attribute the fraud of Cenco's managers to Cenco only if it found that the managers had been acting on Cenco's behalf, and the verdict for Seidman implies that the jury either so found or found that Seidman had not even committed a prima facie breach of duty to Cenco. The former assumption is more favorable to Cenco.

Fraud on behalf of a corporation is not the same thing as fraud against it. Fraud against the corporation usually hurts just the corporation; the stockholders are the principal if not only victims; their equities vis-a-vis a careless or reckless auditor are therefore strong. But the stockholders of a corporation whose officers commit fraud for the benefit of the corporation are beneficiaries of the fraud. Maybe not net beneficiaries, after the fraud is unmasked and the corporation is sued—that is a question of damages, and is not before us. But the primary costs of a fraud on the corporation's behalf are borne not by the stockholders but by outsiders to the corporation, and the stockholders should not be allowed to escape all responsibility for such a fraud, as they are trying to do in this case.

We need not go so far as to predict that the Illinois courts would hold that in any action by a corporation against its auditors an employee's fraud intended to benefit the company rather than the employee at the company's expense will be attributed to the corporation, however lowly the employee. It is true that the lower down the employee is in the company hierarchy, the less likely he is to commit fraud for rather than against the company. But there are overzealous employees at every level—many a corporation has paid heavy damages for antitrust violations committed by low-level sales managers who thought they were acting in the company's best interests as well as their own—and we think it premature as well as unnecessary to decide that an auditor is never liable for the frauds of loyal but misguided company employees that he could have prevented by taking care. But here the uncontested facts show fraud permeating the top management of Cenco. In such a case the corporation should not be allowed to shift the entire responsibility for the fraud to its auditors.

The judgment appealed from is affirmed.

The *Cenco* opinion remains today one of the leading statements on the subject of client misconduct as a defense to auditor liability, although it has many critics.[20] The court addresses the issue of whether the acts of Cenco managers should be imputed to Cenco itself, and therefore frames the issue as one of agency law—imputation of an agent's acts to its principal. But one critic of the case argues that the issue is not imputation at all, but rather that of *in pari delicto* (of equal fault). The question is not whether the acts of the agents should be imputed to the principal—clearly they should—but whether those acts are sufficiently wrongful to deny recovery.[21] And in determining whether the company is equally at fault with the (presumably) negligent auditor, one reviewer argues that courts should look at the extent to which the auditor has properly assessed the client's internal control systems.[22]

* * *

2. Securities Fraud

It may seem odd to focus on such a specialty as securities law in discussing accounting misstatements. However, there is a broad antifraud provision in the Securities Exchange Act of 1934 (the "Exchange Act"). This is a rule, known well to corporate and securities lawyers as Rule 10b-5, which applies to any misstatement in connection with the purchase or sale of securities.

Rules and Regulations under the Securities Exchange Act of 1934

Rule 10b-5, 17 C.F.R. § 240.10b-5

> It shall be unlawful for any person, directly or indirectly, by the use of any means or instrumentality of interstate commerce, or of the mails or of any facility of any national securities exchange,
>
> (a) To employ any device, scheme, or artifice to defraud,
>
> (b) To make any untrue statement of a material fact or to omit to state a material fact necessary in order to make the statements made, in the light of the circumstances under which they were made, not misleading, or
>
> (c) To engage in any act, practice, or course of business which operates or would operate as a fraud or deceit upon any person,
>
> in connection with the purchase or sale of any security.

---

20. For a summary, see Note, Christine M. Shepard, *Corporate Wrongdoing and the* In Pari Delicto *Defense in Auditor Malpractice Cases: A New Approach*, 69 Wash. & Lee L. Rev. 275, 297 (2012).

21. *Id* at 324.

22. See Deborah A. DeMott, *Further Perspectives on Corporate Wrongdoing,* In Pari Delicto, *and Auditor Malpractice*, 69 Wash. & Lee L. Rev. 339, 345–46 (2012).

The rule makes actionable a material misstatement by the defendant upon which the plaintiff relied or which was relied upon by the market in which the plaintiff traded.[23] When the statement was made by the company, the company is liable, and the auditors may be liable as well if the statement was made by them in the financial statements.[24]

Private liability under Rule 10b-5 was implied by the courts decades ago, but courts were left to fashion the *standards* of liability from the very general and unhelpful language of the rule and underlying statute. They turned, predictably, to the common law action for misrepresentation. Building on this common law foundation, one treatise describes the elements of liability under Rule 10b-5 as follows.

> There are five principal elements for stating a claim under Rule 10b-5: the plaintiff must show (1) fraud or deceit (2) by any person (3) in connection with (4) the purchase or sale (5) of any security. Furthermore, since Rule 10b-5, like its parent section, requires deceit or fraud, the elements of common law fraud—materiality, reliance, causation, and damages—are part of a Rule 10b-5 claim.[25]

Although this cause of action may seem more limited than the common law claim discussed in Part A(1) above, Rule 10b-5 has almost totally eclipsed state law as a theory for accounting cases. Unlike the state law claim, which extends to negligence, a Rule 10b-5 claim requires *scienter* or intent to defraud. However, the cause of action is not limited by any tort law concepts of foreseeability as we discussed in Part B(1) above. A Rule 10b-5 plaintiff can take advantage of the Exchange Act's provision for exclusive federal jurisdiction and nationwide service of process.[26] In addition, there is federal preemption of class-action lawsuits involving securities fraud where the class consists of more than 50 persons.[27] The following cases discuss the extent of liability under this federal rule.

United States v. Simon

United States Court of Appeals Second Circuit, 1969
425 F.2d 796

FRIENDLY, Circuit Judge:

Defendant Carl Simon was a senior partner, Robert Kaiser a junior partner, and Melvin Fishman a senior associate in the internationally known accounting firm of Lybrand, Ross Bros. & Montgomery. They stand convicted after trial by Judge Mansfield and a jury in the District Court for the Southern District of New York under three

23. As to the latter "fraud on the market" rule, see *Basic, Inc. v. Levinson*, 485 U.S. 224, 241–49 (1988), which permits the plaintiff to hold the defendant liable even if the defendant did not see or rely on the misstatement, but traded in a market which did so see and rely.

24. The U.S. Supreme Court has held that accountants (and others) cannot be liable for assisting (or "aiding and abetting" in the common parlance) violations of others.

25. Thomas Lee Hazen, The Law of Securities Regulation 770 (1996).

26. See § 27 of the Exchange Act.

27. *See* § 28(f) of the Exchange Act.

counts of an indictment charging them with drawing up and certifying a false or misleading financial statement of Continental Vending Machine Corporation (hereafter Continental) for the year ending September 30, 1962. After denying motions for acquittal or a new trial, the judge fined Simon $7,000 and Kaiser and Fishman $5,000 each.

Count One of the indictment was for conspiracy to violate 18 U.S.C. 1001 and 1341 and 32 of the Securities Exchange Act of 1934. Section 1001 provides:

> Whoever, in any matter within the jurisdiction of any department or agency of the United States knowingly and willfully falsifies, conceals or covers up by any trick, scheme, or device a material fact, or makes any false, fictitious or fraudulent statements or representations, or makes or uses any false writing or document knowing the same to contain any false, fictitious or fraudulent statement or entry, shall be fined not more than $10,000 or imprisoned not more than five years, or both.

Section 1341 makes criminal the use of the mails in aid of "any scheme or artifice to defraud." Section 32 of the Securities Exchange Act renders criminal the willful and knowing making of a statement in any required report which is false or misleading with respect to any material fact.[28] Counts Three and Six charged two mailings of the statement in violation of 18 U.S.C. 1341. Nothing turns on the different phrasings of the test of criminality in the three statutes. The Government concedes it had the burden of offering proof allowing a reasonable jury to be convinced beyond a reasonable doubt not merely that the financial statement was false or misleading in a material respect but that defendants knew it to be and deliberately sought to mislead.

While every criminal conviction is important to the defendant, there is a special poignancy and a corresponding responsibility on reviewing judges when, as here, the defendants have been men of blameless lives and respected members of a learned profession. This is no less true because the trial judge, wisely in our view, imposed no prison sentences. On the other hand, ... our office is limited to determining whether the evidence was sufficient for submission to the jury and, if so, whether errors prejudicial to the defendants occurred at the trial.

....

I.

The trial hinged on transactions between Continental and an affiliate, Valley Commercial Corporation (hereafter "Valley"). The dominant figure in both was Harold Roth, who was president of Continental, supervised the day-to-day operations of Valley, and owned about 25% Of the stock of each company.

Valley, which was run by Roth out of a single office on Continental's premises, was engaged in lending money at interest to Continental and others in the vending machine business. Continental would issue negotiable notes to Valley, which would endorse these in blank and use them as collateral for drawing on two lines of credit,

28. Ed.: The statute makes any "willful violation" of the Securities Exchange Act—including Section 10(b) and Rule 10b-5—a criminal offense.

of $1 million each, at Franklin National Bank ("Franklin") and Meadowbrook National Bank ("Meadowbrook"), and would then transfer to Continental the discounted amount of the notes. These transactions, beginning as early as 1956, gave rise to what is called "the Valley payable." By the end of fiscal 1962, the amount of this was $1,029,475, of which $543,345 was due within the year.

In addition to the Valley payable, there was what is known as the "Valley receivable," which resulted from Continental loans to Valley. Most of these stemmed from Roth's custom, dating from mid-1957, of using Continental and Valley as sources of cash to finance his transactions in the stock market.[29] At the end of fiscal 1962, the amount of the Valley receivable was $3.5 million, and by February 15, 1963, the date of certification, it has risen to $3.9 million. The Valley payable could not be offset, or "netted," against the Valley receivable since, as stated, Continental's obligations to Valley were in the form of negotiable notes which Valley had endorsed in blank to the two banks and used as collateral to obtain the cash which it then lent to Continental.

By the certification date, the auditors had learned that Valley was not in a position to repay its debt, and it was accordingly arranged that collateral would be posted. Roth and members of his family transferred their equity in certain securities to Arthur Field, Continental's counsel, as trustee to secure Roth's debt to Valley and Valley's debt to Continental. Some 80% Of these securities consisted of Continental stock and convertible debentures.

[Note 2 to the 1962 financial statements of Continental read as follows:]

> 2. The amount receivable from Valley Commercial Corp. (an affiliated company of which Mr. Harold Roth is an officer, director and stockholder) bears interest at 12% a year. Such amount, less the balance of the notes payable to that company, is secured by the assignment to the Company of Valley's equity in certain marketable securities. As of February 15, 1963, the amount of such equity at current market quotations exceeded the net amount receivable.

....

The case against the defendants can be best encapsulated by comparing what Note 2 stated and what the Government claims it would have stated if defendants had included what they knew:

> 2. The amount receivable from Valley Commercial Corp. (an affiliated company of which Mr. Harold Roth is an officer, director and stockholder), which bears interest at 12% a year, was uncollectible at September 30, 1962, since Valley had loaned approximately the same amount to Mr. Roth who was unable to pay. Since that date Mr. Roth and others have pledged as security for the repayment of his obligation to Valley and its obligation to Continental

29. From mid-1957 until January 1963 Continental thus advanced more than $16 million to Valley and Valley advanced more than $13 million to Roth. Of the latter sum the payment of approximately $6.5 million would have resulted in an overdraft in Valley's account but for the deposit of a Continental check on the same day.

> (now $3,900,000, against which Continental's liability to Valley cannot be offset) securities which, as of February 15, 1963, had a market value of $2,978,000. Approximately 80% Of such securities are stock and convertible debentures of the Company.

Striking as the difference is, the latter version does not reflect the Government's further contention that in fact the market value of the pledged securities on February 15, 1963, was $1,978,000 rather than $2,978,000 due to liens of James Talcott, Inc. and Franklin for indebtedness other than Roth's of which defendants knew or should have known.

....

III.

The defendants called eight expert independent accountants, an impressive array of leaders of the profession. They testified generally that, except for the error with respect to netting, the treatment of the Valley receivable in Note 2 was in no way inconsistent with generally accepted accounting principles or generally accepted auditing standards, since it made all the informative disclosures reasonably necessary for fair presentation of the financial position of Continental as of the close of the 1962 fiscal year. Specifically, they testified that neither generally accepted accounting principles nor generally accepted auditing standards required disclosure of the make-up of the collateral or of the increase of the receivable after the closing date of the balance sheet, although three of the eight stated that in light of hindsight they would have preferred that the make-up of the collateral be disclosed. The witnesses likewise testified that disclosure of the Roth borrowings from Valley was not required, and seven of the eight were of the opinion that such disclosure would be inappropriate. The principal reason given for this last view was that the balance sheet was concerned solely with presenting the financial position of the company under audit; since the Valley receivable was adequately secured in the opinion of the auditors and was broken out and shown separately as a loan to an affiliate with the nature of the affiliation disclosed, this was all that the auditors were required to do. To go further and reveal what Valley had done with the money would be to put into the balance sheet things that did not properly belong there; moreover, it would create a precedent which would imply that it was the duty of an auditor to investigate each loan to an affiliate to determine whether the money had found its way into the pockets of an officer of the company under audit, an investigation that would ordinarily be unduly wasteful of time and money. With due respect to the Government's accounting witnesses, an SEC staff accountant, and, in rebuttal, its chief accountant, who took a contrary view, we are bound to say that they hardly compared with defendants' witnesses in aggregate auditing experience or professional eminence.

Defendants asked for two instructions which, in substance, would have told the jury that a defendant could be found guilty only if, according to generally accepted accounting principles, the financial statements as a whole did not fairly present the financial condition of Continental at September 30, 1962, and then only if his departure from accepted standards was due to willful disregard of those standards with knowledge of the falsity of the statements and an intent to deceive. The judge declined to give these instructions. Dealing with the subject in the course of his charge, he said that the "critical test" was whether the financial statements as a whole "fairly presented the financial position of Continental as of September 30, 1962, and whether it accurately reported the operations for fiscal 1962." If they did not, the basic issue became whether defendants acted in good faith. Proof of compliance with generally accepted standards was "evidence which may be very persuasive but not necessarily conclusive that he acted in good faith, and that the facts as certified were not materially false or misleading." "The weight and credibility to be extended by you to such proof, and its persuasiveness, must depend, among other things, on how authoritative you find the precedents and the teachings relied upon by the parties to be, the extent to which they contemplate, deal with, and apply to the type of circumstances found by you to have existed here, and the weight you give to expert opinion evidence offered by the parties. Those may depend on the credibility extended by you to expert witnesses, the definiteness with which they testified, the reasons given for their opinions, and all the other facts affecting credibility, * * *"

Defendants contend that the charge and refusal to charge constituted error. We think the judge was right in refusing to make the accountants' testimony so nearly a complete defense. The critical test according to the charge was the same as that which the accountants testified was critical. We do not think the jury was also required to accept the accountants' evaluation whether a given fact was material to overall fair presentation, at least not when the accountants' testimony was not based on specific rules or prohibitions to which they could point, but only on the need for the auditor to make an honest judgment and their conclusion that nothing in the financial statements themselves negated the conclusion that an honest judgment had been made. Such evidence may be highly persuasive, but it is not conclusive, and so the trial judge correctly charged.

....

IV.

Defendants properly make much of the alleged absence of proof of motivation. They say that even if the Government is not bound to show evil motive, and we think it is not, see *Pointer v. United States*, 151 U.S. 396, 14 S.Ct. 410, 38 L.Ed. 208 (1894), lack of evidence of motive makes the burden of proving criminal intent peculiarly heavy and the Government did not discharge this.

....

Even if there were no satisfactory showing of motive, we think the Government produced sufficient evidence of criminal intent. Its burden was not to show that defendants were wicked men with designs on anyone's purse, which they obviously were not, but rather that they had certified a statement knowing it to be false. As Judge Hough said for us long ago, "while there is no allowable inference of knowledge from the mere fact of falsity, there are many cases where from the actor's special situation and continuity of conduct an inference that he did know the untruth of what he said or wrote may legitimately be drawn." *Bentel v. United States*, 13 F.2d 327, 329, *cert. denied*, 273 U.S. 713, 47 S.Ct. 109, 71 L.Ed. 854 (1926). Moreover, so far as criminal intent is concerned, the various deficiencies in the footnote should not be considered in isolation. Evidence that defendants knowingly suppressed one fact permitted, although it surely did not compel, an inference that their suppression of another was likewise knowing and willful.

....

Affirmed.

United States v. Ebbers

United States Court of Appeals, Second Circuit, 2006
458 F.3d 110

WINTER, Circuit Judge.

Bernard J. Ebbers appeals from his conviction by a jury on nine counts of conspiracy, securities fraud, and related crimes and from the 25-year jail sentence imposed by Judge Jones.

Ebbers was the Chief Executive Officer ("CEO") of WorldCom, Inc., a publicly traded global telecommunications company. During the pertinent times—from the close of the fourth quarter of the 2000 fiscal year through the first quarter of the 2002 fiscal year—he engineered a scheme to disguise WorldCom's declining operating performance by falsifying its financial reports. Although the scheme was multi-faceted, the fraud primarily involved the treating of hundreds of millions of dollars of what had always been recorded operating costs as capital expenditures for several fiscal quarters. After a seven-week trial, the jury convicted Ebbers on all counts. He was sentenced to 25 years' imprisonment, to be followed by 3 years' supervised release.

On appeal, Ebbers ... claims that the court should not have given a conscious avoidance instruction and that the government should have been required to allege and prove violations of Generally Accepted Accounting Principles ("GAAP"). We affirm.

BACKGROUND

We must of course view the evidence in the light most favorable to the government and draw all permissible inferences from that evidence in its favor.

Beginnings

As part of its business, WorldCom built a global network of fiber-optic cables and telephone wires to transmit data and telephone calls. It also leased capacity on other companies' network facilities to transmit data and calls. The cost of the leasing was WorldCom's single largest expense-styled "line costs." When the "dot-com bubble" burst in early 2000, WorldCom's business slowed dramatically as some of its dot-com customers were unable to pay their bills and demand for WorldCom's internet services declined. Anticipating growth rather than declining demand, WorldCom had added 10,000 new employees, continued to invest heavily in new equipment, and had taken on long-term line leases with fixed monthly payments. By the end of the third quarter of 2000, as its revenue growth decreased and its expenses increased, the company could no longer meet investors' expectations of revenue and profit growth.

Third Quarter 2000

As a public company, WorldCom was required to file quarterly financial statements and annual reports with the SEC. When it became clear that the company would be unable to meet analysts' expectations in the third quarter of 2000, Ebbers and WorldCom's Chief Financial Officer ("CFO") Scott Sullivan reviewed the monthly revenue reports and discussed the company's options. Sullivan told Ebbers that WorldCom's financial performance had deteriorated and that they should issue an earnings warning to investors. Ebbers refused. Sullivan then told Ebbers that to meet expectations the company would have to make an improper adjustment to the revenue figure. Ebbers replied that "[W]e have to hit our numbers." Sullivan instructed others to increase the publicly reported revenues by adding $133 million in anticipated under-usage penalties to the revenue calculation, even though he believed that those penalties were not likely to be collected.

Earnings pressure. Recall from the *Mattel* case (*In the Matter of Arthur Andersen & Co.)* p. 124, how the pressure to meet analysts' earnings projections can be a major factor in fraudulent revenue recognition practices. You can see the progression of the fraud here in the *WorldCom* saga as we did with *Mattel.*

Soon after, Sullivan learned that line cost expenses would be almost $1 billion greater than expected. He reported that to Ebbers, who reiterated that the company had to hit its quarterly earnings estimates. Sullivan instructed [WorldCom's financial staff] to reduce line cost expense accounts in the general ledger while also reducing reserves in the same amounts, which lowered the reported line costs by about $828 million. As a result, WorldCom's reported earnings were increased by the same amount.

Fourth Quarter 2000

WorldCom's revenues and line costs did not improve in the fourth quarter of 2000. In January 2001, Ebbers and Sullivan agreed that WorldCom would not be able to meet even the analysts' revised expectations if it reported its actual results. Sullivan asked Ebbers if he would again reduce the earnings estimate given to analysts, but Ebbers refused to do so....

WorldCom's line cost expenses were $800 million above analysts' expectations. Sullivan directed ... his staff to reduce[] the income tax reserve by $407 million, and altered other accounts until they were able to reduce the reported line costs by $797 million for the fourth quarter.... The 2000 annual report and Form 10-K also contained the false information.

First Quarter 2001

In early 2001, WorldCom's line costs were still hundreds of millions of dollars higher than the company had predicted.... Sullivan suggested capitalization of the line costs, that is, shifting a portion of the costs out of reported current expenses into capital expenses. Because line costs had always been treated as operating expenses, their unannounced treatment as capital expenses

The WorldCom deferrals. Recall this story on p. 164, "the decision to defer." We also read about the deferral of certain costs in the trash collection business in *In re Chambers Development Corp.* What would be required in order for Mr. Ebbers or Mr. Sullivan to properly defer these line costs?

would disguise the decline in earnings.... At a dinner in Washington in March 2001, Sullivan and Ebbers discussed the line cost problem. Sullivan told Ebbers that the planned allocation of current expenses to capital expenses—in an amount over $500 million—"wasn't right." Ebbers did not deter him from the allocation.

Ebbers approved the capitalization of line costs in a later conversation with Sullivan. He told Sullivan that "[w]e have to grow our revenue and we have to cut our expenses, but we have to hit the numbers this quarter." ... When Ebbers spoke to analysts and the public about WorldCom's first quarter performance in the earnings conference call, he did not mention the change in how the company was booking line costs. Instead, he said "there were no storms on the horizon," urging them to "go out and buy stock."

Second Quarter 2001

Capitalizing WorldCom's line cost expenses left another problem unaddressed: revenues were not growing at the 12% annual rate that Ebbers had predicted. Missing the revenue growth target was likely to lower WorldCom's stock price. Sullivan, Ebbers, and a handful of other executives created a new program called "Close the Gap" to "get [the] operating performance ... up to the market guidance expectations" by finding new items to include in revenue. Each month, and sometimes more often, the business operations group presented revenue data to Ebbers in detail as part of the "Close the Gap" program. Sullivan told Ebbers that there was no basis for including many of the opportunities presented in the "Close the Gap" program in reported revenues. In a voicemail to Ebbers, Sullivan described some of the items eventually included in reported revenues as "accounting fluff," "one-time stuff," and "junk." In July 2001, Ebbers sent a memorandum to Chief Operating Officer ("COO") Ron Beaumont, who was involved in the "Close the Gap" program, asking him "[w]here we stand on those one time events that had to happen in order for us to have a chance to make our numbers." Ebbers and Sullivan were aware that the company's true results fell far short of analysts' expectations, but ordered the improper revenue accounting so that those expectations would be met.

Once again, Sullivan told Ebbers that the company could reach the analysts' estimates only by capitalizing a portion of its line costs. Ebbers attended one of the line cost meetings around this time, and explained to the employees there that his "lifeblood was in the stock of the company" and that if the price fell below about $12 per share, he would be wiped out financially by margin calls. Although the line costs had improved slightly since the previous quarter, the accounting staff still had to capitalize over $610 million in line costs in order to meet earnings estimates.

Third Quarter 2001

In the third quarter of 2001, WorldCom's actual revenue growth rate, as reported internally to Ebbers, had fallen to about 5.5%. However, Ebbers announced that WorldCom had sustained its 12% revenue growth rate when the third quarter results were reported. The "Close the Gap" program added several new revenue items, largely one-time items not previously counted in revenue. Sullivan told Ebbers that the purpose of the adjustments to revenue was to reach the 12% growth target. WorldCom's press release announcing the quarterly results quoted Ebbers as saying the company had "delivered excellent growth this quarter." During the earnings conference call with analysts, Ebbers said "[w]e were able to achieve very solid growth." However, over $700 million in line costs had to be capitalized to create the appearance of meeting the earnings target for the quarter.

....

Fourth Quarter 2001

By the fourth quarter of 2001, even the "Close the Gap" program could not generate enough one-time revenue opportunities to create double-digit revenue growth. Nor could the staff find ways to adjust the line cost expenses sufficient to hit the earnings target. After [the staff] capitalized over $941 million in line costs, [it] still had to adjust the SG & A (sales, general, and administrative) expenses in order to reach the target. On the fourth quarter earnings conference call, Ebbers assured investors that "[w]e stand by our accounting," and later said in a CNBC interview that "[w]e've been very conservative on our accounting."

First Quarter 2002

WorldCom's revenue declined in the first quarter of 2002. The accounting staff added new sources of revenue to improve the results but were unable to bring the revenue up to analysts' expectations. Sullivan informed Ebbers that even with the improper revenue adjustments and the capitalization of line costs, the company would be unable to meet investors' expectations that quarter. The accounting staff capitalized about $818 million in line costs, but WorldCom still had to announce that its results had fallen below investors' expectations.

Investigation, Trial, and Sentence

In March 2002, the Securities and Exchange Commission ("SEC") began to investigate WorldCom. At the end of April 2002, WorldCom's board asked Ebbers to resign, which he did on April 29th.... A month after Ebbers' departure, WorldCom's Internal Audit Department learned of the line cost capitalization and alerted the new CEO. Sullivan was soon fired, and WorldCom disclosed the fraud to the public on June 25, 2002. WorldCom's stock collapsed, losing 90% of its value, and the company filed for bankruptcy.

On September 15, 2004, Ebbers was charged ... with one count of conspiracy to commit securities fraud and related crimes, one count of securities fraud, and seven counts of making false filings with the SEC. *See* 18 U.S.C. § 371 (conspiracy); 15 U.S.C. §§ 78j (b) & 78ff (securities fraud); 15 U.S.C. §§ 78m(a) & 78ff (false filings).

A jury convicted Ebbers on all counts on March 15, 2005.... Judge Jones ... sentenced Ebbers to 25 years' imprisonment and three years' supervised release, and imposed a $900 special assessment but no fines.

This appeal followed.

DISCUSSION

The Need to Prove GAAP Violations

> **Logic drill.** The SEC rule quoted here says that non-GAAP financial statements are presumed to be "misleading" (and thus actionable) under the federal securities laws. Does it necessarily follow that ***GAAP*** financial statements are presumed to be ***not misleading?***

Ebbers argues that the indictment was flawed because it did not allege that the underlying accounting was improper under GAAP, and that the district court should have required the government to prove violations of GAAP at trial. He claims that where a fraud charge is based on improper accounting, the impropriety must involve a violation of GAAP, because financial statements that comply with GAAP necessarily meet SEC disclosure requirements. *See* ... 17 C.F.R. § 210.4-01(a)(1) ("Financial statements filed with the [SEC] which are not prepared in accordance with generally accepted accounting principles will be presumed to be misleading or inaccurate...."). Before trial he moved to dismiss the indictment on those grounds, and after trial moved for judgment of acquittal pursuant to Federal Rule of Criminal Procedure 29 based on the Government's failure to prove violations of GAAP at trial. The district court denied both motions. We review both the denial of a motion to dismiss an indictment and the denial of a Rule 29 motion for judgment of acquittal de novo.

We addressed a similar argument in *United States v. Simon,* 425 F.2d 796, 805–06 (2d Cir.1969) (Friendly, J.), when three accountants asked for a jury instruction that they could not be found guilty of securities fraud if the financial statements in question were in compliance with GAAP. We ruled that the district court properly refused to give the instruction.

We see no reason to depart from *Simon.* To be sure, GAAP may have relevance in that a defendant's good faith attempt to comply with GAAP or reliance upon an accountant's advice regarding GAAP may negate the government's claim of an intent to deceive. *Id.* at 805. Good faith compliance with GAAP will permit professionals who study the firm and understand GAAP to accurately assess the financial condition of the company. This can be the case even when the question of whether a particular accounting practice complies with GAAP may be subject to reasonable differences of opinion.

However, even where improper accounting is alleged, the statute requires proof only of intentionally misleading statements that are material, *i.e.,* designed to affect the price of a security. If the government proves that a defendant was responsible for financial reports that intentionally and materially misled investors, the statute is satisfied. The government is not required in addition to prevail in a battle of expert witnesses over the application of individual GAAP rules.

For example, an addition to revenue used in the "Close the Gap" program may or may not have been improper under particularized GAAP rules. However, where an addition intentionally involved funds that had not previously been used to calculate revenue and were a one-time addition to revenue, investors would not have been alerted to the fact that revenue as previously calculated was actually down. Such an intentionally misleading financial statement violates the statute. For similar reasons, the addition of underusage penalties to revenue may or may not have been proper under some GAAP rule, but was intentionally misleading because the penalties were not expected to be realized. Finally, appellant claims that capitalization of some leases may have been proper under GAAP, but the capitalization of line costs—again an unannounced change in bookkeeping—was based not on an examination of particular leases but on the financial targets needed to keep share price high.

In a real sense, by alleging and proving that the financial statements were misleading, the government did, in fact, allege and prove violations of GAAP. According to the AICPA's Codification of Statements on Accounting Standards, AU § 312.04, "[f]inancial statements are materially misstated when they contain misstatements whose effect, individually or in the aggregate, is important enough to cause them not to be presented fairly, in all material respects, in compliance with GAAP." Thus, GAAP itself recognizes that technical compliance with particular GAAP rules may lead to misleading financial statements and imposes an overall requirement that the statements as a whole accurately reflect the financial status of the company.

To be sure—and to repeat—differences of opinion as to GAAP's requirements may be relevant to a defendant's intent where financial statements are prepared in a good faith attempt to comply with GAAP. The rules are no shield, however, in a case such as the present one, where the evidence showed that accounting methods known to be misleading—although perhaps at times fortuitously in compliance with particular GAAP rules—were used for the express purpose of intentionally misstating WorldCom's financial condition and artificially inflating its stock price.

....

For the reasons stated, we affirm.

Note and Questions

In re Global Crossing, Ltd. Securities Litigation, 322 F. Supp. 2d 319 (S.D.N.Y. 2004), involved allegedly improper revenue recognition practices. Global Crossing's auditor, Arthur Andersen, argued that the accounting practices were "permissible under GAAP, and that they were therefore not "false or misleading" within the meaning of Rule 10b-5.[30] The court responded:

> Even should Andersen prove that these accounting practices were in technical compliance with certain individual GAAP provisions, however, this would not necessarily insulate it from liability. This is because, unlike other regulatory systems, GAAP's ultimate goals of fairness and accuracy in reporting require more than mere technical compliance....
>
> GAAP ... provides no loopholes or shelters. It has a single unified purpose, one that it shares with section 10(b) of the 1934 Exchange Act: to increase

30. *Global Crossing*, 322 F. Supp. 2d at 337.

> investor confidence by ensuring transparency and accuracy in financial reporting. *See* Statement of Financial Accounting Concepts Nos. 1 (Objectives of Financial Reporting by Business Enterprises), 2 (Qualitative Characteristics of Accounting Information). Plaintiffs allege that the Companies' accounting ... amounted to a violation not only of [revenue recognition rules], but also of basic overarching principles of accounting aimed at meeting this goal.[31] ... Even assuming, therefore, that the Companies' accounting ... was arguably consistent with the terms of certain specific accounting standards, this would not insulate them or their accountants as a matter of law from liability under the securities laws, because under both GAAP and the securities laws, business entities and their accountants are required to provide whatever additional information would be necessary to make the statements in their financial reports fair and accurate, and not misleading.[32]

(1) The court cites FASB Statements of Financial Accounting Concepts, which we studied in Chapter 3(B) as "basic overarching" principles of GAAP, as opposed to the primary provisions in the Accounting Standards Codification. Is the Court making the case for treating GAAP as "principles-based" rather than "rules-based"?

(2) The Court also notes, in the last sentence quoted above, that both the federal securities laws and GAAP require supplemental disclosures to make the financial statements not misleading. The authority cited, however, includes only federal laws and regulations. Does GAAP require additional disclosures to avoid misleading readers of financial statements?

Securities And Exchange Commission v. Arthur Young & Company

United States Court of Appeals, Ninth Circuit, 1979

590 F.2d 785

SNEED, Circuit Judge:

This case grew out of the activities of Jack Burke, an oil and gas venture promoter, during 1964–71. In the course of these activities the appellee Arthur Young and Company (AY) performed certain audits and prepared certain financial statements in connection with some of Burke's ventures. In 1973, the Securities and Exchange

---

31. [by the Court] For example, Statement of Financial Accounting Concepts ("Concepts") 6 specifically requires that the costs associated with the generation of revenues should be matched with and set off against revenues as they are recognized. More generally, Concepts 1, 2, and 5 require that a company's financial disclosures should accurately and completely disclose sufficient information to enable potential investors, creditors and other users of financial statements to meaningfully evaluate the cash flows of the reporting enterprise, *see* Concepts No. 1; that they should be reliable, transparent, truthful, and accurately reflect the financial performance of the company, *see* Concepts No. 2; and that revenue recognized by a corporation in its financial statements should accurately reflect the business operations of the company, *see* Concepts No. 5....

32. *Global Crossing*, 322 F. Supp. 2d at 339–40.

Commission (SEC) brought a civil action against Burke and many of his associates charging violations of the antifraud and reporting requirements of the securities laws. The SEC joined other defendants, including the appellee and four of its auditors, charging violations of the securities acts by participating with and aiding and abetting the violations by Burke. Specifically, violations of Section 17(a) of the Securities Act, Section 10(b) of the Securities Exchange Act and Rule 10b-5 thereunder, and Sections 13(a) and 15(d) of the Securities Exchange Act.

After a thorough trial before an experienced trial judge AY and its auditors were found neither to have violated, nor to have aided and abetted the violations of, the securities laws.... The trial court also refused to enjoin AY and its auditors from future violations because "the evidence is insufficient to show a reasonable likelihood or expectation that AY would commit further violations in the future." 426 F.Supp. at 731. The SEC appealed and, because the only sanction sought to be imposed upon AY and its auditors was an injunction preventing future violations, we affirm on the ground that the trial court did not exceed the limits of its discretion in refusing to enjoin AY and its auditors.

....

II.

Standard of Performance Required of Auditors.

Our affirmance rests on our conviction that under the circumstances of this case the trial court did not err as a matter of law in fixing the standards of performance imposed on auditors by the securities laws.... [T]he question is did the trial court impose an insufficiently demanding standard with which accountants must comply to avoid liability under the securities laws. We hold that it did not.

We confess at the outset that our review is hampered by the fact that neither the trial court nor the parties have been pellucid in presentation of their view of what constitutes the appropriate standard. The SEC in the trial court appears to have asserted that AY and its auditors performed their work "with blinders on" and that they should have done "more" to reveal to investors the conduct of Burke and his associates that increased the financial risk of those who invested in his ventures.[33] During oral argument the SEC appeared to take the position that the proper standard is whether the accountant performed his audit functions in a manner that would have revealed to an ordinary prudent investor, who examined the accountant's audits or other financial

33. Uncertainty as to what exactly the SEC contended caused the trial judge to characterize the SEC position as that AY should have done something "more" than it did. 426 F.Supp. at 759. In its brief, the SEC never clearly articulated a standard more stringent than Generally Accepted Auditing Standards (GAAS). "(B)y failing to conduct its audit in accordance with generally accepted auditing standards, AY deprived itself of any chance to discover the fraud...." The one concrete aspect in which the SEC asserts AY's audit was deficient was in not examining more closely the account balance and assets of Fundamental, the corporation through which the funds of all Burke oil and gas programs were channeled. The district court, however, found that GAAS required no more than AY had done. For the reasons set out in this opinion, we find that no more was required.

statements, a reasonably accurate reflection of the financial risks such an investor presently bears or might bear in the future if he invested in the audited endeavor.

AY, on the other hand, contends that good faith compliance with Generally Accepted Auditing Standards (GAAS) under the circumstances of this case will immunize it from liability under the securities laws. The trial court did not explicitly choose between these competing standards; but a careful reading of its findings of fact and conclusions of law convinces us that it did not accept that urged by the SEC during oral argument. Its failure to do so, we hold, did not constitute error.

> The court's broadside here against the SEC is frequently quoted in defendants' briefs in SEC actions. For an equally quotable rejoinder, see the note following the case.

To accept the SEC's position would go far toward making the accountant both an insurer of his client's honesty and an enforcement arm of the SEC. We can understand why the SEC wishes to so conscript accountants. Its frequently late arrival on the scene of fraud and violations of securities laws almost always suggests that had it been there earlier with the accountant it would have caught the scent of wrong-doing and, after an unrelenting hunt, bagged the game. What it cannot do, the thought goes, the accountant can and should. The difficulty with this is that Congress has not enacted the conscription bill that the SEC seeks to have us fashion and fix as an interpretive gloss on existing securities laws.

Under existing law we agree with Judge Pollack when, in *SEC v. Republic National Life Ins. Co.*, 378 F.Supp. 430, 440 (S.D.N.Y.1974), he observed:

> Since an accountant is not a guarantor of the reports he prepares and is only duty bound to act honestly, in good faith and with reasonable care in the discharge of his professional obligations, the elements of fraud if charged must be pleaded with particularity to show a fraudulent breach of duty.

On the facts of this case, AY discharged its professional obligations by complying with GAAS in good faith. The trial court's findings, which are not clearly erroneous, establish beyond dispute that AY and its auditors conformed to this standard.

Moreover, it is clear that the trial court found no basis for the application of *United States v. Simon. Simon* recognized that compliance with Generally Accepted Accounting Principles (GAAP) would not immunize an accountant when he consciously chose not to disclose on a financial statement a known material fact. No such deliberate concealment was found by the trial court to exist in this case. Thus, although we assume arguendo that *Simon* strips the accountant of the protection that compliance with GAAS (*Simon*, incidentally, was concerned only with GAAP) normally affords when he fails to reveal material facts which he knows or which, but for a deliberate refusal to become informed, he should have known, there exists no basis in the trial court's findings for so applying *Simon*. We cannot say such findings in this respect are clearly erroneous.

....

AFFIRMED.

As counterpoint to the court's indictment of the SEC's "conscription" of accountants, an equally famous quotation, taken from *United States v. Arthur Young & Co.*, a case with a similar title but a different factual underpinning, is just as often found in plaintiff's briefs in securities fraud cases.

> By certifying the public reports that collectively depict a corporation's financial status, the independent auditor assumes a public responsibility transcending any employment relationship with the client. The independent public accountant performing this special function owes ultimate allegiance to the corporation's creditors and stockholders, as well as to the investing public. This "public watchdog" function demands that the accountant maintain total independence from the client at all times and requires complete fidelity to the public trust.[34]

This case actually dealt with the existence (denied by the Court, as you might suspect from the above language) of an "auditor-client" privilege in a federal income tax case. The holding of the case has been partially overruled by Internal Revenue Code § 7525(a)(1), which provides: "With respect to tax advice, the same common law protections of confidentiality which apply to a communication between a taxpayer and an attorney shall also apply to a communication between a taxpayer and any federally authorized tax practitioner to the extent the communication would be considered a privileged communication if it were between a taxpayer and an attorney."

* * *

Problem 12-4

LoanStar Corporation is a loan company. It borrows money and lends it to homeowners. In early 2019, LoanStar was short on funds, and borrowed $5 million from First National Bank. LoanStar prepared disclosure documents discussing its five-year results of operations and its five-year future business plan, and a complete set of income statements and balance sheets covering the most recently-completed fiscal years (2017 and 2018). The financial statements were audited by Shure & Serton, a local firm of certified public accountants. Shure & Serton gave an unqualified opinion on LoanStar's financial statements.

Later in 2019, a local newspaper's investigations discovered that LoanStar made loans based on inadequate documentation, continued to accrue interest income on loans in default, and the interest rates on its loans were in excess of state and federal limits. These revelations led to legal actions which reduced the price of LoanStar stock and caused LoanStar to default on its loan to First National Bank.

Loan Star stockholders have sued Shure & Serton under Rule 10b-5, claiming that its audit opinion was misleading, because it should have uncovered and disclosed

34. United States v. Arthur Young & Co., 465 U.S. 805, 817–818 (1984).

these problems at LoanStar. Advise Shure & Serton as to the likelihood of liability in the lawsuit.

Problem 12-5

Auditor has reviewed the financial statements of Client and has concluded that its accounts receivable are partially uncollectible, and that Client's management has no reasonable basis to determine the extent of the problem. Therefore, Auditor has determined to take the unusual step of qualifying its opinion. See the discussion of qualified opinions, pp. 107–08. Auditor issues a standard opinion, that the financial statements fairly present the position of Client in accordance with GAAP, and adds the following language: "While management is of the opinion that the allowance for doubtful trade accounts and notes receivable is adequate, we [Auditors] are unable to determine the adequacy of the provision for uncollectible accounts."

Audit work completed prior to the qualification decision indicated that the extent of the required reserves might be as much as $250,000 (a material amount). However, because Auditor has already qualified the opinion, it does not inquire further into the proper extent of provision for uncollectible accounts, as it does not believe that Client's records will provide any basis for a conclusion.

Disappointed investors have sued Client and Auditor. They allege that Auditor's statement was misleading because it did not disclose Auditor's knowledge that $250,000 in reserves might be required.

Was Auditor's conduct compliant with GAAS? Misleading? Or both? See *Fine v. American Solar King Corp.*, 919 F.2d 290 (5th Cir. 1990).

Index